P9-EMN-876

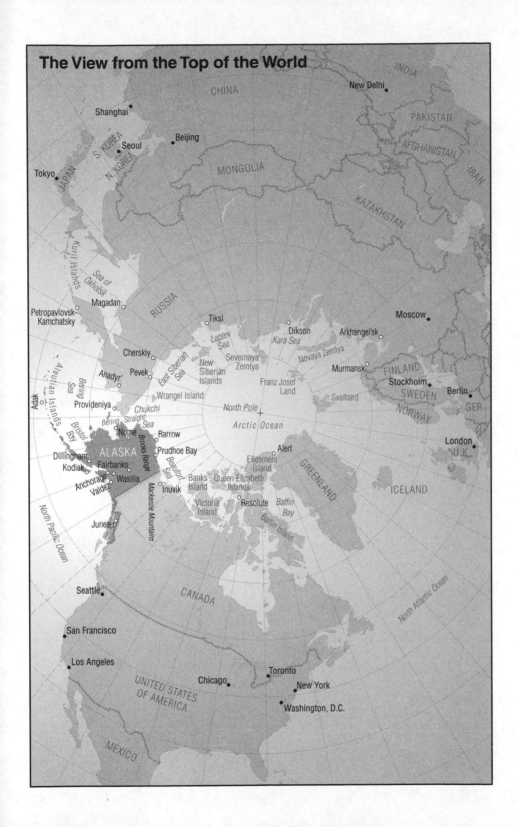

The View from the Top of the World

Going Rogue

Going Rogue

An American Life

SARAH PALIN

HARPER

An Imprint of HarperCollins*Publishers*
www.harpercollins.com

GOING ROGUE. Copyright © 2009 by Sarah Palin. All rights reserved. Printed in the United States of America. No part of this book may be used or reproduced in any manner whatsoever without written permission except in the case of brief quotations embodied in critical articles and reviews. For information, address HarperCollins Publishers, 10 East 53rd Street, New York, NY 10022.

HarperCollins books may be purchased for educational, business, or sales promotional use. For information, please write: Special Markets Department, HarperCollins Publishers, 10 East 53rd Street, New York, NY 10022.

FIRST EDITION

Designed by Got Moxie Design

Map by Nick Springer, Springer Cartographics LLC

Library of Congress Cataloging-in-Publication Data has been applied for.

ISBN: 978-0-06-193989-1

09 10 11 12 13 ID/RRD 10 9 8 7 6 5 4 3 2 1

*Dedicated to all Patriots who share my love
of the United States of America. And particularly to our
women and men in uniform, past and present—
God bless the fight for freedom.*

Contents

Going Rogue

Chapter One

The Last Frontier

I don't believe that God put us on earth to be ordinary.

—LOU HOLTZ

I t was the Alaska State Fair, August 2008. With the gray Talkeetna Mountains in the distance and the first light covering of snow about to descend on Pioneer Peak, I breathed in an autumn bouquet that combined everything small-town America with rugged splashes of the Last Frontier. Cotton candy and footlong hot dogs. Halibut tacos and reindeer sausage. Banjo music playing at the Blue Bonnet Stage, baleen etchings, grass-woven Eskimo baskets, and record-breaking giant vegetables grown under the midnight sun.

Inching through rivers of people with Trig, our four-month-old son, cradled in my arms, I zigzagged from booth to booth, from driftwood art to honeybee keeping to home-brewed salmonberry wine. Bristol and Willow, our teenage daughters, roamed ahead with friends, heads together, laughing, thumbs tapping cell phones. Piper, seven, my constant sidekick since the moment she was born, bounced along at my hip, pinching off fluffs of cotton candy, her reward for patiently accommodating my stop-and-go progress through the crowd. For the most part, she was comfortable watching the grip-and-grin photos and hearing the friendly chit-chat with constituents that I enjoyed as part of my job as governor of the state. Every few moments, I pulled my right arm free from baby duty to shake hands with folks who wanted to say hello.

"Hey, Sarah! You never miss the fair!"

"Oh, my goodness, is that the new little one? Let me say hi to him . . ."

"Price of energy's pretty high, Governor. When are they gonna ramp up drilling?"

A robin's egg sky arced overhead, the brisk kick in the air hinting at winter's approach. Like a family conga line, we wound our way among the vendors and exhibits: from pork chops on a stick to kettle corn, veggie weigh-ins, and livestock competitions. A local dance troupe took to the stage and the music blared, competing with the constant hum of generators and squealing kids on rides. Ahead, on my right, I saw the Alaska Right to Life (RTL) booth, where a poster caught my eye, taking my breath away. It featured the sweetest baby girl swathed in pink, pretend angel wings fastened to her soft shoulders.

"That's you, baby," I whispered to Piper, as I have every year since she smiled for the picture as an infant. She popped another cloud of cotton candy into her mouth and looked nonchalant: *Still the pro-life poster child at the State Fair. Ho-hum.*

Well, I still thought it was a nice shot, as I did every time I saw it on its advertisements and fund-raiser tickets. It reminded me of the preciousness of life.

It also reminded me of how impatient I am with politics.

A staunch advocate of every child's right to be born, I was pro-life enough for the grassroots RTL folks to adopt Piper as their poster child, but I wasn't politically connected enough for the state GOP machine to allow the organization to endorse me in early campaigns.

From inside the booth, a very nice volunteer caught my glance, so I tucked my head inside, shook hands, and thanked the gracious ladies who put up with the jeers of those who always protested the display. With their passion and sincerity, the ladies typified the difference between principles and politics. As I signed the visitors' book, I saw Piper's picture again on the counter and became annoyed at my own annoyance. I still hadn't learned to accept the fact that political machines twist and distort public service—and that, a lot of times, very little they do makes any sense.

Years before, I had seen our state speeding toward an economic train wreck. Since construction began in 1975 on what would become Alaska's economic lifeline, the Trans-Alaska Pipeline, it had grown increasingly obvious to everyday Alaskans that many of their public servants were not necessarily serving the public. Instead they had climbed into bed with Big Oil. Meanwhile, in a young state whose people clung to America's original pioneering and independent spirit, government was growing as fast as fireweed in July.

It didn't make sense.

It seemed that true public service, crafting policies that were good for the people, had become increasingly derailed by politics and its infernal machines. But I had a drive to help, an interest in government and current events since I was a little kid, and I had become aware of the impact of common sense public policy during the presidency of Ronald Reagan. I was intrigued by political science in college and studied journalism because of my passion for the power of words. And I had been raised to believe that in America, anyone can make a difference.

So I got involved. I served first on the Wasilla City Council, then two terms as mayor, helping turn our sleepy little town into the fastest-growing community in the state. Then I served as an oil and gas regulator, overseeing the energy industry and encouraging responsible resource development, Alaska's main economic lifeline. In 2002, as my second mayoral term wound down, my husband, Todd, and I began to consider my next step. With four busy kids, I would certainly have enough going on to keep me occupied, even if I chose to put public service aside. And for a while, I did. But I still felt a restlessness, an insistent tugging on my heart that told me there were additional areas where I could contribute.

From what I could see from my position in the center of the state, the capital of Juneau seemed stocked mainly with "good ol' boys" who lunched with oil company executives and cut fat-cat deals behind closed doors. Like most Alaskans, I could see that the votes of many lawmakers lined up conveniently with what was best for Big Oil, sometimes to the detriment of their own constituents.

When oil began flowing from Prudhoe Bay in 1977, billions of dollars flowed into state coffers with it. The state raked in more revenue than anyone could have imagined—billions of dollars almost overnight! And the politicians spent it. Government grew rapidly. One quarter of our workforce was employed by state and local governments, and even more was tied to the state budget through contracts and subsidies. Everyone knew there was a certain amount of back-scratching going on. But an economic crash in the 1980s collapsed the oil boom. Businesses closed and unemployment soared.

During the oil boom, anyone who questioned the government's giving more power to the oil companies was condemned: What are you trying to do, slay the golden goose? But when the boom went bust, the golden goose still ruled the roost. By then, state government was essentially surrendering its ability to act in the best interests of the people. So I ran for governor.

I didn't necessarily get into government to become an ethics crusader. But it seemed that every level of government I encountered was paralyzed by the same politics-as-usual system. I wasn't wired to play that game. And because I fought political corruption regardless of party, GOP leaders distanced themselves from me and eventually my administration, which really was fine with me. Though I was a registered Republican, I'd always been without a political home, and now, even as governor, I was still outside the favored GOP circle. I considered that a mutually beneficial relationship: politically, I didn't owe anyone, and nobody owed me. That gave me the freedom and latitude to find the best people to serve Alaskans regardless of party, and I was beholden only to those who hired me—the people of Alaska.

Still in the RTL booth, Piper said she was ready to go. She was antsy to stop by the fair's hula hoop contest, so I hurriedly shook a couple more hands and gathered Trig back from the nice lady who had asked to hold him.

I had certainly gotten off on the wrong foot with the Republican Party by daring to take on the GOP Chairman Randy Ruedrich, and then incumbent Governor Frank Murkowski. Party bosses weren't going to let me forget that I had broken their Eleventh Commandment—"Thou shalt not speak ill of a fellow Republican"—even if Murkowski did have a 19 percent approval rating, his chief of staff would later plead guilty to a felony charge, and it appeared corruption was growing at a breakneck pace.

I didn't have time to waste embracing the status quo and never had it in me to play the party's game. That just meant I'd have to work harder, advancing the state not on the currency of traded favors but on the strength of ideas that proved themselves good for the people. This was the only way I'd found to transform a grudging bureaucracy into a team that could try to reform government and shrink its reach into our lives.

Since being elected governor in 2006, I had managed to rack up an 88 percent approval rating, and though I didn't put much stock in fickle polls, I figured my administration must be doing something right. To me, it signaled that Alaskans, with their independent spirit, wanted principle-centered policies, not the same old politics-as-usual. I was grateful. All I wanted was the chance to work as hard as I could, serve the people honorably—and I figured that maybe between changing state government and changing diapers, we'd help change our corner of the world.

In the RTL booth, I smiled, dropped some dollars into the contribution can, and didn't care who might be watching, including local reporters. Alaskans knew my pro-life views—no news there. At that moment, one of my BlackBerrys vibrated me back to work. I was thankful for the excuse to hustle back into the sunshine. Piper tugged on my arm with sticky fingers, whispering reminders that I'd promised if she was patient I'd take her on a roller-coaster ride, too.

"Just this one last call, baby," I told her.

I ducked behind the booth, hoping it was my son Track calling from his Army base at Fort Wainwright. He was set to deploy to Iraq soon, and his sporadic calls were something I lived for.

But in case it wasn't Track, I offered up a silent fallback prayer: *Please, Lord, just for an hour, anything but politics.*

I punched the green phone icon and answered hopefully, "This is Sarah."

It was Senator John McCain, asking if I wanted to help him change history.

2

From Sandpoint, Idaho, where I was born, via Juneau, Alaska, I touched down in the windy, remote frontier town of Skagway cradled in my mother's arms. I was just three months old, and barely sixty days had passed since the largest earthquake on record in North American history struck Alaska, on Good Friday, March 27, 1964.

The southwestern coast had bucked and swayed for nearly five full minutes, shaking down a rock rain of landslides and avalanches. Whole mountainsides of snow tumbled into the valleys. Near Kodiak, tectonic shifts thrust sections of the ground thirty feet skyward, permanently. In Seward, an entire chunk of waterfront detached itself from the coast and slid into Resurrection Bay. Twenty minutes later, a towering tsunami swallowed the shore, carrying with it a flaming sheet of oil that burned on the ocean surface. Along Alaska's Inside Passage, a massive submarine earth slide so destabilized the ground that the entire port town of Valdez had to be relocated to another site.

The quake altered the topography of Alaska forever. Mother Nature showed her might and reminded us that she always wins. But that did not scare my parents, Chuck and Sally Heath, who weren't about to change their minds about pulling up stakes in Idaho, where my dad was a schoolteacher, and settling in America's untamed North. Instead, my parents thought the Good Friday quake—with a 9.2 magnitude, the second largest ever recorded— added to the aura of rugged adventure that lured them to the forty-ninth state, which was then only five years old.

My big brother, Chuck Jr., was two at the time, and my sister, Heather, was one, so they were old enough to sit up by themselves in the Grumman Goose we flew in on, a 1930s-era plane that looked like it came straight out of the movie *Casablanca*. By the time the Heath family arrived, the population of Skagway was only about 650, way down from its heyday in the summer of 1897 when the town boomed with thousands of fortune hunters who streamed in with the Klondike Gold Rush.

The people who trekked north at that time weren't just grizzled old prospectors, but also doctors and lawyers and teachers like my dad. Many of the gold hunters settled in Skagway and from there hauled their hopes and supplies over the thirty-three-mile Chilkoot Trail to the head of the mighty Yukon River. But Skagway itself remained the Las Vegas of the North. The newly wealthy rode in to celebrate and the newly busted drank away their troubles while piano music and the laughter of dance hall girls spilled onto the same raised-plank sidewalks that still lined Main Street when my family moved to town.

One of those wooden sidewalks was the scene of one of my earliest memories: my attempt to fly. I couldn't have been more than four years old and was walking to my friend's house all by myself because in such a small town, little kids gained their independence early. My friend and I were supposed to go to catechism together, and I was anxious to get to her big, busy, Catholic family, which bustled with a dozen brothers and sisters. I kept to the wooden planks that paralleled the town's main dirt road, and as the warm boards echoed under my feet, I got to thinking: I had seen eagles and dragonflies and ptarmigan fly, but I had never seen a person fly. That didn't make any sense to me. Hadn't anyone ever tried it before? Why couldn't someone just propel herself up into the air and get it done?

I stopped and looked up at the summer sky, then down at the dirt road below. Then I simply jumped. I didn't care who might see me. I wanted to fly more than I worried about what I looked like. My knees took most of the impact, and I scraped them both.

Well, that didn't work, I thought. So I got up, dusted myself off, and kept walking.

———

Skagway was a sweet start in life. Mom and Dad rented a tiny wooden house built in 1898 on the corner of First and Main. Alaska's wealthiest banking family, the Rasmusons, owned it. Thirty months after we landed in town, my younger sister, Molly, was born. We added a couple of dogs and a cat, and the Heath family was complete.

Perched on the rim of a harbor at the northern apex of the Inside Passage, Skagway is encircled by mountains. I remember the air smelled of ocean salt and that even though the town was small, it pulsed with boats in port, locomotives churning through to Canada, and the hum of propellers on the gravel airstrip right near the middle of town. I remember lush emerald moss hugging the hillsides. Mom always said she was going to buy a carpet that color some day—and one day, she did.

The southeast Alaska winters are brutal. In Skagway, icy winds tear relentlessly through town. But I don't remember the winters as well. I mostly remember sunny summer days, playing dress-up with my sisters under a wild crabapple tree. I remember community basketball games. And I remember arguing with the nun who taught catechism and tried to teach me to write the letter *E*. It seemed a naked letter to me, so I was determined to reinvent it. I insisted she let me improve it with at least a few more horizontal lines.

I shared a little bedroom with my sisters while my brother, Chuck, slept in a closet, which also doubled as the sewing room. Chuck was all boy. Once he pulled the town fire alarm; the fire chief visited our home, and Dad's hand visited Chuck's backside. Another time, he pulled a burning catalog Dad had used as kindling out of our rock fireplace, dropped it on the living room floor in a panic, and nearly burned Mr. Rasmuson's house down. My sisters and I loved our big brother, and we loved each other, but still, we all scrapped like wolverines.

Mom had agreed to give Alaska a one-year trial run, but our "short stint" in the quaint old tourist town inaccessible by roads turned into five years of Dad teaching and coaching, working summers on the Alaska Railroad, and tending bar in seasonal tourist traps. Mom stayed busy herding four small kids and driving a seasonal tour bus, and was active in community theater and the Catholic church. Both of our folks loaded us up for activities like hunting, fishing, and hiking, carting us on sleds or in backpacks when we were too young to walk.

The lifestyle was a radical departure from Dad's hometown of North Hollywood, California. He was born in 1938 to the celebrity photographer Charlie Heath, who specialized in shooting famous prizefighters. At home, black and whites of James J. Jeffries, Joe Lewis, and Primo Carnera plastered the walls. But when Dad was ten, Grandpa Charlie moved the family to Hope, Idaho, and started a fishing lure business, while Grandma Marie continued to teach school. Grandma was a Christian Scientist who didn't believe in doctors or medicine, and believed that physical illness was merely a manifestation of the mind.

Dad doesn't talk much about his childhood, but through the years I heard enough muffled conversations between my mom and dad to know that his parents' acceptance of pain must have translated beyond the physical. Dad's childhood seemed to me painful and lonely.

Sports and the outdoors were Dad's passion, but his parents thought they were a waste of time. Dad had a choice: he could either abandon his passion or fend for himself. So he rode the bus fifteen miles every day to Sandpoint High School, and hitchhiked home every night after practice. He became a standout athlete, excelling in every sport. He held the school record for the 100-

yard dash for forty-four years, until 1998 (Dad sent the boy who broke it a letter of congratulations), and was recently inducted into Sandpoint's Sports Hall of Fame. Even setting records didn't capture my grandparents' attention, though. Dad worked in a local lumberyard, staying with different families. He went from couch to couch when he couldn't hitch a ride back to Hope, and was virtually adopted by a classmate's kind family, the Mooneys. Dad became his own man early on, and would pass that independent spirit on to his kids.

When I think about Dad's upbringing, it's amazing that he turned out to be such a dedicated, family-oriented father. It seems he was determined not to replicate his family's brokenness in his own.

As for my mom, it's easy to see where she got her nurturing, hospitable personality. Sally Ann Sheeran was born into a large, educated Irish Catholic family in Utah. Her father, Clement James Sheeran—everyone called him "Clem," or "CJ"—was a mediator for General Electric and was wild about Notre Dame. He played football for Columbia University (later renamed the University of Portland) and refereed Washington high school football for years. My grandmother Helen studied at the University of Idaho, then put her talent and intelligence to work as a homemaker, raising six active kids while working for the Red Cross and sewing costumes for the Richland Players. She worked tirelessly. My aunts tell me she was the hardest-working housewife they ever knew; they'd come home from school to see Grandma's bloody knuckles from her reupholstering projects, back when they used hammers and nails to stretch the fabric to re-cover old furniture, which she volunteered to do for all their neighbors. She laid the foundation for volunteerism in the family.

When CJ moved his family to Richland, Washington, he landed a job at the Hanford Nuclear Plant. The Sheerans were one of those big, rambunctious, patriotic families. Grandpa was witty and poetic, wore Mr. Rogers sweaters, ate black jelly beans, and looked like a graying Ronald Reagan. He loved to entertain us with silly poems and Irish songs and sayings. Everybody in the family played Scrabble and took great pride in hoarding *K*s and *Q*s and slapping them down in long, fancy words on triple-letter scores. Even though they lived so far away, Grandma and Grandpa Sheeran and their adult kids would top my "most favorite people" list as I grew up and got to know them all through visits on college vacations.

Smack in the middle of this jovial clan, my mom grew up in a very conventional life of Richland Bomber pep squads, piano lessons, and sock hops. After high school, she attended Columbia Basin College and worked as a dental assistant. When she met my dad, he had already served a stint in the Army. They were lab partners at CBC, and she wouldn't let him draw her blood.

Dad loved teaching and coaching all kinds of sports, but he had grown up reading Jack London novels, and he craved adventure. London himself had arrived in Skagway from California in the fall of 1897 and set out to hike the Chilkoot Trail. The following spring, the author traveled down the Yukon River en route to California, inspired to write *White Fang* and *The Call of the Wild*, novels that called Dad north.

It was just thirty years before London's arrival, in 1867, that Secretary of State William H. Seward bought Alaska from the Russians. The government paid two cents an acre, adding 586,412 square miles to U.S. territory. Critics ridiculed Seward for spending so much on a remote chunk of earth that some thought of as just a frozen, inhospitable wilderness that was dark half the year. The $7.2 million purchase became known as "Seward's Folly" or "Seward's Icebox." Seward withstood the mocking and disdain because of his vision for Alaska. He knew her potential to help secure the nation with her resources and strategic position on the globe. Over the decades, exploration led to the discovery of gold and oil and rich minerals, along with the world's most abundant fisheries. And so, decades later, he was posthumously vindicated, as purveyors of unpopular common sense often are.

In the summer of 2009, I visited Seward's home in the Finger Lakes region of Central New York when Auburn honored him in celebrating Founder's Day. It was inspiring to see the historically rich region, home to heroic figures I had read so much about, including Elizabeth Cady Stanton, Susan B. Anthony, and Harriet Tubman. As a little girl, I had read about Tubman's journeys along the Underground Railroad to secure freedom and equality for others. Now I was standing in her home and walking across her property, which Seward provided to her just down the road from his own. As with Seward, Tubman hadn't taken the easy path. But it was the right path.

Seward was typical of the visionary—and colorful—characters Alaska attracted. The year before Jack London arrived, Skookum Jim Mason and Dawson Charlie met up in the Yukon Territory east of the Alaska border with a gold miner who had been panning near the Klondike River. History is a little fuzzy on who struck gold first, but someone in the party spotted the telltale amber shimmer, and Alaska's gold rush was on.

After his adventures in Tombstone, the legendary lawman Wyatt Earp came north and spent a few years in Nome during the gold rush. On the other side of the law was "Soapy" Smith, a Wild West crime boss whose tight-knit gang moved from Colorado to Skagway. They made a mint cheating gold miners out of their cash. It finally caught up with Soapy Smith: he was killed in a shoot-out with a vigilante gang.

The spirit of Alaska is unique, combining awe for the untamed majesty of nature, a rugged individualism, and strong traditions of mutual aid. People still come to Alaska seeking adventure and a chance to test their mettle in the wilderness.

Good people like Chuck Heath. He arrived for the hunting and fishing but actually hit the trifecta: he got the adventure he yearned for and earned his master's degree in education and got a pay raise to boot. The State of Alaska was paying a premium, $6,000 a year (more than twice what he was paid in Idaho), to attract more teachers. So Chuck and Sally Heath packed up their three babies, all under the age of twenty-eight months, and headed north to Alaska on the adventure that became their life.

In those days, it was unusual for an entire family to pull up stakes and relocate to the Last Frontier. Unless you were a member of a multigenerational Alaska Native family like my husband Todd's, it was usually the family breadwinner who trekked north to seek adventure and job opportunities, while the nuclear family remained in the safe, known confines of the Lower 48.

Five years later Mom and Dad piled our six-person clan into a blue 1964 Rambler, barged it on a ferry to the Alcan Highway, and drove us through part of Canada into Anchorage and a new chapter of Heath family life.

3

We moved to a duplex fifteen miles outside Anchorage so Dad could teach at Chugiak Elementary School, in a town that was a little smudge on the map outside the state's biggest city. Mom worked part-time as the school lunch lady at Eagle River Elementary School, and I loved the fringe benefit of her bringing home leftover homemade rolls from the cafeteria. She later became our school secretary.

My first clear memory of school was when my kindergarten teacher wheeled a black-and-white television into the classroom so we could watch American astronauts land on the moon. The lunar landing had happened in July 1969, before school started, but even watching taped images of an American walking on the moon stirred in me an overwhelming pride in our country—that we could achieve something so magnificent. A similar feeling stirred in me as my class recited the Pledge of Allegiance. I felt proud and tall as we pledged on our hearts every morning. Early on, I gained great appreciation for the words we spoke: ". . . the United States of America . . . one nation under God, *indivisible, with liberty and justice for all.*" I knew those words held power.

And not just those words. I developed a love of reading and writing early on. Leaning on Mom's shoulder in the pew at Church on the Wildwood during a Sunday sermon, I heard the pastor use the word "different."

"I can spell 'different!'" I excitedly whispered in her ear, and scribbled it in the margin of the church bulletin. It was my first big word, and I was proud to have figured it out myself. It was the first time Mom didn't give me her stern don't-talk-in-church look but instead smiled warmly and seemed as proud as I was.

Reading was a special bond between my mother and me. Mom read aloud to me—poetry by Ogden Nash and the Alaska writer Robert Service, along with snippets of prose. She would quote biblical proverbs and ask me to tell her what I thought. She found clever ways to encourage my love of the written word—by reading cookbooks, and jokes out of *Reader's Digest* together, and writing letters to grandparents. My siblings were better athletes, cuter and more sociable than I, and the only thing they had to envy about me was the special passion for reading that I shared with our mother, who we all thought ranked somewhere up there with the female saints. When the VFW announced that I won a plaque in its annual flag poetry contest for my third-grade poem about Betsy Ross, Mom treated me like the new Emily Dickinson. Years later, when I won that patriotic group's annual college scholarship, she was just as proud.

My appetite for books connected my schoolteacher father and me, too. For my tenth birthday, his parents sent me *The Wonderful Wizard of Oz,* and Dad read it to us at night. I appreciate that now even more, realizing he spent all day teaching elementary school science and coaching high schoolers and then came home no doubt a bit tired of kids.

We still had only one old Rambler car, so we walked most everywhere in our small town, even on icy winter days. Our big trips were drives into Anchorage, and on those rare occasions we'd sing along to "Ain't No Mountain High Enough" and "Tie a Yellow Ribbon Round the Old Oak Tree" on the scratchy AM radio.

"Shut your ears!" Dad would holler when the news came on, in case a sports score was broadcast that would ruin the next week's game for us. (We avoided the sports page, too, so that we wouldn't spoil the NFL games we didn't get to watch until a week after they were played because television broadcasts were tape-delayed in Alaska's early days.) There was no need to drive to town often because Mom sewed a lot of our clothes, and we shopped for some via mail order through the Sears catalog.

It wasn't common in Alaska to have many fresh fruits and vegetables from the Lower 48, and transportation costs drove food prices through the roof. So a lot of what Alaskans ate, we raised or hunted: moose, caribou, ptarmigan, and ducks. Dad and his friends became their own small-game taxidermists. Even today, my parents' living room looks like a natural history museum. And when an earthquake hits, Dad can tell the magnitude by how fast the tail wags on the stuffed cougar that crouches on a shelf over their big picture window.

When we were kids, we raised chickens, caught fish, and dug for clams. In summer, we picked wild blueberries, cranberries, and raspberries. We grew produce, like carrots, lettuce, and broccoli, but never could compete with the world-record-setting cabbages like you see at the Alaska State Fair. (The 2009 cabbage winner was a Valley farmer who grew a 127-pounder—twice as big as Piper!) We usually baked our own bread and drank powdered milk that was sold in big red-and-white Carnation boxes.

In so many ways, Alaska is a playground. When Lower 48 parents tell their kids, "Go play outside!" there may be limited options in suburban backyards. But Alaska kids grow up fishing the state's 3 million lakes in the summer and racing across them in winter on snowmachines, kicking up rooster tails of snow. We hike, ski, sled, snowshoe, hunt, camp, fish, and fly. We have the highest number of pilots per capita in the United States.

In Alaska, we joke that we have two seasons: construction and winter. As I grow older, it seems construction season—summer— never lasts long enough. Even in a good year, summer speeds past in a three-month flash, from mid-May to mid-August. In contrast to our long winter darkness, the blessed summer light creates a euphoria that runs through our veins. Hour after hour, there is still more time and more daylight to accomplish one more thing. If we told our kids to be home before dark, we wouldn't see them for weeks. The never-ending sun so elongates the days that by September, newcomers to the state (or "Cheechakos") say they're exhausted enough to hibernate until spring.

In the early '70s, after two years outside Anchorage, my parents saved enough to buy a little house about an hour up the road in the Matanuska-Susitna (Mat-Su) Valley in the one-horse town of Wasilla.

Growing up, there was always work to be done: canning, picking, cleaning, and stacking, stacking, and stacking more firewood, which we burned to heat our home. (My sister and I were re-reading our girlhood diaries recently, and we must have stacked firewood every day, because on nearly every page we wrote about it!) When it came to chores, there was no arguing: you did them. We always ate at home because there were only a few restaurants around, and after dinner our routine was always the same:

"I'm washing!" Heather would say.

"I'm rinsing!" said Molly.

"I'm singing!" I said.

Then Heather washed the dishes and Molly rinsed, while I sat on the washing machine, which was squeezed up against the sink in our sunflower yellow kitchen, and sang until the dishes were dry. Then I put them away.

I remember banging on the upright piano in the living room and twirling around the floor to Heather's first record, *The Sound of Music,* which she bought after seeing the movie. My sisters and I stayed out of trouble, seeming to find it only when hanging out with Chuck and his typical mischief. Like the time he and I snow-machined down an empty dirt road and got pulled over by one of the few state troopers in our part of Alaska. It was Christmas Day; we were out in the middle of nowhere, a couple of kids on a snowmachine up against a big dude with a gun and a badge. I couldn't help wondering about his priorities, if he really didn't have more important things to do, like catching a bad guy, or maybe helping a poor old lady haul in her firewood for the night. Looking back, maybe that was my first brush with the skewed priorities of government.

—————

Not far from home, near the Talkeetna Mountains, I learned to hunt. Traveling on skis and snowshoes, we harvested ptarmigan and big game. I love meat. I eat pork chops, thick bacon burgers, and the seared fatty edges of a medium-well-done steak. But I especially love moose and caribou. I always remind people from outside our state that there's plenty of room for all Alaska's animals—right next to the mashed potatoes.

In our northern state, with some communities located hundreds of miles from big grocery stores, Alaskans have for generations lived on local, organic protein sources. Anti-hunting groups are clueless about this. It always puzzled me how some of the people who think killing and eating animals in the wild is somehow cruel have no problem buying dead animals at the grocery store, wrapped in cellophane instead of fur.

Ever since I can remember, Dad would take us up to Mount McKinley National Park, named after President William McKinley of Ohio who had never traveled to our state. A vibrant sanctuary for most every big-game animal, woodland creature, and bird in Alaska, the park is also home to the highest peak on the continent, Mount McKinley, or "Denali," rising 20,320 feet. Alaska is home to seventeen of the twenty highest peaks in North America, in addition to other wonders, like the ever-shifting glaciers, one larger than the state of Delaware, and dozens of active volcanoes.

At the national park, we'd dress in white sweatshirts and quietly, carefully, creep near herds of majestic dall sheep with their thick curled horns. We weren't to bother the sheep, just get close, be still . . . and enjoy. It was one way Dad taught us to appreciate the pristine beauty and wildlife in Alaska.

One year, while stalking sheep, I disappeared. I was only about eight years old, and for a couple of anxious hours of climbing hillsides and calling my name, no one could find me on the crags and snowpack. Finally, Dad found me—sound asleep in the sunshine on a rocky slope near a grazing herd. While watching the animals, I had simply dozed off, camouflaged in a sweatshirt as white as the sheep were, so no one could spot me, even with binoculars. Dad said he played it cool while I was lost, but inside, he was pretty frantic. My main heartache was that I had taken a rare Hershey's chocolate bar with me, planning to graze on it while I sheep-gazed. But by the time Dad woke me, my coveted candy had melted into an inedible mess.

Every spring, Dad would bring his sixth-grade class up to the park on the Alaska Railroad for a weeklong field trip to experience what they'd studied all year about animals, geography, geology, and the environment. I was happy to tag along and appreciated that what his students learned during the school year in Mr. Heath's classroom was what I got to learn every day from Mr. Heath, my dad.

Dad would give us a quarter for being the first to spot a moose or a bear on our hour-long drives into Anchorage. And you'd think we'd have tired of seeing yet another caribou or dall sheep along Alaska's roadways. But then, as now, our wildlife inspired excitement, and even today we'll still pull over to look, and take a picture. My parents instilled in me that appreciation; we were not to take for granted the wonder of God's creation.

To this day, we still call each other even in the middle of the night to report an awe-inspiring aurora borealis display. We never tire of the dazzling Northern Lights, shimmering like the hem of Heaven. So it's not uncommon to get a midnight call from friends or family: "Quick! Look out the window! They're dancing!"

By the mid-1970s, Alaska's economic advantages had begun capturing as much attention as its natural beauty. Construction of the eight-hundred-mile-long Trans-Alaska Pipeline was under way. High-paying pipeline jobs brought thousands of new workers to the state. It was a new gold rush that sent truckloads of cash into the state's economy. Jobs were plentiful, and Dad had many opportunities to leave teaching and start making real money on the oil pipeline, along with thousands of others who would capitalize on this huge piece of infrastructure. But he loved teaching and he loved his students, so he chose making a difference in kids' lives over making money.

The employment boom and energy production were the upside of development. The downside was the concurrent spike in social problems. Without the law enforcement resources to keep things in check, prostitution, gambling, and illegal drugs proliferated in the growing population, especially in pipeline towns like Fairbanks. The boom also stressed local infrastructure, including schools and health care facilities. Meanwhile, some Alaska Native leaders knew they must aggressively protect the natural resources to which they were spiritually and physically connected.

Thankfully, the young state's founding fathers and mothers ensured that the state Constitution contained specific language guaranteeing equal rights and protections to all Alaskans, and empowered the First People's participation in the state's economic and political life.

One of those participants was Todd's mom, Blanche Kallstrom, who was among those who helped work on the Alaska Native Claims Settlement Act. The legislation would ultimately secure land and money to establish Native corporations, and ensure their inclusion in future resource developments that came from their aboriginal lands.

4

It was during these early years that Mom became interested in an expanded faith. She sought further spiritual fulfillment in addition to the liturgical traditions of the Catholic Church. In Wasilla, she volunteered as a secretary at the Presbyterian church on weekends and traveled to northern Alaska Eskimo villages on mission trips.

At about that time, her best friend, Mary Ellan Moe, a newly transplanted Texan, invited her to attend an evangelical church in Anchorage. There Mom found a depth of spirituality she had been seeking, the filling of what the French writer Blaise Pascal called "the god-shaped vacuum" in every human heart.

Back in Wasilla, the most "alive" congregation was our local Assembly of God, so my siblings and I attended Sunday School there and enjoyed attending the youth group with our friends. There weren't many churches in our small town, and though my family would eventually worship at a nondenominational Bible church, a lot of kids joined the youth group because it did a great job with activities that were what people used to call "good, clean fun."

One summer, I attended a youth Bible camp in Big Lake and understood for myself what Pascal was talking about. Looking around at the incredible creation that is Alaska—the majestic peaks and midnight sun, the wild waters and teeming wildlife— I could practically see and hear and feel God's spirit reflected in everything in nature. I reasoned that if God knew what He was doing in this magnificent creation, how much more did He know about me? If He is powerful and wise enough to make all this and thought also to create a speck like me, there surely must be a plan, and He'd know more than I did about my future and my purpose. I made the conscious decision that summer to put my life in my Creator's hands and trust Him as I sought my life's path.

My siblings and I were baptized together in Big Lake's freezing, pristine waters by Pastor Paul Riley. I got into the habit of reading Scripture before I got out of bed every morning and making sure it was the last thing I did at night. Ever the pragmatist, I also tested God's promises. For example, God says in Scripture, " 'Bring the whole tithe into the storehouse, that there may be food in my house. Test me in this,' says the LORD Almighty, 'and see if I will not throw open the floodgates of Heaven and pour out so much blessing that you will not have room enough for it.'" As a kid, to me that meant that if I earned five dollars, I put fifty cents in the offering plate. Later, Todd and I saw that there were many other ways to share our blessings with others, like buying a tank of gas for a bush pilot so he could fly supplies to a remote village. Not only was doing those things personally rewarding, but God continually proved His promises true, blessing our giving with giving of His own.

Dad wasn't into organized religion so much, and he was usually busy Sunday mornings getting ready for our afternoon ski trips or hunts or hikes; he said it was in the great outdoors that he "did church." But he did his fatherly duty, making us answer to him if we ended up skipping church for any reason. And Mom never let us get by with any weak excuses. Looking back, I'm grateful to them for "forcing me" to go. Without that foundation of faith, we would never have been able to get through some of the tests and trials that have come our way.

One such test came when I was in elementary school. The telephone rang during dinner. Dad left the table, picked up the beige wall phone in the living room, listened for a few minutes, and hung up. Then he turned away and stood stock-still, gazing silently out the big picture window. Looking at him, I was pretty sure he'd just received some bad news.

Dad's best friend, Dr. Curt Menard, had been working with his son, Curtis Jr., to drape fluorescent flagging over a power line that ran low across their homestead property. Curt, a dentist who had moved up from Michigan, was, like so many Alaskans, also a private pilot. He wanted to increase the visibility of the power line so that he could land his Citabria safely at home. While Curtis was holding the bottom rung of the metal ladder and Doc was standing on the top step slinging the flagging over the wire, the tip of his finger brushed the line. Current licked out like a snake's tongue, snapped his right hand around the wire, and shot enough electricity through his body to melt the ladder rung he'd been standing on, fry the outside of his legs and torso, and stop his heart. When the wire finally let him go, Doc plunged to the ground. Medical workers said later that the impact probably started his heart again and saved his life.

Miraculously, Curtis had let go of the ladder a split second before the accident and was physically unharmed.

When Dad took the phone call, he found out that physicians had to amputate Doc's right arm. I'll never forget the stricken look on Dad's face. I could see that he was crying. I had never seen him cry before.

Until then, I remember our family life being pretty idyllic. No real tragedies. No deaths among close family. After Doc lost his arm, Mom and Dad explained to us that every family goes through struggles and times of testing.

"We haven't really been through that yet," Mom said in a gentle warning.

That scared me at first. But then she comforted me, saying, "Maybe our challenge will be to care for other families who do."

For me, that conversation laid the foundation that you help other people. That everyone has a struggle and that when you don't, you comfort and support those who do. Plato said it well: "Be kind, for everyone you meet is fighting a hard battle." The conversation also warned me to not take our comfort for granted.

Doc fought his battle bravely. He retrained himself to be a left-handed, one-armed dentist. His staff would be his right arm, he said. My dad volunteered to be one of his first patients. Doc went on to serve as our borough mayor and in our legislature. For nearly four decades our two families' lives intertwined like flourishing vines, so much so that Curtis Jr. even grew up to be my firstborn's godfather.

5

In the Heath home, very little time was spent watching the "boob tube," as my folks called it. Even in the '70s, television shows were still tape-delayed in Alaska by as much as a week, and a lot of news was old news by the time it filtered up north. It was sometimes easy to fall out of the news loop, but still, in 1974, I noticed that the newspapers kept running front-page stories on what they were calling Watergate. News broadcasts kept repeating the same theme: President Richard Nixon was in trouble.

That year, when I was ten, we traveled back down to Skagway for a visit. Chuck, Heather, Molly, and I stayed with the Moores, the big family whose house I had been on my way to the day I tried to fly. During our visit, Mom and Dad took some friends mountain-goat hunting and trekking. Sometimes Dad guided in the summers and would take groups of travelers on the Chilkoot Trail, the same route used during the Klondike Gold Rush. One summer it was a Florida businessman named Tad Duke and a group of his friends. (Many of those people started out as tourists and wound up as lifelong Heath family friends; Tad Duke was one who ended up helping me thirty years later on the campaign trail.)

Our family loved that rugged Chilkoot hike, and Dad was happy to be out on the trail again that summer. I distinctly remember my folks returning after a week away and walking into the Moores' big kitchen. They hadn't had access to television or newspapers for days.

"Well, who's our president?" Dad asked.

Omigosh, that's right, I thought. *He doesn't even know that Richard Nixon resigned. America has a new president!*

I had been keeping track and was fascinated with the civics

lesson that unfolded across America that summer. It amazed me that the whole country seemed riveted, unified by watching the events unfold. It was the first time since the moon landing that I'd seen that, so I knew this Watergate thing had to be big. When Gerald Ford took over, I knew who he was because I remembered reading about him and seeing a picture in a scholastic magazine. He'd been America's vice president then, sitting parade-style atop the backseat of a convertible, waving at the crowd. Now he was our president!

Looking back, it seems significant that many of my clearest childhood memories involve politics and current events. I don't remember my ten-year-old friends being especially interested in who the president was, but to me it was a pretty big deal.

We finally got a TV at home, but Dad was clever with his limitations on it. He and his Idaho buddy Ray Carter, by then a fellow Wasilla teacher, built an unheated, gravel-floored garage attached to our house. On top of the structure they built what they called a family room, uninsulated and unfurnished, with only a wood-stove to heat it. It was rarely worth chopping and hauling extra firewood, stoking the flames, and waiting hours for the frozen room to heat up enough to enjoy watching anything—a dynamic that Dad was well aware of when he put the TV out there. But on Friday nights we sometimes braved thirty-below temperatures to watch *The Brady Bunch,* huddling together in down sleeping bags, so cold that when Greg, Marcia, and the gang finally solved the family problem of the week, we fought over who would have to venture out to change the channel. On Sundays, it was *The Lawrence Welk Show, 60 Minutes,* and *The Wonderful World of Disney.*

In our teen years, if we stayed awake long enough, we'd sneak upstairs and watch *Saturday Night Live.* Having grown up in a house where "butt" was a bad word and we had to say "bottom," we assumed we had to sneak. It wasn't until years later that we learned our parents got a kick out of *SNL's* political humor, too.

My folks were smart: less TV meant more books. From *The Pearl* to *Jonathan Livingston Seagull* to *Animal Farm* and anything by C. S. Lewis, I would put down one book just long enough to pick up another. The library on Main Street was one of my summer hideaways. I wandered through the stacks, thumbing through the smallish collection as though it were a secret treasure. One of my dad's buddies said that he never stopped by the Heaths' house when we didn't have our noses in a book or one of the magazines we subscribed to, including *National Geographic, Sports Illustrated,* or *Ranger Rick.*

The 1970s also ushered in the running craze across America, and my family was hooked. Mom and Dad had their friends training for marathons even on subzero winter days, and in the summertime, we ran together in the sunlit nights. On weekends, we squeezed in 10k family fun runs. My parents and sister Heather became decent marathoners. Dad qualified for the Boston Marathon and proudly represented Alaska twice at the Big Show. Mom, who was not at all athletic growing up, won her age group in the 26.2-mile Mayor's Midnight Sun Marathon, a testament to how Alaska can change a person.

At the time, running with my family was just a fun and expected thing to do, but it became a lifelong passion for me. For one thing, you don't have to be particularly coordinated or talented to do it. Eventually, though, I realized that the road, and especially marathon training, holds invaluable life lessons. That to reach your goal you have to put in the tough, drudging miles. That the best rewards often lie on the other side of pain. And that when it seems you can't take another step forward, there is a hidden reservoir of strength you can draw on to endure and finish well. Some would call it something spiritual, others would call it personal resolve, but I believe that reservoir resides in all of us. We all have opportunities to tap it. A couple of decades and four kids later, I finally reached my goal of running a sub-four-hour marathon. By a few seconds. When I finished that hellish exercise, I considered it one of my greatest accomplishments because it just hurt so bad.

Every year in school I ran for something in student government—vice president, treasurer, something. Curtis Jr. was usually president, and I always served with him. One year, I served as one of the student representatives for the Mat-Su school board. Our rival school, Palmer High, sent a representative who was the undisputed queen of the Mat-Su Valley, a dazzling and brainy cheerleader, Kristan Cole, who would play an important role in my future.

We were all expected to participate in most everything offered in our hometown: *of course* we'd be in 4-H, and Campfire Girls, and Scouts and ballet and band. *Of course* we'd take foreign-language courses and join the National Honor Society. And we went from sport to sport to sport.

One part of athletics I really appreciated was our local chapter of Fellowship of Christian Athletes, which I co-captained under the leadership of the Wasilla Warriors' wrestling coach, Mr. Foreman. At least sixty of us met in public school classrooms for Bible study and inspirational exchanges that motivated us to focus on hard work and excellence. In those days, ACLU activists had not yet convinced young people that they were supposed to feel offended by other people's free exercise of religion.

As an athlete who advanced more on tenacity than talent, I wanted sports to be my future but was realistic enough to know I wouldn't always be a player. That's why with my passion for both sports and the written word, becoming a sports reporter seemed like a natural fit. There were few women in the field, but

I couldn't see any reason why more women shouldn't bust through and succeed in this arena. Lesley Visser had already shattered the ceiling, breaking into the profession when the rules of the press box were plainly printed on media credentials: NO WOMEN OR CHILDREN ALLOWED.

I set out to follow that path, even memorializing in my high school yearbook my goal of someday working in the broadcast booth with Howard Cosell. Granted, conventional wisdom at the time was that sports reporting was a man's world, but in my family, gender was never allowed to be an issue. My parents gave us equal opportunity and expectations. We were all expected to work, build, chop, hunt, fish, and fight equally. I'm a product of Title IX and am proud that it was Alaska's own Senator Ted Stevens who helped usher through the federal legislation in 1972 to ensure girls would have the right to the same education and athletic opportunities as boys. I was a direct beneficiary of the equal rights efforts that had begun gaining traction only the decade before. Later, my own daughters would benefit, participating in sports like hockey, wrestling, and football, which had been closed to girls for decades.

I didn't subscribe to all the radical mantras of that early feminist era, but reasoned arguments for equal opportunity definitely resonated with me. It was a matter not of ideology but of simple fairness. Standing on the shoulders of women who had won hard-fought battles for things like equal pay and equal access, I grew up knowing I could be anything I wanted to be. Years later I came across a book by fellow Alaskan (and former basketball rival from Fairbanks) Jessica Gavora called *Tilting the Playing Field,* about the liberating effect of Title IX on women's sports, and I agreed with a lot of what she wrote: "Instead of reflecting and, indeed, reveling in our expanded horizons, the feminism of the National Organization for Women and other so-called 'women's groups' . . .

depicts women as passive victims rather than the makers of their own destinies, and overlooks our individuality in favor of a collective political identity that many of us find restrictive."

Sports empowered me to plow through some Neanderthal thinking that still permeates corners of our culture, including some parts of that thing we call American politics. Jessica and I are from the same era and have the same Alaska spirit, so it's no surprise that we consider ourselves more liberated than some women's rights groups would have us believe we are.

———

Dad coached many of our teams, Mom was an assistant running coach, and they expected us all to participate and work hard, no matter what our talent. We lived by the creed that passion is what counts. Our parents were as proud of us when we won little awards, like the Presidential Physical Fitness patch, as when we won bigger ones, like the time I was named MVP of our high school cross-country team.

My siblings all won many more sports awards than I, as I wasn't equipped with anything close to their natural talent. But I once overheard Dad say to another coach that he'd never had an athlete work harder. Overhearing those words was one of the most powerful experiences of my life. Maybe God didn't give me natural athleticism—other athletes could run faster, jump higher, and hit the basket more often—but I loved competition. I loved pushing myself and even relished pushing through pain to reach a goal. I realized that my gift was determination and resolve, and I have relied on it ever since.

Because Dad was our coach, there was extra scrutiny and pressure. It seemed to me that he went out of his way to dispel any perceived nepotism. I felt a jealous twinge, and even hurt sometimes, when he'd give other athletes an inspiring word or comforting arm around the shoulder but would give me the proverbial slug in the arm and tell me to "work harder." I know now why he did that, and what seemed a double standard at the time did make me work harder and become stronger.

There were practical benefits of having Dad coach, though. He knew how much I disliked playing in the pep band after a tough basketball game, but it was required of all band students that we play for the boys' games following ours, so Dad would tape my fingers and I'd explain to the conductor that I needed to be excused yet again from the flute section: "It's those darn sprained fingers again, sir!"

But there was no excuse for not giving my all to sports—especially not boys. One night at the dinner table, Dad noticed some ink marks on my hand.

"What's that?" he asked.

I quickly put my hand under the table. "Nothin'."

"Looked like somebody's name to me."

I didn't say anything, just stared down at my spaghetti.

"You have a choice between boys and sports," Dad said sternly. "You're at the age where I start losing my good athletes because they start liking boys. You can't have both."

I stood up, walked to the sink, and washed the kid's initials off my hand. Some might see that as the wrong way to set parameters. But for me, it was fine to have these high expectations made clear.

Just because Dad steered me away from an early crush didn't mean he couldn't appreciate that I had a softer side. Early one morning when I was a teenager, he and I went hunting before school. Dad bagged a moose pretty quickly and began field dressing it right away so we could both get to school on time. Killing two birds with one stone, he could fill our freezer plus bring in specimens to dissect for his students.

"Here, hold these," he said. "I want to show them to my science class today."

I looked down to see the moose's eyeballs lying in his palm, still warm from the critter's head. But when he saw me wrinkle my nose and shake my head slightly, he set them aside. He realized that even though he had raised me to be a solid hunting buddy, I had my limits.

In between sports and school we worked. I cleaned a small local office building by myself, every Sunday night, through all four years of high school, for $30 a weekend. I babysat. I waitressed. My sister and I picked strawberries in the mud and mosquitoes at Dearborn's local farm for five cents a flat. We inventoried groceries on dusty shelves at the local store. We swept parking lots to raise money for our next softball tournament and raked leaves to make money for trips to basketball camps and track competitions in Texas. We did not think to ask our parents to pay our way. I was proud to be able to buy my own running shoes and sports equipment.

I took pride in my work, and my parents took pride in my working. The expectation was that we would all go to college and pay our own way, no questions asked.

It was in softball that Coach Reid Smith taught me another lesson that served me well for years. He told one of our rookie outfielders, who was almost as weak a player as I was, to quit jumping around and acting all gleeful when she successfully caught a fly ball.

"That's what you're supposed to do, girl!" he yelled. "Quit acting surprised when you do what you're put there to do!"

Early in my political career, I would remember that lesson. When things went right under my administration's leadership, sometimes I'd look around and wonder why no one but me was jumping with joy. Then I'd recall Coach Smith's holler from years ago: "You were put there to do this, so don't act surprised." (And don't look to anyone else to cheer you either.)

In high school, I played basketball, my name next to number 22 on the varsity roster all four years. I mainly rode the bench during close games, until my senior year, because I played point guard behind a much stronger player, my sister Heather. Our team was made up of a group of best girlfriends, like Kim "Tilly" Ketchum and Karen Bush, who shared everything, including our faith. (Tilly taught me to drive her sister's VW stick shift on the way to practices, and she and our other girlfriend, Adele Morgan, were my partners in shop class, which we took to avoid home ec.) We were the Cinderella team my sophomore and junior years, having fallen short in hard-fought state championship games in back-to-back years. But as soon as Heather and her senior team-mates graduated, the B-team finally had the opportunity to prove we had it in us.

6

By my senior year of high school, I had been praying that God wouldn't have in mind for my future one of the local boys I'd grown up with. I loved those guys a lot, but I looked at them all like brothers. I had just about given up hope that I would ever meet a guy I could really like as more than just a buddy. Then a new kid came to town.

In late August 1981, my dad drove to Wasilla High to get his classroom ready for the start of the school year. That night at dinner, he had news to share.

"Stopped by the gym to talk with some of the coaches today," he said. "That new kid, Palin, was there. I watched him practice for a while. I can tell you right now, he's the best basketball player Wasilla's ever had."

My ears perked up. A week later, between our pickup basketball scrimmages in the Warrior gym, I finally met this mystery guy. When I saw him, my world turned upside down. I actually whispered, "Thank you, God."

Todd Palin roared into my life in a 1972 Ford Mustang. Handsome and independent, he was part Yupik Eskimo and had moved to Wasilla from Dillingham, a fishing town on the chilly, rugged shores of Bristol Bay. Todd was only sixteen and had come to town to play his senior year of basketball on a strong Warriors squad, a goal that coincided with career opportunities for his parents. His newly remarried father, Jim Palin, was in line to run the local electric utility. His stepmom, Faye Palin, would move up to vice president at the telephone company.

Todd was so different from any kid I'd ever known. He made all his own decisions, from finances to future plans. Not only was he one of the only kids in town who owned his own ride—he owned *two*, the Mustang and a 1973 Ford F-150 long-bed pickup that he used to haul a pair of Polaris snowmachines. By the time I met him, he had honed an independent spirit and a sterling work ethic that drew me like a magnet, and would help define me and clarify my life's priorities more than anything else.

Todd thought nothing of doing things like driving the fifty miles into Anchorage by himself anytime he wanted to, which was a big deal to the rest of us, who had neither vehicles nor parents who would let us do such a thing.

Todd had purchased his rigs himself, which blew us away because not many Valley kids had such luxuries, much less owned them outright. He didn't come from a wealthy family but from a very hardworking family. He was a commercial fisherman, drifting for red salmon in the rich waters of Bristol Bay. It was his Native family's tradition to make their livelihood and subsist on the water. Todd made more money as a young teen in one fishing season than I'd made with all the jobs I'd ever held, combined over many years.

Todd's grandmother Lena, who is almost ninety, is a Yupik Eskimo elder and was one of the first female commercial fishermen on the bay. His grandfather Al Andree was a boatbuilder. Together Al and Lena helped start the Bristol Bay fishery in the 1930s, drifting for salmon from sailboats, navigating the frigid winds and ebb and flow of the tides, figuring out even on windless days how to get fish to the tenders, where they sold for just a nickel apiece. The women braved the icy chop, the fish slime, the blood, and the stench, out there fishing with the men, and Lena was one of the first.

Todd started fishing Bristol Bay at a very young age and grew up in this multigenerational industry. Lena saw the fishery as a God-given resource that provided for the family. She believed in sweat equity. Using commercial fishing as an economic bootstrap, Todd's family owned and operated the town's hardware store, hotel, mechanic shop, and other businesses, ultimately employing scores of people. Their efforts in free enterprise became an economic engine in the region.

The Palin-Kallstrom family was also the most generous I have ever met, willing to give the shirts off their backs for those in need. Todd's mother, Blanche Kallstrom, ran her businesses that way and has been materially blessed for being so generous to others.

———

Todd has always had great respect for Alaska's environment. Through meeting him and his family, I began to truly appreciate not only Alaska's natural diversity but its social diversity, too. Todd came from a different world than I, with this huge, exotic family that splintered off in several directions and was impacted by some of the societal ills that plague Native villages in Alaska. Though his upbringing was unconventional and tough at times, Todd bore down and built a reputation for working harder than men twice his age—men who had far more tools and advantages than this kid who shuffled among parents', grandparents', and great-grandparents' homes. Todd had what is uniquely beautiful in our Native culture—"cousins" everywhere. It's tradition that even a second or third cousin is referred to as "cousin," and his family seemed to have hundreds.

Todd witnessed things that many Americans never will. There are tough conditions in some villages, and the harsh circumstances lead some to abuse both alcohol and each other, and societal ills that include despondency and suicides. Todd saw it all. He also saw opportunities to react to circumstances in productive ways.

Despite his steel core, Todd was shy and quiet in demeanor, typical of Yupik men, who, unlike some others, don't feel the need to fill up the air around them with words all the time. He was also incredibly well-mannered and polite to my parents, who were smitten with his work ethic and his constant offers to help anyone who needed anything. He stacked firewood for Dad and drove my mom out to the mountains so she could find the perfect skiing conditions. He picked up Molly and me for practices so we wouldn't have to walk. Todd and Dad hit it off because not only could Todd fix anything, but Dad had never met anyone who had an even greater respect for Alaska and her wildlife than we did.

My family fell in love with Todd right along with me.

Coming from a family full of very strong, independent women, Todd didn't find me a surprise in that way. But he tells me that he was most attracted to my solid family. He was crazy about my parents and knew that if they were such good family people, we had the potential to continue that tradition. As we grew up and grew together, our priorities became apparent. Neither of us was into heavy-duty materialism. We weren't into fancy food, fancy clothes, fancy anything. He was very practical: he bought his car because he needed transportation; he bought his truck to haul his snowmachines.

We certainly had differences.

I was broke. I was nerdy. I played the flute.

He cussed. He chewed. He didn't go to church.

But when he told me he had become a Christian and had been baptized at a sports camp a few years earlier, that was the clincher for me.

Amidst our hometown group of friends' shared interests, difference after difference struck me with Todd. He seemed so much more enlightened than the rest of us and had such a sense of justice. He hated gossip and pretension. He hated prejudice. He opposed any physical disrespect of the land, from litter to irresponsible development. He talked about respect for nature, especially for the waters he was born and raised on. He truly was a conservationist and was adamant about using every part of any animal he hunted.

I admired Todd's great reverence for his elders, especially his wise grandparents. At the time, I felt I barely knew my grandparents, and I envied his Native culture, which taught him to know well and honor those who had helped raise him. I learned from Todd that Native youth are taught to listen and learn from their elders and not to run their mouths.

Todd absolutely loved children. He had a cousin with Down syndrome whom he cherished, and even with all my babysitting jobs I had no experience with children with special needs. I always wondered how I'd handle someday meeting this special relative.

Our senior year, when my girlfriends were receiving the standard "cool" gifts, like Van Halen cassette tapes and L.A. Lakers sweatshirts, Todd gave me gold nugget earrings, nestled in a grass-woven Native basket instead of a gift box, the consummate Alaskana gift. He didn't worry about money as much as my friends and I did because he knew he'd fish the next season and would be rewarded according to how hard he worked the waters.

Because Todd had been exposed to conditions in rural Alaska many of us cannot imagine, he'd made tough decisions on his own from a young age. Because of that, principles like honesty, justice, and accountability became crucial to his life perspective, and he understood intuitively that you get to *choose* how to respond to circumstances around you—even those out of your control. You get to decide what's really important and what your attitude will be.

Our background differences were exciting to me and opened up my more sheltered world. We spent more and more time together, and when we couldn't, we still stayed connected. With four teenagers in our house, our single landline phone was off-limits for long boyfriend-girlfriend calls. But Todd and I discovered we could close the five miles between our homes if we stood on our back porches and used the handheld VHF radios he used on his fishing boat in Bristol Bay. For months, we snuck whispered nighttime chats until we discovered that the commercial truckers barreling through town could hear us.

I snuck other things with Todd, too: Copenhagen dipping tobacco, which I tried for the first time about an hour before I met his mother, Blanche. (Todd cracked up watching me trying to make conversation with her, while I gagged with dry heaves and cold sweats caused by the nauseating chew.) My first chug of beer, with Todd and Tilly the summer after we graduated. My first PG-13-equivalent movie, which Todd and I watched on the VCR at my friend Karen's house.

Then, on the drive home in his Mustang, he tried to kiss me for the first time. But the truth was, I was a never-really-been-kissed nerd. As soon as Todd hit my driveway, I jumped out of the car, scared to death that this suave worldly guy that I was crazy about would find out what a wallflower I was.

The next day, my sheltered little world felt shattered when he told the boys in the locker room—my "brothers" whom I'd grown up with—that I didn't even know how to kiss. I was mortified. He thought it was sweet and figured it reflected innocent modesty, but I was humiliated, sure that the whole school now knew the story. My young, crushed spirit learned a lesson about guys that day: even the good ones can act like jerks.

7

My friends and I lived for basketball, and at the beginning of my senior year, we counted down the days until the season began. A reporter from the Mat-Su Valley *Frontiersman* asked for my preseason prediction. Speaking for the team, I declared that we'd go all the way, that we wanted a state championship. To us, losing state for a third straight year would be intolerable.

I spoke off the cuff and from the heart, but walked away from the interview with a sense of dread, fearing that my words would be interpreted as cocky and naive. When the sports page came out, I swallowed hard, read what I'd said, and decided I'd have to work that much harder to live up to my bold proclamation.

It was supposed to be a rebuilding year for the Warriors. But Karen and I, and other benchwarmers, like Jackie Conn and Michelle Carney, Amy, Wanda, Katie, and Heyde, resented the years we had spent riding the pine. We were determined to make up for it, to show our respected Coach Teeguarden and Coach Randall what they'd been missing out on, and to seize the opportunity to win. As a captain, I played furiously; I drew a lot of fouls, but I brought everything I had to every practice and every game. I left everything on the court because I simply wanted the team to win.

I was certain I wanted victory for my team more than any opponent wanted it, and that would be the key to reaching my goal of a state championship, even though we were an underdog team. When I have opportunities to speak to athletes today, I always ask these kids what I asked myself that season: Who wants it more? Who will work harder for it? And who will be most prepared when the opportunity arises to score and win?

I was bold but pragmatic. I reminded my teammates that through all our years playing the sport together, all our camps, our practices, games, seasons, our obsession with it all, at one time or another we had defeated every one of our opponents. So there was no reason we couldn't beat them one more time in that final, shining season.

Game by game, week by week, our scrappy but determined team surprised everyone by piling up victories. As the season progressed, I recalled my newspaper prediction and thought that maybe we had a shot at making it come true. We were on a roll. But then I stumbled. It was hard, painful, and very public.

During a game in the regional tournament a week before state, I came down wrong on my right foot, twisted my ankle underneath me, and felt a sickening pop. Coach Teeguarden carried me off the floor and the rest of the team carried us to regional victory. I was devastated to think that my season, my dream, was over.

It was just days before the state tournament, and I refused to see a doctor because I didn't want to hear him say something was broken. I hobbled around and sat on the bench through a week of practices with my foot planted in a bucket of ice. But after all we'd been through, I decided it would be over my dead body that I'd sit the bench in the state tournament.

At state, we battled through the bracket and made it to the championship game. Our little Wasilla Warriors team faced the big Anchorage squad, the Service Cougars. Coach T. knew how badly I wanted to play. I had shown him through four seasons that I would give 100 percent effort no matter the cost, so he took a chance and gave me a shot. He put me in the game. I made it up and down the court, not gracefully but playing as hard as I could. I'd never worked so hard for anything in my life, because I'd never wanted anything so badly. I felt like I couldn't pull my weight, but I encouraged the team: if we stayed together and played selflessly, I promised them we would win. My teammates were tenacious, intense, and focused, and we never let up. I scored only one point that game, a free throw in the waning seconds. But we pulled off the upset.

That victory changed my life. More than anything else to that point, it proved what my parents had been trying to instill in me all along: that hard work and passion matter most of all.

Everything I ever needed to know, I learned on the basketball court. And to this day, my right ankle is a knobby and misshapen thing, a daily reminder of pushing through pain.

———

In May 1982, Todd and I walked together during our graduation ceremony in the Warrior gym, dressed in caps and gowns to match our school colors, red and white. Over the next six years, we kept walking together, though we'd be thousands of miles apart.

Todd headed off to play basketball at a college in Seattle but eventually felt drawn back to Alaska, to the kind of hard work he thrived on. He earned his private pilot's license in Prescott,

Arizona, along the way. I kicked off college by taking a semester to thaw out; along with Tilly and two other girlfriends, we flew to Hawaii for our freshman year of college. Our intention was to play basketball there, but we made it to only a few tryouts and then decided we'd better concentrate on our studies . . . and the beach. It turned out that Hawaii was a little too perfect. Perpetual sunshine isn't necessarily conducive to serious academics for eighteen-year-old Alaska girls. Besides, we were homesick for mountains, cooler seasons, and even snow. After that first semester, we realized we'd better transfer back to something closer to reality so we could actually earn our degrees.

Tilly and I opted for a more conventional and affordable campus, choosing Idaho because it was much like Alaska yet still "Outside" (Alaskans' alternative term for the Lower 48). I still desperately wanted to earn a journalism degree and to put my passion for sports and writing to work as a sports reporter.

After our freshman year, Tilly and I returned to Wasilla for summer work at a little diner. While we were home, our friend Linda Menard, Doc's wife, talked me into entering the local Miss America Scholarship Pageant with the promise of tuition for college.

I thought it was a horrendous idea, at first. I was a jock and quite square, not a pageant-type girl at all. I didn't wear makeup in high school and kept my hair short because I didn't like wasting time primping. I couldn't relate to the way I assumed most cheerleader types thought and lived, and figured it was those girls who were equipped for the pageant thing.

On the other hand, there *was* the scholarship money. I knew I wasn't a good enough athlete to get a Division I scholarship, but I did want to graduate debt-free. Was there some way I could make this work?

I thought about it for a couple of days. My stomach knotted up at the thought of parading around onstage in a swimsuit, especially since I'd packed on the famous "Freshman 15" and wasn't in the best shape of my life. It would be humbling at best, risky and embarrassing at worst. But a scholarship was a scholarship, and in the end, pragmatism won out. Half seriously, I wondered if the pageant organization would accept for the talent portion of the competition a fancy display of right- and left-handed dribbling. But Linda suggested I play the flute, something I'd been doing since age ten.

Linda also reminded me that the scholarship money was generous, especially if I won individual competitions within the pageant, in addition to the Miss Wasilla crown. I enlisted the advice of a former pageant winner, my friend Diane Minnick. Then I shocked my friends and family, put on a sequined Warrior-red gown, danced the opening numbers, gave the interview, and uncomfortably let my butt be compared to the cheerleaders' butts. I played my flute, and I won. In fact, I won every segment of the competition, even Miss Congeniality.

The Miss Wasilla Scholarship paid my college tuition that fall. The following summer, I progressed to the next round and was crowned second runner-up and Miss Congeniality in the Miss Alaska Scholarship Pageant. I had to admit it was good tuition money, as well as a good testing ground for public speaking and issue advocacy, and I was happy to be even more involved in the community via this nontraditional adventure that took me out of my comfort zone. I went on to pay for two more years of college the same way.

Recently, my sister Molly unearthed an old pageant video, a Q&A exchange with a judge that I had completely forgotten about. Molly laughed as she recounted the exchange about the fact that not much has changed, besides the '80s pageant hair.

JUDGE: Geraldine Ferraro recently became the first female vice presidential candidate representing a major American political party. Do you think a woman can be vice president?

ME: Yes. I believe a woman could be vice president. I believe a woman could be president.

JUDGE: Would you vote for a vice presidential or presidential candidate just because she was a woman?

ME: No, I would not vote for someone just because they were a woman. I would vote for the candidate that reflected my political beliefs and had strong character and family values.

JUDGE: What do you think are Alaska's best attributes?

ME: One of the best attributes of Alaska is its beauty, and everything that the great Alaska outdoors has to offer, from hunting and fishing to snowmachining in winter. And Alaska has amazing potential in drilling for oil on the North Slope. But unfortunately some Outsiders don't understand Alaska's potential in developing our vast natural resources.

That exchange, a quarter century ago, now seems either strangely coincidental or a Providential signpost pointing toward my future. And I don't believe in coincidences.

8

Idaho's down-home feeling and gorgeous campus on the rolling hills of the Palouse helped lessen the homesickness I felt for Alaska. Childhood friends from the Carter and Carney families attended the University of Idaho with me, and even Chuck and Molly were fellow Vandals. They pledged Greek, so I enjoyed extended Sigma Alpha Epsilon and Alpha Phi families through them. But I, ever the independent, was proudly GDI.

I was amazed when my education became an issue in the vice presidential campaign. "Well, look at that," the pundits said, "she went to all those different schools, and it took her five years to graduate."

Yes, it did take me five years because I paid my own way. Tilly and I came home to Alaska between semesters and worked so we could earn money to pay for the next term. Sometimes we had to take a semester off and work until we could afford tuition again. I remember when that was an honorable thing.

At UI, I lived in an all-girls dorm. I planned on a political science minor because I loved studying U.S. history and government and knew poli sci would mesh well with a journalism major.

Although my family wasn't political, and certainly not obsessively partisan, I registered to vote in 1982, at age eighteen, and proudly checked the Republican box on the registration form. I had read both major party platforms, and the GOP just made sense for someone like me, a believer in individual rights and responsibilities rather than heavy-handed government; in free-market principles that included reward for hard work; respect for equality; support for a strong military; and a belief that America is the best country on earth.

I looked forward to every poli sci lecture. I attributed my enthusiasm to patriotism and a fascination with current events. I was also eager because this was the 1980s and our studies centered on one of the most inspiring individuals ever to occupy the White House, President Ronald W. Reagan.

I was in high school the day Reagan took the oath of office. On the same day, minutes after he was sworn in, a band of Iranian militants released fifty-two Americans, after having held them— and our national pride—hostage for 444 days. I had followed the Iran hostage crisis and remember wondering why President Jimmy Carter didn't act more decisively. From my high schooler's perspective, I thought the question was, Why did he allow America to be humiliated and pushed around? The new president being sworn in radiated confidence and optimism. The enemies of freedom took notice. In years to come people would ask, What did he have that Carter didn't? To me the answer was obvious. He had a steel spine.

I appreciated Reagan's passion and conviction, and the way he so plainly articulated his love for our country. Like millions of others, I related to him personally—he was one of us. I liked him, and I liked the fact that he was never afraid to call it as he saw it.

During the previous decade, we seemed to have slid into a darker period as a country: Vietnam, Watergate, the energy crisis, the perception of environmental abuses, the Iran humiliation (made worse by the abortive hostage rescue attempt). Reagan's optimism restored our faith in ourselves. Yes, maybe our nation had veered off course, he seemed to be saying, but not only could we right ourselves, America's best days were still ahead.

As Reagan's presidency unfolded, I also appreciated his focus on a handful of overarching themes, such as reining in the intrusiveness of government, building a strong national defense, and cutting taxes. I knew the previous administration had left a legacy of soaring unemployment, sky-high taxes, and rampant inflation. Reagan's plan for growing our economy made common sense: reduce reliance on government by cutting taxes and putting more money into the hands of the people who earned it.

At the peak of Soviet military power, Democrats had retreated into an embarrassed pacifism, cutting defense projects and reducing our troop strength. But the new Republican president I was studying in school unabashedly set out to make the United States the strongest power in the world. Reagan's plan for national defense was logical: to build up our military while pursuing diplomacy with the Soviet Union. Critics derided him as a warmonger, but as the violent twentieth century came to an end, Reagan's position ultimately led to a climactic victory for freedom and peace with the collapse of the Iron Curtain and the liberation of millions from the tyranny of Communism. Reagan won the Cold War without firing a shot.

"America is still the abiding alternative to tyranny," Reagan said. "That is our purpose in the world—nothing more and nothing less."

Ideas and speeches like that inspired me. I had always subscribed to concepts like Providence and purpose, that people aren't just random collections of molecules stumbling aimlessly through history. I believed—and still do—that each person has a destiny, a reason for being. So Reagan's sense of national purpose resonated with me. His speeches on the subject evoked in me the sense of national pride I had felt even back at Eagle River Elementary School when I watched our astronauts explore the Final Frontier. As Reagan said, America was more than a place in the world; it was a world-changing *idea,* founded on a set of principles that had weathered many storms. Reagan restored our faith that those principles would prove themselves again.

During semesters in college and summers back in Alaska, I interned at a couple of TV sports desks. I covered high school and college sports, putting together packages and writing sports copy for many anchors, including the two guys who gave me a chance— John Hernandez and John Carpenter. On weekends during one season, I anchored the sports desk live. I loved the intensity of the newsroom, the deadlines, the adrenaline. Unmarried and with no kids, I spent hours and hours at the station. I felt I was on my way.

I also began paying more and more attention to the chatter from the news desk, especially at Anchorage's NBC affiliate,

KTUU. It was always politics first and everything except natural disasters second. In Alaska, we don't have big-league professional sports teams or many celebrities (except famous dog mushers), so for many up here politics is just another sport. So even as I covered sports, my interest in public policy and how it affected people continued to grow.

In Alaska, much of our local news involves natural resource issues, balancing human needs with environmental ones. The Alaska Constitution charges state government with managing natural resources "for abundance"—for equal access to plentiful supplies—and that takes conscientious stewardship. For many in Alaska, being "green" isn't about wearing Birkenstocks and driving a hybrid; it's about survival.

Throughout this time, Todd and I continued to see each other. Though miles apart during college, we wrote letters, made phone calls, and saw each other during vacations. But it was challenging trying to stay together while so far apart. It was a huge relief when I graduated, grabbed my diploma, and beat feet back to Alaska, happy to be in the same state as Todd.

I joined him on the Bristol Bay fishing grounds. During slow salmon runs with Todd, I worked messy, obscure seafood jobs, including long shifts on a stinky shore-based crab-processing vessel in Dutch Harbor. Another season, I sliced open fish bellies, scraped out the eggs, and plopped the roe into packaging. All of us on that job thought it was hilarious that the company would slap a caviar label on the . . . er, delicacy . . . and sell it to elite consumers for loads of money. Practically every kid in Alaska has spent at least one summer working some kind of "slime line."

At the end of one summer, twenty-one-year-old Todd finished up the salmon season by celebrating over beers with his fishing partners in Dillingham. Then he jumped into his truck to drive the empty dirt road home—and got busted for a DUI. It was a humiliating mistake, a big wake-up call to be charged with drinking and driving in his hometown. He'd later tell an employer in a job interview that it was his most critical lesson, because it woke him up to the danger of making stupid decisions. He said it changed his life.

In the summer of 1988, I fished again with Todd, but this time during slow runs I waited tables at the rowdy Bristol Inn, where drunken fishing crews doled out more in tips than I earned on the water all season. Still, money was tight because we had to reinvest our earnings in new nets and boat motors that season.

By the end of summer, Todd and I didn't want to spend more time apart. So we took our broke butts down to the Palmer Courthouse and lassoed a magistrate to pronounce us man and wife. Our witnesses would come from where they often do at this courthouse, across the street at the old folks' home.

I walked over to the Palmer Pioneers Home to see who was available, and Todd followed me in the car, saying, "See if you can find a couple of people who can make it to the car without wheelchairs."

I couldn't find any who fit the bill. But I found a nice elderly man with a walker and a kindly old lady in a wheelchair who agreed to see us into matrimony. They couldn't squeeze into Todd's little Honda coupe, so we had no choice but to escort them across the street, where, on August 29, 1988, those nice Alaska pioneers witnessed the beginning of two lives joined together at the Palmer Courthouse. The magistrate, Mrs. Fife, was young and brand new to the position, and she cried as she read the boiler-plate vows. Then we walked our witnesses back across the street and stopped by the Wendy's drive-thru for our wedding dinner.

Very much in love and oblivious to the idea that we needed to do anything conventional for anyone else's sake, we left flowers on our parents' front porches with notes announcing that we'd eloped. I heard later that Mom bawled. I'd do the same. I tell my kids now that I'll wring their necks if they do what I did. I want my kids to have the wedding I didn't have.

Todd moved into the apartment that my sister Heather and I shared in Anchorage, and the three of us undertook a whirlwind work schedule that turned our tiny apartment into a revolving door. Todd worked as a baggage handler for an Alaska Airlines subsidiary during the day and worked at night plowing snow and clearing the steps of the BP Exploration Alaska office building until the fishing season would start again. I worked customer service at an Anchorage electric utility during the day and reported for a local station part-time in the evenings and on weekends. Heather put her college degree to work, working with audiologists in special needs children's classrooms.

Todd applied for a full-time job with BP working in the North Slope oil fields. We hoped he'd land the kind of Slope job so many young Alaskans dream of so he could work a schedule that would allow him to enjoy as many of our outdoor passions as possible while making a good living. While he waited, he worked. I remember him working so hard that he dropped to about 150 pounds from handling the bags in the belly of the plane. (Surely it couldn't have been my newlywed cooking skills that contributed to that.)

While he slimmed down, I porked up, pregnant with our first child. As the months went on, Todd's prayer was answered by an offer for a permanent position with BP: he'd move up from plowing parking lots to working a week-on, week-off schedule in the rich oil patch that BP partially controlled in Prudhoe Bay near the top of the continent, earning a king's ransom of $14 an hour.

When I made the happy announcement that Todd would be a Sloper, Dad responded, "Is that good news or bad news?"

He knew the pros and cons of the physical separation endured by Slope families. He'd seen many of his students whose parents' marriages collapsed under the demands of Slope life. Todd and I were excited about it, though. We'd been together but separate for many years already, so we figured we could handle whatever life dished out. We put it all in God's hands.

9

On April 20, 1989, my life truly began. I became a mom. I had no idea how this tiny person, my son, would turn me inside out and upside down with the all-consuming love that swelled my heart from the second he was born. As clichéd as it sounds, that was the happiest day of my life.

The two previous days, however, were not.

On April 18, I went into labor. I called Todd and asked him to fly home early from his weekly hitch on the Slope—a mere 858-mile commute, one way—to meet me, my mom, and Blanche at my parents' house. I had set up camp there for the night, trying to find comfort while ignoring Dad's attempt at humor: "I'm sticking close to home for the next few days," he told a buddy on the phone. "Sarah's ready to calve."

I was quite a cocky young mom-to-be. I'd gone through the requisite childbirth class (we were going to use the Lamaze method), and, being an athlete used to pain, I figured, *How tough could giving birth be?*

Oh. My. Gosh. I thought I was going to die. In fact, I began to pray that I *would* die.

A laserlike searing rolled through me in waves, from my knees to my belly button. Had any woman ever hurt this much? I didn't think so. I gritted my teeth and willed myself not to scream.

Todd made it down from the Slope the next day. Between nuclear-level contractions, I couldn't climb into our truck, so I squeezed sideways and backward into the passenger seat of Mom's Subaru, my belly poking out like a medicine ball, and Todd drove me to Valley Hospital. We saw the sign where we were supposed to go—DELIVERIES—and followed the arrows.

He parked the car, helped me out, and we entered through a rear entrance. Struggling down hallway after hallway, stopping for contractions in the industrial zone, I glanced over to see Todd near a janitor's closet telling a maintenance worker: "You guys need better signage to get people through to deliveries!"

Since I thought I was dying, I didn't care that we were in the warehouse part of the hospital. I figured I'd just die there near the delivery trucks. I even came close to thinking that someday we'd laugh about it.

All through my perfect, healthy pregnancy, I had pictured this peaceful Earth Mother birth experience, the lights low in the delivery room, maybe even some of that nature-sound music playing in the background. Like a pioneer woman, I would bravely deliver our firstborn, Todd beaming beside me, with the Alaska wilderness waiting outside to welcome our son, the newest addition to Nature's grand march of creatures great and small.

Instead, by the time the nurses got me prepped, I was sweating and panting, trying to do those infernal breathing techniques, when what I really wanted to do was scream bloody murder and beg for drugs. Blessed Mother of Jesus, I finally got them!

The delivery room was chaos: the doctor and nurses bustling around; Todd and my mom saying sweet, soothing, irritating things; my mother-in-law angling for a better shot with a video camera that I cursed every time she aimed it.

Many hours later, though, chaos evaporated when Track CJ

Palin was born. The world went away, and in a crystallizing instant, I knew my purpose.

As the nurse laid my son gently in my arms, Todd and I laughed and cried together. It was a profound moment, unexpected, overwhelming. In the space of a few minutes, we'd gone from being two individuals to being a family.

My nature-loving dad became a grandpa for the first time that spring day. He said he'd never forget the day because it's when the geese return north to migrate. He liked Track's name, but he mistakenly assumed it signified adventure.

"Track, right?" he said. "Like tracking an elephant?"

I explained that no, it was because obviously we loved sports, and the baby was born during the spring track season.

"What if he'd been born during wrestling season?" Dad asked. "Would you have named him 'Wrestle'?"

"No," I said, smiling, "we'd have named him 'Mat.'"

"And if he'd been born during basketball?"

"We could've called him 'Court.'"

"And hockey?"

"What's wrong with 'Zamboni'?"

Todd and I had been counting down the days to meet our son, always referring to him as Track, so we were used to the sound of the name. It took us aback to realize that the name sounded odd to others. After so many people did a double take, we sighed and gave in, joking that his real name was "Track? Oooh . . . Track!"

Later, Track would come home from kindergarten and declare that he wanted a change. "I want to be named something *normal*, Mom!"

"Okay, son, what should we change your name to?" I said.

He turned his tiny face up, brown eyes blazing. "Like I told you, something *normal*. I want to be called 'Colt'!"

"Normal" is a subjective concept.

From the beginning, I was head over heels in love with him and convinced that I was the most important person in his world. He had my heart then (and now). Becoming a mom mellowed my drive toward making it as a big-time sports reporter. I didn't want to leave Track with anyone, so I only worked weekends at a couple of network affiliates in Anchorage. Heather babysat at her house near the studio and brought him by when I couldn't stand another minute without inhaling the soft scent of his downy hair and baby skin.

When Track was just a couple of months old, the commercial fishing season began. Todd was low man on the BP totem pole, so he couldn't take much time off to work our leased site on the shores of Bristol Bay. We depended on the season's catch as part of our annual household income, so Dad and I, along with our fishing partner, Nick Timurphy, a full-blooded Eskimo, fished it without our captain. Nick often spoke Yupik to me, especially when I was too slow picking fish.

"Amci! Amci!" he'd yell. It meant "Hurry! Hurry!"

Nick used to flavor it up with Eskimo quasi-cussing. When I'd throw the wrong buoy over the bow or stumble around trying to pull anchor, he'd shout, *"Alingnaafa, Sarah!"* It meant, "Oh, my goodness, Sarah!" Or so he claimed.

One summer (before Todd and I married) my hair was too long and my messy bangs kept getting in the way out on the water, so Nick cut them with a pocketknife. Later, he carved me an ivory ring in the shape of a seal. I used it for my wedding ring the day I eloped.

I headed to the Bay to work the site when Track was just ten weeks old. Mom came along to babysit. It broke my heart to leave him for whole days at a time while I was out on the water plucking salmon from the nets, but I did what I had to do.

Just before Track was born, Todd and I moved to a small apartment in Wasilla, next door to our good friend Curtis Menard, Jr., who by now was a dentist like his dad. Curtis was like a brother to me. We asked him to be Track's godfather. Todd and I shared one car, and we loved our little life together, though with the Slope and fishing schedule we still didn't see each other very much. I was surprised by how much I loved motherhood. We desperately wanted another baby right away, so I was excited when I learned I was pregnant again. We were sure it was another boy, and we decided to call him Tad, a combination of Todd and Track.

I loved the fact we had planned so well and that events were falling neatly into place in our well-ordered lives. Our babies would be a year apart, right on schedule. At the beginning of my second trimester, I went in for my monthly exam. Todd was on the Slope. He had always been good about leaving me short love notes before he left, but as I drove to the doctor's office, his latest replayed in my head because it had a special addendum: "I love you, Tad!"

At my exam, the doctor listened for the baby's heartbeat. When she didn't smile, I didn't worry; she was known for her mellow demeanor. But I noticed that she kept moving the stethoscope around. And she didn't hand it to me as doctors usually do, so the expectant mother can listen to the sound of life.

"Let's do a quick sonogram," she said.

I agreed, eager to confirm that Tad was a boy—or to be surprised.

We moved to another room, and I lay down on a sheet-covered table. The doctor spread gel on my belly and began sliding the transducer back and forth. I waited expectantly for the familiar *shoosh-shoosh-shoosh* sound of the baby's beating heart.

But it didn't come. And the sonogram picture looked empty.

The doctor said coldly, "There's nothing alive in there."

Her bluntness shocked me. I felt sick and hollow, and burst into tears.

"You have a couple of choices about getting rid of it," she said.

"It." That's what she called our baby, whom we'd been calling Tad for three months.

She went on to explain that I could go home and let "it" pass naturally. Or I could have a D&C.

I wasn't listening. I was praying. *Why, God? Why?*

I was stunned and felt so very empty.

It was my first taste of close personal tragedy, the kind that rocks a relatively untested faith. I dressed, then walked numbly through the waiting room and out to the parking lot and drove myself home. Mom came over to watch Track. A friend stopped by. But I just lay on my bed feeling like the world had stopped spinning.

As my mom had warned me years before, everyone goes through trials. Our friend Mary Ellan called to echo the same thoughts and to pray for me. A miscarriage is often dismissed as something a woman needs to shake off quickly, but it's impossible to explain the devastation and loss unless you've experienced it.

Todd flew home to be with me when I had the D&C. When the doctor's bill arrived in our mailbox, it came with a typo. In the box describing the procedure, someone had typed, "Abortion." Instead of starting over with a fresh form, they painted it over with a thin layer of Wite-Out, and retyped, "Miscarriage." For some reason it just felt like salt in the wound.

I had lost three of my grandparents and a very good friend by then, but my heart ached more for this baby than for anything else. The miscarriage carved a new depth in my heart. I became a little less Pollyanna-ish, a little less naive about being invincible and in control. And I became a lot more attuned to other people's pain.

10

We were more cautious with our next pregnancy but also more thankful that God was again blessing us with new life. The next year a beautiful, healthy baby girl joined our family on October 18, Alaska Day. Her shock of black hair, chubby cheeks, and dark, lively eyes showed off her Native heritage, and Todd grabbed the birth certificate before I could get to it, declaring that his first daughter would be named "Bristol." He proudly told everyone we'd named her for the Bay he'd loved since childhood. I claimed that the name was the substitute for my plan to become a big-dog sportscaster in Bristol, Connecticut, home of ESPN.

With Todd away, I was busy with two active little ones in our first house, which we purchased on Arnold Palmer Drive in a tidy little subdivision called Mission Hills. Track was the clingy one and always needed me in his sight, while Bristol was quite independent. As she grew she manifested her little mama's heart by nurturing her siblings and cousins and always begging to babysit. One evening just before she turned eight, Bristol was camped out in my bed, as the kids often were when Todd was on the Slope. I was lying next to her reading when she rolled over and screwed her eyes down into a commanding stare.

"You," she decreed, "are going to rent me a baby for my birthday!"

She was a neat freak and perfectionist. She potty trained herself at fourteen months. Meanwhile, Track was an adorable and rambunctious fireball who threw temper tantrums whenever I had to leave him, even in front of his cousins in Dillingham when the fish were running and I had to get out on the water. Bristol, on the other hand, would shoot her older brother a look of annoyance and calmly ask what time I'd be returning. Kind of an old soul, mature beyond her years, she grew up with an uncommon work ethic and a great disdain for drama. She didn't like gossip or wasting time.

I'd left the TV sports desk when Track and Bristol were babies, pouring my energy into my kids. Like most moms, I also sought an outlet to prevent stir craziness, and I still craved getting out to sweat. I found both on an exercise floor with a group of future best friends. Our kids would grow up together, and the group of us gals would support each other through tragedy and triumph, divorces and deaths, new births and birthdays. And politics. I love my girlfriends, the "Elite Six" as one of them facetiously dubbed us, because we're the antithesis of "elite"—a diverse group of two Democrats, two Republicans, one Independent, and one who still won't tell us what she is. Our friendship has spanned two decades now. We can talk about everything and we don't scream at each other about anything, especially not politics.

I also kept my hand in journalism, working a couple of days a week at the *Frontiersman* as a proofreader and submitting a sports column every once in a while. So I didn't suffer too much guilt over leaving the kids for a few hours.

Track grew into a daredevil who was obsessed with sports. He started playing hockey as soon as he learned to walk, and I'd spend hours with him in the hallway. I'd read the newspaper from beginning to end while firing rolled-up balls of duct tape at him, with him deflecting them like an NHL goalie. He never tired of it.

Obviously, the older he got, the less dependent he was. On his first day of school, with the apron strings fraying a bit, I kicked myself for ever having been annoyed with his clingy "Mom! Watch me! Watch me, please!" moments. I thought I'd seen every bike trick and skateboard flip ever attempted and sometimes wondered why he needed me to see yet another one. Now, if I had it to do over, I'd stop every time he asked me to, give him my full attention, and cheer as if it were the first time.

———

On Good Friday, March 24, 1989, I baked a cake for Dad's fifty-first birthday. It started out a great day, but turned into one of those "where were you when . . ." moments. When Ronald Reagan was shot, I heard about it over the intercom upstairs in the library at Wasilla High; when the space shuttle *Challenger* exploded, I was watching it on TV while standing in my dorm room at UI.

On this day, I was in our apartment on Peck Street in Wasilla when the phone rang.

"Sarah, turn on the TV!" It was Blanche. The intensity of her voice did not spell good news.

I flipped on the TV and was smacked with live footage so surreal it seemed broadcast from another planet. I listened to a somber voice-over explain the images that were coming from Prince William Sound, America's northernmost ice-free port, our busy shipping inlet on Alaska's coast about 260 miles from Wasilla. Growing up, we had driven many times to the fishing community of Valdez and taken the choppy ferry ride across to Cordova. We'd chug through the clean, steel gray waters past rocky, tree-sheltered shores that were part of the Chugach National Forest. The waters were full of incredible sea life that is typical and abundant along our coast.

Now, though, on the television screen, the Sound appeared as a vast dark field of heaving sludge. The oil tanker *Exxon Valdez* had run aground on Bligh Reef and some of its cargo of 53 million gallons of North Slope crude was pouring into the water.

Instantly, Alaskans thought of the fisheries. Most everyone in the Valdez-Cordova area relied on the fishing industry for livelihoods and subsistence. They supplemented their purchased groceries with clean, healthy organic salmon, halibut, and other seafood. The industry employs thousands of people—in fact, fisheries are the state's top private-sector employer. More people work seafood jobs than oil and gas, tourism, mining, and forestry combined. The commercial fishermen in the Sound lived much the same lifestyle as our Bristol Bay fishing family.

I remember Todd used the word "heartbreaking" to describe what he saw as he watched the coverage. The land and sea are sacred to Native families, who seem instilled with a special connection to God's creation that can only be described as spiritual. "How?" Todd wondered aloud. "How will this ever be cleaned up?"

It was a good question. Ultimately, the tanker would spill 11 million gallons of oil into the water, which spread across 10,000 square miles of coastal seas—an area larger than Connecticut, Delaware, and Rhode Island combined—and contaminated 1,500 square miles of shoreline. Many Americans remember the *Exxon Valdez* spill as a series of tragic environmental images: Litters of dead seabirds slicked in shrouds of slime. Sinister black muck surging against the rocks. Workers in fluorescent haz-mat suits swabbing the faces of oil-drenched ducks and sea otters. But in addition to being one of the worst manmade environmental disasters in history, the spill was an economic and social disaster. And like the earthquake that had rocked the state on Good Friday exactly twenty-five years before, the spill would change Alaska forever.

Although the spill's epicenter hammered communities along the Sound, the effects rippled through the state like aftershocks. Todd knew immediately that it would have an effect on all wild Alaska fish products, which today make up an $8 billion industry and produce more than 62 percent of all the United States' wild seafood.

"There will be a taint on our fish, too, Sarah," he told me, referring to the harvest from Bristol Bay, as well as fisheries farther north. "Buyers will assume all Alaska salmon is oiled. Watch our price drop this summer."

He was right. Fishermen watched helplessly as fish processors posted the price they'd pay for our wild salmon caught that season; it plummeted by 65 percent, from $2.35 to 80 cents a pound. The fish still fetched ten times that much once it hit markets in the Lower 48 and overseas, but processors insisted they could pay the fishermen only minimal prices for a product perceived as "tainted." With the polluted Sound unfishable and incomes dried up, banks repossessed scores of commercial fishing vessels, leaving hundreds of people jobless, unable to pay their mortgages and other bills. Entire commercial salmon and herring fisheries closed after the disaster. And the fallout yielded more fallout—not only bankruptcies and foreclosures, but (due to poor choices sometimes made in the face of adverse circumstances) divorces, alcohol abuse, and even suicides.

Most everyone we knew was directly affected, knew someone directly affected, or went to help clean up the spill. Todd was just starting his full-time Slope job with BP; we wondered if the job would still be there when the smoke cleared. The rumor was that Alaska's oil production would shut down, which I believed would be an unnecessary, knee-jerk reaction that would destroy our state's ability to recover. Molly, Chuck, Dad, and many of our friends headed to the Sound to drive skiffs and scrub shoreline rocks, steam down recovery vessels, and rescue and wash animals slicked in oil.

After a long clean-up effort, as days rolled into weeks, then months, then years, Alaskans' frustration mounted as Exxon-

Mobile steadily refused to step up and pay the penalty the courts decided it owed for destroying the livelihoods and lifestyles of so many families and communities. And no one in local, state, or national government seemed able to hold the corporate giant accountable.

ExxonMobil's litigation compounded the suffering, especially for Cordova and Valdez fishermen. Court challenges stretched on for two decades. It took twenty years for Alaska to achieve victory. As governor I directed our attorney general to file an amicus brief on behalf of plaintiffs in the case, and, thanks to Alaska's able attorneys arguing in front of the highest court in the land, in 2008 the U.S. Supreme Court ruled in favor of the people. Finally, Alaskans could recover some of their losses.

When the *Exxon Valdez* hit Bligh Reef, I was a young mother-to-be with a blue-collar husband headed up to the Slope. I hadn't yet envisioned running for elected office. But looking back, I can see that the tragedy planted a seed in me: If I ever had a chance to serve my fellow citizens, I would do so, and I'd work for the ordinary, hardworking people—like everyone who was a part of my ordinary, hardworking world.

Chapter Two

Kitchen-Table Politics

Criticism is something we can avoid by saying nothing,
doing nothing, being nothing.

—ARISTOTLE

Whil first got into Wasilla city politics, I wasn't even sure how to pronounce the mayor's name. I kept up with state and national politics, but Mayor John Stein was relatively new to the community and was elected while I was away at college. Then I came home, got married, and got busy raising babies and living life.

It was Nick Carney, the self-proclaimed local mover and shaker and president of the Wasilla Chamber of Commerce, who set me on the path of public service. Wasilla was *his* town. His wife led the local library board. The two of them were big golfers and liked to wear visors and golf shorts around a town where a lot of folks wore Carhartts and Bunny Boots, the fat rubber army boots that are incomparable for keeping your feet warm and dry (and the more duct-taped they are, the more Alaskan you are).

Nick was running for Seat F on the six-member Wasilla City Council, and in 1992 he recruited me to run for Seat E. He told me about a group that called itself WOW (Watch on Wasilla) that was looking for young, "progressive" candidates. "The city would do well to have you serve," he said. In those days, the word "progressive" wasn't necessarily associated with liberalism, although that's what they meant by it. I took it in the more common sense spirit of "progressing" our young city by providing the tools for the private sector to grow and prosper. The group, which was backed by the local newspaper, the *Frontiersman,* also supported Carney and Mayor Stein. I fit the demographic they were looking for: as the newspaper editor put it, a "young, sharp Wasilla resident who lived inside the city limits."

Finding a young, sharp person in Wasilla proper wasn't difficult; finding someone willing to brave the swamp of local politics was.

I talked it over with Todd. On the one hand, I was a typical busy mom, not too familiar with the low-level intrigue of a small-town city hall. On the other hand, Wasilla was starting to grow beyond its prior claim to fame as the "Home of the Iditarod," and the city's leadership was on the verge of making decisions that would affect my family and my community for a very long time. Todd thought it was a great idea. He knew that I wanted to make a difference, and he encouraged my instinct that it was time to get involved.

My first campaign was exciting, and exactly what you would expect for a small town. I focused on reducing property taxes and redefining government's appropriate role. Without knowing that I was setting a pattern for years to come, I ran an ultra-grassroots campaign with hand-lettered signs that read, POSITIVE-LY PALIN.

Track and Bristol were still tiny, so I went door-to-door asking for people's votes, pulling the kids through the snow on a sled.

At the time, believe it or not, Wasilla didn't even have a police force. The Alaska State Troopers had patrolled the area but said that Wasilla had better grow up because we were big enough to support our own police department.

Of course, we'd have to pay for it. There were two options on the table: increase property taxes or adopt a sales tax. I didn't like either, but raising property taxes meant more government control over what residents owned. A sales tax would be fairer and more optional, with a broader base of support in a town like Wasilla, which is a hub for commerce and tourism.

So in the campaign I supported the 2 percent sales tax only if it correspondingly reduced property taxes. That got me off on the wrong foot with some local Republicans who heard the word "tax" and assumed I actually *wanted* one.

When the polls closed, the sales tax had passed, Nick won Seat F, and I won Seat E, defeating a guy who was married to Mayor Stein's secretary.

After the election, I went to meet the mayor. We both assumed we would be allies since he and the Carney crew had recruited me to run. We were both wrong.

The city council chambers had once been next to my second-grade classroom, before the old school was converted to City Hall. It also doubled as a polling station, and when I later became mayor, my office was directly above.

The council met twice a month on Monday nights, and among its members, I stuck out like a Brownie at a Cub Scout meeting. Most of the guys were around my grandfather's age. In some ways, they had a kind of paternalistic way of governing. For example, they wanted to regulate how many kids a mom could babysit in her home, whether signs on businesses should be allowed to flash, and whether the town barber pole should be permitted to spin— should one ever be installed. But Valley residents, like other Alaskans, are not "master-planned-community" kind of people. We are extremely independent, no community organizers necessary. Not a lot of zoning regulations needed either. We are do-ityourselfers. (As proof, after our local Wal-Mart broke the world record for duct tape sales, Wasilla was named the honorary Duct Tape Capital of the World.) I agreed with that spirit of independence, and I voted in ways that honored people's ability to think for themselves.

Sometimes council members' plans went beyond paternalism to conflicts of interest. For example, Nick tried to spearhead a development plan that would require people living in homes built in new subdivisions to pay for weekly trash removal instead of hauling their trash to the dump themselves, as most Valley residents did and I still do. It was a convenient proposal: Nick owned the town's garbage truck company. I opposed that, too.

Now, Nick was the de facto leader of the council, and even though he said Wasilla would do well to have me serve, he became extremely annoyed when I didn't vote the way he did. That didn't bother me; I had to live with my own conscience, so I voted according to my principles and let the chips fall where they may. A vote on garbage seems like small potatoes. But it was not a little thing to me. I wanted our local government to position itself on the side of the people and preserve their freedom so that Wasilla could progress, and not restrict opportunities.

Almost immediately, my fiscal conservatism kicked in. For one thing, Mayor Stein, Nick, and others on the council wanted to raise the mayor's pay. I thought he made enough money and that there were people whose roads needed fixing before the mayor's paycheck did. I voted no, but the pay raise happened anyway.

Because Todd was on the Slope a lot, the Carter family usually babysat Track and Bristol during the Monday-night meetings. Later in my first council term, the kids started school and I got involved in the PTA. Then our third child, pretty little Willow Bianca Faye, came along. I went into labor with her on the Fourth of July while kayaking with the Menards on Memory Lake. I so wanted a patriotic baby that I paddled as hard as I could to speed up the contractions, but she held out until the next day. After she was born, I took Willow to council meetings with me, toting her in her car seat and tucking her next to my legs under the old wooden council table. I didn't care too much what the good ol' boys said about it either.

Away on the Bristol Bay fishing grounds, Todd missed Willow's birth but sure made up for it. Later he would take time away from BP to run our business, Valley Polaris, a snowmachine and ATV dealership and mechanic shop where Willow was pretty much raised on his hip for a few years. She grew into a little motorhead and spoke the mechanics' lingo. To this day she is our athletic powerhouse, riding snowmachines and ATVs with more skill and confidence than a lot of guys twice her age. (She's at the age now where she can't figure out whether she'd rather kick a guy's butt racing across the snowpack or not muss up her hair under the helmet. I tell her my vote is to kick butt.)

While I served on the council, a local politician asked me to cut a radio ad for his campaign. I liked his conservative message and said I'd help. Into the KMBQ radio studio I brought my hungry, grumpy baby in a Snugli, and the only way to calm Willow was to inconspicuously nurse her while we rolled tape. I acted like I didn't see the shocked look on the politician's face as he turned red and pretended it didn't bother him at all.

As a council member, I focused on what I believed to be the key functions of local government: infrastructure development, fiscal responsibility, and simply being on the side of the people. At the time, I thought the issues we were tackling in our small town were the political be-all and end-all. And in some ways they were. It's a serious responsibility to be elected and make decisions about how to spend other people's money. As much as any policy that rolls down from Capitol Hill and state houses, the policies coming out of City Hall hit people in their pocketbooks and at their kitchen tables.

That's why I poured my heart into the responsibilities of Seat E. Maybe the nerd in me kicked in again, but I made it my business to know every line item in the budget, to review every word of proposed regulations and ordinances, and to really know my constituents' concerns. One Christmas Eve, a man called me at home to give me his take on the city's burdensome sewer system. I talked to him for *two hours*. Here I was surrounded by little kids and all the wonderful clutter of Christmas and Todd making "wind it up" signals, and I'm talking to this guy about sewer systems. I knew I couldn't be rude, so I gritted my teeth and let him talk, thinking, *Someday I'm going to look back on this as proof that I really cared about my job.*

In local politics, your constituents are your neighbors, family, friends, and sometimes even your enemies. You see them at the grocery store, the post office, and the hockey rink. Often politicians who make it to state and national office forget that those good people—the gas station mechanic, the local farmer, the scores of mom-and-pop shop owners who form the backbone of our economy—put them into office, and they are the ones who should be at the forefront of our minds.

At the time, I had no political aspirations beyond local public service. But when hard work, life, and Providence later took me to the governor's mansion and the vice presidential trail, I vowed not to forget that.

2

I served three years on the city council, campaigned again, and was elected to three more. Then John Stein came up for reelection.

Wasilla has a "strong mayor/manager" form of government. That means the office isn't a ceremonial position; it's a full-time administrative job. You're the CEO of the city, a multimillion-dollar entity. Stein's background was in city planning. He wasn't a born-here, raised-here, gonna-be-buried-here type of hometown guy. He was more into the technical aspects of growth, planning, and code compliance. I once heard a voter bark at Mayor Stein that he wasn't impressed with his public administration degree. "I can't support a guy whose degree is in public management," the guy hollered after a local debate. "The public does not need to be *managed!*"

A key question arose that convinced me that the town needed new leadership, and it went right back to my concerns about heavy-handed government. The issue was forced annexation. Stein and some council members were fine with forcing other areas of the Mat-Su Borough to become part of the City of Wasilla. With a bigger footprint, the city would increase the size of its tax base, plus gain political power in Juneau. But they tried to sell it with rhetoric like "Government's here to help; trust us, you need better public services." For me, it went back to people being able to think for themselves. If they wanted Wasilla's services—and Wasilla's property taxes—then they'd *choose* to be part of Wasilla. I supported annexation by invitation instead.

It was evident during my years on the council that the mayor and I had sharply differing ideas about the future of Wasilla and how to make that future happen. He was for more government control; I was for smaller government and more individual freedom. I wanted government to appropriately provide the private sector with infrastructure tools to increase opportunities. Stein supported expanding land-use restrictions and building codes. I wanted to eliminate property taxes (since we now had the sales tax), slow down the rate of government growth, and build roads and water and sewer systems. And I would support capital projects if the people voted for them and acknowledged that they'd be expected to fund them.

I decided to challenge the mayor in the upcoming election in order to effect greater change than I could as a council member. The city's chief executive position provided much more responsibility and more opportunities to see where change could be effected. Besides, as every Iditarod musher knows, if you're not the lead dog, the view never changes.

We had a two-term-limit law, but Stein had been grandfathered, so he was running for his fourth term. I ran another very grassroots campaign, mostly with the help of my girlfriends. We painted pink-and-green signs with my familiar slogan, "Positive-ly Palin," and posted them all over town. (Pink and green because no one else ever used pink and green.) And when it was time to knock on every door in the city again, I pulled Track and Bristol in a little red wagon, and this time toted Willow in a toddler backpack.

I promised new energy and an end to politics-as-usual. I raised some eyebrows by promising to cut property taxes. I also promised to take a pay cut. It would be a money-where-your-mouth-is move. If I was going to run as a budget cutter, I figured the cutting had to start with me. Plus, as a council member I had just voted against a mayoral pay raise, and it would be hypocritical to conveniently forget that vote if I were elected mayor. Todd wasn't enthused about the pay-cut promise. But Curtis Jr. had once shared an observation with me: "In politics, you're either eating well or sleeping well." I wanted to sleep well.

I also wanted to speed things up in our little town, to keep us growing and prospering by embracing laissez-faire principles and promoting Wasilla as a pro-free-enterprise kind of town.

During the campaign, the chamber of commerce sponsored a debate at the Mat-Su Resort, a rustic post-and-beam restaurant that overlooks Wasilla Lake. I squared off with a number of challengers, including Stein. After the debate, a fellow who was part of our local network of well-meaning good ol' boys walked up to me.

"You know, you'll do fine in the campaign," he said. "But you're not going to win because you have three strikes against you."

I thought, *Okay, I know what he's going to say:*

Strike one: At thirty-two, I was too young. I'd be the youngest mayor in Wasilla's history.

Strike two: I couldn't win because I was a woman. I would be the first woman elected under the strong mayor form of government.

And strike three: I knew he'd tell me I didn't have enough experience.

I looked at him and waited.

"The three strikes against you," he said, "are Track, Bristol, and Willow."

My kids are *strikes?*

Oh man, the Mama Bear in me rose up then. For one thing, Stein had *four* kids. The mayor before that had had a bunch of kids. The only difference was that they had wives.

After that, of course, I was more fired up than ever. All the more reason to get out there, work hard, win, and start shaking things up.

When the votes were tallied on that October election day, our victory was seen as a huge upset of the political apple cart. I won by a handy margin, so I knew the voters were mandating *no more politics-as-usual.* The day after I got elected, I put in my time in Track's first-grade classroom—I had previously committed to volunteering that day—and then went down to City Hall. I wasn't sure how the transition of power would work, so I just showed up and wanted to know, well, who's going to show me where the light switches are, and let's get this show on the road. But no one jumped out of their swivel chairs to say, "Welcome! Here's what you'll do when you take over." It was a pretty cold reception in the mayor's office, but it was understandable: the mayor's secretary was still the same woman whose husband I'd defeated in the council campaign four years before.

When I was finally sworn in a couple of weeks later, I walked into my first staff meeting and saw all of the department heads sitting around a long table. Among them were the city planner, the public works director, plus the police chief and the town librarian, who it was rumored were good friends. I knew that most of those folks, along with some council members like Nick, had campaigned vigorously against me. And they'd had every right to do so. But the campaign was over now, and it was time to get to work on the changes that the voters had just mandated. They sat with their arms crossed, staring at me. Some of them had been in government about as long as I'd been alive. Their collective stare transmitted a single message: *"You're* going to tell *us* what to do?"

I attempted to turn them into allies. "Thank you all for coming," I began. "I know you guys weren't really rooting for me, but I'm anxious to work together. Are you ready to go, team?"

Yeah, right.

I didn't have in mind to replace them, except for the museum director. Our city had only been incorporated for twenty-two years, so I knew we didn't need a full-time cabinet member to "curate" such artifacts as license plates from the town founder's tractor—not when our roads still needed paving. So I eliminated the position. As for the rest, I figured their experience was valuable.

When it became obvious that the "team" wasn't gelling and Stein's players continued to campaign informally against the new administration, I did what many incoming executives do and requested letters of resignation to keep on file in the event that I decided to replace these political appointees. Only two of them complied—so I knew those two would be team players. The rest refused.

Nick, who had originally recruited me to serve on the council, confronted me personally to announce that he intended to make my life difficult. He launched a recall effort. Within days, he and his cronies began holding public meetings around town, drafting a petition that said I was too inexperienced to do the job. When I cut my own pay, as I'd promised to do, they accused me of trying to shoehorn myself into a lower tax bracket.

Hmmm, I thought, *wish I'd thought of that.*

Meanwhile, my efforts to rally a team composed of someone else's players weren't working. The police chief was their quarterback. He was rarely seen out of uniform, except every afternoon when he put on his shorts and headed to the local aerobics class that I used to attend with my girlfriends. He was now a regular there. He liked to stir the pot and was known for it. I felt our city government was growing too fast and was getting in the way of the private sector's progress. I asked the department heads to prioritize their operations and show me how they could accomplish an across-the-board cut so that I'd have more budgetary options.

The chief's response was an outright "Nope. I won't do it."

He claimed he wouldn't be doing his job if he cut the budget.

"You won't even give it the ol' college try?" I asked.

His answer: "No. My department can't be cut."

Finally, after too many months of *me* giving it the old college try, in the hope that he would come around and join the team, I knew I would have to shake things up at City Hall even more.

3

One day, an elderly resident insisted on a private meeting in my office. It was all very hush-hush. On the appointed day, she sat down across the desk from me. I had used a pretty marble table from my own kitchen. I'd known it was just a matter of time before the kids thrashed that table with Sharpie markers and Matchbox cars, so I rescued it by moving it to my office. People thought I had this big, fancy desk when it was really just a kitchen table.

I smiled at the lady who had come to see me. "Okay, what's this about?"

Her brow furrowed with deep lines of concern, she said, "Well, I want you to know that I'm here for you if you need help. Know that I'm praying for you and am so sorry."

I was a little confused. "Sorry for what?"

She hesitated, then plunged ahead. "Your children. We understand that your daughter was caught smoking pot."

I opened my eyes wide and creased my face into a worried look to equal her own. "She got caught?" I asked incredulously. "Dang! Which daughter? My toddler or my kindergartner?"

Momentarily flustered, the lady pressed on. "Well, this is what's been going around on our prayer chain. We've been praying for the mayor's daughter. I'm sure it was the mayor's daughter."

Yeah, well, wrong mayor. Another mayor nearby did have a teenage daughter who may have been smoking weed. Still, I was thinking, *Are you kidding me? I appreciate the prayer support, but . . .*

you're going to believe unsubstantiated rumors and then repeat them to other people?

It would be a few more years before I learned that some people make a living and even earn prestigious awards for doing exactly that.

Every Friday morning, I drove down to a local café called the Country Kitchen to have breakfast with the regulars. It was the kind of small-town joint where waitresses who could have been named Flo and Ruby poured your coffee into thick off-white ceramic cups and asked after your kids. My kids still remember going there with me for an occasional treat before school. They'd have pancakes and I'd drink coffee, sitting with all these lovable old dudes who owned the plumbing store and the construction company and the septic pumpers, and younger blue-collar workers who were actually building the town. I would just listen to what they had to say about how the town's business was being handled.

They loved to gripe about this and that and tell me how to do my job. I loved listening to their ideas and showing them that I cared. I usually agreed with their take on the world. I learned a lot from them, mostly that I wasn't off base in my thinking about what the people expected from their government. They just wanted it on their side.

I finally slowed down on that Friday-morning routine when I was pregnant with Piper. Nearly every pregnant woman has something that can make her instantly ill, and the cigarette smoke inside the café kind of nauseated me. Instead of supporting a much-talked-about citywide smoking ban at the time, though, I just stopped going to that restaurant. It eventually went smoke-free on its own, which is the way things like that should work.

My friends and I still did a lot of things together, including clay shooting, and I continued to visit the range while I was pregnant. So in a nod to our Second Amendment, my friends Kristan Cole and Judy Patrick threw me a baby shower at the Grouse Ridge shooting range—complete with a cake in the shape of a Piper airplane.

Piper Indi Grace was born March 19, a Monday. Todd flies a Piper plane, but I just liked the name. "Indi" for "Independence" (though the Indy 500 is pretty cool too) and "Grace" for "God's Grace." The next day, I took her by work when I checked in on City Hall. She was a fun and accommodating kid from the start, even arriving exactly on her due date.

I hadn't been mayor long when a certain Wasilla resident established herself as the town critic. She showed up for nearly every council meeting on Mondays and a lot of planning commission meetings on Tuesdays. A Birkenstock-and-granola Berkeley grad who wore her gray hair long and flowing and with a flower behind one ear, she always had something to say, usually about her clogged culvert. She demanded to come to cabinet meetings to make sure my door was literally open—to which the cabinet answered, in unison with me, not just "No," but "Hell no!" This town crier would later become an "expert" on all things Palin when I ran for vice president.

She was a big supporter of the small city library, where the librarian wasn't exactly on board with my administration. I was already mixing it up with the librarian's good friend, the police chief, and maybe that wasn't sitting well with her.

As I had with every department head, I asked the librarian for a meeting to let her know that I was there to help. We talked about library policies, the budget, maintenance issues, and operating hours. Then I brought up an issue that was all over the news at the time. That week in Anchorage, everyone was talking about book banning, and I was curious what her selection policy was.

"What if a mom came in and said she didn't like a book near the children's section?" I asked. "What's the common policy on selecting new titles?"

This was one question among many I asked as I tried to get to know her a little better and smooth the way after a rocky start. The next thing I knew, a *Frontiersman* reporter wrote a story suggesting that I was on the road to banning books. The librarian didn't come out and correct the story, so I confronted her about it.

"Oh, that reporter took what I said out of context," she said.

"Um . . . can you correct it, then?"

"Sure. I'll try."

She didn't. Not long after the story came out, there was an advisory Friends of the Library meeting that I was scheduled to attend. The head of the group was Nick Carney's wife. I walked in and found the participants all wearing black armbands.

Oh, no, I thought, *I wonder who died?*

Then I realized it was in protest of me.

And here I was expecting coffee and cake.

Even though I never sought to ban any books, this incident was falsified years later during the presidential campaign. Odd, because some of the books I had supposedly banned had not even been written yet.

But in the end, remembering that we all teach our kids that life is too short to hold a grudge, when Nick was home recovering from knee surgery, I knocked on his door. He hobbled to it in pain. It was "Good Neighbor Day in Wasilla." I brought him a pretty white Peace Lily.

At times I felt like the mayor of Peyton Place. In spite of that, I loved my job and I loved my town—I've always been so proud of the Valley. I couldn't wait to push forward with more of my campaign promises. I cut taxes—lots of them. I eliminated small business inventory taxes, I got rid of personal property taxes, I gave the boot to burdensome things like business license renewal fees, and I cut the real property tax mil levy every year I was in office. I worked to pass these cuts with a new group of conscientious, conservative council members who worked with me to develop the city's infrastructure. We had our share of debates, but all of us ultimately shared the same vision for Wasilla.

In the mid-1990s, many of the city's main roads were still made of dirt. Even the runway at the municipal airport was gravel. I knew businesses—and thus jobs—wouldn't locate in Wasilla if the tools weren't there for the private sector to grow and thrive. So, in an effort to attract businesses, we built and paved roads, and extended water and sewer lines. Within a few years, established mom-and-pops were growing, new ones sprang up, and stores like Fred Meyer, a Wal-Mart Superstore, and other national chains opened their doors in our city.

In 2002, we put a city bond measure before the voters that would fund construction of a multiuse sports center. Voters approved it and the half-cent sales tax to pay for it, and we broke ground on this project, which for decades had only been a dream for Valley residents. The arena was named after our good friend Curtis Menard, Jr. The year before, Curtis Jr. was piloting family members back and forth between a Cook Inlet sport-fishing site when his small plane went down, and our dear friend was killed at age thirty-six. The community felt honored to name the arena after such an enthusiastic and generous soul.

As a result of our common sense conservative efforts, Wasilla became a booming, bustling town—the fastest-growing area in the state, and an independent financial auditor (Mikunda, Cottrell & Co.) reported that Wasilla was "the envy of other Alaskan cities."

Unfortunately, things hadn't gone as well on the police chief front. I thought maybe he'd come around and work with me on the budget. But the issues multiplied, and he forced my hand. So I fired him.

This gets at my approach to management. I have a bulletin board filled with coffee-stained, dog-eared quotes tacked up along with family photos that has followed me from office to office since 1992. One of my favorite quotes comes from author and former football coach Lou Holtz, on how to build your team: "Motivation is simple. You eliminate those who are not motivated."

Admittedly, I didn't know the protocol for firing the chief—of course, no one else did either because we had had only one chief in our entire history. But I was well within my authority to fire him—his position was an at-will political appointment. Still, he sued. He claimed sexual discrimination. He said in the suit that I must have been intimidated by him because he was a big power-ful male and I was a woman, and he couldn't help that, so it was "wrongful termination."

I told our city attorney, "Give me a break. I've been living in a 'man's world' all my life—when I hunt, when I'm on a commer-cial fishing boat, when I was reporting sports from men's locker rooms." I was no stranger to these bastions of masculinity.

It took almost three years to defend against that lawsuit, but in the end a judge agreed with me.

When I ran for reelection, John Stein again challenged me for the job. In one debate, Stein referred to me as a "cheerleader" and a "Spice Girl."

A cheerleader? I thought. *Come on, don't insult cheerleaders like that.* I was just a jock and I couldn't hold a candle to their pep and coordination.

"At least get it right," I laughed when it was my turn to re-spond. "Call me 'Sporty Spice'!"

I thought the whole thing was hilarious because a TV station was covering the debate and I knew that his sexist remark would play to my advantage. (As Napoleon said, "Never interrupt your enemy when he is making a mistake.") A young female reporter, brand new to Alaska, caught Stein's "Spice Girl" comment.

"I can't believe what that candidate just said about you!" she told me, appalled and sympathetic.

I shook my head in a "can you believe what we women have to put up with?" way and milked it for all it was worth. "I know, I know," I said. "But you just have to rise above all that and plow through! Look, we have to work twice as hard to prove we're half as capable as men think they are."

Then I gave her a wink and whispered the old familiar punchline, "Thankfully, it's not that difficult."

I won the election with about 75 percent of the vote in a three-way race. In my second term, I had the honor of serving my peers from around the state as president of the Alaska Conference of Mayors. In that position, I led dozens of other mayors in dealing with statewide issues, such as municipal revenue sharing and advocating for local control of government. I loved being able to help other communities, and it allowed me to expand my contacts around the state.

4

So often in life, the first hint of tragedy arrives with a phone call. Early in the morning of September 11, 2001, our police department called me at home to tell me to turn on the news. Thousands of miles away, at the epicenter of our country's financial markets, the World Trade Center atrocity unfolded before our eyes. Surreal reports continued: The Pentagon had been hit. A plane had crashed in a Pennsylvania field. For the first time in history, the Federal Aviation Administration had ordered every plane out of the sky.

Like all Americans, Alaskans wondered where the terrorists would strike next. The terrorists had struck at our military and financial center, and had meant to hit another seat of power in Washington. Officials thought the Trans-Alaska Pipeline could be on the list of possible targets. In Anchorage, the Air Force scrambled fighter jets, while FAA air traffic controllers frantically tried to make contact with at least one foreign jet still in the air out of communication with towers. In Wasilla, I monitored the early-morning events from my office as we prepared the Valley's public safety building as an emergency center. Later I gathered with area residents at the Wasilla Presbyterian Church to pray for the thousands of victims.

My parents would travel from Wasilla to New York in the aftermath of 9/11 to work near the World Trade Center. Their temporary job with the USDA Wildlife Services involved keeping predators and pests away as detectives searched through evidence and remains transported to the nearby Fresh Kills landfill.

By the time I was thirty-eight, my second term was winding down and I was about to be term-limited out of office. Meanwhile, several people approached me saying they hoped I'd stay in public service. Not politicos, just ordinary people.

As president of the Conference of Mayors, I saw so many needs around the state, places where I felt I could help. But I had no interest in running for the state legislature. I did not think I would do well in a place where you had to scratch disagreeable backs in order to secure a nameplate in the caucus.

About that time, candidates started lining up for the lieutenant governor's race, the bottom half of the ticket led by the popular and powerful U.S. Senator Frank Murkowski, who was coming home to run for governor.

Alaska was just coming off eight years of a Democrat governor, Tony Knowles. Knowles was quite liberal—he was later considered by President Barack Obama for a cabinet position—but also very much supported by Big Oil. Polls showed Alaskans were ready for a change. Many looked at Murkowski's candidacy as a welcome-home to a public servant who had represented us in D.C. for more than two decades and was now returning to serve us more personally.

Like most Alaskans, I viewed Murkowski as a respected elder statesman, a bigwig pol on the national level. By then, he'd served twenty-two years in Washington, where he'd chaired powerful committees, like the Energy and Natural Resources Committee, and helped usher Arctic National Wildlife Refuge (ANWR) legislation through to President Bill Clinton's desk—before Clinton vetoed it. Murkowski was our junior senator; the senior was Ted Stevens, who served for four decades in the Senate and even chaired the coveted Appropriations Committee. Alaska's only representative, Don Young, has served for over three decades, chairing influential committees like Transportation. This created what was arguably the most powerful congressional delegation in the nation, and they did bring home the bacon: more federal money per capita than any other state. I would eventually argue with them against the notion that Alaskans should be known as "takers," when we were finally becoming able to contribute more to our nation instead.

Meanwhile, family life swirled. Todd was building a new house for us on Lake Lucille, and we had to pack up and sell the one we were living in on Wasilla Lake. He was still full-time on the Slope, plus commercial fishing. He and his partner had recently sold our business, Valley Polaris; we were both busy shuttling around three kids with a full slate of homework and sports; and we'd just had our fourth baby. I was also coaching youth basketball, helping with hockey, and counting down to the big Iron Dog snowmachine race. This meant that Todd, when he wasn't on the Slope, would be in full training mode, cutting hundreds of miles into the snow in the middle of winter nights and working on his machines in between. And I was still the mayor—working full-time for the fastest-growing city in Alaska.

Still, the lieutenant governor's spot seemed like a good next step for me. It was an administrative position where I could put my executive experience to good use.

During that time, I was reading Willow a book called *The Flyaway Kite*. The metaphor of this book worked its way into my spiritual life and my whole way of thinking. I wrote a contemplative prayer in my journal that summer that I recently came across. I had written: "Let me not become disconnected from You, Lord. Like that red kite, let there be a connecting string between You and me, so that I can fly high and safe as You've created all people to do. With that string, I will go where You want me to go. I'll be what You want me to be. Thank You for Your grace."

Somehow I knew that God was working on something significant in our small-town life, and I felt myself seeking something ahead. Still, I prayed to be content with what I had, even if that meant that my political career would end in Wasilla City Hall.

I didn't have a campaign organization, and I certainly didn't have any extra time, but I decided to give it a shot. There were about half a dozen in the race, most with state-level experience, statewide name recognition, and strong finances. One of my opponents was a former Speaker of the Alaska House, and we were both working parents with a political background and deep Alaska roots. During the campaign, however, she emphasized that I lacked something the front-runners had: state-level legislative experience.

"The one big difference," the Speaker told reporters, "is that if, Heaven forbid, something were to happen to Murkowski, I'm prepared to step in and run the state government. I don't think Sarah is."

I couldn't have disagreed more. For one thing, my opponents had no executive experience. And I didn't think legislative experience constituted any greater preparation, particularly in a state legislature where the trading of favors seemed to run through the ventilation system as a substitute for air.

I told reporters what I still believe today: government experience doesn't necessarily count for much. A friend and campaign volunteer, Karen Rhoades, summed it up in a letter to the editor pointing out that all of my opponents agreed it was "time for change." Yet among them, they'd accumulated decades of government service during which to enact change, but they hadn't done so.

My other opponents included a couple of state senators. It seemed as if they viewed the post as a brief stopover on the way to the Juneau mansion. While campaigning, I emphasized the fact that I was running for *lieutenant* governor, not governor. If I were elected, I joked, Frank Murkowski wouldn't need a food taster.

The campaign was also my first opportunity to introduce my fiscal philosophy to all Alaskans. In national politics, some feel that Big Business is always opposed to the Little Guy. Some people seem to think a profit motive is inherently greedy and evil, and that what's good for business is bad for people. (That's what Karl Marx thought too.)

But theories like that pretty much get run over on Main Street. Big Business starts as small business. Both are built by regular people using their skills, gifts, and resources to turn their passions into products or services, supplying demands and creating jobs in the process—like Todd's family, with its roots in the Alaska fishing industry. I had put a free-market, pragmatic philosophy to work in Wasilla, implementing conservative fiscal policies conducive to economic growth, and I got to explain this as I campaigned for lieutenant governor.

Having advocated for local control across the state as president of the Alaska Conference of Mayors, I added that principle to my campaign platform. I had great respect for the need for state government to preserve locally enacted policies. Likewise, I believed that national leaders have a responsibility to respect the Tenth Amendment and keep their hands off the states. It's the old Jeffersonian view that the affairs of the citizens are best left in their own hands. So when I discussed economic policy, I wasn't shy about calling myself a hard-core fiscal conservative. Some folks liked what they heard, and I picked up a couple of endorsements here and there and won some opinion polls. But I wasn't part of any political machine, or the Juneau good ol' boys club, so I was definitely seen as the outsider.

I used this statewide platform to tell voters about my vision for Alaska: responsible resource development, less intrusive government, and respect for equality. Those were the GOP's keys to unlocking the state's future and moving beyond political entrenchment and stagnancy after eight years under a liberal Democrat.

Though I hated to admit it, part of what made the lieutenant governor's campaign tough is that a statewide race is expensive, and I was uncomfortable asking people for funds. In my journal that season I wrote, "Unlike some other candidates, I can't just be-bop all over the state raising money."

"The front-runner's doing a heck of a job out there," I wrote. "I just don't want to have any regrets. I don't want anyone associated with my campaign to have any regrets."

But as the months wore on, it appeared that regrets were definitely going to be on the menu. While the other candidates' war chests ballooned to six figures, I managed to scrape together only about $40,000. My heart just wasn't in soliciting donations.

"I'm going one step forward and two steps back," I wrote in my journal. "And this is my laughable attempt at running?"

Of course, I realized the problem: My campaign theme was "New Energy," but, unfortunately, I did not run an energetic campaign. I had always burned with purpose, but this time I was stretched so thin that there was just no room for another log on the fire. My energies remained in my full-time job as mayor and in raising my family.

There were times when I thought, *You know what I could really use? A wife.*

I wish I would have listened to my mother when she warned me that as a working mom I would have to make tough choices. She never said that one couldn't "have it all," but it was becoming clear that maybe one couldn't have everything at once. With tiny children at home and Todd on the Slope, some things would have to be put on the back burner for a while.

Looking back, I should have known that without that fire in my belly, it would be a futile effort. I didn't take to heart the words of Martin Luther King Jr.: "Set yourself earnestly to discover what you are made to do, and then give yourself passionately to the doing of it." I wasn't living my own creed in that 2002 race: Do it right, or don't do it at all.

But even with my lackluster campaigning, I continued to win a few opinion polls that conventional wisdom said I shouldn't have won. It was an indicator that people were eager for change at the state level.

Local campaigns were heating up too. Two months before the lieutenant governor election, Todd and I had a bit of a blowout concerning one of those campaigns.

Todd had turned on the local news to hear about the Wasilla

mayor's race, which was just around the corner. In one report, a candidate claimed gleefully that I had recruited her to run for my job.

Todd turned and stared at me, and his ice-blue eyes got icier. "Is that true?" he asked.

I was busted.

With my mayoral term in its twilight, candidates had been throwing their hats into the ring to replace me. One of them was Todd's stepmom, Faye Palin, a sharp, very professional leader in the city's business community. I'd always said our parents were too smart and too nice to get into politics, yet now Faye was offering to serve Wasilla in a new capacity. But the rumor was that John Stein was thinking about running yet again, and I'd be darned if he was going to get back in and wipe out the progress we'd made in Wasilla with his liberal agenda. So I had approached a couple of well-known council members who shared my conservative free-market views and asked them if they'd consider running. To beat Stein, I thought we needed a safer bet than Faye, whom I feared wasn't as well known as the council members. Plus my political detractors would take it out on her because of our relationship.

This did not go over well with my husband. "That's two-faced," he said.

Instead of instant remorse, I jumped on defense. "That's not *entirely* true," I said and quickly tried to spin my way out of trouble. I loved Faye and knew she'd be a great mayor, but I didn't know if she'd defeat a former multiterm mayor. It was a lame excuse for a lame deed, and deep inside I realized it.

Todd stood his ground and pierced me with those eyes. "No. That's two-faced."

"Well, if I backed my own mother-in-law for mayor, people would scream, 'Nepotism!'" I said self-righteously. "I can't afford to be accused of that!"

"My family has *always* supported you. Why wouldn't you support her?"

"Hey, it's *my* family stuffing all the envelopes and stuck with all the babysitting!"

"Are you kidding me? I'm with these kids—*and your sister's kids*—so much that I don't even get to go do my own stuff!"

"Your *own* stuff! What about the Iron Dog? What about all those hours you spend tinkering in the garage?"

"*Tinkering?!*"

It didn't go exactly like that, but if you've ever been married, you know the kind of stupid bunny-trail argument that normal couples have. It was a nasty brew, mixing local politics, which is notoriously contentious, with family politics, which can be just as bad. The truth was, I had let the heat of politics get in the way of family. Faye would never have done that to me. In fact, even though we disagree on some issues, when I later ran for VP, she worked incredibly hard for John McCain and me, traveling around the nation to campaign for us. She and Jim helped lead successful efforts in some of the western states. But that's what politics can do to you if you don't catch yourself: the heat of battle causes a little core of self-centeredness to harden in your heart, so subtly that you're not even aware of it.

As it turned out, we both lost our races that year. I came in a close second, coming up short by only about 2 percent of the vote despite being outspent five to one. I had managed not to ingratiate myself with anyone just to fill my campaign coffers, though, so that was some consolation. Deep-pocketed lobbyists don't always write fat checks out of the goodness of their hearts. It was encouraging to know I would not be beholden to special interests going forward—if there was a political "forward."

The way things unfolded for the victor, I realize now that it was a blessing not to have won. It would have been very tough to serve in that office. As the years spun out, communication

broke down so completely between the governor's and lieutenant governor's offices that they literally closed the doors
between them.

Looking back, my lack of passion in even contemplating gun-
ning for the job should have been a sign. My basketball coaches
used to say, "Practice how you play." If I was going to run this
kind of halfhearted campaign, was that some indication of how
I would have performed in the job? Reading my journal entries
from those days, I detect the note of apathy that I absolutely
loathe in today's political culture. I'd made a mistake, but that's
the way we learn life's most important lessons. I would not make
the same mistake again.

5

After I lost the lieutenant governor's race, I hit the campaign trail
and stumped for Murkowski's general election bid, at one point
whistle-stopping across the state with Senator Ted Stevens for
two weeks. Alaskans still saw our senior senator as the World
War II veteran who had volunteered on Dwight D. Eisenhower's
presidential campaign, served as a U.S. Attorney, and spearheaded
Alaska's efforts to be admitted into the Union. He had served in
Congress since I was a kid. He was the author of the Magnuson-
Stevens Fishery Conservation and Management Act, the primary law governing marine fisheries management in U.S. federal
waters; and, of course, he helped usher in Title IX legislation to
ensure gender equality.

Those were glorious, pressure-free travels and so much more
fun than the trips I'd taken alone during my own lieutenant governor campaign. We stopped amidst the fjords of Kodiak, where
emerald green mountains plunge straight down into brilliant blue
waters surrounded by picturesque fishing villages. We crisscrossed
Southcentral Alaska, Fairbanks, and the Kenai Peninsula, where

glacier-covered mountains form a spine that juts down the coast. We stopped in the small communities along Prince William Sound, ringed by green islands rising out of waters that house whales and copious sea life, tidewater glaciers, and the towering trees of the Chugach National Forest.

It was refreshing and comfortable to stump for someone else, to speak highly of someone else's record and vision, and to know I wasn't the aim of the spotlight—the other guy was.

I agreed with Murkowski's vision of resource development, though not wholesale and in every particular. I also supported his talk of fiscal conservatism. In stump speeches, I noted that if Murkowski's opponent, a Democrat, got in there, we'd be paying sky-high taxes to fund all the government growth that ticket promised.

On election day, Murkowski won with nearly 56 percent of the vote. He then had to resign from Congress. The national press was buzzing about who he would appoint to take over his Senate seat. He released a short list of potential candidates. My name was on it, along with several current and former state lawmakers, and prominent businessmen in the state.

I had mixed feelings about being on the U.S. Senate short list. As before, I wasn't sure I'd fit in to a group that required loyalty to a party machine.

There were a few U.S. senators whom I'd admired from afar, especially those in whom I saw an independent streak as they bucked party politics whenever they felt it was good for the people as a whole. I didn't know if there'd be room for one more maverick on Capitol Hill. Still, the idea of serving in the Senate where I could contribute on a national level was definitely appealing.

As the days ticked down for Murkowski to announce his pick, there was a dramatic crescendo in the state and local press. Newspapers ran detailed profiles of all the candidates, pegging their strengths and weaknesses and even placing odds as though we were horses in a race. After the governor whittled his list down to just a handful of candidates, I was called in for an interview.

Todd drove me into Anchorage in our Ford Extended Bronco on a sunny but frigid November day. We were supposed to meet with the governor and his newly chosen attorney general in the Anchorage governor's transition office.

Todd drove laps in the parking lot to keep the truck warm while I rode up in the elevator. Walking into a large office, I found the governor, silver-haired and reminiscent of a large, gruff, but relatively friendly insurance salesman, along with the new AG, a lobbyist from D.C. who had come up to run Murkowski's campaign. His appointment as AG was the first big controversy Murkowski had generated. Transplanting a D.C. lobbyist who had to join the Alaska bar quickly to practice law legally in our state raised eyebrows and questions about the new governor's political judgment. Later, this AG would leave office under a cloud of alleged self-dealing involving some stock he owned, and Murkowski would appoint yet another lobbyist, this time from the oil industry, as the state's next attorney general.

The interview began, but instead of the anticipated litany of questions on my policy positions and goals for the state, Murkowski barely touched on those.

"What's your key issue?" Murkowski said.

"Energy," I answered instantly. "Resource development so we can grow more jobs in Alaska."

That wasn't the last word I said, but it was pretty close. Murkowski immediately launched into a soliloquy on how tough it was on a family to serve in the Senate. Although it was a bit of a weird segue, it felt like a fatherly talk, and I remember thinking that he must be a caring parent who had the welfare of his family uppermost in his mind.

"What would be your plans for your kids?" Murkowski said.

"I'd bring them with me. They'd go to school in D.C., but we'd probably do some back-and-forth to Alaska because I wouldn't want them to lose touch with home—"

"You don't understand," he interjected. "This is really tough on kids."

He repeated a few more times those same sentiments.

It was then that I knew I wasn't getting the gig. It seemed to me that though he thought me competent enough to make his short list, the father in him felt compelled to protect me from the storm that is national politics.

Murkowski then talked a little about the logistics of Senate service, touched on our common goal of energy development, but again he repeated his mantra about working and kids and the shredderlike nature of Washington politics.

About thirty minutes passed, and then we were done. I thanked the governor and the mostly silent AG, said my good-byes, and elevatored down to meet Todd in the parking lot.

"Well, it's not going to be me," I told him, shaking off the cold inside the truck's warm cab.

Todd steered the truck back out into the street. "Why not?"

"Governor Murkowski kept repeating how tough it would be on the kids. But it will be interesting to see who he picks. It's not going to be a woman with a family."

We were disappointed . . . for about seven seconds. We talked about the way the "ball bounces." We reminded each other how UCLA Coach John Wooden had captured our thoughts in a book we'd read about him.

I told Todd, "Coach Wooden said, 'Things work out best for the people who make the best of the way things turn out.'"

We said in unison, "Or something like that!"

Then we drove home through the gorgeous winter landscape,

making it back in time for Bristol's basketball game and Track's evening hockey practice.

Soon afterward Governor Murkowski made his big announcement. He'd chosen the "most politically aligned Alaskan to replace him in the U.S. Senate," he said. He then handed what was called the most coveted government job in the state to his daughter, Lisa, a mom with two young kids.

———

I guess Murkowski took me seriously when I said my most important issues were energy and resource development. A couple of months into his administration, he offered me a job as chairman of the Alaska Oil and Gas Conservation Commission (AOGCC). Established during the days when Alaska was a territory, the commission is a quasi-judicial regulatory body that has a range of duties, many of which affect people, companies, and markets in the Lower 48 and around the world. It was confirmation that having lost out on the lieutenant governor's position and the U.S. Senate appointment were actually blessings. Working at AOGCC, I could still live in Wasilla while working on the issue I cared most about for the state and our nation. The salary was eye-popping, to me, at $124,400 a year.

As the entertainment industry is to Los Angeles, corn is to Kansas, and markets are to New York, so is the energy industry to Alaska. More than 85 percent of the state's budget is built on petroleum-based energy revenues. For more than thirty years the big oil companies like British Petroleum (BP), ExxonMobil, and ConocoPhillips have extracted the oil underneath Alaska lands and sold billions of barrels of it to very hungry markets. But oil is not a renewable resource. Once it's gone, it's gone, so it has to be dealt with prudently. Many Alaskans were aware that these huge multinational energy corporations had been leasing oil-rich chunks of land on the North Slope, but were just sitting on the leases, in some cases for decades. And as long as they held the leases, other companies couldn't come in and compete for the right to tap our resources, so parts of the oil basin were essentially locked up.

When Murkowski appointed me AOGCC chairman, one of the first things I told him was that we needed to make sure our resources were not being wasted and hold the oil industry accountable to its contracts.

AOGCC functions include maximizing oil and gas recovery, minimizing waste, approving oil pool development rules, and maintaining state production records. The commission also lends a hand in protecting the environment from contamination during drilling and also ensures environmental compliance in production, metering, and well abandonment activities, so federal agencies like the EPA as well as private interests and environmental groups have key interests in the commission's activities. In my view, the nation deserved an agency that was a fair, impartial body with the best interests of Alaskans and the country in mind.

I hadn't been there long when it became clear that that wasn't necessarily the case. Nor did I have any idea how my involvement would lead me into a head-on confrontation with the forces of corruption in the highest levels of the state and my own party.

The AOGCC is led by three commissioners appointed by the governor, one each representing expertise in petroleum engineering and geology, plus a representative from the public sector—the post I filled. A geologist, Dan Seamount, an experienced, nonpolitical outdoorsy type who was friendly and especially knowledgeable in coal bed methane development, was already serving on the commission. Randy Ruedrich, a former general manager of Doyon Drilling and a contractor for the oil company ARCO, was named to the petroleum engineering position.

It was Murkowski's third eyebrow-raising appointment in his short tenure. But this one was especially troublesome because Ruedrich was the state Republican Party chairman and would remain so during his tenure. He was also a member of the Republican National Committee.

Ruedrich was jovial, and he was very smart when it came to extracting and selling oil. He said once that he was the only person who could chair the Alaska Republican Party because he had lots of money *from* that oil extraction and "no one else could afford to do it for free."

Ruedrich was the key fund-raiser for the GOP and naturally solicited party dollars from the oil and gas industry players we were to be regulating, something that should have immediately been pegged as a conflict of interest. Of course, being married to Todd, I was also accused of literally being "in bed" with the oil industry. I had to explain that as a blue-collar union hand, a production operator wearing a hard hat and steel-toed boots, Todd wasn't calling the shots for the corporate bosses in London. In fact, I told Alaskans, "Todd's not in management. He actually *works*."

The state determined that there was no conflict of interest with Todd's Slope job. Ruedrich, though, had held his former position as Doyon's GM during the period when the company pled guilty to federal felony charges for environmental crimes on the North Slope. In July 1995, Ruedrich testified before the U.S. Senate Energy and Natural Resources Committee (chaired by then-Senator Frank Murkowski) that a new method of disposing drilling waste back down wells had boosted environmental safety because it eliminated unsightly "waste pits." But just a month later, a whistle-blower reported that Doyon was actually injecting illegal and hazardous substances down wells in order to save money. The FBI and EPA investigated Doyon and BP. BP paid a $500,000 fine, and Doyon paid a $1 million fine.

When Ruedrich became an AOGCC commissioner, there were whispers on the staff and among the public about the fox guarding the henhouse. And the trouble began almost immediately.

I began commuting into Anchorage five days a week, diving headlong into a learning curve that would deepen my knowledge of Alaska's energy resources, the energy problems facing the country, and the close relationships clouding judgment on both.

When Murkowski tapped me for the commission, he quickly named me chairman. That meant I also became the ethics supervisor of the staff, a job that turned out to be more than just a compliance title. When a staffer hinted right away that Ruedrich seemed to spend a lot of time running the Republican Party from his new AOGCC office, plus dealing with GOP operatives as a National Republican Committeeman, I mentioned it to the party boss–slash–commissioner.

Then another problem cropped up: Ruedrich involved himself in adjudicating two cases that were closely intertwined with his old Doyon illegal dumping case. Commissioner Seamount and I urged Ruedrich to recuse himself, but he refused. An administrative assistant took me aside to say she suspected Ruedrich of sharing confidential commission information with a coal bed methane company we were supposed to be regulating. She was right: he was passing agency information to the company's lobbyist.

I was dealing with the issue while observing my own chain of command. I spoke personally to Ruedrich numerous times. Dan Seamount also raised concerns. But no one, including my own ethics supervisor, seemed to take the concerns seriously. He was a young guy who was a political appointee of Murkowski's and a good friend of Randy's. In fact, Randy mentioned often that he was like a grandfather to the ethics supervisor's child.

At one point, an angry Alaskan's e-mail arrived in my inbox:

"Mr. Ruedrich's continued service calls into question the purpose and credibility of the AOGCC as well as its ability to act in an unbiased way to protect and conserve the resources of the state. Aggressive lobbying in favor of developments he obviously doesn't fully understand and continued use of his office in improper ways to press forward his agenda and that of the Republican Party reduced the commission to an ineffectual, biased body the public cannot trust."

As commissioner, I was prohibited by law from publicly discussing my concerns, but I responded to this citizen with a message that I meant with every keystroke: "This will not be swept under the rug."

I got a call from a Democrat state legislator. "Hey, we know what's going on over there," he told me on the phone. "If you don't stop this, I'm going to blast Ruedrich's corruption all over the state."

"I'm with you on this conflict issue. I promise you I'm not sweeping this under the rug," I said. "Will you trust me?"

Since the chain of command seemed to be ignoring the conflict of interest and the concerns of commissioners, lawmakers, and citizens, I went to Governor Murkowski's chief of staff. I laid out what I knew so far, including potential conflicts of interest that staff was observing. He assured me he'd take care of it.

"That's what a chief of staff is for!" he said.

A few days later, I stopped Ruedrich in the hall at work. "I think Murkowski's chief is going to be calling you, Randy," I said.

"Oh yeah, he called me."

I thought, *Whoa, he must be shaking in his boots.*

"He calls me every Sunday afternoon."

"Really?" I said.

"Yeah, we talk politics, what's going on in the administration, that kind of thing."

That's when I knew the chief had done nothing. My ethics supervisor was doing nothing, the AG was dismissive of the concerns I repeatedly shared with him, and the public was rightfully questioning the commission's integrity. I wrote a letter to Governor Murkowski. Basically, I told him that his appointee, the chairman of his party, was perceived as trashing the reputation of a state agency. Shouldn't he do something about it?

As I typed out the words, I thought, *This is it. I'm taking on the party and putting it in writing. My career is over. Well, if I die, I die.*

Then the strained peas hit the fan. The staff was becoming more vocal. Democrat lawmakers broke their silence, as did others, and I couldn't blame them. Then reporters started calling. One weekend evening my home phone rang. I picked it up in my bedroom.

"Sounds like Randy Ruedrich is through," a local television reporter said. "What do you know about it?"

I sat down. "I don't know anything about it. What do you know?"

"Sounds like the governor gave him a choice, resign or get fired. We hear he's gone."

He was gone, but I hadn't been told about it, and the problems would still brew. Outside the commission, people began turning up the heat. While I pushed for somebody higher up than I to do something to salvage the regulatory commission's reputation, I took fire from both sides. GOP operatives accused me of speaking ill of a fellow Republican and "jumping on board with the Democrats," warning that I was through politically. Democrats accused me of covering up for the GOP. And no one in the administration would tell me the status of any investigation into the mess. Meanwhile, I was living under a Department of Law gag rule and paying a high price for my silence.

Finally, I wrote Governor Murkowski another letter. I reminded him that I had warned him and the rest of the chain of command about all this for months, and I detailed my communications with all of them. I concluded the letter with the suggestion that for the good of AOGCC, to salvage its reputation, and to prove a commitment to transparent government, as chairman I should be allowed to speak publicly about all this.

Nothing happened.

So I had to *make* something happen. I prayed long and hard. I loved the job. And I had to consider that by making any drastic moves I would be crossing swords with the most powerful men in my own party. My political career would be over. My whole future was before me. But I also knew I couldn't sit there and be a party to all of this.

I knew what I had to do, so I resigned—stepping away from the ethical lapses and hierarchical blinders to effect change where I could—on the outside.

After I left, a state assistant AG issued a sixteen-page ethics complaint against Randy, who eventually agreed to pay the highest civil fine in Alaska history. He retained his GOP chairmanship.

Out of a job but sleeping well again, I knew that any shot I might have had to become a GOP insider was gone, which was fine, but I wanted Alaskans to be able to believe in the party ideals again. I knew the GOP planks made the strongest foundation upon which to build a strong state and country.

Later that winter, the gag order was finally lifted and I was able to talk about what had really happened at the AOGCC and how Seamount and I had tried to preserve the integrity and work product of the conscientious geologists, engineers, and other professionals who served in the agency. Lawmakers on both sides of the aisle, such as Democrat State Senator Hollis French, told the *Anchorage Daily News* that they had gotten to know and respect me through all that as I tried to uncover the truth.

The Democrats and the media both praised my efforts, but obviously only because it was the GOP getting hammered in that episode.

"Sarah has been tortured by this for a long time," French said. "I feel she has never had a chance to let her story out."

Funny, five years later, when I ran for VP, he would personally make sure I didn't get my story out then either.

6

The snow melted, the sun rose again, and summer rounded the corner—a glorious time up North! I stayed busy with the girls and traveled with Track's hockey team as the team manager. The boys were a handful of mischievous fun, and they made my work rewarding. My years in politics were a fine training ground for dealing with small-town dramas involving coaches and referees. (Any soccer mom or dad knows what I'm talking about.)

In the meantime, there was drama in my own family, too. In 2001, my sister Molly had married a guy named Mike Wooten who'd recently moved to Alaska. Molly has always loved kids and had been concentrating on her job as a pediatric dental hygienist and helping out with her nieces and nephews, because by now the extended family was growing rapidly. Around the time she turned thirty, this new guy came along and swept her off her feet. She did not know that he, only in his mid-twenties, had already been married and divorced twice. Or that he'd already filed once for bankruptcy, or that infidelity had been a problem in an earlier marriage. What Molly saw was a big, charming guy who cared for her; he was fun and was also persuasive even if he was known around town for stretching the truth.

When I was serving as mayor, Mike asked me to write him a recommendation for the Alaska State Trooper Academy, as I did for lots of people applying for different programs and scholarships. After he became a trooper, though, it became clear that there were some problems. He was seen drinking alcohol while driving a patrol car. In 2003, after using graphic terms to challenge his young stepson's masculinity, he shot the child with his state-issued Taser gun. Later, after Molly found out the guy was having an affair, Track and I witnessed a domestic dispute in which we both heard the man threaten to harm my dad. If Dad helped Molly retain a divorce lawyer, he screamed while wearing his trooper gun belt, "he'll eat a f***ing lead bullet!" Part of his job was to arrest hunters who illegally shot game, but he also illegally shot a moose while hunting with another local cop, and the other cop had to confess to seeing it happen.

Everyone, including Molly and Mike, seemed relieved when Molly filed for divorce in 2005. The divorce would be final, the drama's volume would be turned down, and he would go on to marry (and divorce) a fourth time. Much later we found out, as did the rest of the state when the union released his personnel file, the results of an internal trooper investigation stemming from citizen complaints which listed ten different unethical or illegal incidents.

This was during a time when Alaska law enforcement's reputation was taking a beating because other abusive actions were being reported in the media.

I was asked to comment on my former brother-in-law's actions as a cop—and I spoke candidly about how unfortunate it was that a few bad apples were perceived as spoiling the whole bunch. I had great respect for law enforcement and fought to provide the tools it needed to do its job. But just because this particular character was a former member of the family, I wasn't going to pretend that his actions should be accepted as the norm. The chapter for our family was closed, and Molly moved on to concentrate on her work and raising three beautiful kids, Payton, McKinley, and Heath.

This sad family episode would later be twisted and used as a political weapon against me and John McCain.

———

Winter 2004 came and with it the unique blanket of darkness that covers our coldest months. For me it was a time of restlessness, the kind when you know in your soul you're supposed to be preparing for something, that there's something else out there, but the next open door is not yet revealed. I remember waking up in the middle of the night knowing there was something else, knowing there was room for more.

The kids were growing up quickly, and we moved through fun holiday seasons into the rebirth of spring. Track got his driver's license, and I trained for a marathon. It was a very contemplative time, and I focused on my family while considering what I might do next. The long runs provided me with the clarity needed to weigh my options. As the soles of my shoes hit the soft ground, I pushed past the tall cottonwood trees in a euphoric cadence, and meandered through willow branches that the moose munched on. A grassy culvert ran parallel to the road where I logged my long miles. On lucky days, my newly licensed sixteen-year-old drove the route ahead of me, placing water bottles at intervals inside the culverts, along with notes of encouragement. "Run, Mom! I love you!" and "Don't give up!" For any mom, it just meant so much that somebody would do that, especially a busy teenager. It was a great season.

Soul-searching continued, though, tugging at my heart most when I paused to really consider life's purpose. When Piper was born, Blanche had given me one of those wonderful glider rockers covered in soft suede. I remember waking up to fresh, fat snowflakes falling outside my bedroom window, the sky as black as India ink. I would pick Piper up from her bed, snuggle her in a worn flannel quilt, and rock with her in the stillness of the night. The gas fireplace would kick on when the temperature dropped to just the right degree, and I could feel the flickers of light and heat near my feet. There was a longing inside me that winter, a sense of purpose hovering just beyond my vision. Was it ambition? I didn't think so. Ambition drives; purpose beckons. Purpose *calls.*

I definitely wasn't *driven* toward any particular goal, like power or fame or wealth. So what was it? I wondered, as Piper's sweet breath against my neck matched the rocker's rhythmic glide. I prayed again that if I was to resign myself to what felt like a public service career cut short, that I'd embrace being home full-time. I asked that the fire in my belly, and whatever was feeding it, would simmer down.

I thought of a passage from the book of Jeremiah 29:11–13: " 'For I know the plans that I have for you,' declares the Lord. 'Plans for peace and not for calamity, to give you a future and a hope. When you call upon Me I will hear you, when you search for Me you will find Me; if you seek Me with all your heart.' "

It irked me that too often women are made to feel guilty for seeking the next open door, no matter what career choices we make. That seems universal. But one doesn't just *create* passion, nor consciously generate the feeling that there's a door standing open somewhere, even if you can't see it yet. And it wasn't anyone who pressured me: "Sarah, you've got to get out there and fly! Go do more!" But I knew there *was* something more.

I thought of the graduation speeches I had been honored to give over the years as mayor and began to apply their message to myself. I often told the kids to ask themselves: "What gets you excited to wake up in the morning? Is it science? Art? Children, animals, books, sports, mechanics? What is the desire of your heart?"

I'd add: "God put those in you not to tease or frustrate you—He created them in you to give you direction! To put you on the right path—He bridles your passion! So stop and think about what you love to do, then look for signposts along the way that confirm you're on the right path to doing that—doors opening, people with your best interests at heart supporting what you're doing."

I wasn't sure what I was to do next, yet. But I also knew I was blessed with a supportive family and a husband who took joy in my working hard, so I knew I had options. As I rocked my daughter all those dark nights, I knew that what still stirred passion in me was the desire to make a positive difference for others, not just in my family and community but in the wider world as well. I resolved to seek confirming signs along the way—the open doors—to show me the right road.

Chapter Three

Drill, Baby, Drill

*Our land is everything to us. . . . I will tell you one of
the things we remember on our land. We remember that our
grandfathers paid for it—with their lives.*

—JOHN WOODEN

I stuck my head out the window of my black Jetta and shifted
into fifth after cresting Thompson Pass. It was winter 2005.
The girls were finally asleep, and I needed another gulp of
ten-below-zero air to keep from joining them. I fumbled with the
CD changer, loaded the kids' Toby Keith, and cranked up "How
Do You Like Me Now?!"

It was the middle of the night, and I had just emptied my last
sugar-free Red Bull. I was already second-guessing my decision
to drive the twelve-hour round-trip to the Valdez meet-and-greet
campaign event in the middle of winter—a distance like going
from Raleigh, North Carolina, to New York City. Thompson Pass
is treacherous in the winter, with an average snow dump of fifty
feet, and I kicked myself for not driving Todd's big Dodge truck
even though it was cheaper to drive my little diesel car. I read
once that the winter of '52–'53 had dumped eighty-one feet of

snow in the area. I pictured that while I sought familiar land-marks ahead in the dark distance.

There wasn't a doubt in my mind that I was on the right road now, but it was a tough road to barrel down in the dark.

I'd finally decided to toss my hat in the ring to replace Frank Murkowski as governor, and I was having a ball working long, intense days. Road trips became our campaign MO since we didn't have funds to fly, especially when I wanted to take the kids to a campaign event. One-day round-trippers like this one weren't ideal, but they were necessary and usually a lot of fun as I worked to cover the state during the yearlong gubernatorial campaign.

Now, with the dark ribbon of highway unfurling in the head-lights, my thoughts drifted back to a question my friend Rick Halford had asked me that summer: "Do you remember the story of David and the five stones?"

A former State Senate president, Rick was the quintessential Alaskan: an outdoorsman and private pilot who flew between his home in Chugiak and the fishing village of Aleknagik. Quiet and deeply thoughtful, he was a veteran public servant who I felt had served for the right reasons and had been smart enough to get out while the getting was good—about a term before corruption grew deep roots in Alaska's State House. We first met back in 1992 at a Wasilla community forum, where he heard me speak about my vision of a fiscally conservative government as I was campaigning for city council. Rick had recently married one of Todd's childhood friends from Dillingham. Over the summer of 2005, he had called a few times to share his concerns about the direction of the state.

"You have the five stones," Rick said in one of those calls. "You have the right positions on ethics, on energy, on government's appropriate role. It's an out-of-the-box idea and you won't get the establishment's support, but I think you should run for governor. Our state is ready for change."

Rick wasn't an establishment Republican in the derogatory sense of the term, but he was definitely influential in the mainstream party. And he was the only person like that—a quasi-insider, who reached out and encouraged me to run. I considered Rick's encouragement to run for governor as one of those signposts on the right road.

Some of his colleagues would think it was a horrible idea, he acknowledged. That intrigued me, of course. As Murkowski had, Rick warned how tough the job would be on my family. He knew what he was talking about: as a young senator, he'd had three daughters with his first wife, then divorced, remarried, and had three sons.

In spite of the challenges, he said, I should seriously consider running. "You're different. Alaska needs something different."

I respected Rick and took what he said to heart. On the other hand, I took what another caller that summer, Andrée McLeod, said with a grain of salt.

In 1997, after losing an eighteen-month battle seeking a permit to sell falafel on street corners, Andrée the Gadfly, as many called her, ran for mayor of Anchorage. City officials had spiked Andrée's falafel stand idea, deeming homemade chickpea sandwiches a potential health hazard, and she was ticked. But she lost the mayor's race. In 2002, she ran a losing campaign for the state house with yard signs that featured an ill-advised logo of giant red lips and the slogan "Kiss off special interests." She lost again two years later.

Andrée, who had once listed her occupation as "whistleblower" on a candidate survey, was a too-frequent caller to my home. My kids dreaded hearing her voice, but the only way I could get anything done during her long, one-sided conversations was to put her on the speakerphone while I'd go on cooking dinner and washing dishes. She ranted in the background, dumping piles of compliments, complaints, and curses on my head. She implored me to run for office and wrote glowing letters to the editor about me, but her motivation in communicating with me wasn't so much "pro-Palin" as "anti–everyone else." In those days, her target was Murkowski, and she thought I needed to bring him down.

Another day during that season of soul-searching, my telephone rang again.

"You don't know me," said a deep, confident voice on the other end of the line. "But corruption in Juneau is disgusting, and we gotta clean it up or Alaska will get left behind."

The caller introduced himself as John Reeves, and he went on to say that he lived in Fairbanks, had five kids, and worried that they wouldn't have the opportunities he'd had to build and produce and succeed.

John said he was ready for Alaska to get on the right track with responsible development of our natural resources, and he was sick and tired of backdoor deals struck between politicians and special interests, especially the oil companies. If I was game to take on entrenched interests in Juneau, he'd back me. "You should think about running for governor," he said. "I'm a Democrat, and I'd support you."

John and I talked a lot about our kids' future and the threats to their opportunities and freedom. Corruption was spreading in Juneau, and the state's future was in trouble. He knew I wanted to tackle it.

A lot of sincere, hardworking people called to give me their two cents' worth that summer. They were basically saying the same thing: the growth of government bureaucracy was out of control; the oil companies were sitting on their leases instead of drilling, thus withholding jobs and development opportunities from Alaskans; and people were sick of politics-as-usual. After the AOGCC issue erupted and rumors began to swirl about FBI corruption probes in Juneau, it was pretty certain that some state officials were on the take.

By the end of that summer, the bottom line for me was clear: voters wanted change, and they should have a straightforward choice about what kind of change it would be. As always, Todd supported me and encouraged me to do it. So on Alaska Day, October 18, 2005, I kicked off the gubernatorial campaign with about fifty friends, family, and reporters in my living room. It also was Bristol's fifteenth birthday, so of course we had cake.

Now here I was headed home from Valdez, still toting kids on campaign trails, except this time (with longer distances to cover) using a Jetta instead of a sled. Ironically, and typically, the trip cost me more than I managed to raise.

The Valdez event had been a typical grassroots affair. The local mayor, Bert Cottle, an old friend, had invited me to meet a few folks for cookies and coffee in a small venue. I talked about the potential Alaska had if we protected our Constitution and unshackled the private sector. Most people recognized that Wasilla had thrived while I served there, so I had to touch only briefly on what we'd done. Basically, we'd gotten government out of the way.

Throughout the campaign, I made a point of praising the good work ethic and personal responsibility of our pioneers. Then I would tie the state's history to the significance of the election.

Always thinking of their kids and mine, I'd tell the voters, "There's a lot riding on this election, including the trust of future generations. We need new energy and someone with a stiff spine to fight for you. I'll put government back on your side." I promised that if they hired me as their governor, there would be no more politics-as-usual, and I had a record to prove it. "I won't let you down."

In 2005, I was the first Republican to file for governor because I didn't want to play the political "wait your turn in line" game to see if Murkowski, the incumbent, would seek reelection. I knew I wouldn't have the backing of the party machine anyway, so my reliance on a grassroots effort required an early edge before the other guys started lining up.

Clark Perry, a high-energy, redheaded high school friend who worked for the state's Department of Corrections, came to the house the day I kicked off my campaign. His wife, Kris, had been president of the Wasilla Chamber of Commerce when I was mayor, and Clark told me he liked my common sense politics. I liked him because he is one of the funniest and nicest guys I know, and because he was smart enough to marry Kris, who is one of the sharpest women in America.

Clark helped get everything off the ground. He would drive 120 miles round-trip every day from his worksite at the Palmer Correctional Center in Sutton to our campaign office on Fifth Avenue in Anchorage—prime real estate most commuters had to drive by every day. My friends and I spent our Thanksgiving vacation painting the interior Warrior red and painting the Alaska flag on the main wall. Besides coordinating the early work, Clark was in charge of cool things like handing out warm red "Palin for Governor" headbands at high school football games and community road races, as well as red wristbands that could be seen all over the state.

In the primary, I was running against Governor Murkowski, of course, and his friend Randy Ruedrich was still the state GOP chairman—a bad omen to some but to us a motivating challenge. To win the primary, I'd have to go through both of them. It also meant we'd have no backing from the state party. I found my underdog status and the outsider label quite liberating. If there were only a few politicians bold enough to hook up with us, that was fine too. We built a network of nonpolitical, hardworking Alaskans who were tired of politicians bending with the wind.

Our friends volunteered, adamantly believing it was time to put state government back on the side of the people. As the campaign expanded, Kris did what a lot of strong women do: she kindly asked her husband to step aside on this particular venture and she took over the leadership role. Never having been involved in a campaign before, she succeeded because she has good instincts, works tirelessly, and was there for the right reasons.

Kris had grown up in Wasilla but was younger than I. We'd had babies at the same time who'd grown up in school and sports together. Her active community volunteerism proved her servant's heart. At twenty-two she had become general manager of the local cellular service provider. Kris had about as much patience as I did for political nonsense. Both of us held high-pressure jobs. And we were wired to handle that pressure through faith in Providence and our knowledge that, at the end of the day, we could only do our very best. As long as our kids were healthy and happy, everything else could melt away and we'd march on just fine. Those similarities—and the fact that Kris is a kick-butt, tell-it-like-it-is soccer mom—helped us forge a deep bond during the campaign, and she became my closest confidante.

Our campaign would focus on cleaning house in government and facilitating the private-sector development of energy resources, specifically ramping up production of America's energy supplies and building the 3,000-mile, $40 billion natural gas pipeline that other administrations had been promising to build for decades. It could ultimately go from the North Slope to hungry Midwest markets out of a Chicago hub. No more time wasted recycling the same old arguments and excuses as to why it couldn't be done. I was determined that Alaska was going to start contributing more to the nation.

We promised to shine a bright spotlight on ethics reform and to clean up the favor factory known as the Capitol Building. An undercover FBI investigation of the Alaska State Legislature was bubbling to the surface. In the week after the primary election, federal agents served more than twenty search warrants, many of them at the offices of state legislators—five Republicans and one Democrat. It turned out that the feds had been investigating links between some lawmakers and VECO Corporation, the oil field services giant. The warrants authorized agents to search computer files, personal communications, and official reports, as well as any items emblazoned with the phrase "Corrupt Bastards Club," or "CBC."

The CBC had started as a barroom joke after a newspaper opinion piece highlighted eleven lawmakers who had received large campaign contributions from VECO and who appeared to cast votes according to the corporation's demands. The name stuck—and some of the lawmakers thought it was so funny they had hats printed up that said "CBC."

It wasn't so funny after the feds showed up.

Alaskans were disenchanted and felt disenfranchised from their own government. We were going to change that. Of course, the minute you start campaigning on ethics reform, critics start trolling to see what kind of dirt you've got under your fingernails. During the primary campaign, I remember one reporter heading down that road with me. I invited him to dig deep and even offered to help. "Look, I got a D in a college course once, and I yelled at the wrong kid this morning for not taking out the trash," I said. "You got me. Those are the skeletons."

My campaign theme of "change" was palpable and sincere, and we walked the walk every day of the race. While never pretending to have all the answers—which of course is a change in itself—I made it clear to voters that I would gather the information I needed and base my decisions on principle and sound ideas, not cronyism or political expediency. I ran on my record as an executive and told Alaska voters that I would govern according to conservative principles, and if I were to err, it would be on the side of those principles.

I wanted to shake every hand on the trail. I wanted to meet the people who would be my bosses. While the other candidates jetted between big cities, our team drove *way* up to tiny towns like Tok and Delta Junction, where the permafrost heaves in the road make you feel like you're riding ocean waves. It's not unusual to see bear and moose and buffalo and an occasional wolf loping down the middle of the highway. Like stars in the northern sky, Alaska has hundreds of tiny towns and villages flung across it, and the people who live in them are the state's heart and soul. When we visited, sometimes whole towns turned out, from little kids to Native elders bearing *akuutaq* and blueberry muffins and salmon strips.

In almost every community, I drew on local connections as I shared my message, like pointing out one of Todd's cousins in the crowd, or recalling a summer job I'd had years before in the area. Or I'd mention my parents' travels that would have taken them to some adventure nearby. Before leaving, I told folks I wanted the job of serving them as governor; I asked them to hire me. Then, the kids would usually be loaded down with homemade goodies, I'd grab coffee-to-go, and we'd barrel down the road again.

On one return trip from Glennallen, we stopped late at night in the middle of nowhere to drop off a campaign sign. Todd had spotted the unmarked dirt road we needed to take, and we rumbled down a narrow lane lined by tall, spindly black spruce until we came to a tiny wooden cabin hidden in the woods. The elderly couple who lived there had called in to a political radio show and voiced their support, so we'd looked them up and promised to deliver them a yard sign, even though you wouldn't be able to view it from the main highway.

These good folks were exactly the type of Alaskans who supported us: hardworking, unpretentious, patriotic, and ready for honest leadership. They treated us to slices of homemade rhubarb pie, then gave us a whole blueberry pie that we shared with friends after our 800-mile, 40-hour round-trip, driven to the sound of the Black Eyed Peas and an old LL Cool J remix we found in the glove box.

Every part of our campaign shouted "Change!" A change in campaign financing: we ran on small donations from all over the state, mostly from first-time political donors, and we turned back some large checks from big donors if we perceived conflicts of interest. A change from photo-op stops to honest conversations with actual voters. A change from emphasizing politics to emphasizing people. A change from smooth talk to straight talk—even then.

We were amused a couple of years later when Barack Obama—one of whose senior advisers (come to think of it) had roots in Alaska—adopted the same theme. Kris and I joked about it: "Hey! We were change when change wasn't cool!"

2

During the Republican primary, I attended dozens of candidate forums, debates, interviews, and events. Near the August vote, a crucial debate was broadcast between the front-runners: incumbent Governor Murkowski, wealthy-businessman-turned-state-senator-turned-wealthier-businessman John Binkley, and me.

I knew I could capitalize on the studio's round-table seating arrangement because I could anticipate the guys would toss barbs at each other, revealing their conventional ways of politicking. Sure enough, Murkowski made an erroneous suggestion that Binkley had never gotten much of an education. Then Binkley shot back something about the private jet Murkowski bought in defiance of everyone and used to zip off on pricey junkets. Back and forth they went until the moderator couldn't get a word in edgewise.

We switched to more serious topics like gross versus net oil taxes, but they kept their claws out. I sat back in my chair and let them bicker. Then, just as their ears turned red and they had to come up for air, I leaned forward and let the mom in me flow out. "Come on, guys," I said, "I really think Alaskans deserve a better discourse than this." I spent a couple of moments turning down the volume of their spat, then pivoted back on message. It was another good night for us.

It wasn't the last time I'd find that there's no better training ground for politics than motherhood. At one point during the general election, motherhood became the focus of a unique line of questioning. In my responses to a series of debate questions on abortion, I remained consistent and sincere, explaining how personal and sensitive the issue is and that good people can disagree.

But the debate moderator decided to personalize his hypotheticals with a series of "What if . . ." questions. He asked:

"If a woman were, say, raped . . ."

". . . I would choose life."

"If your daughter were pregnant . . ."

"Again, I would choose life."

"If your teenage daughter got pregnant . . ."

"I'd counsel a young parent to choose life . . . consider adoption," I answered.

I calmly repeated my answers to all of his "what-ifs," then

looked pointedly to my right and my left, to one opponent, then the other. Then I returned to the moderator and said, "I'm confident you'll be asking the other candidates these same questions, right?" Of course, he didn't.

On election day, we shocked everyone. We won the primary, pulling 51 percent of the vote in a five-way race. We won by taking on the entrenched interests and the political machine. With no negativity and with a highly energized grassroots campaign, we moved on to the general election, where we continued to have a ball. I put in twenty-hour days, with Todd and the kids by my side.

In the six-way general election, we were routinely tag-teamed by our main opponents, two-term former Democrat Governor Tony Knowles and former two-term Republican State Representative Andrew Halcro, now running as an Independent. Halcro was a wealthy, effete young chap who had taken over his father's local Avis Rent A Car, and he starred in his own car commercials. He would go on to host a short-lived local radio show while blogging throughout the day, all of which were major steps up from a previous job as our limo driver at Todd's cousin's wedding. During the campaign, Halcro had asked to meet with me many times to request that I run as his "partner"; though I was way ahead of him in the polls, he asked me to quit so we could run as "Co-Governor partners." I finally had to tell him, firmly, *No.* Months later my new press secretary, Meghan Stapleton, and my acting commissioner of natural resources, Marty Rutherford, and I chuckled when we discovered that Halcro had asked all three of us to run with him at different times during the campaign.

As a candidate, Halcro was an ardent proponent of letting the natural gasline project be handed over to the Big Three oil companies to develop however they wanted instead of creating competition. We didn't know at the time that his brother-in-law was a bigwig in the London headquarters of BP. In the governor's race, Halcro pulled 9 percent of the vote. He later asked for a job in my administration.

Later on, during the vice presidential campaign, Halcro—along with the Wasilla town crier mentioned previously, plus the falafel lady Andrée McLeod—would be touted as "expert" sources on all things Palin by the national press.

The gubernatorial election required a couple dozen more debates, events, and joint appearances with my opponents. We faced off against one another so often that I pretty much had Knowles's retread of his past campaigns' rhetoric memorized by October. It was fun to draw out the contrasts between us, and enlightening for voters to learn, through those contrasts, what our priorities were—he as a liberal, and me as a conservative.

One beautiful but solemn day about six weeks before the final vote, 3,500 Alaska-based troops were about to be deployed to a war zone overseas. I sat in the crowd on that chilly autumn day on the military base to honor those brave souls, knowing that far too many wouldn't be seen by us again until their pictures flashed across some news screen announcing they had made the ultimate sacrifice for America.

The candidates and I had already met numerous times in various public forums. There were a dozen more scheduled in the upcoming weeks. The chamber of commerce held its weekly luncheon, and the candidates were invited to attend our umpteenth event to debate pretty much the same topics in front of pretty much the same crowd. The forum was on the same day as the Airborne Infantry Brigade's deployment ceremony. I chose the troops, the other guys chose the luncheon. Sean Parnell, who had just won the GOP primary for the lieutenant governor's race and so was now teamed up with me on the ticket, was to attend the chamber luncheon in my stead because the front-runners and I had already been together at another forum earlier that same day.

My opponents and the press had a field day with that one: "Palin a No-Show at Chamber of Commerce Luncheon Debate." The guys' campaigns raised such a fuss about it that they wouldn't let Sean participate; he was permitted to give only short opening remarks. I couldn't make the media understand why I had chosen to skip another rubber-chicken campaign stop and instead attend this significant military exercise. I tried to explain: the chamber of commerce would be here next week; our troops would not.

———

Despite such occasional pettiness, my family continued to enjoy the campaign immensely. Everyone was involved, including Todd's eighty-seven-year-old Yupik elder grandma, Lena. She was a one-woman Eskimo whistle-stop tour!

Lena grew up in Dillingham on Bristol Bay. Her history sounds like something out of a Herman Melville novel. Her father, "Glass Eye Billy" Bartman, was a Dutchman, a sled-dog freighter and caretaker of the Alaska Packers saltry, a salmon cannery, on the Igushik River. Her mother was a full-blooded Yupik Eskimo who grew up in a *barabara*—a sod-roofed dwelling excavated from the earth and built partially underground to protect its residents from the wicked arctic winds that screamed across the tundra in the village of Tuklung.

Lena's first husband died of tuberculosis—a lot of villagers did. Her second husband, Al Andree, was a boatbuilder and Bristol Bay fisherman. Lena is a tough frontier woman. How many American women do you know who can weave a grass basket; sew squirrel skins into a garment and adorn it with intricate beadwork; haul a thousand salmon out of the ocean, get them to market in a sailboat, then take some home, fillet them, and serve them for dinner?

During the campaign, Lena went around Dillingham talking with the Yupik elders.

"Do you know my grandson Todd?" she would ask.

Everyone in Dillingham knew Todd.

"His wife is running for Boss Alaska."

Like Lena, we were tireless, because every vote and every voter mattered. Most of our volunteer staff had never been involved in a campaign before, yet they made sure we were always visible and viable.

Campaign staff kept it real by bringing their kids, along with ours, on the trail as much as possible. We'd stop to take pictures of them standing by frozen waterfalls along the highway or with a double rainbow over the tundra in the background. We all memorized every Big & Rich, Martina McBride, and Travis Tritt song ever recorded, singing at the top of our lungs to stay awake on the road.

My media campaign was the essence of simplicity—which would also be my communication strategy as governor. My two themes were "New Energy for Alaska" and "Take a Stand." I ran a few upbeat commercials that featured my family and Alaska's natural beauty, highlighting our Piper Super Cub airplane, reading to our kids who attend public schools, and thanking law enforcement officers. It wasn't so much to portray a "Little House on the Tundra" scene as to let the visual imagery speak to my priorities. In those ads, I promised that I would fight to protect our state's future. I was as sick and tired of the corruption and politics-as-usual as the majority of Alaskans were, but I kept an optimistic message flowing to show how we'd turn things around for the people.

3

Triumph on November 7, 2006!

On election night, hundreds of us filed into a ballroom at the Hotel Captain Cook to celebrate our victory. We were so thrilled and thankful—and finally tired—as the results poured in. We won with nearly half the vote in a six-way race. Volunteers joined me that morning, and in the days leading up to the election, waving signs in the freezing cold with a diesel-generated spotlight that Dad and his buddies jury-rigged to shine on an enormous Palin sign along the highway in the dark winter hours. We were there in the Captain Cook to warm up and celebrate.

After our victory speech and between enthusiastic thank-yous to our volunteers, we quickly discussed our next morning's press conference and then tried to hit the hay in the hotel before the few remaining nighttime hours turned into our new day. It was a rowdy night, though, because the hallway was full of our celebrating kids who were eating lots of cake.

Dad and his buddies Adrian Lane and Don Benson went to a local bar called Humpy's, which they said was like a funeral inside. Apparently a lot of the Knowles camp was there. Some drunk guy walked in and announced, "Tony Knowles got jacked up!" Dad led the cheers in the bar—for all three of them who'd cheer anyway.

All through Alaska's history, the inaugural swearing-in had taken place in the capital city of Juneau. But in a break with tradition, I selected Fairbanks, the Golden Heart City, as the location for the December 4 ceremony. The fiftieth anniversary of statehood would take place during our term, so we wanted to celebrate the Alaska

Constitution, which was written in Fairbanks. That was what I wanted to honor that day. Thanks to our state's simple and concise founding documents, our founding mothers and fathers had provided a level of opportunity and prosperity that other states, even other countries, could only dream of. I believed then—and still do now—that in addition to God's grace, the credit for Alaska's prosperity should be given to our Constitution's framers.

We chose as our venue the Carlson Center, the arena where the Nanooks, the University of Alaska Fairbanks' hockey team, play. Looking up at the team banners hanging overhead, I remembered the many days I'd spent in this arena, cheering young athletes, keeping score and compiling stats, bandaging bruised bodies, organizing their journeys up north and then home again after the games. During the ceremony, floorboards protected the ice, which was covered with fresh blade marks carved by kids who were full of hope and goals and energy. Instead of a sterile conventional venue, the arena was the perfect place for our inauguration celebration.

As the ceremony began, Alaska Native dancers and singers, bagpipes, and my friend Adele Morgan's beautiful singing moved the crowd to roars of applause; the thunderous and pulsating foot stomping in the arena felt like the low, strong trembles we never quite got used to when another Alaska earthquake struck. I looked at my family onstage to my left, Grandma Lena on one end, five-year-old Piper on the other. From the podium, I waved to more family in the first few rows in front of me: five generations were represented. As I kicked off my speech, I joked that we had all cleaned up pretty well—I couldn't spot a Carhartt or a Bunny Boot in the entire bunch!

The ceremony was held around lunchtime to take advantage of the winter light. It was freezing outside, but I looked up to the rafters and pointed at the students who'd been able to skip school that day: "You are what's warmed up the place—thank you!" It was a magnificent moment; I was so thankful for the journey. My campaign staff had traveled such a long way, and, really, their efforts drove me to that stage. I winked at Kris Perry and her family, and saw Frank Bailey and Ivy Frye, the Ketchums, the Menards, my aunt Kate and uncle Tom, who had flown up from Washington. Nick Timurphy and Todd's relatives had come in from far-flung towns all over the state.

Libby Riddles, the first woman to win the Iditarod, the famed 1,100-mile sled dog race, had just introduced me as the first woman governor of the state. I had specifically invited her to emcee the inauguration in keeping with the unconventional nature of the event.

"It's more significant than perhaps you think, Libby, accepting my invitation to speak here today," I said while roars of applause for Libby continued to erupt. I went on to tell her that while other college students had had posters of Metallica or Michael Jordan on their dorm room walls, mine had been plastered with a *Vogue* magazine spread of Libby Riddles.

"She was an underdog, a risk taker, kind of an outsider, she was bold and tough," I told the crowd. I felt so proud to share the stage with this genuine trailblazer. "She shattered an ice ceiling, and thank you for plowing the way!"

When the applause died down, I began my first speech as governor of Alaska by honoring the framers of our Constitution, created to guide our state. "It demands that Alaskans come first. It will keep my compass pointed true north. It's the tool to build Alaska with strength and with order."

I hit on the issues critical to our state: responsible energy resource development, cleaning up corruption, putting Alaskans to work in good jobs, reforming education, and nurturing that most precious resource—our children—because in every one of their lives there is purpose and destiny.

I emphasized my priorities of improving public safety and tackling substance abuse. Then I concluded with plain talk on the role of government, stressing fiscal restraint and the importance of competition and free enterprise. "Alaskans, hold me accountable, and right back at you!" I said. "I'll expect a lot from you, too! Take responsibility for your family and for your futures. Don't think you need government to take care of all needs and to make your decisions for you. More government isn't the answer because *you* have ability, because you are Alaskans, and you live in a land that God, with incredible benevolence, decided to overwhelmingly bless."

I could feel the energy in that arena, and I knew it could flow across the entire state—we *were* shaking things up—and there'd be new energy for a new future!

There was more celebration after the speech, as some of our homegrown talent entertained us, including Atz Kilcher, the father of the pop singer Jewel. Piper sat happily for most of the ceremony, her bright red dress unruffled and her new black patent leather shoes swinging. Her sisters had placed a tiny toy tiara on her head and told her to be patient.

She hung in there with just a hint of weariness, though she never got bored with her dress. She wore it to all the inaugural events and never tired of dancing in it.

———

The next morning, I kissed the kids awake and Todd helped each one of them get ready for their day. I headed to my new office on the seventeenth floor of the silver-mirrored State Building in Anchorage. Most of the staff, many lawmakers, and by far the greatest number of constituents are in the Anchorage area. Until a road is built to Juneau—an idea that didn't have much support from legislators—less than 10 percent of Alaskans can conveniently get to their capital. So an obvious part of the new, transparent way of conducting the people's business would be to serve where the people are. That's why I would often work in my Anchorage office, in addition to the one in our much smaller capital city.

It was my first day in office, and my core gasline team and I were meeting to kick off our top agenda item. The governor's office has one particularly enviable view, south across the city toward the beautiful mountains of Chugach State Park. From one window I could also see an active volcano, and from another window, Mount McKinley. We overlook Cook Inlet, abundant with sea life, including salmon, halibut, and beluga whales, all safely coexisting with offshore oil rigs for the last thirty years. Almost symbolically, my office also looked directly into the towering gold-mirrored building occupied by the oil giant Conoco-Phillips. This mélange of views served as a constant reminder of my mission in office to develop our state's resources in the best interests of the environment and of the people—including getting a gasline built.

It was a humbling experience to step in to lead an administration that would serve a state of this size and diversity. But I knew we could face the challenge with anticipation and without a sense of overload if we observed Ronald Reagan's principles: pick your core agenda issues and focus on those; empower and motivate your departments and staff to implement your vision in other areas. Reagan concentrated on a few key issues and knocked them out of the park. That gave him the political capital to effect change in many other policy areas. I knew if I kept my campaign promise of overhauling the state in the areas of resource development, fiscal restraint, and ethical government, I would also be able to turn attention to equally urgent issues such as education, services for special needs and the elderly, job training, unemployment, and social ills in rural Alaska. We'd be able to do so with reprioritized funding to help the private sector provide opportunities in a way that would help Alaskans stand tall and independent.

Ethics reform was already under way, with some lawmakers already under arrest, so to kick off the Palin-Parnell agenda, we started with the natural gas pipeline on our first day in office.

For Alaskans, the term "gasline" is as familiar as "irrigation" is to Californians or "Wall Street" is to New Yorkers. Except that Californians and New Yorkers already reap the benefits of these economic lifelines, while Alaskans have been waiting more than fifty years to realize the benefits of the state's vast reserves of natural gas. At least 35 trillion cubic feet of proven natural gas reserves lie untapped on the North Slope, and geologists say there are hundreds of trillions more, both on- *and* offshore. Our oil and gas supplies would be enough to provide ten years of total energy independence for the entire country.

Construction of a gas pipeline to transport this safe, clean energy supply to the Lower 48 was originally authorized by the Federal Energy Regulatory Commission in 1979. At the time, a lot of folks had high hopes. Not only would the pipeline become a second economic pillar for the state, creating jobs and development opportunities, but it would reduce our dependence on foreign supplies and therefore our reliance on unfriendly nations.

Cheap natural gas from other countries had delayed the project for years. And for years the big producers who held leases on the gas fields sat on their contracts, preferring instead to develop projects in countries with fewer labor and environmental restrictions. It was unfortunate that our government's well-meaning policies had driven producers to other parts of the world where there were no restraints on their activities. That was no way to protect the environment or heat the economy.

With my background, I understood the concerns of all the parties: as a free-market capitalist I understood the bottom line for the oil producers; as the spouse of an oil worker I understood the Slopers and their families' reliance on oil jobs; as a mayor I understood the communities' dependence on oil's economic contributions; as a lover of the land I understood as well the environmentalists' and Alaska Natives' concerns.

Any corporate CEO is tasked with looking out for the bottom line. My business was to look out for Alaskans' bottom line. Our state Constitution stipulates that the citizens *actually own* our natural resources. Oil companies would partner with Alaskans to develop our resources, and the corporations would make decisions based on the best interests of their shareholders, and that was fine. But in fulfillment of my oath, I would make decisions based on the best interests of *our* shareholders, the people of Alaska.

So, in my Anchorage office, amidst the family pictures already on my desk, a hide of a grizzly bear shot by my dad draped over the couch, my collection of military coins and flags, and Piper's hand-painted artwork taped to the credenza, we established the ground rules for the gasline team.

"I won't pretend to have all the answers," I told them, "and I won't micromanage you. You guys are the experts; that's why I want you here."

I believed then and now that I had the best gasline team ever assembled anywhere. Acting Commissioner Marty Rutherford, a brilliant and yet incredibly humble single mom, had followed her father, the former mayor of Valdez, in committing to public service. Marty had been a firsthand witness to the Good Friday earthquake and Good Friday *Exxon Valdez* oil spill, so she knew perhaps better than most the importance of safe development and respect for the power of nature. Other commissioners included Tom Irwin, a calm, gentle, grandfatherly man, who, after years of bringing Alaska's other resources to market, was determined to do the same for our natural gas. Pat Galvin was a brilliant young family man with an incredible combination of financial and resource development knowledge. Oil and gas gurus Kurt Gibson and Bruce Anders rounded out the core team. Kurt had left a lucrative position in the oil and gas industry to return home and help bring Alaska's gas to market. Bruce is a dear friend who shared passionately my core conservative principles and instinctively knew my direction on the gasline. I also considered the lieutenant governor to be a key member of the team, and he met with us that first day. We were Republicans, Democrats, and Independents, all working together, bound by our fierce determination to do things the right way, based on free-market competition and a transparent government.

Our goal was to commercialize Alaska's treasure of oil and gas by opening up the North Slope basin to long-term exploration and production, thus creating jobs and ensuring a stable energy supply. We also planned to bring new players to the table. Instead of negotiating over cocktails with the Big Three oil producers, I intended to craft a bill that would create a framework within which any willing and able company could compete.

Most of us spent my first two days in office in a windowless conference room, convening with oil executives to listen to their opinions on the pipeline's future. The producers had heavily backed Murkowski in the primary and Knowles in the general election. I walked into those meetings with coffee in hand, cookies to serve our guests, and thought to myself, *Hmmm. You just spent a year trying to kick my ass. I just spent a year trying to kick yours. And now we're in this room together.*

Out loud I asked, "Want a cookie?"

———

Under Murkowski's administration, gasline negotiations had taken place behind closed doors. Along with five others, Marty had left her position in the administration about a year before I was elected in protest of Murkowski's firing of their team leader, Tom Irwin. The group became known statewide as "The Magnificent Seven." Murkowski hadn't appreciated Irwin's efforts to make resource development deals competitive and transparent by opening them to public scrutiny.

Evidently, my friend Tom had told Murkowski one too many times that the secret gasline deal he was negotiating with Exxon-Mobil, BP, and ConocoPhillips violated the state's Constitution. Among other things, his approach relinquished state sovereignty, and would unwisely lock in tax rates for decades into the future despite volatility in the markets. Murkowski didn't like being questioned. Tom loved his state too much to be part of something that would ultimately hurt it. So he did what I had done when faced with my AOGCC decision—he left so he could be effective elsewhere. Tom went home to Fairbanks, and the rest of the Magnificent Seven also found other jobs.

During my campaign, I reached out to Tom and Marty and asked them to come back if I were elected. They were happy to share their expertise. While the other candidates suggested tweaks to Murkowski's plan to hand over state sovereignty to Big Oil, Tom and Marty and I were confident that no amount of "tweaking" could save it. So I put my name and commitment behind a proposal to open bidding to the private sector. I ran as the candidate who would begin anew with a process that would not and could not be tainted by previous secret negotiations and corrupt legislative votes.

During our first week of conferencing with the oil executives, every man—and they were all men—who entered that room knew things had changed. I made a point of saying "We're leaving the door open." Their inches-thick proposals would be displayed out in the reception area for the public and the media to see.

Our approach to moving the gasline forward was both innovative and simple: Explain the importance of gasline development to ordinary Alaskans. And get them involved. That meant our war room became every kitchen table, town hall, classroom, and living room across the Last Frontier. We reached out. We asked citizens, "These are your resources, so what do you think?"

Internally, our natural gas mantra was "Greenies, Grannies, and Gunnies."

Greenies: Natural gas is the cleanest nonrenewable fuel.

Grannies: Production of a domestic supply from Alaska would help those on fixed incomes, such as the elderly, by increasing supply and lowering costs in a more stable price environment.

Gunnies: Alaska's energy supplies would help lead America toward energy independence and greater national security.

Greenies. Grannies. Gunnies. So Alaskan. So politically incorrect. Perfect.

4

The size of Alaska is difficult to comprehend for anyone living in the Lower 48. It is huge, one-fifth the size of the entire continental U.S. When the kids and I moved to Juneau in January 2007, Todd and I worked more than 1,300 miles apart. To put that into perspective, it would have been closer for one of us to work in Houston and the other in Minneapolis. Adding to the challenge, you can't drive between Prudhoe Bay and our capital city, of course, even if you were up for a four-day road trip. In fact, no one can drive to Juneau. You can fly in or hop a ferry, but not many people want to brave the frigid swells on the Inside Passage waterways in January during the legislative session, so Juneau's always been known as the most inaccessible state capital in America. I wanted to change that too.

After the Palin-Parnell swearing-in ceremony and gasline meetings, my daughters and I boarded the state's single prisoner-transport plane (available for the governor's use when the Department of Public Safety isn't using it). I was determined not to use the corporate jet that former Governor Murkowski had bought against everyone's wishes.

About a two-hour flight from Anchorage, Juneau sits at the base of Mount Juneau, enclosed by Auke Bay and hemmed in by dense forests. I think it's the nation's prettiest capital. We could look out the window and see mountain goats and soaring eagles and an occasional avalanche pouring snow down chutes carved in the mountains. One morning, Willow jumped out of bed in the Governor's Mansion to see a mama black bear and her two cubs waddling down the road right outside our door. She dragged her sisters and sleepover friends outside in their pajamas to take a look.

Track was in Michigan during all this, traveling with a competitive hockey team, and he wouldn't return until almost time for his Wasilla High School graduation. We missed him terribly, but he was doing what he loved best that semester, playing some of the most competitive hockey for his age in the country. He missed the First Family official photo at the mansion, so he's represented in the picture by a pair of hockey skates hanging from the fireplace over our shoulders.

Our initial arrival at the mansion was a bit like walking into a storybook. The home was decorated for Christmas in the whimsical theme of a gingerbread house. Outside, large white lights trimmed the eaves and colored lights sparkled in a pine whose upper branches soared past the rooftop. We had fought hard to get there, and now here we were, reaching for the door handle of our new home.

The last time I had tried to enter the Governor's Mansion was back in high school. One of my heroes, Jay Hammond, had been governor then. He was another commercial fisherman, married to an Alaska Native from Bristol Bay—also very independent. I traveled to Juneau for a basketball tournament and stopped by to ring the doorbell, but no one was home—or at least no one wanted to open the door to a curious and historically minded teenager. Now, twenty-five years later, I stood before that same door with my own basketball-playing teenage daughters. Life has a fascinating way of coming full circle.

The Governor's Mansion in Juneau may not be as grand as other governors' digs, but by our standards, it's a beautiful and stately old home, and one of the most historic residences in the state. Built in 1912 and first occupied by Territorial Governor Walter Eli Clark, the home has hosted President Warren Harding, Charles Lindbergh, and President Gerald Ford. It was like living at the turn of the century but with modern appliances—and plumbing that usually worked. Our first official event, however, was a dinner for friends and family that was interrupted by a leak dripping water through the ceiling onto the grand piano. We had buckets under ceilings for two years until Todd helped track down leaks, and repairs were finally finished.

The layout of the mansion is quite open and inviting. The red-accented dining room seated a couple dozen people and would become the center of activity for many receptions, late-night meetings, and dinners for traveling high school and college sports teams. The living room boasted the beautiful grand piano where Piper took her lessons. She almost mastered "Chopsticks" by the time we left office. In the blue study, an oil portrait of Secretary William H. Seward hung above the fireplace. Downstairs there was a wine cellar that I never did find a key to, but I saw pictures of it that showed duct-taped labels left by the former governor that read DON'T TOUCH; meanwhile, we had a kitchen with a pantry large enough to earn the nickname "Costco."

Alaska's NBC affiliate, KTUU, sent its main anchor, Maria Downey—one of my old bosses from sportscasting days—to record our homecoming. It was the first time in years that little kids had lived in the mansion.

Bristol, Willow, and Piper bounded upstairs, eager to see the rest of the home and stake claims to their bedrooms. The girls had never lived in a home with an attic, so it frightened Piper when Bristol tugged on a door in the ceiling and watched as the attic stairs "fell down." Bristol and Willow climbed up to take a peek. Maria recorded Piper, standing below, scolding the girls, "I'm gonna tell *Mom!*"

The first night in our new home, I tried to light a nice, cozy fire for the kids in one of the eight fireplaces. Problem was, it hadn't been used in years. I didn't know the dampers were closed, so the house filled with smoke and alarms summoned the local fire department. Next some revelers "welcomed" the First Family on our lawn, and our neighbors had to call the police department. It was nice to meet Juneau's first responders.

We got the house in order by the next day, just in time for Juneau's annual cookies-and-cider open house. We couldn't have done it without our patient and kind house manager, Erika Fager-strom, and her fun family full of teenagers, who would become friends of the Palin kids. And after thousands of people came through the mansion for Juneau's annual event, staff member Diane Diekman and her helpers turned the formal house back into a home.

Later, after Trig was born, the staff became even more like family. They'd come to work early and we'd all congregate in the kitchen and have a cup of coffee together before our official work-days would begin. Before friends would arrive to help take care of Trig, and I headed off to the Capitol, the staff would kiss Piper good-bye and send her on her way to school.

We had a lot to do to get settled in: enroll the kids in new schools, sign up for sports and music—and serve this huge state. The chef, the staff, the security—it was all exciting and kind of fun; but where some saw luxuries, I saw budget cuts. It was all a bit too much. I had asked my department heads to trim their budgets, so it was only fair to trim the mansion budget too.

The place came with a personal chef, but I unbudgeted the position. When we hosted meals and receptions at the mansion, I figured I could have them catered. The chef seemed so darn bored because the kids didn't want anything fancy to eat, and I didn't want them thinking life entitled them to have paid staff cooking for them. I never pretended to have a huge culinary repertoire, and thankfully, the kids weren't picky and loved my specialty, moose chili. So they wouldn't starve. But they also realized that Grandma Sally had some kind of magic kitchen mojo that I didn't.

One day when Track was little, he looked up at me from his bowl of chili, the third one that week, and said, "Even the fruit tastes better at Grandma's house."

I also trimmed the state food budget by keeping our home's freezer stocked with the wild seafood we caught ourselves, as well as organic protein sources hunted by friends and family. We kept an interesting variety of food that way. If any vegans came over for dinner, I could whip them up a salad, then explain my philosophy on being a carnivore: *If God had not intended for us to eat animals, how come He made them out of meat?*

As governor, though, hunting *was* an issue. I would face pressure from Hollywood to halt hunting, ban guns, and end our state's wildlife management practices, such as controlling predators. I said no to all of that nonsense: gun bans would destroy the Second Amendment, and as a lifelong member of the NRA (Alaska has the highest NRA membership per capita in the nation), I had plenty of backup when telling Hollywood liberals what I thought of their asinine plans to ban guns. And we *had* to control predators, such as wolves, that were decimating the moose and caribou herds that feed our communities. One animal rights group recruited a perky, pretty celebrity to attack our scientifically controlled, state-managed wolf-control program. It was ironic that she opposed using guns to kill predators that would cause Native people to starve, but apparently not opposed to taking movie roles in which she'd use guns to kill predatory people.

People outside Alaska are often clueless about our reliance on natural food sources. (You know you're an Alaskan when at least twice a year your kitchen doubles as a meat-processing plant.) They don't use common sense in considering why our biologists need responsible tools for abundant game management. But as the ninety-year-old Alaska Native leader Sydney Hunnington told Todd, "Nowadays, common sense is an endangered species."

Todd couldn't be there for many of the mansion functions, so I always sat at the head of the table as official host, plus I often carried the conversation as the official hostess too. That role tradi-tionally fell to the First Lady, but I wore both hats as best I could and relied on Bristol to help with some of the finer details, such as choosing flowers, centerpieces, and name-tag fonts. I loved it when Piper joined us at the table for important meetings. We moved in when she was in kindergarten, and she was always very polite when she slipped into a dining room full of dignitaries and asked if she could help pour coffee, serve cake, or just sit on my lap. I wasn't about to shoo her away, especially during func-tions with partisan lawmakers, who were gracious and kind over dinner, then pulled the typical political 180 the next morning with less-than-gracious comments in the press. Piper usually had important whispers to share with me at the dinner table, about one of our puppies or what she needed for school the next day. She always kept me grounded and reminded me of what really mattered.

I particularly enjoyed personal lunches we hosted for Senators Ted Stevens and Lisa Murkowski and Representative Don Young; a lunch for Bill Kristol, Fred Barnes, Dick Morris, and other journalists who stopped in Juneau on cruise ship tours; and one very memorable lunch and tea that Todd hosted for all the former First Ladies of Alaska. Two years running, at the end of February, Todd rushed off the Iron Dog trail to hustle back for his official First Gentleman duties, which included accompanying me to D.C. for meetings of the National Governors Association. It seemed he barely had time to tear off his Arctic Cat gear and rip the protective duct tape off his face before settling in to sip fine tea with Laura Bush and other First Ladies of state at the White House. (He was getting good at those tea parties!) I remember teasing him later—"What? Did you chat about your snow-machine suspension? Did they ask about top-end speed and size of carbides?" Todd was a good sport and an awesome First Dude.

Todd would develop his own role in contributing to Alaska's progress while we served in office. His family had long struggled against the tide of increasing state and federal intrusion that was creating a climate of government dependency for our rural areas. Tucked high in the frigid North, Alaska's Native communities are often isolated and dark, sometimes both literally and figuratively. Todd's hometown of Dillingham is one of the larger "hubs." Some villages are as small as a couple dozen people, isolated hundreds of miles from grocery stores and modern amenities, or what people Outside may think of as civilization. Some areas are reminiscent of a third-world country, without sewer systems or roads. Cell phones and Internet service are of little value in these most remote areas. Many people receive their mail and living essentials via bush pilots who land on frozen rivers and sandbars more often than they land on runways, to keep rural Alaskans connected to other parts of the world. "Survival mode" is what hearty residents adopt in the remote areas. This choice of lifestyle is rugged, it's raw—it's not an easy living, but it's a good living.

Todd's family had worked hard to escape a rut that some find themselves in when faced with harsh conditions. They saw that when government programs started growing, sometimes citizens became dependent on the programs and abandoned the strong work ethic of their elders. This resulted in too many young people giving themselves over to a dependent lifestyle that often leads to fractured families, abuse, subpar education, and other problems. Todd and his family appreciated the opportunity we had as First Family to help share a message of family strength and unity, and a work ethic that should be both expected and rewarded. Todd was, to me, a perfect spokesman to help spread that positive message to all Alaskans, especially those in our rural communities.

When I became governor, he devoted himself to workforce development, including vo-tech education designed to get kids excited about real-life work experience and break young men and women free of dependency and the limits it imposes, which are as real as any prison bars.

Some First Spouses maintain an office in their state capitols and often travel with an assistant or staff, but Todd did not. Sure, the critics still accused him of being "The Shadow Governor," but that's because they couldn't find anything legitimate to criticize him about.

The girls fit into their new city right away. All three would visit me at the Capitol Building after school. Most of the staffers had authentic Piper Palin artwork hanging in their offices. And when the Menards gave us a puppy to bring to the mansion (for which I still don't forgive them), Willow named her Agia—a pretty name that really stood for the Alaska Gasline Inducement Act, which was the name of our administration's signature project. Once after school, Willow hid the puppy in her purse and snuck her into my office. The Senate Rules Committee chairman busted her and sent me a letter with some kind of official citation attached. Heaven forbid any lawmaker would catch Willow carrying her furry four-pound puppy into my office in violation of the new NO DOGS ALLOWED sign. (Surely just a small distraction for this senator—he was later busted by the FBI and convicted on federal corruption charges.) The kids had another pup too, named Indi.

Juggling car pools is part of raising kids, but as governor I had to be a bit more careful. The mother of one of Willow's dear friends on the basketball team was a lobbyist, and I had a rule that my staff and I would not hang with lobbyists.

Worried about even the whiff of impropriety, I told Willow, "Sorry, honey, you'll have to find another ride."

Willow set me straight and insisted that the ethics laws for my staff would ruin her life. "That's not what those laws mean anyway, Mom!" she said. "People aren't going to pick on you if you don't do anything wrong."

"You'd be surprised," I said.

I compromised with Willow and let her hang out with her teammate, but in my official state financial disclosure forms I went so far as to reveal the friendship and noted that when she traveled with her basketball team she received rides from this lobbyist, who was a very nice lady.

Still, I told Willow, "You may never even take a Gatorade from the family."

You haven't seen teenage eye rolling until you've seen Willow roll her eyes.

The honeymoon lasted a while for the kids. But when it ended, it ended abruptly, and their perspective changed entirely. In that first year, I was alerted to threats against Willow by students at her Juneau school, one particularly disturbing. Someone posted a note on an Internet site threatening to gang-rape her at school. I never felt as safe for her after that. Later, the same thing happened to Bristol. And during the VP campaign, among so many other threats, a guy from New Jersey wrote that he would "shoot her pregnant body from a helicopter."

Those were the ugly times, but there were precious times too. My fondest memory from the mansion is Piper learning to ride her bike in the yard. A little kid hadn't lived in the house for decades, so we put in a buoy swing and a trampoline for ours (which I suspect some of the neighbors didn't think was very stately). Someone let Piper use an old bike, a blue one for little boys, and that's what she learned to ride on. My happiest day at the mansion was on a sunny weekend afternoon. We were in the yard, and after many unsuccessful tries, she finally managed to ride her bike upright in a great big circle all the way around the trampoline.

Of course, being able to ride doesn't mean being able to stop, and she crashed headfirst into the bushes bordering the lawn. But for Piper, it was the ride that mattered, and she jumped up from the bushes, pumped her fist in the air and yelled, "Yay, me!"

She was victorious! She was proud of herself! And she got to shout it to the world with no one to shush her or to tell her to be humble and quiet. For me, standing there in the sunshine, it was one of those Mom Moments when your heart feels like it just might burst, and I thought, *May every little child have an abundance of "Yay, me!" moments.*

5

I built my circle of close advisers carefully. The opportunity to pull in the perfect partners was challenging because few prospective candidates wanted to make the long commute to the state capital. So I shook things up a bit and made concessions more readily than other governors about where my staff's home base could be. New communication technologies allowed this. I wanted the right people for the job, and if Juneau's location was the main stumbling block, I wasn't going to mandate that families uproot and move to a beautiful but isolated panhandle, especially when the previous governors had spent so much time in Anchorage and traveling out of state.

Early on, I announced a number of commissioners, including Walt Monegan as the commissioner of the Department of Public Safety. I also announced other appointments, including my chief of staff, my legislative director, and my communications director, Meghan Stapleton. They were a young, motivated staff with lots of energy.

Some of the team had worked on my general election campaign. The new legislative director had lobbied for the chief of staff slot, but I knew he wasn't ready for that, so a hint of internal rivalry cropped up immediately.

Meg Stapleton was well known from her years as a political reporter and news anchor at our local NBC affiliate. She had national political experience from her days on Capitol Hill with the Republican National Committee and her work for GOP power-broker Fred Malek, as well as corporate experience with an Alaska-based telecommunications company.

I also added my campaign manager and confidante Kris Perry as director of my Anchorage office, and she soon had everything running like a Swiss watch. During the vice presidential campaign, she would become the lone state staffer the McCain campaign allowed to accompany me on the trail.

———

Politically, Juneau always had a reputation for being a lot like Animal House: drinking and bowling, drunken brawls, countless affairs, and garden-variety lunchtime trysts. It's been known at times to be like a frat house filled with freshmen away from their parents for the very first time. At other times, the capital city's underside was even darker: clandestine political liaisons and secret meetings, unethical deeds and downright illegal acts. When the legislative session begins, the good and decent people who live in Juneau can witness some of these extracurricular pursuits at places like the Red Dog Saloon and the Baranof Hotel. Others around the state read about them in newspaper gossip columns. During the 2006 gubernatorial race, the FBI handcuffed a number of lawmakers.

In short, it was a lot like Washington, D.C.

With a state to run, a husband on the Slope, and an active family to shepherd, I didn't have time to follow all the shenanigans. And though some held it against me that I didn't spend time on the cocktail circuit, I was confident of my priorities. Meanwhile, there were many talented people who served in Juneau for the right reasons, and I enjoyed spending time with them, as their good work demonstrated their servants' hearts.

I attributed part of the corruption problem, besides the obvious self-dealing motives of politicians, to Juneau's inaccessibility. Foreign tourists on cruise ships had better access to lawmakers in session than 80 percent of the citizens of the state had. That makes Juneau an island of sorts, isolating legislators and staff from the people who elected them. Until access improves, the political atmosphere there will not change much. And I know there are a handful of legislators who would prefer just that.

———

Just as I took the helm, the results of an FBI investigation that had percolated between Juneau, Prudhoe Bay, and Washington, D.C., began bubbling to the surface. Bill Allen, the longtime CEO of VECO Corporation, the powerful oil field services company, had for years held court in Juneau's Baranof Hotel, where his firm maintained a suite. For decades, he was a big-time political fund-raiser, and, following the *Exxon Valdez* oil spill, his company was the prime oil services contractor. Like other business owners, Allen pressed for legislation that would benefit his company. But he pressed harder than most. Allen was friends with Governor Murkowski and his chief of staff, and with powerful Republican lawmakers.

FBI undercover surveillance video of the VECO suite in Room 604, which would become infamous, even showed the VECO executive pressing cash into the palm of a Republican legislator. Months of videotaping and recorded phone calls earned VECO executives a long visit with federal agents, during which they admitted having bribed several lawmakers to push through legislation favorable to the oil industry. Allen pleaded guilty to extortion, bribery, and conspiracy.

His mea culpa led to other pleas, including one by Governor Murkowski's chief of staff, who eventually copped to a single count of conspiracy. All told, a dozen lawmakers, staffers, and oil company executives would be found guilty of multiple charges, including wire fraud, bribery, conspiracy, and extortion.

Alaskans said the Democrats weren't any better—they just hadn't been caught that go-round. But the reality was that it was the Republicans this time. And some of them didn't like it when my administration rode in on the horse of ethics reform. At a press conference after my first State of the State Address, we released a white paper on ethics coauthored by one Democrat and one Republican. As Meg and I left the conference room and walked back to my office, she commented on the anticipated favorable coverage in the media. "You reached across the aisle," Meg said. "I think Alaskans will appreciate that."

But my legislative director wasn't so happy. He had fought the release of the ethics paper because he knew it would rub legislators the wrong way—and would shut the revolving door between the administration and outside lobbying jobs. He was right: the moment the press conference was over, he delivered the unsurprising news that GOP lawmakers were furious and wanted a meeting in my office. *Now.*

About a half a dozen paraded in. They brought me a message: "Don't come down here and expect to change things. Don't paint us all with the broad brush of corruption. You go clean the administrative house, but don't touch ours."

I reiterated the need for reform. They reiterated their vast experience and implied my equally vast naïveté. Then we all smiled graciously as I noted that, yes, we would be working hard to change the rules for the executive branch, too.

Later, one lawmaker called Meg to his office to continue the conversation. "I can tell you right now which bills will pass this session and which won't," he said. "It's based upon one thing: relationships—and who is sleeping with whom."

Wow. Shocking to hear it from the horse's mouth. But instead of being discouraged by that, we took it as a challenge and set out to prove that we'd live up to our promise of reform and positive change.

I had been in office two weeks when the Alaska Supreme Court issued an order requiring us to offer health benefits to the same-sex partners of state employees. The issue split conservatives and liberals.

I support the traditional definition of marriage. One man and one woman make a marriage. And I don't support efforts that can lead to changing that definition.

But on this issue in Alaska, the court was the lawful interpreter of the state Constitution. The promise I had made when being sworn into office was to uphold the Constitution. That meant I would be bound by the judiciary's ruling. So when conservatives in the legislature passed a bill that would prohibit state benefits for same-sex couples, the court ruled it unconstitutional, so I vetoed it.

A few angry lawmakers visited my office, outraged that I hadn't bucked the court. A couple of them said I should have been willing to go to jail over the issue.

The unhappy legislators knew how I felt personally about benefits for homosexual couples; there was no need to preach to the choir about it during our meeting. I bit my tongue and didn't ask them why, as lawmakers who'd been serving in office for many years—and I'd just gotten to Juneau—they hadn't been able to usher their desired outcome through the legislative process or at least get the issue onto the ballot for Alaska voters to decide.

As governor, I meant to follow the law. Therefore, even though legislators passed a law that reflected my personal views, I vetoed it. It wasn't about me; it was—and is—about respecting the Constitution and the separation of powers.

And if the people want to amend the Constitution via referendum, I told the lawmakers, they have the right to battle it out and do so.

6

I remembered reading a survey once that said most CEOs, if they had to do things over again, would hire back only 20 percent of their original staff. For me it was the opposite: I would rehire 80 percent of my great team of dedicated public servants, including my office administrative staff.

But the 20 percent on which I'd ask for a "do-over," well, they were doozies.

My first legislative director was one of these. He turned out to be a BlackBerry games addict who couldn't seem to keep his lunch off his tie. He relished the perception that he was a "player" in Juneau politics, but we were never sure which team he was on. In one of our first meetings with lawmakers, he bragged that he was buddies with all of them and swore he knew exactly "how to handle them." He had worked in the Capitol and used to be a lobbyist. He was an "insider," and we thought we should hire at least one of those to show us where the light switches were.

"These guys need to be reminded that you were elected on your promise of 'no more politics-as-usual,'" he said. "You gotta go in there and tell lawmakers up front, 'All of you here are in need of some adult supervision.' Trust me, I know this stuff, they want to hear it."

So I followed his advice. I had my come-to-Jesus meeting with legislators. They didn't quite *want* to hear it.

When the fallout began after that meeting, I looked at the legislative director. He looked at the ground and shrugged as if to say, "Wasn't me."

Well, I figured, I had already won a Miss Congeniality sash back in the day. Though my girls had thrashed it over the years while playing dress-up, I wasn't looking to replace it.

The guy was right about this much: a few of our forty representatives and twenty senators did appear to need adult supervision. Alaska's part-time legislature meets for just ninety days each year, from January to April, but somehow required tens of millions of dollars to get its job done. The public noticed how much time the legislature spent discussing such weighty matters as whether to name an official state dog, debating whether Marmot Day should replace Groundhog Day or whose birthday should be celebrated on the House floor, as well as traveling out of state and country. They passed plenty of laws—that wasn't the concern; in fact, some of them wanted to pass too many laws, and I told one of the Democrats that for every law they passed I wanted to see two repealed. That didn't go over very well, either.

Meanwhile, Alaska's annual budget growth was unsustainable and we needed to slow it down.

Managing a $14 billion budget as the chief executive of the largest state in the Union with thousands of employees is more complex than managing a city like Wasilla, and certainly weightier than managing a household of seven. But lessons learned on the micro level still apply to the macro. Just as my family couldn't fund every item on our wish list, and had to live within our means as well as save for the future, I felt we needed to do that for the state. I had four core principles as the foundation of our budget: live within our means, expand resource development and industry, focus on core services (education, infrastructure, and public safety), and save for the future. And I reminded my staff: never forget you're spending other people's money; that should make us more prudent and serious than anything.

Almost all of our state budget depends on development of Alaska's energy resources. The petroleum resource is nonrenewable. When it's gone, it's gone. Not only is it finite, its value fluctuates. In 1999, the price of a barrel of oil was $9; in 2008, it was $140. Price is dependent upon so many factors—a war in a third-world country, a hurricane off the coast, an angry petro-dictator, new oil discoveries in foreign lands. And our revenue department has to estimate every year what the price of a barrel of oil will be in order for us to build the budget.

Alaskans know the pain of wildly fluctuating oil prices. We learned our lesson about saving for the future the hard way. During the heyday of the Trans-Alaska Pipeline, we were living the good life. The price of oil was high and the boom was on, creating a gold rush of state revenue, which government spent as quickly as possible. We were still a vast, undeveloped frontier outpost in need of infrastructure. So the state spent fast.

Then the smack-down: oil bottomed out at $9 a barrel. There hadn't been much planning for the bust times. Alaskans began driving around with bumper stickers that read, DEAR GOD, GIVE US ANOTHER OIL BOOM AND WE PROMISE NOT TO PISS IT AWAY THIS TIME.

When that next boom came during my administration, we were determined to be conservative and accountable to future generations. (As Thomas Paine said in 1776: "If there must be trouble, let it be in my day, that my children may have peace.") Yet getting certain legislators, including Republicans, on board with budget cutting in a time of surplus was like turning off a free tap at the Red Dog. I was told more than once that I was crazy for not spending the money while it rolled in, because, as in every state, there were a lot of "needs"—especially "for the children."

At the time, both parties, nationally and locally, were spending uncontrollably. No wonder voters couldn't tell Republicans from Democrats. How can the GOP claim fiscal conservatism when we let our own party's congressional delegations fund things in the federal budget like the new monument to honor the mules

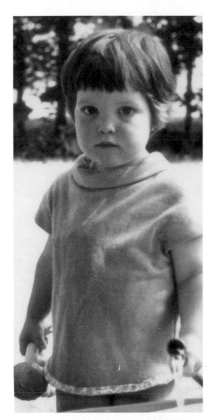

ABOVE: In 1964 Mom bundled me up with a cloth diaper for a scarf to watch the Fourth of July races in windy Skagway. *Courtesy Chuck Heath*

LEFT: We visited our grandparents for a week or so every few years. I was three years old in this picture, taken in Richland, Washington. We stayed longer that summer because Dad had a severe case of hepatitis and was bedridden. *Courtesy Chuck Heath*

Grandma Heath visited us in Skagway and helped pull the wagon of groceries and Baby Molly down the gravel road to our house on a sunny summer day. The wooden sidewalks are the scene of one of my earliest memories. *Courtesy Chuck Heath*

TOP: On a Sunday-afternoon drive up the new Parks Highway we got a much-needed caribou and carried it back to Wasilla atop the trunk of our old blue Rambler. Dad would offer a quarter to whichever kid first spotted a moose or caribou. Everyone must have had better eyes than I did because I rarely got that quarter. *Courtesy Chuck Heath*

MIDDLE: Molly, Heather, and I with our wonderful family dog, Rufus, a faithful companion and protector for thirteen years. *Courtesy Chuck Heath*

BOTTOM: Dad shows our Skagway neighbor Blythe, and Heather, me, and Chuck Jr., how to skin a harbor seal. It was legal to harvest the seals for their meat until the Marine Mammal Protection Act of 1972 banned hunting them (a 1994 amendment allowed for hunting by Alaska Natives). Grandma Sheeran sewed coats and mittens for us out of the hides. *Courtesy Sally Heath*

Growing up, I was of the mind that basketball was life and the rest was just details. I was cocaptain and point guard of the Wasilla Warriors 1982 State Championship team. It was a season that changed my life. *Courtesy Jackie Conn*

BELOW LEFT: My fellow track teammates Katy Port, Chris Koeneman-Triplett, and Kim "Tilly" Ketchum standing in front of me in our school parking lot, where we had to practice all events during spring breakup seasons. *Courtesy Chuck Heath*

Our state cross-country running meet was held in the snow at Settlers Bay Golf Course. Dad and Dan Giffen were our coaches and inspired us to be not only determined runners but good students too. The whole team was on the honor roll. I'm in the first row, far left; Heather is the blonde on the far right. Behind us are Lincoln Fischer, Rocky Moreland, Benny Welch, Elwyn Fischer, Curtis Menard, Darin Swift, Grant Smith. In front stand Dena Ludington, Marie Carter, Chris Erickson, Michelle Carney, and Karen Bush. *Courtesy Chuck Heath*

May 1982. Todd and I walked together in Warrior colors at Wasilla High School's graduation ceremony. Twenty-eight years later, we're still walking together, but maybe have picked up the pace a bit. *Courtesy Jim Palin*

LEFT: Graduation day, 1987, at the University of Idaho. I loved my years in college as a Vandal but was ready to return to Alaska and get busy on a full-time career. This picture is in front of "The Tower," an all-girls dorm where I lived for three years. *Courtesy Anna DeLaCueva*

RIGHT: Spring of 1982. I'm standing in front of the rig that Todd took great care of—his 1972 Ford Mustang Grande, which he bought from his hip grandma in Oregon, Margaret Denny. And I'm sure I looked pretty hip in the Members Only jacket I borrowed from Todd for this picture. *Courtesy Faye Palin*

My group of lifelong girlfriends, the "Elite 6"—as we jokingly refer to ourselves, because we're anything but "elite." I'm on the far left, and special needs assistant Patti Ricker sits by me. Next are EMT/ambulance driver Sandy Hoeft and personal trainer Juanita Fuller. On the floor are investigator Amy Hansen and food bank volunteer and election poll coordinator Deb Remus. We've been through tragedies and triumphs, births and deaths—together. They're trustworthy, faithful, down-to-earth *true* friends, and they help keep me grounded despite the politics that constantly swirl. *Courtesy Deb Remus*

On July Fourth, 1994, while visiting the Menards, I take to kayaking on Memory Lake with Bristol and Chuck Jr. to try to kick up the contractions. Baby Willow was overdue, and I thought it would be great for her to be born on the Fourth of July, but alas, I must not have paddled hard enough because she wasn't born until the next day. *Courtesy Linda Menard*

LEFT: Here Nick Carney and I take the oath of office as we're sworn in as Wasilla City Councilmen in City Hall, in 1992. Finance Director Erling Nelson administered the oath. I used to babysit Erling's kids when I was a teenager. *Courtesy Todd Palin*

RIGHT: After serving my first term on the City Council, I was reelected in 1995 to serve another term, before I ran for mayor. It was a pleasure serving my hometown, and I wouldn't trade the experience for much of anything. *Courtesy Judy Patrick*

BOTTOM: Our 1996 campaign for mayor took to Palmer's Alaska State Fair parade right before the local elections. Our campaign theme, "Positive-ly Palin," was delivered with pink and green signs—because no one else ever used those colors. *Courtesy Heather Bruce*

The family lines up for a weekend snowmachine ride, where we take off from our front door on frozen Lake Lucille. There are plentiful trail-riding opportunities all over our state, and, in fact, if you're tough enough, you could travel all the way from our house to Nome, like Iditarod mushers and Iron Doggers do. *Courtesy Todd Palin*

BELOW LEFT: Here I'm panning for gold on a creek near Eureka, which is near Glennallen. This find is after three of us panned for two days in the freezing creek. BELOW RIGHT: Commercial fishing in Bristol Bay on a nice day like this is a family affair. Track and I prepare the net to set from Nushagak River's beach, which requires me leaving the skiff, tromping through the mud, and then working the ebb and flood of the tide to catch healthy, clean, wild Alaska salmon. *Courtesy Todd Palin*

ABOVE LEFT: Dad and his granddaughter Willow clean silver salmon at our favorite sport-fishing hole. We dry the eggs to use as bait, often for ice fishing. I'm not hard-core enough to thaw the frozen eggs in my mouth before baiting an ice-fishing hook; Dad's a good man—he usually takes care of that. *Courtesy Todd Palin*

ABOVE RIGHT: Our wonderful friend and commercial fishing partner Nick Timurphy, originally from the Native village of New Stuyahok, is ready to help me field dress the caribou I just shot. It may not look like a trophy, but it's good eating, and I'm thankful to help fill our freezer with some of the cleanest organic protein on God's green earth. We eat, therefore we hunt. *Courtesy Todd Palin*

Todd and I pull in the net to haul a catch of red salmon that we'll sell to a Bristol Bay processor. Todd's the hardest-working fisherman I know. He goes days without sleep and picks salmon from the nets with amazing skill and speed. He's been at this for nearly forty years. He hires a crew, sometimes greenhorns, to join us every summer, and if they start off not knowing what hard work is, Todd makes sure they know what it feels like by the end of the season. *Courtesy Kaleb Westfall*

and pack animals in California? And Democrat politicians aren't any better, but at least their fiscal liberalism is expected. Take the New York senior senator's recent million-dollar request for a museum to pay homage to the Woodstock Music Festival, widely criticized as a "taxpayer-funded LSD flashback."

My own fiscal restraint was considered by some Alaska lawmakers too sharp a contrast to the last Republican administration's lack thereof, and I was warned by lawmakers *not* to shake things up so much. Governor Murkowski was a nice man, but he had spent twenty-two years in D.C. where the budget does nothing *but* grow, so he was just doing what came naturally. Murkowski was so nice, in fact, that he unveiled his last capital budget while donning a Santa Claus hat. I don't mean figuratively. He put the hat on and signed a budget full of "gifts" for lawmakers.

Not that he didn't trim here and there. He did cancel a senior care program for needy elders who had come to rely on it for their monthly income. Then he turned around and bought the jet.

That darn jet. Both the public and the legislature had told Murkowski not to buy it. It was very expensive to operate, and pilots couldn't land it on gravel strips, making it practically useless for travel around a lot of Alaska. After I was elected, I listed the thing on eBay and an agent finally sold it.

I asked my own staff to develop efficiencies and gave them budget-cutting goals. And I didn't exempt the First Family from this. We saved tens of thousands of dollars in our very first year just by discontinuing the perks like fancy meals. (As I would go on to say in my VP nomination acceptance speech, my kids still hold that against me.)

When I was outside Juneau, I accepted the normal meal per diem of $60 but refused the per diem checks for the other six eligible First Family members (including a $100+ check made out to Piper—I handed it back and said, "Piper can't eat that much in a month"), and we refused the housing per diem as well. I also stayed in our own house in Wasilla while working in the Anchorage office and when plumbing repairs kept us out of the mansion for months, rather than have the state put me up—as it had for previous governors—in an expensive hotel or a rented apartment. In fact, we slashed living expenses, and I drove myself to the Anchorage office and to most meetings and events. I was never paid to sleep in my own home, and I accepted only a meal per diem, despite what some critics would later accuse me of doing.

This while Juneau's own legislators, including Senator Kim Elton who lived right there in town, pocketed more than $20,000 in food and housing per diem payments in just one year.

Meanwhile, I'm still trying to find a hotel in Anchorage that will put up a family of seven and feed five hungry kids for sixty bucks a night.

———

In Juneau, the one thing that's required during the session is passing a budget, and that one task is the subject of endless hours of discussion, deliberation, bartering, and whining. Again I was thankful for my training grounds as a mom.

My first budget was initially assembled by Murkowski's administration on its way out the door, so I cut $150 million out of it right off the bat when I handed it over to lawmakers. I asked my legislative director to draft a letter to lawmakers to make them aware that I wanted a smaller, smarter budget and that I wouldn't be afraid to use my veto pen to achieve it. My thinking was that we could be proactive about the whole process: if they didn't send me pork, I wouldn't have to kill it. Simple.

The director's letter was to convey two messages. First, I wanted lawmakers to know that to be approved, their funding requests must be centered on core services that government appropriately provides: public safety, education, and infrastructure. Second, I asked them to prioritize their funding requests because I assumed that they were in contact with those on the front lines in their districts and that they could better tell me where cuts could be made.

There would be cuts one way or another, which the letter was to make clear. I took a firm stance, but I didn't want to sound adversarial. My door was open, I was willing to listen. I just wanted them to know where I was coming from.

On the lawmakers' end, part of the budget process was of the smoke-filled backroom variety and ultimately was in the hands of just a few powerful politicians. They crafted the budget and voted it into law at the eleventh hour, then dropped it in my inbox and rocketed out of town.

That first year, what they turned in was a budget that didn't look prioritized and was so lacking in detail that on some pages it was simply a subject ("Batting Cages for Kids") and a number ("$100,000"). And so began our marathon budget breakdown.

It was late June 2007, just after the solstice, and we worked late into the night with the warm midnight sun still pouring through my office windows. My chief of staff and our budget director were there. Meg (who was nine months pregnant and ready to meet her first baby at any moment), Kris, and another budget staffer sat with me around my conference table. Pens in hand, we combed through the budget, line by line, page by page—my inner nerd coming out again, just like Wasilla City Council days.

I felt a serious sense of responsibility for this. It was other people's money we were spending, and I was the one who had to sign off on this multibillion-dollar budget. I had to know what was in there, or I wasn't doing my job. We spent days trying to decipher who put in what and why.

Late one night, I looked up from the table and asked our veteran staffers, "What did past governors do? How did they get through these budgets with so little detail?"

"They didn't," was the response.

Before, others skimmed through it and governors signed off on it.

Well, it was a new day, and we sifted through funding requests for schools, roads, ports, AstroTurf and batting cages, blueberry farms, and, believe or not, a lawmaker's friend's suicide memorial.

State spending increases were unsustainable. I was looking for cuts. Lawmakers long ago learned that they could get almost anything through if they couched it as "It's for the children." Thus, one year, a lawmaker didn't bat an eye in his request for $43,000 for a landscaping project at a school in his district. Apparently some shrubs had died and due to the leafless twigs, according to the funding request, "The risk of a child impaling themselves on the shrubs is substantial."

Killer shrubs!

I asked the obvious: was there some reason the district couldn't remove the potentially lethal shrubs using part of the *billion dollars* we had already allocated? Or maybe have the local Girl Scout troop volunteer to chop to them down?

During my 2007 budget powwow, the legislative director should have been at the table with us so that there would be no surprises in the state house come veto time. Occasionally, he would wander in and out, plop down in the chair at the end of the table, nibble cookies, and absently thumb his BlackBerry. Every now and then a tired staffer on a bathroom break would pass behind him, glance down, then mouth over his head, "It's Brick-Breaker."

One day Meg and I caught up with him in the hallway to ask about his communication with lawmakers because we were getting mixed messages from city officials regarding their project priorities, and I was ready to announce the budget cuts. Slouching against the wall, he assured us that, yeah, he had everything under control, mission accomplished. The fact that his shirt was buttoned one button off and his shirttail was poking through his open fly didn't exactly inspire confidence.

Trying not to telegraph the last problem with my eyes, I said, "Legislators *do* know I'm going to be making a lot of cuts, don't they?"

"Yeah, they know why you got elected."

"They're fine with a whole lot of vetoes that are coming?" Meg said.

"Sure."

"And they understand my funding criteria from the letter you sent—right?" I added.

His eyes subtly widened, as if he were just remembering something important he had neglected to do. "Yeah," he said. "They're all set . . . um . . . gotta go . . ." He hustled off, one of the last times we saw the fellow.

My budget priorities weren't all about slashing. We increased education funding and committed to putting a billion dollars into where I wanted to go with "forward funding" education so that local school districts could know how many state dollars they could count on every year. We also increased school services for children with special needs and beefed up funding for public safety officers to handle alcohol abuse and domestic violence in rural villages. But even with increased funding for public safety and infrastructure projects, by the time we had reprioritized the budget, I had made the largest veto totals in the state's history. It wasn't the easy path, but it was the right path.

But it soon became obvious just how little the legislative director had done to inform the legislature this was coming. And we got a taste of state-level political turf wars, as legislators threw their heads back and howled.

"Palin blindsided us!"

"If you're going to change the rules, you should have told us!"

"It was only a hundred thousand dollars for a blueberry farm! What's the big deal?"

"Where's my killer shrub money?"

As legislative staffers scrambled to locate defibrillator paddles to resuscitate their bosses, press releases showered down like propaganda flyers before an air raid:

Palin destroys city! Women and children in peril!
Governor vetoes animal shelter expansion! Imminent death for
*   puppies and kittens!*

Later we learned the legislative director had been too busy with his personal affairs to attend to much state business. He had spent years in Juneau's political circles; we had thought we needed someone with that kind of experience to get our new administration off the ground. So much for my idea that I needed to hire an "insider." Lesson learned.

Not long after we released the budget, with walking papers in hand, he quickly popped up as a staffer for a legislator who immediately transformed from one of the administration's biggest allies to one of our sharpest critics.

7

Prior to the election it had been revealed that BP had been trying to save money for years by cutting corners on oil pipeline maintenance on the North Slope. This was very serious: leaks and spills from corroded pipelines were all too common and harmed the environment plus led to production slowdowns. So one of my first priorities was to establish the Petroleum Systems Integrity Office (PSIO). With the creation of the PSIO, Alaska became the first state to require industry operators to document their compliance with maintenance and quality assurance standards, and to share that information with the state. Unfortunately, the next year the House Finance subcommittee gutted more than a third of the PSIO budget. I fought to get it restored and finally succeeded.

To avoid the caterwauling and turf wars of our first-year budget process, we set up a new process for assembling the capital budget heading into my second year. This time lawmakers knew that when we said cuts, we meant cuts. With the price of a barrel of oil at record highs, we had a major revenue surplus. My fiscal plan included saving the money before lawmakers spent it, and finding a way to give it back to the people because it was theirs to begin with. Being a fiscal conservative during a time of scarcity isn't nearly as difficult as being one during a time of plenty. It's easy to tighten the belt when you have no money to order a feast. Using our surplus, we paid down debt and set aside billions of dollars in savings for the day when the price of oil would plummet. Again I wanted lawmakers to prioritize their requests, and again I promised to veto. This new budgeting process had to be open and transparent to fulfill my promise of changing the way business was done. Many legislators again resisted the idea. I wanted them to encourage town hall meetings in their districts so that constituents could weigh in and help prioritize the spending of public money, *their* money. By the third year, many legislators were sitting down with me and explaining each line-item request ahead of my vetoes. It became a very good process to prioritize public monies.

When you talk about a city's needs, the buck stops with the person ordering potholes filled and equipping the local police department—the mayor. My philosophy has always been that the most responsive and responsible level of government is the local level. Local government is best able to prioritize services and projects. That's the basis of the Tenth Amendment to the U.S. Constitution, which, paraphrased, says that the powers not delegated specifically to the federal government or prohibited by the states are reserved to the states or the people themselves.

My insistence on this, as well as my commitment to trickling down state resource development revenues to local governments—known as municipal revenue sharing—infuriated some legislators. They saw it as a usurpation of their power. In their eyes, I was bypassing them as the keepers of the state purse strings and responding directly to the people.

I released my budget, having trimmed it as much as I believed the public would stand for. At the same time, I insisted on showing the real numbers, including a "true up" of eight hundred existing state positions that previous administrations had funded off the books. This led some critics to claim that I had grown government by eight hundred people. No. These positions already existed. Prior administrations had simply refused to disclose it on the books.

I welcomed public scrutiny and invited the legislature and the public to look hard at other places to cut. I honestly hoped the people would find more government programs and projects they wanted cut. Then we put our state checkbook online for all the world to see—we weren't the first, but it's a practice that has spread to other states.

———

The House of Representatives introduced my administration's ethics reform bill, a rawhide-tough package of measures meant to pry state government away from special interests and put it back on the side of the people. Our bill followed that period of embarrassing political scandals that occurred before I was elected. Ordinary Alaskans were expressing outrage at what was going on in Juneau, and I had promised to clean house.

The ongoing FBI investigation had revealed legislative conflicts of interest, so our ethics package required that lawmakers report outside income. In addition, we shoved a wedge into the employment revolving door between special interests and the Capitol. Remember the young political appointee who was supposed to be the ethics supervisor over AOGCC? In 2006, he was working as Governor Murkowski's chief legislative aide, representing the state in gasline negotiations with ExxonMobil and other companies. A few months later, he was earning $10,000 a month lobbying the state *for* ExxonMobil. The public's obvious question: whose side are these guys on?

We wanted Alaskans to have faith that the people in state government were working for the people's benefit and not simply greasing the skids for their own future.

In early March, the Senate passed its own ethics bill, authored by Democrat Senator Hollis French. It was watered down. It rejected all but one of the amendments we had asked be included from the tougher House bill. In particular, I was astonished that French and the Senate didn't adopt provisions such as a ban on gifts from lobbyists.

The Senate's action was politics-as-usual. We were determined to keep the pressure on.

That pressure paid off when legislators approved an omnibus ethics bill. It included my administration's ethics proposal, as well as the House's muscular amendment that imposed criminal penalties on lawmakers who traded votes for campaign contributions. Plus, any legislator convicted of a felony would forfeit his or her state pension.

We were pleased that no one could claim pride of authorship on this. Finally the Capitol had pulled together and passed a strong bill. A Democrat lawmaker noted: "This is one of the best pieces of work I've seen come out of the legislature because it came out as a policy document and not a political document."

It was music to my ears: *policy,* not politics.

━━━

As with ethics reform, my team and I were determined to fundamentally change the game when it came to the natural gas pipeline. Instead of negotiating behind closed doors with the monopolistic industry, we wanted to get back to competitive free-market principles, ethically employed. To that end, we built a team of energy experts and lifelong Alaskans whose focus was on crafting a bill that would provide a framework within which any company could compete.

This was a multibillion-dollar project, the largest private-sector energy project in North American history. It was a once-in-a-lifetime opportunity. So we had to demand that the resource owners' needs be met.

To get the project off the ground after decades of politicians just talking about it, we tried a "newfangled" approach: free-market principles. We asked willing and able companies to compete for the right to build Alaska's gasline. Our approach would be open and transparent, with no behind-closed-door deals. The plan also included a series of mandates, or must-haves, including specific timelines, provisions related to pipeline access and expansion, reasonable tariffs (or transport rates) so more energy could affordably flow through the natural gas pipeline, and better energy prices for Alaskans.

Those provisions would allow local consumers to benefit appropriately from a pipeline running through their backyard. For instance, rather than pegging Alaskans' gas price to the price paid in Chicago, the AGIA bill insisted that the project sponsor licensee essentially provide a "pay for what you need" transport rate, allowing Alaskans to pay transportation "tolls" relative to the distance the gas had been transported.

Some accused us of taking too hard a line with the oil companies. I knew we were acting appropriately to hold the companies' feet to the fire.

This project would cost the private sector a tremendous amount in government fees and prep work to get through local, state, and federal regulatory and environmental processes, so it made sense, along with the state's number of must-haves, for us to put some skin in the game by reimbursing the winning bidder for some of the up-front bureaucratic costs.

Therefore, in crafting what would become the landmark Alaska Gasline Inducement Act, or AGIA, we promised to reimburse up to $500 million in matching funds for the exclusive gasline license.

Throughout the process, it was our goal to take one of the state's most historic—and most technical, buzzworded, boring-to-read—bills and boil it down to the common sense level—because that's my world. We had to articulate clearly and simply what we were doing so that Alaskans could trust us to do it right. While our gasline team crunched away on the technical issues and lawyers, economists, scientists, consultants, and specialists from around the world provided drafts of potential language, the communications team—Marty, Bruce, Meg, and I—would cut to the chase like Ronald Reagan used to do and just talk to the people in plain language.

The task was all-consuming: many hours a day for many months with office meetings, conference calls, cabinet meetings, town hall meetings, legislative discussions, e-mails, video messages, and media interviews. None of it felt like work though. Instead it was exciting and exhilarating because we felt we were making history.

We knew we were headed in the right direction when the threats from some oil industry players began—everything from nasty e-mails to multimillion-dollar ad campaigns. Though none of the Big Three oil companies wanted to move away from their relationships with the previous administration, ExxonMobil seemed particularly hostile. As we got ready to present AGIA to the legislature, ExxonMobil's chairman, Rex Tillerson (we called him "T-Rex"), told journalists at an energy conference in Houston, "I don't really know where we are. I don't think it looks like Alaska knows where it wants to go, either."

Privately, I was frustrated with the industry's posture against the new competitive environment we hoped to create. Publicly, I tempered my comments:

What bothers me is that Alaska tried it Exxon's way. The result was a contract [Murkowski's] that is not viable. It did not have the support of the public or the legislature. That's why we need a competitive, open, and transparent process. It's painfully obvious that ExxonMobil does not want that process. We know exactly where we're going and have a plan to move forward. Exxon doesn't like that plan because it puts the interests of Alaska and the nation first—and not Exxon.

Still, Big Oil slammed us in the media—again, confirmation that we were making the right decisions. Soon after, we introduced AGIA to the legislature. That new word, "ah-gee-ah," quickly became part of the 49th State's vernacular.

When I was labeled "anti-business," it wasn't difficult to connect the dots back to Big Oil. The motive was clear: it would spend millions of dollars to paint us as bad for Alaska because it no longer had control of the state's decisions. The smear campaign was obvious to many, thank goodness. I attribute that to the fact that we conducted business out in the sunshine for everyone to see. And the people appreciated that: my administration's approval rating hit an all-time high.

After much debate, the legislature adopted AGIA. In the end, only *one* lawmaker voted against the measure. Interestingly, it was the legislator who had told Meg early on that bill passage is all about relationships and who is sleeping with whom.

We were tremendously excited about signing the bill into law. We planned the ceremony carefully: we wanted to bring this historic law, decades in the making, outside the state offices and directly to the people. After all, it was their bill—this was truly their future. We decided to hold the ceremony at the Fox Visitor Center right outside Fairbanks, next to the Trans-Alaska Pipeline.

On the morning of the signing on June 6, 2007, friends, family, and staff all headed to Fox. I wore my best pair of Carhartts, clogs hand-painted by the Alaska artist Romney Dodd, and a T-shirt that said FREEDOM.

We placed a podium underneath the pipeline. Across the street, John Reeves (the Fairbanks Democrat who had encouraged me to run for governor) parked his bulldozer with the blade spray-painted red: CONGRATS AGIA! His sign included: THANKS GOV PALIN, TOM & TEAM—FROM CONSUMERS, D.O.B. 6/6/07.

During the ceremony, I spoke of the historic economic and political juncture represented by AGIA's success. Piper and her cousin McKinley stood beside me throughout the dedication, representing the future of Alaska. The gasline team had reason to be proud: after decades of bureaucrats just talking about it, we were ushering in change just six months after taking office, with new energy standing beside me and proven, reliable energy flowing past me in the pipeline. The hard work of the last six months had culminated in this moment.

Except for one thing.

The bill wasn't real. The legislative director had a little snafu. The actual bill hadn't made it from Juneau in time.

"How did this happen?" our press people asked him. "We've been waiting for this moment for decades."

"No one will ever know it's not a real bill," he said. "We're fine. We can fake it."

"But we knew this day was coming . . . ," I said.

"Look, we'll sign a ceremonial bill today and the actual bill tomorrow. It's fine."

Fine wasn't good enough. I cared about the possibility that anything we did with regard to this much-anticipated bill would be perceived as fake or insincere. But we couldn't cancel. So the bill-signing ceremony turned out to be . . . well, ceremonial. And I explained it that way.

When the real bill finally arrived in Anchorage, the director had to drive it out to Wasilla, and, as with most significant events in my life, I signed it near my kitchen table.

———

During the AGIA education process, I participated in a series of town hall meetings across the state to help citizens understand what we needed to do. On May 4, I was with Tom Irwin, speaking at an AGIA meeting in Barrow, the northernmost city in America, when my BlackBerry buzzed. I slipped out of the meeting and retreated to a corner of the local museum to take the call, surrounded by baleen carvings and historic Native harpoons.

"Governor Palin, it's Special Agent Toni Fogle"—special agent in charge for the state of Alaska. With the corruption investigation boiling in Juneau, it wasn't the first time the FBI had called me.

"I've got a confidential briefing for you," Fogle said.

"Okay," I said, "I'm in a good area. No one can hear me."

"I have agents standing outside the Capitol Building. More arrests of state legislators today. We're looking for one of them right now."

Special Agent Fogle ran through the details that were being made public.

After the call, I snuck back into the AGIA town hall meeting, where Tom was still speaking. By the time the event was over and we were headed to the airport for the 1,400-mile journey back to Juneau, the news was out: this time, three lawmakers would be standing handcuffed in a federal courtroom while they were arraigned on charges of extortion and bribery.

The arrests continued to expose an entangled network of corruption throughout state government. Oddly, it was as if every time a monumental issue was unveiled in Juneau, another oil executive, lawmaker, or former state staffer was indicted. Some wound up in orange jumpsuits. Others walked free. But enough proven guilt emerged to expose the corruption of at least one piece of key legislation—oil taxes crafted under the previous administration. That legislation was called the Petroleum Profits Tax, or PPT.

PPT was the latest formula the state and oil companies used to calculate Alaskans' share of oil revenues. The majority of legislators wanted oil companies to share with the state 25 percent of the profit they made selling Alaska's oil; others wanted the rate sky high; some wanted virtually nothing shared with the true resource owners. The debate was cut short when Murkowski unilaterally proposed setting the rate at the lowest number seriously under consideration, a deal the oil companies liked very much.

Heading into the governorship, I knew something needed to be done about it. An analysis of PPT showed that it was generating far less revenue than legislators had advertised—$800 million less in the year or so since it had passed. Also, PPT called for the state's share of oil revenues to be tallied as a percentage of oil companies' profits. Interestingly, after PPT passed, producers' reported operating costs suddenly doubled. Beyond the numerical haze, the arrest and indictment of a half-dozen lawmakers involved in PPT's passage created a cloud of suspicion that I believed would be dissipated only by a healthy blast of sunshine.

To that end, I called a special session of the legislature to deal solely with this issue. My feeling was that not only did PPT need the absolute attention of the legislators, Alaskans needed to know the details weren't buried in the politics and lifestyle of a normal legislative session.

Throughout the summer, the revenue and natural resources team discussed the clearest way to put a value on our resources. We pored over options. One idea was to scrap PPT entirely and create a more transparent valuation system based on a formula that was clearly understandable and would increase public confidence. We needed to improve the state's audit function, enabling us to obtain forward-looking cost data from producers. We also felt it was critical to introduce economic information sharing between the departments of revenue and natural resources and the Alaska public, something that was sorely lacking under PPT.

After my astute team of experts put their heads together, we arrived at an entirely new way of calculating Alaska's share of revenue derived from resource development: a hybrid system that included a minimum tax on gross receipts for the North Slope's oil fields, plus part of a net profits tax to encourage new development and reinvestment in existing infrastructure via incentives we'd provide entrepreneurs keen on new exploration. It allowed for tax credits on future work, restricted capital expense deductions to scheduled maintenance, and implemented strong audit and information-sharing provisions. The new formula would incentivize the industry to produce more, while protecting the public.

If that kind of explanation makes your eyes cross, it's because we didn't yet have a catchy name for our proposal. Everything in government attracts an obligatory acronym, it seems, so we figured the one assigned to this plan might as well be memorable and positive. Political terms are meant to paint a picture. For example, liberals prefer the term "social justice" over "welfare" and why conservatives prefer "marriage protection amendment" over "gay marriage ban." In the case of our new valuation formula, it was Pat Galvin's wife who came up with the name. Late in the process, she woke up early in the morning, shook Pat awake, and said, "I've got it! ACES!" She explained to him why.

Pat presented it to me the next day. "Governor, what do you think of ACES—'Alaska's Clear and Equitable Share'?"

"Perfect!" I said. The Alaska Aces, the state's only professional hockey team, was a winner—and this new clear formula was a winner, too.

Once again, it all came down to a discussion around the kitchen table. The night before I was scheduled to publicly outline the restructured resource tax, Galvin, my special assistant for oil and gas, and others stopped by the Wasilla house for pizza and one more review of our plan. We crunched and recrunched the numbers, trying to predict every conceivable economic scenario and producer loophole. Numbers don't lie; the ACES formula was best for all parties.

ACES represented a major philosophical shift in the role of government. As resource owners, Alaskans literally had a "working interest" in energy exploration and development. Traditionally, the sovereign's role is to passively collect resource royalties, but under this value structure, we would shift toward an active role in incentivizing resource development. Our state and nation needed it. Our ACES proposal would provide more value to Alaskans when the price of oil was high but would provide substantial relief to the oil companies when prices fell.

In the special legislative session held in October and November 2007, legislators on both sides of the aisle agreed with our approach. The measure passed with overwhelming public support. Of course, I took the political hits as the oil companies launched a smear campaign that we were raising taxes on industry. But we persevered, and I'm glad that we did. A year later, vindication came when industry officials admitted that the legislation was working and had even significantly increased their profits while spurring them to invest more in exploration and new development in Alaska. We had struck that sweet spot where industry and the public interest were mutually served.

8

I loved every part of my job, but the toughest part was meeting with the families of fallen soldiers. As governor, I attended many military funerals—too many. Lieutenant Governor Sean Parnell and I made sure one or both of us made it to as many military events, services, deployments, and glorious homecomings as we could. We would cancel other scheduled events in order to attend.

I attended deployments where I spoke to thousands of soldiers headed to the war zones. I spoke at their homecomings and noted with a heavy heart that there were fewer than we had said good-bye to a year earlier. I spoke at memorials and cried with Blue Star moms who had to endure the mournful call of taps, the twenty-one-gun salute, and the final roll call. And I was nearly speechless with grief when I saw those moms change their blue stars for gold ones.

As governor, I was commander in chief of the Alaska National Guard and was privileged to visit Alaska troops in Kuwait in 2007, stopping in Germany to visit wounded warriors at the Landstuhl Regional Medical Center. I traveled without staff because the U.S. State Department wanted me to travel with federal officials from the Pentagon instead of local officials. I saw our Alaskans sweltering in conditions that had the mercury soaring 150 degrees above the temperatures they'd left in some of their towns and villages. They were half a world away from their families, their beloved mountains and crisp air, the alpenglow in the evenings, and their hunting and fishing. Yet I never heard a complaint from any of them. I had a couple of Alaska-style town hall meetings over there and conducted reenlistments in the desert; and when a number of them decided to drive down the road into Iraq to conduct the ceremony, we did.

Instead of complaining about the war or the hardships they

faced, what our soldiers wanted to know was, how were the king salmon runs? And since it was almost moose season back home, they asked me, was there any way I could finagle our Fish and Game Department into extending their hunting permits until they returned? I promised I would do that.

Two summers later I would head overseas again to visit our Guard in Kosovo and spend another day visiting the wounded at Landstuhl. Amidst the peace-keeping mission we were undertaking in Kosovo, I was impressed with the troops' hospitality as they served me smoked salmon and a big Alaska flag cake that we shared under an Alaska Aces hockey jersey. Pictures of home decorated the entire base, the Big Dipper proudly displayed everywhere I looked.

The spirit of the medical team at Landstuhl will change your life if you experience it. This talented medical staff, who could have been anywhere, chose to be there, tending our wounded warriors. USO volunteers are there too, selflessly giving their time and energy to lift the spirits of our soldiers. During my last visit, I met two soldiers whose legs had been blown off just a couple of days earlier. One had just been given the news by doctors the day before. And yet when I had the privilege of shaking his hand, he only wanted to ask about his fellow soldiers down the hallway who had also taken the IED blast.

Another young soldier, who reminded me of my son, was concerned that the surgeon would mess up the newly inked tattoos on his upper arms; "Watch my artwork, Doc!" he told Landstuhl's staff before he was wheeled in to surgery. One soldier there was on life support; doctors were helping him hang on until his family could arrive from the United States so they could say good-bye.

I loved those men and women in uniform and all those who were supporting them with the mission. The troops were sacrificing so much. I obviously saw my own son in their eyes, but in

addition, as I felt that sweet healing spirit of selflessness in Landstuhl's medical staff, I saw the very best of America.

———

During his teen years, my biggest argument with Track was
whether he'd play the hockey position he wanted to play, or skate
a position I wanted him to. I thought, *Great, if all I have to fight
about with my teenagers is where they'll be in the lineup, we're doing
pretty well.*

From the time he could walk, Track skated. He played other
sports, but hockey was his passion. From the moment we first
laced up his skates for him, like every other Alaska kid's, his
dream was to play in the NHL. I didn't want to shatter that dream
by reminding him that less than one percent of athletes make it
to the big show, but I did occasionally mention that some dreams
are thwarted by career-ending injuries. He answered that with a
concession: "Ah shoot, if I can't go to the NHL, I'll just play in
the NFL." As it turned out, Track was injury-prone because he
was a grinder, a player known for workhorse toughness first, and
finessing the puck second. He relished hitting the boards—and
opponents. He drew a lot of penalties. I remember at a rink once,
a clean-cut young man walked up to me.

"Are you Mrs. Palin?" he said.

I said I was.

We shook hands.

"I just wanted to tell you that I played against Track for a
whole bunch of years!" he said.

I was thrilled and was about to ask him for memories when he
provided one on his own.

"Yeah, Track broke my hand."

My face fell. "Oh. I hope he said he was sorry."

It wasn't only his opponents who took a beating. Track had

chronic shoulder problems, including a right shoulder that persistently popped out of the socket.

One spring, he was playing for the Alaska All-Stars and trying out for an older elite juniors team when I got an emergency call from his coach. Track had suffered a devastating hit that blew out his shoulder again. The coach had him in the hospital emergency room; they'd been there for hours.

The hospital hadn't been able to reach me because I was fifty miles away at a track meet with Bristol and the area had weak cell coverage. Guilt enveloped me for being out of touch and too far away from a son who was in pain. I quickly wrangled rides for the other kids I'd brought to the track meet and took off for Anchorage.

In the ER, I was shocked when I saw Track sitting on a gurney, disheveled, ashen, and shaking. They'd cut off his jersey, and his arm dangled at his side, useless. He looked so worn out and hurt.

"I asked for a cup of water, Mom," he said. "They said I couldn't have one until you got here."

I turned to the nurse, and my eyes said more than words could have. "I am so sorry," she said. "I really am. But we can't treat him until you sign consent forms because he's a minor."

I willed myself to remain calm. "He's seventeen. And he needs a drink of water."

Apologetically, the nurse explained that they couldn't even let him walk down the hall to the drinking fountain because if he needed surgery his stomach should be empty, and they couldn't treat him without me. Of course I understood, but I still fumed inside. I even wondered out loud about why this big, strapping, nearly grown man who was overcome with pain couldn't even get a drink of water without parental consent, yet a thirteen-year-old girl could undergo a painful, invasive, and scary abortion and no parent even had to be *notified*. The nurse seemed to agree with me, and on the spot I mentally renewed my commitment to help change Alaska's parental notification law so that our daughters would have the same support and protection we give to our children in other medical situations.

Track never wanted me in the room for the aftermath of his shoulder injuries, but he always asked me to pray for him before I stepped outside, and this time was no exception. From the waiting room, I heard his groan when the doctors popped his shoulder back in.

Later, he would have surgery to correct the problem. As the injury healed, he said he wanted to scar the shoulder up some more—with a tattoo.

"No way," I said. "How could you choose something to live with for the rest of your life? You want a tattoo to define you?"

The answer turned out to be yes. On his eighteenth birthday, he and his buddy Jack Nelson headed to the local parlor, and Track had a Jesus fish inked into his skin. He knew I couldn't object to *that*. Soon after, he did it again, this time with a map of Alaska tattooed over his bum shoulder. He knew I couldn't argue about that one, either.

In his senior year, when Track left Alaska to play on a traveling squad near Kalamazoo, Michigan, he bunked with the Holmes family, a troop of dedicated hockey heads whose lives revolved around early rink times and coughing up retirement savings for monthly ice bills. Track had traveled outside Alaska many times before, but never so extensively, and it was while bouncing around the Lower 48 with the Holmeses that he fell in love with his country. He would call home in wonder about the diversity and the nice people and the heartland neighborhoods with American flags hung from doorposts in every town. The city of Boston, to which we had traveled for hockey tournaments before, fascinated him with its deep, historic roots. Being from a very young state himself, he asked me over the phone one night whether I thought kids who lived in historic cities just took it all for granted. He hoped they could appreciate what America means.

I was elected governor the season he was away. It was convenient for him, since it meant he could avoid the political spotlight, which he did not like. But Todd and I did get to travel to his big Thanksgiving tournament near Dallas, and we were able to meet and thank the Holmeses for the first time. I would later run into them again on the front row at a Michigan town hall meeting that John McCain and I held.

Eventually, Track's injuries and shoulder surgery made him realize he'd be hanging up the blades. But he was still drawn to the team culture of brotherhood and camaraderie, and a tough environment where he had to push through challenges to meet a goal. He had seen some of his older buddies floundering around right after high school and knew that wasn't for him. He's like me in that respect. He has an appreciation for the most valuable resource God gives us—time—and time is limited. He doesn't like to waste it.

Track started revisiting Army recruiters he'd first met in the cafeteria at Wasilla High School. Then, the week his first term at college started and with Todd on the Slope, Track and his high school buddy, Johnnie Bates, enlisted in the U.S. Army as infantrymen. On September 11, 2007, they took the oath at the recruiting office in Anchorage as Johnnie's mom, Nicki, and Kris Perry and I looked on, blinking back tears of pride.

These are just kids! I thought. *Yet they're doing all they can to protect and serve the greatest country on earth. Are the rest of us doing as much?*

9

Two weeks later, I flew to New Orleans to keynote an oil and gas conference. I had noticed some peculiar yet familiar physical symptoms, like the smell of cigarettes making me feel more nauseated than usual. For a few weeks, I brushed these things aside. But by New Orleans, I had begun to suspect something else.

There was no way I could buy a home pregnancy test in Alaska. The cashiers would know, the people in line would know, and the next thing I'd see would be a headline. The last time I'd tried, about seven years before, one of the Elite Six had caught me at the grocery store trying to hide one in my cart. That was when I was mayor. As governor, I knew that my life was even more of an open book, and there were a few things that I thought were not for public consumption, at least not at first.

Since nobody knew me in New Orleans, I asked my security guy to drop me off at a Walgreens. Back at the hotel, before my speech, I followed the instructions on the pregnancy test box. Slowly a pink image materialized on the stick.

Holy geez!

Todd and I had always dreamed of a big family, and he, especially, dreamed of having another boy—bookends for his daughters. I quickly prayed about this surreal situation. First, that I'd even be able to fathom it. I was happy that we'd finally have our Starting Five. But I could hear the critics now:

"She'll be distracted from state business."

"She won't be physically up to the job."

"That's what we get for electing the first woman governor."

My administration was making great progress on issues important to the state. No one could deny we were on a roll. I dreaded the reactions and comments from the Neanderthals who would think of this pregnancy as a distraction.

I sighed and stared at the ceiling. *These are really less-than-ideal circumstances.*

And for a split second it hit me: *I'm out of town. No one knows I'm pregnant. No one would ever have to know.*

It was a fleeting thought, a sudden understanding of why many women feel pressured to make the "problem" go away. Sad, I thought, that our society has elevated things like education and career above the gift of bringing new life into the world. Yes, the timing of this pregnancy wasn't ideal. But that wasn't the baby's fault. I knew, though, what goes through a woman's mind when she finds herself in a difficult situation. At that moment, I was thankful for right-to-life groups that affirm the value of the child. That say, *yes,* every child has value and a purpose and a destiny.

Without that message out there, it would be easy for women to wonder, well, am I the only one who thinks maybe there is some purpose for this baby? Am I off base in believing that what's easiest isn't always what's best? If not for those groups providing an affirming voice, it would be so easy to go along with what society wants women to believe: that it's easier to end a pregnancy than to bring the baby into this world. Society has made women believe that they cannot do both—pursue career, or education, or anything else, and still carry a baby. Pro-life and pro-adoption groups affirm the power and strength of women. Even if it's just a seed of faith the pro-child message plants in a parent's mind, that bit of faith can grow. I reassured myself that it was going to be okay, that giving this baby life was the right choice. It wouldn't be the last time I had to hold on to that seed of faith.

My thoughts ran the gamut, from the fact that I was no spring chicken to the reality that now I wouldn't be looking at an empty nest for a *long* time. I remembered the Old Testament story of

Isaac's parents. *Yes Lord,* I thought. *My name is Sarah, but my husband isn't Abraham. His name is Todd!*

Unlike the Sarah of old, though, I couldn't laugh with delight. Not yet.

I didn't want to tell Todd on the phone, so I concentrated instead on my role at the conference for the rest of the trip. I discussed with representatives of other oil- and gas-producing states what America's needs are and how we can become energy-independent. I also assumed chairmanship of the Interstate Oil and Gas Compact Commission, where I could help influence Congress and the White House on energy and security issues.

After my New Orleans speech, I headed home but missed Todd, who had gone straight from Canada, where he was visiting a workforce development program with my commissioner of labor, back to the Slope. Between my job and his we kept missing each other, so it was a few weeks before we were in the same room and I told him about the baby. He was ecstatic. For him, it's always been the more the merrier, and he especially wanted another boy.

We kept our news to ourselves. We had always been private about our pregnancies. We didn't tell anyone about Piper until I was five months along. Our lives were an open book in virtually every other way, so for us this was just a special, sacred time, the one thing it seemed that just we two could know and enjoy together.

Later, I saw my doctor, Cathy Baldwin-Johnson, at our Health Care Commission conference, where I had appointed state officials and private professionals to discuss free-market solutions to the state's health care problems. I addressed the group and then looked for Cathy, whom we called "CBJ." She had been named the Family Physician of the Year by the American Academy of Family Physicians in 2002 and had also launched a facility for sexually abused children. She was admired by many around the country for her extraordinary skills and especially her compassion for patients. I had witnessed that firsthand. Between Willow and Piper, I had had a second miscarriage. But instead of treating our loss as if it were something to ignore, CBJ had been so kind, so caring; she even cried with me when she had to deliver the news that we'd lost the baby. After that loss, in my own heart, I'd also noticed a change. My first miscarriage had sent me into a valley of despair, but I'd made it through to the other side. Like everyone else, I coped differently with each episode of grief. I grieved when I had that second miscarriage, too, but with so many people now depending on me, I had to react differently. Life does toughen up your reactions to devastating news.

At the health conference, I spotted CBJ and smiled at her when I slipped her a note on the way to the exit. I wrote: *I need to come see you!*

———

At about twelve weeks along, I visited CBJ at her Wasilla family practice. After the exam, we sat down together in her office decorated with Alaska quilts, some of which she sews herself and gives to babies she delivers, like the Noah's Ark–themed blanket she'd sewn for Piper years earlier. She looked at me kindly. "Well, you're forty-three, so there's a higher chance of certain abnormalities." Then she showed me some statistics, one of which said I had about a one-in-eighty chance of having a child with Down syndrome.

"We discussed all this when you had Piper, and I remember you said abortion wasn't going to be an option, so I just want you to keep in mind that there is some chance everything isn't going to be as easy or perfect as your other pregnancies."

I wasn't worried. I was healthy as a horse with four perfectly healthy children. Besides, my sister Heather already had a special needs son, Karcher, who had autism. He was our family's angel boy. In our family, we always said God knew what he was doing when he gave Heather, the most nurturing of the Heath sisters, the child with special needs. Among all of us, she was the one with the tender spirit who could not only handle but even *thrive* with a child with "challenges." And in fact she had chosen working with special needs children in public schools as her profession.

CBJ said she'd like me to have a sonogram, so I walked into the office across the hall. The technician was a sweet, funny older lady who'd been doing the procedure for decades. She prepped me, and we joked about a lot of things while she pressed the wand across my belly. Then she got a little quieter. Suddenly I flashed back to the grim sonogram I'd had when that first stoic doctor said, "There's nothing alive in there." Now my breath caught, waiting.

Then the technician smiled. "I see boy parts . . . would that be good?"

Relief blew through me like the Mat-Su Valley wind. "Yes, that would be perfect!" *God is so good!* I thought. *He knows what's best.*

She kept passing the transducer across my abdomen, more slowly now. It seemed to be taking a long time. "Oops, sorry. Not sure on the boy parts after all. Your baby might be a girl."

By then she was taking so long that I didn't care whether it was a boy or a girl. A healthy fourth daughter would be great. Yep, just fine. Please tell me all is fine.

Then the technician said, "The baby's neck is a little bit thicker than what we would normally see . . ."

My first thought was, *Twelve weeks along and you can already measure the baby's neck? Amazing!* Then, a bit more somberly, I remembered that somewhere along the line I had heard that that was a sign of Down syndrome. A whisper of fear tugged at my heart, but I brushed it away with a thought: *God would never give me anything I can't handle. And I don't think I could handle that.*

God knew me: I was busy. Got to go-go-go. I'd always yapped about how lucky I was that my kids were all healthy overachievers, self-sufficient. Now, I thought, I've got a tough job and other kids who need me. I just couldn't imagine how I could add a baby with special needs and make it all work.

Unless He knows me better than I know myself, I thought a bit dismissively, *God won't give me a special needs child.*

═══

CBJ called me the next day. Combined with my age, she said, the sonogram pictures meant there was now a one-in-twelve chance the baby had Down syndrome.

So? I thought. *That still means about a 90 percent chance that everything's fine.*

"There's a doctor in Anchorage I want you to go see, a geneticist," she added. "I'm also offering you an amniocentesis"—the common prenatal test for genetic abnormalities.

I had always flippantly declined the amnios before, thinking they didn't matter, since I confidently asserted I would never abort anyway. But this time I said yes. This time I wanted information. If there was something wrong, I wanted to be prepared.

Todd was out of town on the day of the appointment, so I visited the geneticist alone—through a back door, under my maiden name. I felt a bit of fear. Three days later, I was in my Anchorage office when CBJ called. I thought it was strange she would give me the results. I could have sworn that the nurse said *she'd* be calling. I still remember what time it was: 2:22 p.m.

"I have the amnio results," she said. "I think you should come to my office in Wasilla. Can you come now?"

"No, no, just give me the results over the phone," I said, indulging in a little denial. If I just steeled myself, I thought on some wishful level, if I just took the medicine straight, maybe God would reward my guts with good news.

CBJ hesitated, then said, "No . . . I really think you need to come out here."

"Cathy, I've got *so* much to do here today. It's okay . . . whatever it is, it's fine, just go ahead and tell me now."

"Okay," she said softly. "This child will be born with Down syndrome—"

"I'm coming to Wasilla," I interrupted and hung up the phone.

I was shocked beyond words. Shocked that this was happening. How could God have done this? Obviously He knew Heather had a special needs child. Didn't He think that was enough challenge for one family?

I drove the forty-five minutes to Wasilla gritting my teeth. *I'm not going to cry. I'm not going to cry.*

My stoicism in difficult times had always bugged and puzzled my friends and family. Bristol once asked, "Mom, why don't you ever cry? The rest of us are watching some movie, crying our eyes out, you're just sitting there." Shoot, my mom used to cry during the "Mean Joe Green" Coca-Cola commercials!

Though I didn't tell Bristol this, I choke up all the time—at "The Star-Spangled Banner," at any military event, seeing newborn babies—but secretly, where no one can see. Maybe it was because I'd grown up hunting and fishing with the guys, throwing elbows on the basketball court. Even when my heart was breaking on the inside, I just never wanted to seem weak. Now, as I pressed the accelerator past the speed limit toward Wasilla, my eyes stayed dry and my mind raced.

Maybe the test is wrong.

Maybe my results are switched with somebody else.

Maybe it's a mistake. God . . . are you listening?

But when I got to CBJ's office, she showed me the pictures. There was an extra copy of chromosome 21.

"It's a boy," she said.

"A boy? You're sure? Thank you, God." For me, that was a glimmer of light, and I let it warm me as CBJ walked out of her office and returned with a book for expectant parents of babies with Down syndrome. I thanked her and laid it in my lap, unopened. I just wasn't ready; my sisters were the ones who could handle this, not me. Did I have enough love and compassion in me to do this? Don't you have to be wired a little differently to be gifted with the ability to raise a special needs child, a child who isn't "perfect" in the eyes of society? I didn't know if I should be ashamed of myself for even thinking these things.

I read that almost 90 percent of Down syndrome babies are aborted—so wasn't that a message that this is not only a less-than-ideal circumstance but that it is virtually *impossible* to deal with? Now, just a couple of hours into this new world, I could not get my arms or heart around it. That fleeting thought descended on me again, not a consideration so much as a sudden understanding of why people would grasp at a quick "solution," a way to make the "problem" just go away. But again, I had to hold on to that seed of faith.

—————

Todd finally returned a few days later. He plopped down on the bed, still in his winter coat. I handed him the sonogram pictures, and that's when the dam broke. I could let my guard down.

"It's a boy," I said between the tears. "It's definitely a boy."

He looked up at me, and *his* eyes filled with tears. "See, Sarah? God knows what He's doing! This is great."

I stood beside the bed. I didn't know how to say it any other way but straight. "The baby has Down syndrome."

Todd didn't speak. I remember him lying back on the bed, holding the sonogram pictures and flipping through them. He'd look at one, put it in the back of the stack, look at the next. Over and over, silently, as though looking for answers.

Finally I sat down next to him. In his subdued way, he did not offer a reaction. So I had to ask him. "Well . . . what do you think?"

"How can they tell?" he asked quietly. "Are they sure?"

"Yes. There's an extra chromosome."

He set the pictures aside and turned his face toward mine. "I'm happy, and I'm sad," he said.

I thought it was pretty perfect the way he said that, because that's the way it was. That's the way I felt, too.

Todd said, "It's going to be okay."

I asked if he had the same question I had: "Why us?"

He looked genuinely surprised by my question and responded calmly, "Why not us?"

From that moment on, Todd never seemed to worry about it. Instead, he'd think out loud, wondering what the baby's gifts would be. "What will he want to do?" he wondered. "Will he want to tinker with me in the garage? Will he want to ride on the four-wheeler and drive the skiff? I'm going to build him a buoy swing. I bet he'll love to fly with me."

He started asking other people with special needs children a lot of questions: What does your kid do? Does he play any sports? Heather and her husband, Kurt, had a nephew with Down syndrome, in Kurt's hometown in North Dakota, who was about eleven years old and played Little League baseball on a "regular" team. The whole town loved this little kid. Todd asked about him. Todd later saw his cousin, who had Down syndrome, at a hockey game; he was now thirty-two, loving life and having a ball cheering on the Aces.

From the start, my husband was much more accepting and optimistic than I was. His attitude was kind of like "Well, okay . . . here we go!" But I was still having a hard time wrapping my head and heart around it. So we didn't share the pregnancy with anyone else, even our children. It was such a tough thing to explain, and I just wasn't ready to grapple with it yet or answer any questions. I had always faced life head-on, but here was something that had humbled me into silence.

10

"None who have always been free can understand the terrible fascinating power of the hope of freedom to those who are not free."

Pearl S. Buck wrote those words many years before the lean, proud, newly shorn young men standing before us were even born. The bleachers chilled our backsides as moms, wives and girlfriends, and contemplative military dads, many teary-eyed, watched soldiers march in unison across a Fort Benning field in January 2008. As we watched rank upon rank march in front of us, it seemed true what they say about boot camp changing boys into men. I knew what Track and his friend, Johnnie, had looked like when they had left for basic training months before, and now all these young men looked tall and strong and serious. And they were headed into a mission that asked them to be ready to sacrifice all in a fight for freedom. Yet that freedom had never been absent for them. How did they know how imperative this was?

We hadn't spotted Track yet, but if he looked anything like his fellow soldiers, I knew that my boy had become a man. I turned to Todd, who sat between my mom and me in the second tier. "Can you spot him?"

Piper searched, shaded her eyes, then clapped her hands for all the soldiers. "He's right there!" she said, pointing left.

"He's right there!" Todd said, pointing right.

"No, that's him!" I said, "I think. Maybe not . . ."

"They all look alike," we all said in unison.

"That's the point," some top-brass character whispered over his shoulder.

The boots on the ground at boot camp graduations on every base paint the picture of what is right in America. Left, right, one step at a time, it is straight ahead for those who, it can only be assumed, have a special quality that gives them a sense of honor and selfless duty. What else explains their choice, amidst so many other possibilities, to serve in the U.S. military?

I recalled Senator John Kerry's comment to California college students in 2006: "You know, education, if you make the most of it, you study hard, you do your homework, and you make an effort to be smart, you can do well. And if you don't, you get stuck in Iraq."

What a loon, I thought. *What an elitist loon.*

Now I was in a position to know firsthand what I had always implicitly hoped: the kids enlisting are smart and observant and have made the most of the opportunities America has given them. So they choose to put other desires and ambitions aside for a while to protect our opportunities. I knew it because my son and his buddies were part of a culture that enjoys comfortable luxuries and choices, boys who knew that once they graduated high school the world was their oyster. And here they chose to make sacrifices and give up luxury and comfort. They have within them a willingness and drive to fight for freedom, the absence of which they do not even know, and that fascinates me. I thanked God for this second greatest generation, marching in front of us, because if not them, who?

It had been quite a journey for Todd, Sally, Piper, and the Bates family to get there that day. I had scheduled our trip for Track's graduation a month prior. My chief of staff made sure the state

Senate president knew I'd be taking two days outside Alaska to attend. (The sixty-nine-year-old Republican was a fixture in state politics and was one of the gang not happy to see a new administration rock the boat.) We gave her the date. A letter was sent. We did this because after I was elected, the rules for governors' travel seemed to have changed with no notice. I attributed it to my inauguration speech, when I had promised to be a "protective mom" to the state, though I referred to it as protecting Alaska's interests the way a mama grizzly protects her cubs. But now, it seemed, a few lawmakers didn't want me to leave Juneau. Ever.

Our official January calendar was printed with my scheduled State of the State Address to be delivered in front of the legislature on January 15 at 6 p.m. My plan was to leave immediately afterward to fly through the night, making all the stops and plane changes necessary to arrive in Georgia in time for the graduation ceremonies.

Then the Senate president changed her mind. She claimed she had not known when I would need to travel. She decided the 6 p.m. time slot on January 15 wouldn't work for her, and as president, she insisted, she needed to be in the legislative chambers for the address. The lawmakers had just arrived in Juneau for their session, and she was just getting settled in her suite at the infamous Baranof Hotel, where she'd lived for years.

Alaskans had just voted to shorten the legislature's session from 120 days down to 90 because the public was tired of seeing lawmakers waste the first few weeks, or months, not accomplishing much. There was nothing else going on in Juneau the night of January 15, so my staff was flabbergasted to hear the senator say, "Sorry, that time just won't work after all." We explained to her again that my trip to see Track graduate had been set in stone a month before. And we had proof that I had notified the legislature of that fact. But she dug in her heels.

Believe it or not, this became a public issue. In fact, it was a top story in the news, with reporters breathlessly asking, "Is this the bellwether? Who will be in control of Juneau this session?" Finally, it came down to: Will the Senator Let the Governor Give Her Speech So She Can Get to Georgia in Time?

Good grief. It was more politics-as-usual silliness. *Let her be "in control,"* I thought.

My administration's ideas and common sense conservative agenda were good for Alaskans; we would win on those ideas in the court of public opinion. As an olive branch, I offered to give my speech earlier in the day to accommodate the senator. Or two days later, after my return. It became so ridiculous that we had liaisons running back and forth between offices, trying to broker a deal. *Government dollars at work.* I was game for anything that would let me make my flight connections, which are no small deal when trying to make it from Juneau to Georgia in record time so that I would be out of the Capitol Building for only a minimal number of hours.

I wouldn't be traveling with staff or security, though our previous governors did, even on vacations, because I knew a double standard would apply, this time with accusations that I was using state resources for personal gain. So Todd and I had made the trip arrangements ourselves; we needed to keep with the schedule.

I sensed that the senator was enjoying the media attention that this "showdown" brought. She rallied a couple of radio talk hosts to her cause, and they were milking the drama, such as it was. Some drama: it must have been a slow news week. One particularly caustic host proclaimed my "selfishness" for trying to leave Alaska for two days when the legislature would just be getting under way. Supporters tried to explain to him that most governors steered clear of the Capitol Building during the session so they wouldn't be perceived as interfering with a separate branch of government's work.

The radio host said, "Hell, boot camp? It's no big accomplishment to be graduating from boot camp. What's the big deal?"

I knew when my eighteen-year-old son enlisted and would be deployed to Iraq that the country was lucky to have him and every other patriot who volunteered to serve. And I was determined to be there to say "Thank you."

I ended up being able to give my State of the State Address on the scheduled day, but at a different time, so we missed Fort Benning's family-day events. But we got there in time for Todd to place the blue cord around our son's right shoulder, to watch our boy become a man, to see the U.S. military gain another of America's finest. And it *was* a big deal.

———

I was busy shuttling back and forth to Juneau, with energy and education reform issues stacked on our administration's plate. Todd and I kept thinking, *knowing,* that we had to tell Track, Bristol, Willow, and Piper about the baby, but I still didn't look pregnant, so I figured we still had time. Every once in a while I'd drop hints for them: *Sometimes life throws you a curveball, but how thankful we should be that life is never boring. Sometimes surprising challenges pop up; then we see what we're made of as we make choices about how to react to the circumstances.*

I'd always journaled throughout my life, and now I also began writing a letter about the baby to our family and closest friends. In my research on Down syndrome, I learned that these special kids most often bring joy into their family's lives. While they had developmental challenges, they were also affectionate, generous, and cheerful. Rather than focus on what could be perceived as negative, I wanted our loved ones to focus on the fact that this baby, every baby, has purpose, and that not only would he learn from us, but we would learn from him.

I decided to write the letter as though it were from Trig's Creator, the same Creator in whom I had put my trust more than thirty years before. I hoped that even though this new baby would present challenges, we'd trust that God knew best, that He didn't make mistakes:

I am blessing you with this surprise baby because I only want the best for you. I've heard your prayers that this baby will be happy and healthy, and I've answered them because I only want the best for you!

I heard your heart when you hinted that another boy would fit best in the Palin family, to round it out and complete that starting five line-up. Though another girl would be so nice, you didn't think you could ask for what you really wanted, but I knew, so I gave you a boy.

Then, I put the idea in your hearts that his name should be "Trig," because it's so fitting, with two Norse meanings: "True" and "Brave Victory" . . .

Then, finally, I let Trig's mom and dad find out before he was born that this little boy will truly be a GIFT. They were told in early tests that Trig may provide more challenges, and more joy, than what they ever may have imagined or ever asked for. At first the news seemed unreal and sad and confusing. But I gave Trig's mom and dad lots of time to think about it because they needed a lot of time to understand that everything will be OK. . . .

This new person in your life can help everyone put things in perspective and bind [you] together and get everyone focused on what really matters. The baby will expand your world and let you see and feel things you haven't experienced yet. He'll show you what "true, brave victory" really means as those who love him will think less about self and focus less on what the world tells you is "normal" or "perfect." . . .

Trig will be his dad's little buddy and he'll wear Carhartts while he learns to tinker in the garage. He'll love to be read to, he'll want to play goalie, and he'll steal his mom's heart just like Track, Bristol, Willow, and Piper did. And Trig will be the cuddly, innocent, mischievous, dependent little brother that his siblings have been waiting for . . . in fact Trig will—in some diagnostic ways—always be a mischievous, dependent little brother, because I created him a bit different than a lot of babies born into this world today.

Every child is created special, with awesome purpose and amazing potential. Children are the most precious and promising ingredient in this mixed-up world you live in down there on earth. Trig is no different, except he has one extra chromosome. Doctors call it "Down syndrome," and Downs kids have challenges, but can bring you much delight and more love than you can ever imagine! . . .

Trig's mom and dad don't want people to focus on the baby's extra chromosome. They're human, so they haven't known how to explain this to people who are so caring and are interested in this new little Alaskan. . . . Some will think Trig should not be allowed to be born because they fear a Downs child won't be considered "perfect" in your world. . . .

Many people will express sympathy, but you don't want or need that, because Trig will be a joy. You will have to trust me on this.

I know it will take time to grasp this and come to accept that I only want the best for you, and I only give my best. Remember though: "My ways are not your ways, my thoughts are not your thoughts . . . for as the heavens are higher than the earth, my ways are higher than yours!"

I wrote that all down for you in the Good Book! Look it up! You claim that you believe me—now it's time to live out that belief!

Trig can't wait to meet you. I'm giving you ONLY THE BEST!

Love,
Trig's Creator, Your Heavenly Father

Writing that letter was the best and most loving way I could find to share our news with the people we loved. I had no idea that a year later during the vice presidential campaign a hostile journalist would use it to mock my family and the Christian faith, saying I was so self-absorbed that I even wrote a letter "in the voice of God."

11

Todd is a four-time champ of the Iron Dog race, the world's longest and toughest cross-country snowmachine race. The teams consist of two hard-core racers from anywhere in the world on a pair of sleds ("snowmobiles" in Minnesota talk). They buddy up to pound their bodies 2,200 miles across Alaska in windchill temperatures that can dip to minus 60 degrees in whiteout blizzard conditions. The race is held in the middle of February, our coldest time of year, and Iron Dog widows usually spend Valentine's Day checking GPS coordinates on the Internet to see if their sweethearts are still alive.

Women have raced too, and someday they'll win. "I really want to run the Iron Dog," I cockily told Todd one night as he settled down for a few hours' rest between 120-mph training rides by himself in the middle of the night.

"Can you wrench your own machine?" he asked.

"Nope."

"Can you get the back end of a six-hundred-pound machine unstuck by yourself with open water up to your thighs, then change out an engine at forty below in the pitch black on a frozen river and replace thrashed shocks and jury-rig a suspension using tree limbs along the trail?"

"Nope."

"Then go back to sleep, Sarah."

Iron Doggers race through snow-packed mountain ranges and skip across the open water of the Bering Sea, avoiding ice chunks in the dark of night. They swerve to avoid moose on a trail at 100 miles per hour while sleep-deprived under a disorienting Northern Lights–filled sky. Todd stays in shape year-round for the race but still drops about fifteen pounds along the trail between Big Lake, Nome, and Fairbanks every year.

The racers pair up for safety reasons, I suppose so that if one guy crashes into an iceberg, his partner can mentally mark where the body lands. Todd's partner is a racing icon, Scott Davis, who's taken the crown seven times. The guys look alike in their race gear, with slim, muscular builds and, by now, salt-and-pepper hair. You can't even tell them apart once they get their duct tape on. All the guys wear it to protect exposed skin from frostbite. It's not a pretty sight when they rip it off their faces at race checkpoints and chunks of skin come with it.

Trailbreakers move through to mark the trail before the racers take off. A couple of years ago one of them was caught in an avalanche. It took ten days to find the guy's body buried in the snow. We've lost a few friends that way.

In 2008, Todd and Scott, the defending champs, were on pace to finish up just fine. Four hundred miles to go, and they reached the village of Galena. Flying across the snowpack at 80 miles per hour, Todd was trailing Scott when he slammed into a hidden obstruction buried in the snow-covered trail. The impact launched

Todd 70 feet through the air, and he landed with a thud and the crack of bone. Scott raced to the crash site to see if his partner was still alive. Todd hobbled to Scott's sled, and they soldiered on to the next stop before returning to fix Todd's sled. They rested up at the Hunnington family's house and then kept riding 400 miles to an honorable fourth-place finish in Fairbanks.

After the race, we visited a health clinic, where Todd's broken right arm was casted. He kept it inside his jacket sleeve during that night's award ceremony. Back home, he used a pair of heavy shears to cut the cast off and handed it to Piper for playing dress-up.

I asked if he was still in pain after racing with the broken bone.

"Nope, just still mad about the oil drum."

I joked, "Dang oil companies. Still haunting us."

For the second consecutive year, after the race we boarded an airplane and traveled to the White House for the National Governors Association meeting, where Todd had another tea party with Laura Bush and the governors' wives.

These motorheads are revered up North, but nothing like our other celebrities—those whom we lazier folk vicariously live through: our Iditarod mushers. Both the Iron Dog and Iditarod races pass through rural Native villages, where the kids treat racers like NBA stars, asking for autographs and cheering on the teams of a dozen or more dogs.

The Iditarod Trail Sled Dog Race is another uniquely Alaskan event that puts us on the map. It started after a desperate, harrowing 1925 diphtheria serum run to Nome and was first known as the Great Race of Mercy because diphtheria was rampant and the serum cure had to be delivered by sled dogs from the port of Seward to victims in the far and frigid North. The lead dog's name was Balto. There's a statue in New York's Central Park honoring the heroic canine.

After the long-shot racer Libby Riddles became the first woman to win in 1985, Susan Butcher nabbed four victories, and our bumper stickers boasted, ALASKA! WHERE MEN ARE MEN AND WOMEN WIN THE IDITAROD! Martin Buser also won four times. In fact, this charismatic, always-smiling guy from Switzerland became the first international winner in 1992 and has set the course record for the 1,049-mile race across the Last Frontier in a blistering eight days, twenty-two hours. Martin appreciates America more than most people born and bred here. He became a naturalized citizen and was a perfect spokesperson for the individual freedom and opportunities we enjoy and can't take for granted. We were honored that Martin joined us on the campaign trail to spread that patriotic message across the country.

The tradition is for the governor to call the Iditarod winner, no matter what time he or she crosses under the famed burled arch on Front Street in Nome. My first year in office I called the winner, Lance Mackey, to congratulate him. He was in his midthirties, a throat cancer survivor, a lifelong Alaskan, and an amazing athlete with a world-class team of dogs. His lead dog's name was Larry. My call would be broadcast around the world, so I made sure everything was set up from the mansion as I watched on live TV while a reporter handed Lance the phone. With high emotions and very little sleep Lance exuded relief and honor when he took his first call from the governor. "Hey! How ya doing, sir?"

There was just a tiny bit of a hush. The reporter mumbled, "Um, our governor's a woman." Lance perked up. "Oh, yeah! Right! Yeah, it's Murkowski, I met her before! Hi there!"

Oh, I fell in love with that musher and his lead dog, Larry, right then and there.

"Lance, can you hear me? You just made this state very, very proud!"

The next day at a press conference, Bill McAllister from KTUU asked me just how embarrassing *was* that international moment?

"Are you kidding?!" I asked Bill. "More power to him! Good he's not a politico—I like him even more now."

Bill pointed out that his canines, with names like Hobo, Lippy, and Fudge, were more important to mushers than any politician's name. The mushers and the veterinarians on the trail loved and cared for their animals so much they'd practically lay down their lives for the dogs.

By the second year, with another Mackey victory to celebrate, I placed the call again, this time at 2:46 a.m., to tell the musher he was an inspiration to all of us. Lance was just as proud, and I was just as prepared to be humbled.

A reporter teased him this time, "Now, Lance, remember who this is this time!"

"Got it, got it," he said. Then he picked up the phone, said "Hello" with a grin, and told the world he couldn't forget the governor's name this go-round. He'd named one of his dogs "Sarah."

———

Before we knew it, I was seven months along. I hadn't put on a lot of weight and with winter clothes and a few cleverly draped scarves, no one saw my girth or suspected I was pregnant. A blazer was getting tight enough that Willow looked at me one day and said, tactfully, "Geez, Mom, you're porking up!"

"Oh, hush," I said. "Now pass me the Häagen-Dazs. Chocolate, with peanut butter."

I hadn't quite finished writing my letter about Trig. But at that point in March we shared the news with family and a few close friends that I was pregnant. The kids, of course, were overjoyed. Shortly after that, we decided to go public. The city of Kodiak was putting on a big reception in Juneau for legislators to celebrate their promising seafood industry. This year, I couldn't wait to get there—I was starving for king crab and scallops.

Todd and I decided to get the baby announcement out there, so I called a few reporters near my Capitol office. KTUU's Bill McAllister, AP reporter Steve Quinn, and Wesley Loy from the *Anchorage Daily News* would be there in a minute, they said. I had a great relationship with those guys. We spoke on a regular basis and we had each other's personal cell phone numbers. This time, I asked them to meet Todd, Piper, and me in my office lobby before the reception, and then we'd all walk over to the seafood spread together.

All three showed up and were no doubt expecting me to talk about stalled legislative proposals or maybe timely fishery issues. I knew I could have just spoken candidly and said, "Hey, I'm going to have a baby . . . ready to go eat?" Something short and sweet. Instead, I decided to have a little fun.

"Hey guys," I said with a grin, "I wanted to let you know that the First Family is expanding."

They all just looked at me. Dead silence.

Okay . . . let me try something else.

"Remember when I promised to 'deliver' for Alaska?"

Nothing. But now they took out their notepads and pens. Big scoop coming, they could feel it.

Finally, I gave up on the jokes and went direct: "Guys, I'm pregnant. I'm having a baby in two months!"

Three mouths fell open, and three pairs of eyes dropped straight to my stomach. I laughed out loud. The guys whipped out their cell phones as I waved good-bye. Within ten minutes, the news was all over. And by the time we reached the reception, the room was bubbling with smiles and congratulations.

The next month, Todd and I checked into a hotel in Dallas. The following day I was scheduled to keynote another oil and gas conference. My pregnancy was going fine, and with five weeks to go, I felt great. But at 4 a.m., a strange sensation low in my belly woke me and I sat up straight in bed.

It can't be, I thought. *It's way too early.*

Moments later, I shook Todd awake. "Something's going on."

He sat up in bed, instantly alert. "I'm calling CBJ."

"No, don't do that. It's one a.m. in Alaska."

I didn't want to call anyone yet. I just wanted to take stock and see whether this baby was really coming. I also wanted time to pray and asked God silently but fervently to let everything be okay. Desperation for this baby overwhelmed me.

Please don't let anything happen to this baby.

It occurred to me, once and for all. *I'm so in love with this child, please God, protect him!* After all my doubts and fears, I had fallen in love with this precious child. The worst thing in the world would be that I would lose him. God knew what He was doing.

Over my protests, Todd called CBJ. I told her that I felt fine and absolutely did not want to cancel my speech and disappoint the folks at the conference, including my cohost, Texas Governor Rick Perry. We agreed that I would stay in contact with CBJ through the day, I'd take it easy, give my speech, then catch an earlier flight back to Alaska. I still had plenty of time.

Later that afternoon we entered a packed house at the energy conference, where I'd speak on the urgent need to tap conventional supplies and innovate on stabilizing renewable sources. I was anxious to tell them how Alaska could lead on a needed national energy plan. Governor Perry introduced me with some humorous remarks about things we had in common, like loving the outdoors, and something about how we love people who cling to their guns and religion, and how we've faced down the good ol' boys. Then I took the podium and opened by teasing the audience about how great it was to be in our "little sister state of Texas."

Big laughs. More contractions.

Then I introduced everybody to Todd, Alaska's "First Dude," who, instead of sitting at the head table, was standing at the back of the hall, giving me the "get on with it, let's keep it short this time" look and practically holding the door open for our quick exit to the airport.

I told the gathered industry officials that Alaska was suspending its fuel tax—giving relief to consumers at the pump—and outlined our "three-legged stool" approach to meeting our energy needs: conservation, responsible development, and renewable energy sources. Thus we set a goal of drawing 50 percent of our electricity generation from renewable sources—an unprecedented policy goal in the United States. We would also use the earnings from a multimillion-dollar Renewable Energy Fund for projects like hydropower, along with wind, geothermal, and biomass. Those projects could not even flirt with snake-oil science, I insisted; they must be doable, economical, and real. Finally, Alaska would lead America toward energy security and a cleaner, safer world through responsible development of our conventional sources as we built our AGIA gasline. And I reminded Texas that there is an inherent link between energy and security, energy and prosperity, energy and peace.

The audience graciously gave me a standing ovation. Then I handed the mic back to Rick and walked off the stage.

"Hey," Rick drawled over the sound system with a chuckle, "we're not finished with the program!"

I turned around, smiled, waved, and kept moving.

"I know you're pregnant," Rick said, joking into the mic. "But don't tell me you're going off to have the baby right now!"

The audience laughed. I smiled and waved good-bye. *I thought, if you only knew!*

I reached Todd at the exit, and he eyed me with a grin, "Love this state, but we can't have a fish picker born in Texas." It was a calm, relatively restful flight home. The flight crewmembers, cheerfully representing what's got to be the most accommodating sector of customer service, were their usual impressive selves. One brought me tea while I confessed to Todd that I may not have handled the whole pregnancy announcement thing right. "He'll be here so soon, I didn't have time to prepare anyone, not even the kids," I said. "I should have given everyone that letter already. I feel guilty knowing that I'll put them through more shock when he's born." Todd said he didn't know if we handled it right, either. He held my hand and we prayed together that God would prepare other hearts, since we had not. I asked again that I'd be prepared, too.

Many hours and two plane flights later, with Todd and our daughters nearby, I delivered Trig Paxson Van Palin into the world at Mat-Su Regional Medical Center. When the nurse placed him in my arms, I was overwhelmed with love and with wonder. I knew God had answered my prayer so completely. He just nestled softly into me as if to say, *Aaaah . . . I'm here, Mom.*

I was glad God brought him to us early. We were so anxious to meet him. I hadn't known what to expect. I didn't know what he would look like or how I would feel. But when I saw him, my heart was flooded with unspeakable joy. I knew that not only had God made Trig different but He had made him perfect.

The girls gently cooed and cuddled and quietly helped swaddle their new baby brother. Todd beamed. I heard him whisper to CBJ, "Hmmm, he doesn't look Downs."

CBJ looked up at Todd and gave him a kind, knowing smile. When I look at my beautiful son today, I know what her smile meant. She sees it in the eyes of other parents who have a child that perhaps our world doesn't consider precious or prized. I see photos of Trig and can recognize the physical traits that let all Downs children look like brothers and sisters, the characteristics that may puzzle some who, just like me a few months prior, don't yet understand. But looking at these children in real life, we see only perfection.

12

"Go to hell, but resign first."

The message was pithy and concise. And it reflected the sentiments of some in the oil industry toward me and my team. But this particularly crisp instruction was sent to DNR Commissioner Irwin by a North Slope oil services company employee.

Tom Irwin's recent actions had prompted the e-mail. For the twenty-second time, ExxonMobil had submitted its plan to begin drilling in the Point Thomson Unit but still had not drilled. These domestic supplies of energy were needed. So, with my full support, Tom played hardball and took steps to prove that ExxonMobil was in default of its lease agreements. My administration announced that for the state's and country's sake, ExxonMobil would no longer be allowed to just warehouse America's resources. After all these decades, if the largest company in the world wasn't going to abide by its contracts to drill, we would rebid the leases and find a company that would.

That resulted in the kind note to Tom from an industry player about his employment future and eternal destination.

Adjacent to the much-discussed ANWR area, Point Thomson is a North Slope parcel of state-owned land that holds trillions of cubic feet of clean natural gas and an equally enormous amount of oil. The leases in question were the subject of a prior expansion agreement that would substantially enlarge the area in which ExxonMobil was permitted to drill. Of course, the big question was, why would DNR approve an expansion when ExxonMobil had sat on the unit for more than twenty-five years and had never successfully sunk a drill bit?

The Murkowski administration had even recognized the injustice of this situation and had begun taking steps to force Exxon-Mobil to drill or relinquish its leases. ExxonMobil had recently been fined $20 million for not drilling. The company paid the fine. To them, it was a drop in the bucket. When my administration moved into Juneau, we agreed with the Murkowski team's opinion and told ExxonMobil its leases would be history unless we saw action. The oil giant's MO is to tie up issues through litigation. It threatened to sue. We said, okay, we know the way to the courthouse too.

When you deal with oil executives, you have to remember that they are used to winning. They also spend a lot of time in foreign countries dealing with leaders who carry pistols and whose bodyguards carry AK-47s. Meanwhile, the executives themselves are armed with bottomless bank accounts and highly trained platoons of fire-breathing lawyers. Thus, reminding our friends in Big Oil that they have a contract that they're obligated to fulfill was really not going to scare them. A $20 million fine? Pocket change. But with their leases on the line—permanently—the question ExxonMobil executives finally had to ask themselves was, do we really want to give up prime parcels that are loaded with billions of dollars' worth of natural resources that the public and our shareholders want us to develop?

As AOGCC chair, when I wasn't butting heads with the state GOP, I was getting a thorough education in issues surrounding oil and gas recovery and production. I also learned that in the energy industry, you have to send messages independently to each group: To explorers, you speak of expansion and access to get their new discoveries to market. To producers, you speak of inducements such as a stable investment climate. To pipeline owners, you speak of open seasons and shipping and tariff rates that let them recover costs. Most important, to the resource owners—in this case the people of Alaska—you speak of getting the oil safely out of the ground into our cars and homes and businesses to provide economic and security benefits.

Two days after my first State of the State Address, I spoke to a group of energy explorers at an industry breakfast. It provided me with the perfect opportunity to set that stage and let our most powerful industry know how I would lead. Among the messages that I wished to send: Alaska is now open for business.

"You in the industry make your living by providing the goods and services necessary to get Alaska's resources to market," I said. "You live by contracts and legal obligations. . . . Leases and unit agreements are contracts. Lessees must develop the public's resources or give back their leases."

ExxonMobil needed to develop now or let others compete to do so. In the larger scheme of things, I also knew that unless we accessed our known reserves on state lands, it would be more difficult to argue for access to federal lands such as ANWR. We had to prove we could do so safely and ethically before the feds would let us develop in more controversial areas. It all dovetailed together. As a state chief executive sitting across the table from well-heeled, lawyered-up oil executives, it was a given: you have to be committed to the position that is right for the people who hired you. You can't blink. And we didn't.

Once we put our foot down, we won ruling after ruling after ruling.

May 1, 2007: Superior Court Judge Sharon Gleason denied a motion filed by producers in the former Point Thomson Unit to stay their appeal of our lease termination.

May 22, 2007: Judge Gleason refused the producers' motion to separate issues on appeal and also denied their request that the court not give deference to DNR's expertise.

December 26, 2007: DNR was found to have acted properly when it rejected ExxonMobil's plan.

When you know you've made the right call, you stand your ground. DNR had made the right call. We would now see development.

Victory! Two years into our term, Rolligons packed with drilling equipment started driving up the long ice road to Point Thomson to deploy hundreds of new workers in their hard hats and steel-toed boots. Exxon began ordering parts and supplies and buying equipment in order to develop rich reserves for the industry, the state, and the nation. This was a bipartisan victory that created the mutually beneficial relationship between government and industry we had sought all along.

———

In the first two years of my administration, there would be many bipartisan victories. I had a fine working relationship with state house Democrats, a fact that quite often showed up in the press.

Interviewed for a story on women in leadership, House Minority Leader Beth Kerttula, a Juneau Democrat, told *Newsweek* she was impressed that I had invited others to share their opinions so we could make the most informed decision. Beth was amazed that I had invited members of her party back to my office three times over ten hours to hammer out a solution on AGIA.

I got a kick out of another comment she made, about my being Alaska's first female chief executive: "I finally get to go to the restroom and talk business with the governor," Beth said. "The guys have been doing this for centuries."

In February 2008, Anchorage Democrat Les Gara, a representative, told *Alaska* magazine, "Anybody that comes to Juneau and says, I'm not going to do my party's bidding deserves credit. We had some very dark years under Frank Murkowski, and it has been nice to see something different."

The press was decent and fair concerning my working relationship with both parties my first years in office. The positive news reports slowed down drastically, though, that final year. Since the Point Thomson development was good news, the press was relatively quiet. Still, we celebrated. In early 2009, I would speak at a packed-house luncheon at the Dena'ina Civic and Convention Center in Anchorage to thank all the players who had come together to get Point Thomson rolling. Before my talk, I met with ExxonMobil officials to shake hands and talk about our commitment to work hard and work together. This progress was such great news for all parties involved. Even some ExxonMobil officials from Australia were there for the event, and as a gift of goodwill, they presented me with a jar of Vegemite. I felt bad that I didn't bring a jar of smoked salmon to offer in return.

"Take it home and share it," the folks from down under said of their gift. "See if your children like it."

That night, I tried Vegemite for the first time and realized ExxonMobil wasn't trying to thank me with the gift. They were trying to kill me.

13

The staff understood my agenda of fiscal conservatism and knew that to implement it, we'd have to work as a team. Only one cabinet member voiced criticism of the agenda to slow the growth of government, and he taught me another lesson about how difficult changing bureaucracy is when the team is divided.

A few days before I announced my 2008 preliminary budget, Public Safety Commissioner Walt Monegan held his own press conference to announce his department's funding requests, which included a budget increase. My Deputy Chief of Staff Randy Ruaro was livid.

"What team is Monegan playing on?" Randy asked. "Because you sure can't tell!"

Monegan was using an old political trick, speaking out in public to pressure his boss into accepting his entire funding wish list—which happened to align with the wish list of the union representing some state employees. Democrat Senator Hollis French stood beside Monegan to lend his official support.

Hollis "Gunny" French—he earned the nickname from military veterans who found it unbelievable that he would list himself as a Marine Corps private and imply one year of "military service" when he merely attended a weeks-long military course during college—was one of the ringleaders of the politically motivated investigation that would become known as "Troopergate."

Some union members and Democrat friends were offended when I later branded Monegan's behavior "insubordinate." Is there a better term for it? As I write this, I'm thumbing through a thesaurus . . . still looking . . . still looking . . .

Nope. Seems like insubordination to me. I had the final say on the budget. It was my responsibility to make it efficient. If Monegan wanted to be responsible for a government budget, I thought he should run for office. (He later did; months after his stint in my administration ended, he ran for Anchorage mayor and snagged 8 percent of the total vote.)

Monegan didn't share my commitment to earmark reform, either. We would eventually slash federal earmark requests by 85 percent. My cabinet knew of my commitment for Alaska to lead other states in becoming more self-sufficient and not contributing to the nation's ever-growing multitrillion-dollar debt.

So I was surprised when I learned that Monegan had gone to Washington, D.C., to lobby for earmarks.

He knew my priorities for the Public Safety Department: I wanted him to fill the many vacant state trooper positions. He had failed to do so, yet he still wanted more money. Then we caught wind of a second lobbying trip he was planning to D.C. I knew we couldn't defer the problem any longer.

I'd already been through one episode with a team member who acted as though he wanted to be traded. Making that change with the legislative director had worked out well for everyone. So I offered to reassign Monegan to the Alcohol Beverage Control Board, where he could work on alcohol abuse problems throughout the state. He said he'd think about it for a few days. But instead, the next day he announced he would leave the administration. The day after he resigned, he wrote a nice farewell e-mail to his colleagues admitting his failure to communicate effectively and encouraging them not to make the same mistake.

Soon after that, Democrat legislators and the union spun up a false story that Walt had been fired for personal reasons— purportedly because he wouldn't fire my ex-brother-in-law, the problem-prone trooper. Strange, I thought, because not only was that not true, but Monegan himself debunked the false accusation—until he started getting props from the union for being "a victim" of the governor's office. He told the *Anchorage Daily News,* "For the record, no one ever said fire [the trooper]. Not the governor. Not Todd. Not any of the other staff." The press even printed his statement the day after I was announced as the VP candidate.

We later learned that our old friend Andy Halcro had helped create the story on his blog, a small-town site that was cited as an authoritative source by local media—and later, astonishingly, by national media too lazy to sift fact from fiction. Halcro's false report would ultimately blossom into the "scandal" known as Troopergate, or, as people who knew the facts called it, "Tasergate."

Any governor has a right to pick the right team members for the right positions at the right time, for the good of the team. Monegan was a political, at-will, exempt appointee. Any governor, any mayor, any *president,* can replace any cabinet member at will.

First, the press got it wrong when they reported that I had "fired" Monegan. We were transferring him. But he had turned that down and left without discussion except to say that he understood my decision. My chief of staff and I didn't see a need to publicly get into all the reasons for it, especially since it was a personnel matter. Reporters kept asking, though, so I explained that Walt had been leaving state trooper positions vacant and hadn't been recruiting for them. It was unacceptable to keep them funded and on the books if we didn't need them. Plus, we had other budget issues that he was not helping to resolve. Overall, the job had seemed overwhelming for him and he just hadn't been getting it done.

What Monegan *was* getting done, apparently, was the bidding of union leadership. With union prompting, Monegan quickly changed his story, making a follow-up announcement that suggested that his reassignment had been "unfair." He also had the audacity to claim to a credulous reporter that during all that time we worked together, I had deigned to meet with him only four times in the year and a half he served.

My staff and I just about fell out of the Atwood Building over that one. "Then who the heck was that you traveled around the state with all those days, and had in our offices for all those meetings, cabinet meetings, receptions, and all the other events for the last seventeen months?" Mike Nizich joked with me. "If that wasn't Walt, we need the FBI on this stolen identity case, pronto!"

14

In the months following the AGIA vote, I was glad I'd trained for marathons. I'm superstitious about cutting any corners when I jog, believing the few extra steps can make a difference in a long race. The race for a natural gas pipeline had spanned more years than there are miles in a marathon, but with AGIA now law, we felt the finish line was finally in sight, and our DNR and revenue commissioners worked around the clock on the application process. We wouldn't cut any corners.

AGIA's free-market principles drew five applications from around the world, plus another entirely new competing gasline proposed by BP and ConocoPhillips in lieu of working through AGIA. The applicants' response to the new, open bidding process was proof positive that competition works. Now it was up to the commissioners to vet the applications and recommend the one licensee they felt would best maximize the benefits for Alaskans. As the commissioners worked hard on their end, I accepted opportunities to speak with reporters nationwide about oil and gas—even if they didn't want to hear it. We were bombarded with interview requests, including, believe it or not, a *Vogue* magazine profile of Kansas Governor Kathleen Sebelius and me in a fashion shoot. Mine, of course, was the Last Frontier theme, complete with our Piper Super Cub airplane as the backdrop, Bunny Boots in some of the shots, and a thick winter jacket hiding my pregnant belly. Since fashion trends weren't my top interest, I kept bringing the *Vogue* writer's questions back to national security and energy independence. That made it tough for her, as she was doing her best to write for readers who cared about the latest Fifth Avenue styles and probably wouldn't be caught dead in a pair of Sorels. She finally had to stop me and nicely say she'd heard enough about energy. I just couldn't pivot from hydropower to high fashion, so the interview wasn't that great for her readers, I'm sure.

The competitive bidding process we created with AGIA unlocked the Big Three oil companies' development monopoly and threw open Alaska's doors to true competition and free enterprise. Suddenly, even other nations were bidding on the multibillion-dollar project. We had anticipated Canadian interest but were surprised to receive a proposal from China. The bid, by Sinopec, bothered me. There was little doubt that the company could muster the manpower, technology, and funding necessary to do the job, but this proposal skated on the razor's edge between the free market and national sovereignty. An energy-thirsty Communist nation controlling Alaska's natural gas reserves was not in the best interests of the state or our country. It turned out Sinopec's application was incomplete anyway, and the commissioners rejected it for that reason. Early in 2008, the DNR and revenue commissioners finally announced their AGIA recommendation: the Calgary-based pipeline building giant TransCanada-Alaska, a firm that had not only met every single enforceable requirement of AGIA but exceeded them. We were ecstatic. *I* was ecstatic: there would be hundreds of steps yet to take, but we could almost envision the tape draped across the finish line.

We handed over the license recommendation to the legislature to consider during a special legislative session that summer. We knew AGIA's success hinged on communicating with Alaskans, so we constantly gave our constituents information, competing with the well-financed ad campaigns hawking the competing BP/ConocoPhillips idea to someday build their own gasline, an idea that had attracted the interest of the Russian energy firm Gazprom. The summer of 2008 was also about reeducating lawmakers who had just voted "Yes" on AGIA months before, but now, feeling the heat from Big Oil again, were suddenly feigning shock over the plan to build the gasline project.

We jumped in and did what we do best—town hall meetings, op-eds, weekly gasline briefings, TV and radio interviews. If tea parties had been in vogue back then, I would have thrown the first one to get people involved and energized in their government's decisions. We even hired a communications firm to get us access to a few editorial boards (who no doubt thought, "Great. An op-ed from Sarah Palin . . . who's that?"). I wrote op-eds every week, and we sent them to any publication that would spare a few column inches for our message. Our messaging began making progress happen fast. The gasline team and I hit all the local and major media players who were talking about America's energy challenges that summer and interested in a substantive debate, including Neil Cavuto, Maria Bartiromo, and Glenn Beck. Twice I joined CNBC's Larry Kudlow. I like his energy—even the yelling—and I was clearly in sync with his mantra of "Drill! Drill! Drill!"

With all these folks, I discussed issues such as congressional opposition to drilling in the ANWR; my meetings with the Federal Energy Regulatory Commission, members of Congress, and White House officials; and the national security issues involved in building the gasline. I hit the same topics in detail with reporters from the *Wall Street Journal, Time,* the Associated Press, *Investor's Business Daily,* and *Forbes.* (Perhaps that's why I was so shocked during the VP campaign when Katie Couric wondered which papers and magazines I read. Maybe I should have asked her what *she* reads. She didn't sound very informed on our energy issues.)

The combination of our commissioners' hard work, our outreach to the people, the national media barnstorming, and careful consideration by Alaska lawmakers paid off. On Friday, August 1, 2008, Alaskans won again: the legislature overwhelmingly voted to award the AGIA license to TransCanada-Alaska. We still had a long way to go until our clean, safe energy flowed south to the Lower 48, but after a thirty-year wait, we had turned the idea of commercializing our natural gas for Alaska's economic future from pipe *dream* to pipe*line.*

By then my governorship was only twenty months old. It had been a season of incredible change, both in Alaska and in my own life. I had been elected governor of the state I loved. And in just the past year, we had kicked off the pipeline, overhauled ethics in state government, slashed state spending with my vetoes, saved for the future, and put money back into the hands of the people. Plus, we radically changed the way Alaskans would be secured in the future with the natural resources they owned.

On a personal level, we said "Hello!" to the new Palin son at one end of the childhood spectrum and clung in our hearts to the other Palin son, to whom we had to say, "See you soon!" Then came more life-changing news. The month after Trig was born, Bristol came to Todd and me and told us the shocking news that she was pregnant.

Truthfully, I was devastated for my daughter. It wasn't the morality of the situation—what was done was done. It was that I saw her future change in an instant. Bristol knew what our reaction would be, and that's why she said giving us the news was tougher even than labor. It took a while to absorb it, too. We prayed about this next step in all our lives and began preparing to welcome this new child into a loving extended family. Though things would not be easy for Bristol, we knew that with God somehow we could draw good from this change.

In Alaska, we view change a bit differently. For example, wild-fires in the Lower 48 are often treated as natural disasters. Up here, we often let them burn, knowing that from fire-blackened lands new growth will spring. Often, a searing burn opens dead ground to new light and under the soil, long-dormant seeds ger-minate, covering fields in blankets of a tall, bright pink flower called fireweed. Here in the Great Land, fireweed grows wild every year. We mark out our summer as its blossoms open from bottom to top, starting low on the stem around May and popping open higher and higher as the weeks pass until the last bloom on top turns to new seed.

Month by month in the summer of 2008, from Bristol's news in May, to Trig's first smile, to Track's readiness for Iraq, to the awarding of the AGIA energy project in August, my life tracked the fireweed's fuchsia climb. By the time John McCain called me at the State Fair in August, the blooms had reached their peak, the sign that a new season was only a few weeks away.

Chapter Four

Going Rogue

I am convinced that life is 10 percent what happens to me
and 90 percent how I react to it. And so it is with you . . .
we are in charge of our attitudes.

—CHARLES SWINDOLL

I t was pitch black when we touched down in Arizona, the home state of Senator John McCain. Late on August 27, 2008, with the help of a McCain staffer, Davis White, my assistant and friend, Kris Perry and I had managed to slip out of Anchorage on a private jet. It was no small feat as the entire media world was on veep watch and we were attempting to duck out of a place where most everyone at our local airstrips knew us. But it seemed we'd pulled it off. In Arizona, we emerged from the plane into a warm, dry darkness, and a small knot of men whisked us into a tinted-window Suburban.

We drove to the private home of Bob Delgado, John's friend and the CEO of Hensley & Co., Cindy McCain's beer distributorship. As the dark streets and green foothills of Flagstaff flashed by, I alternated between tapping out state business on my BlackBerry and marveling at the way doors sometimes open before us—doors that we have neither anticipated nor sought. Yet when God presents those doors, we think, *Yes. This is right. This fits.*

There had been rumors that John was considering me along with many others as his VP pick, and a nice guy named Adam Brickley had started a Web site trying to rally ordinary folks to draft me for the job. Several national reporters who interviewed me about AGIA that summer had dropped off-camera hints to that effect. But I was very busy with state business and the whole veep thing was such a long shot that I hadn't even considered it a real possibility.

I had met the McCains in February 2008 at the National Governors Association winter meeting in D.C. During a reception at the J.W. Marriott Hotel, Todd and I had spoken with the senator and Cindy, and the four of us really connected over our families, especially when the McCains talked about their sons, Jack, who was set to graduate from the Naval Academy in 2009, and Jimmy, who had been serving in Iraq. As Cindy and I talked, I was pleased to find that this elegant, beautiful woman was really a down-to-earth mom who is as crazy about her kids as every other mom.

When the conversation turned to us watching our own son go off to war, Cindy said, "You're really going to be on your knees in prayer more than you'll ever expect."

Senator McCain insisted we call him John. I had always admired the Republican senator for his independent spirit and his passion for keeping our homeland safe. I sincerely respected him. Both Todd and I found him a kind, respectful man, not at all worn down either by decades in Washington or, miraculously, by his five and a half years as a POW in Vietnam. Instead, he seemed full of an inspiring inner joy. Later in the campaign, I would see this joy again and again. I'll never forget it: we'd be at these huge, potentially history-making events, and John would clap me on the shoulder, rub his hands together with a grin, and say, "Let's just go have fun!" It seemed to me a perspective forged in the kind of fires that make even the pressure cooker of a presidential campaign seem quaint by comparison.

As we rolled through the Arizona darkness, with Davis up front and Kris tapping on her BlackBerry beside me, I was excited to have another opportunity to meet with John.

For some reason, when the call came at the State Fair, it didn't come as a huge shock. (Perhaps after the year I'd had, nothing could shock me.) I certainly didn't think, *Well, of course this would happen.* But neither did I think, *What an astonishing idea.* It seemed more comfortable than that, like a natural progression. I'd known it was only a matter of time before others saw Alaska's potential to contribute to America's future. Now the time was right.

After that cell phone chat at the fair, I took Piper on the next carnival ride as promised. Then I called Todd on the Slope, and Kris, and they both began working to make the Arizona meeting happen without alerting the press. It was a big deal to try to pull it off. Information security was a huge concern. By that time, just five days before the Republican National Convention, the veepstakes ran end-to-end through daily news coverage. Bureau reporters had staked out the homes and offices of the major contenders, eyes peeled for the slightest clue. I remembered that during the Democrat veepstakes, they'd even put surveillance on Joe Biden's mom.

But Governor Sarah Palin of Alaska? That was too far out of the box.

We did have our local reporters, though. Getting past them would be a trick. And how would we keep this a secret from my staff, especially if I got the nod and went straight to the convention in Minnesota? I was always at work. When I served as mayor, I had Piper on a Monday and was back at work on Tuesday, stopping by with her tucked in a car seat. When I had Trig, my staff brought me state paperwork to do, and I signed a bill into law from the hospital bed. I didn't miss much work for any reason. To my staff, it would be inexplicable that I wasn't in the office on an ordinary Thursday morning.

In discussing logistics for getting me out of Alaska undetected, the McCain people delivered one piece of news with the potential to change the course of the entire campaign: if John picked me as his running mate, Todd would have to confiscate our three teenagers' cell phones—*without* an explanation, *when they weren't even in trouble.* This, of course, would be scarier than anything the Obama-Biden camp could throw at us.

Now in Arizona, we pulled into the driveway of an imposing home surrounded by trees that soared into a star-spangled sky. When I stepped out of the car, I was again struck by a blast of warm nighttime air, the day's heat still baking up from the earth. Alaskans don't get to enjoy a warm, starry night—ever. If it's dark enough to see the stars, then it's quite cold, so the balmy air felt foreign and exotic.

Moments later, Bob welcomed us into his beautiful home, where he'd laid out a generous spread. Davis made the introductions. First, Steve Schmidt, veteran campaign manager, an imposing, gruff-voiced guy who wore sunglasses atop his bald head in the middle of the night. Schmidt, aka "the Bullet," told me he'd managed Arnold Schwarzenegger's gubernatorial campaign, handled press relations for Dick Cheney, and worked on George W. Bush's 2004 reelection campaign.

I knew instantly that Schmidt was business-to-the-bone. I respect that in a person, as I'm not one for a lot of chitchat either, and we were very comfortable with each other right off the bat. As a public relations troubleshooter, Schmidt specialized in shaping public opinion. His peers later told me he has a laserlike ability to spot chinks in an opponent's armor. He is a guy who inspires loyalty: in spite of his steely exterior, people who work for him really want to please him.

Similar to the McCain campaign's struggles, the Bush 2004 campaign had its points when morale was terrible, people on the inside told me. Prior to Bush's debate against Democrat challenger John Kerry, the campaign had been pretty well positioned to continue its lead in the polls if the president performed well at the debate. But the postdebate feeling among some staffers was that it was a disaster. The next day at campaign headquarters, morale was in the tank . . . for everyone except Schmidt. Because Schmidt was focused. He was looking for the advantage, and he thought he had found it in Kerry's assertion during the debate that the United States of America needed to pass a "global test" before choosing to act militarily.

While the press and the Kerry team were picking apart Bush's performance, Schmidt had found a single, unspent shell he would use to make war.

He told one staffer, "We're going to ram 'global test' right up John Kerry's ass."

People said Schmidt was the kind of guy who was in politics because the thirst for competition ran in his blood. He was good at managing the media, at using the press to communicate a message—and he was very good at setting traps for his opposition.

Next was McCain biographer and confidant Mark Salter. He was friendly and quieter than Schmidt. Still, I could tell he was soaking up every detail. I later learned that he had once taken a punch from an activist who was agitating outside John's Senate offices, then wrestled the man to the ground and kept him pinned until the cops showed up. I also learned he was one of the few people who could change John's mind.

We all sat around a coffee table in Delgado's dimly lit living room, talking first about my position on the war in Iraq, my record on energy, and Alaska's economy. We discussed the makeup of my cabinet and staff, which included Republicans, Independents, and Democrats, and the fact that I subscribed to Lincoln's "team of rivals" approach.

I was impressed with these guys. They were thorough. For example, they already knew that Bristol was pregnant, a development that I thought only loved ones were privy to at the time. "You have to be aware that nothing will stay secret during the campaign," Schmidt said.

"That's okay," I said. "I have nothing to hide."

I admitted, though, to the one skeleton I'd kept hidden in my closet for the past twenty-two years. It made me nervous and sick to my stomach, but I felt obligated to confess that D in the college course twenty-two years before. Schmidt didn't bat an eye but instead switched back to the war in Iraq. He wanted to know whether I understood the origin of the conflict, the history of the Middle East, and how thirteenth- and fourteenth-century differences had evolved into today's murderous rivalry between the Sunni and the Shia.

I knew the history of the conflict to the extent that most Americans did. We talked about my perspective, then I added that it was also personal to me: as commander-in-chief of our state's National Guard and as the mother of a son headed to Iraq, I was paying close attention to what was going on and keenly aware of the war's progress and the issues on the ground.

It turned out that conflict in the Middle East was Schmidt's preferred issue, and he seemed very knowledgeable about the subject. It would later concern me that when the tanking economy began pushing the war out of the headlines, Schmidt was slow to turn the campaign's ship into the wind. When I look back at that evening's interview, it seems clear that there was an assumption at the center of the McCain camp that the war would retain center stage come hell or high water. In fact, Schmidt gave me books on the subject, plus stacks of videotapes and DVDs to review as we traveled from city to city so that I could review the war's history at 37,000 feet.

As the vetting discussion entered its second, then third hour, Kris and I gravitated to our usual powwow spots on the floor, propping our backs against the couches and arranging our Black-Berrys and cell phones beside us like playing cards as we did during informal staff meetings at my house.

"What about Walt Monegan?" Schmidt said.

The public safety commissioner I'd reassigned. I gave Schmidt the background on Walt, his budget problems and insubordination, his changing story. I also told him about the "independent" investigator on the case, a guy who had previously worked with both Monegan and the Democrat lawmaker pushing the ginned-up scandal.

"My replacing a cabinet member was legal, normal, and necessary, and had nothing to do with a former brother-in-law," I said. "This is a nonissue."

"Okay," Schmidt said. Then he changed gears, shifting the topic to social issues. He seemed impressed when I told him that people in my own family disagree on some issues like abortion, but that we don't argue over it at the dinner table. I have one relative who expresses her pro-choice position articulately. My own pro-life opinion diverges from hers by 180 degrees, and we've had great, civil discussions on the topic. It would later amaze my family and friends that the Obama-Biden camp and their media friends painted me as rigid and intolerant. It was assumed that I refused to hear alternative points of view and used topics like abortion and homosexual marriage as a political litmus test. I explained that I had never asked anyone, including the Democrats I appointed, what their position on abortion was, and I didn't discuss my opinion on homosexuality with cabinet members or judicial appointees, either.

Schmidt seemed surprised and pleased, even when I reiterated that I was solidly pro-life and hoped they would never try to temper my position on the issue.

Then we talked about gay marriage. That's when I told them about Tilly, my junior high friend and college roommate, who, after college, decided to openly live the lifestyle she chose with her partner. To me, she was still Tilly. I loved her dearly—loved the whole Ketchum family. I explained to Schmidt that I opposed homosexual marriage, but that didn't seem too controversial in the campaign since the Democrat candidate for president held the same position.

<hr>

Once in a while, the guys would take a break and I would go into another room to visit via telephone with the source of all the information the guys out front already had on me: Arthur B. Culvahouse, Jr. Culvahouse is the longtime chair of O'Melveny & Myers, an international law firm with a thousand lawyers, some of whom seem to exist entirely to eat, breathe, and sleep information. The McCain campaign had hired Culvahouse, a former White House counsel to Ronald Reagan, to head up the VP search. The sixty-year-old D.C. veteran had once served on the Counterintelligence Advisory Panel to the U.S. Senate Select Committee on Intelligence. By the time his team of attorneys finished peppering me with questions, I decided that if a person had ever done a single dark and secret thing in their lives, Culvahouse's people would not only find out about it but get eyewitnesses, photos, and blood samples.

These guys knew stuff about me that I had long forgotten: They knew how I had voted on issues during my days on the city council. They reviewed copies of my tax returns. They had transcripts of sermons that visiting pastors had preached at a church I had not attended regularly since I was a teenager. And they were the ones who told Schmidt that Bristol was pregnant.

I was impressed. I also thought, *Good. They know exactly what they're getting.*

⸻

Back out in the living room with Salter and Schmidt, the conversation turned to the topic of theories of origins. And that, it seemed, was when the big guy hit the pause button. He knew my position: I believed in the evidence for microevolution—that geologic and species change occurs incrementally over time. But I didn't believe in the theory that human beings—thinking, loving beings—originated from fish that sprouted legs and crawled out of the sea. Or that human beings began as single-celled organisms that developed into monkeys who eventually swung down from the trees; I believed we came about through a random process, but were created by God.

"But your dad's a science teacher," Schmidt objected.

"Yes."

"Then you know that science proves evolution."

"Parts of evolution," I said. "But I believe that God created us and also that He can create an evolutionary process that allows species to change and adapt."

Schmidt winced and raised his eyebrows. In the dim light, his sunglasses shifted atop his head.

I had just dared to mention the C-word: creationism. But I felt I was on solid factual ground. My dad, who is not particularly religious but certainly sees God's hand everywhere he looks in

Alaska, had spent many evenings around our dinner table discussing treasures from his classroom with me and my siblings. Mr. Heath's classroom featured an exquisite collection of everything exotic and fascinating for his young science students. He kept an albino skunk, scary tarantulas, and an eight-foot-long boa constrictor that had swallowed its five-foot-long roommate. He kept turtles and fish and birds and other amazing things that found their way to our house on weekends and summer breaks. Our home's decor included fossils and petrified wood, pelts, animal skeletons, and jars of dissected creatures.

Dad's curriculum was cleverly all-Alaskan. His spelling tests included words like "ptarmigan" (Alaska's state bird) and *"akuutaq"* (Eskimo ice cream). We learned the difference between glacial crevices and crevasses, and a cave's stalagmites and stalactites. His lessons spilled over to the dinner table. We ate together every night, and I just assumed every kid learned clever acronyms for planet alignments and the elements of the periodic table between forkfuls of caribou lasagna. Didn't every family talk about what differentiated a grizzly from a brown bear? And the difference between king salmon fry and red salmon species, and which world-renowned mountain ranges were located on what continent, and the effects of a river's erosion, and fossil proof of evolutionary patterns that one could actually view as evidence of a grand design?

But in eighteen years of impromptu supper-table lessons and expert-guided field trips to America's national parks, never had Dad or anyone else convinced me that the earth had sprung forth conveniently stocked with the ingredients necessary to spontaneously generate life and its beauty and diversity; in fact, I thought that idea flew in the face of the evidence I saw all around.

I got where Schmidt was coming from. I know the word "creationism" evokes images of wild-eyed fundamentalists burying evidence for *any* kind of evolution under an avalanche of Bible verses. But I needed the campaign to know they weren't going to put words in my mouth on this issue. I would go with them reasonably to a nuanced position, based on facts. But I wouldn't parrot a politically correct line just because some voting bloc might get upset. And, by the way, I saw nothing wrong with students debating the merits of evolution in the classroom. If William F. Buckley—a devout Catholic and a world-class intellectual—could believe in the divine origin of man, why couldn't I?

2

The next morning, we drove to the McCains' ranch in Sedona. The rose-colored morning was perfect, warm and dry. A rugged gravel road unrolled across the dusty hills, and I looked out the Suburban's windows, wishing I could run the rest of the way. I'd just left the coolness of Alaska's lush vegetation, and here we wound through desert canyons with cathedrals of soaring red rock rising near forests of ponderosa pine. I craved stretching my legs on a long, hot run through what looked like the scene of an old western movie.

The McCains' ranch was upscale southwestern, a small compound with a scattering of guesthouses. They had partly raised their kids there, and you could tell that; the place had a lived-in feel rather than the aura of some perfectly groomed, untouched retreat. We parked near the main house. John, sharp as usual in a button-down shirt and creased slacks, was waiting on the porch and greeted me warmly. We walked down across the lawn to comfortable chairs, close to a creek that ran through the property near a line of trees and boulders. I couldn't take my eyes off the water, which seemed to flow red because of the famous Sedona rock.

Some kind of hawk wheeled overhead, and John pointed it out, naming the genus and species. The creek gurgled nearby. I could see tiny lights strung in the trees, and fans to propel the cool creek air into the seating area.

"How do you feel about running for vice president?" John asked me.

"I'll do whatever I can to help our country," I said.

We were both pretty excited, but he looked at me very seriously. "It would be tough on your family."

"I know," I said. "I'm sure it is tough."

Though I knew it wouldn't compare, I thought about how, in some ways, serving for years in local office had been even tougher than serving as governor. In local office you're serving your friends and neighbors. That means you receive a lot of input, a lot of criticism. As mayor, I'd had people calling me in the middle of the night to complain about the neighbor's dog barking and stopping by my house to tell me their property tax assessment was off by a few bucks. When I was governor, I heard a thousandfold more citizen concerns from people all across the state—but at least a lot of the complainants wrote letters instead of ringing up at all hours.

"My kids have grown up with it," I said. "Working on the Slope, Todd's always had an unconventional schedule. The family's always been flexible and adaptable, and that's not unusual in Alaska. It works for us."

"What does Todd think of all this?" John said.

"He's very supportive, John. He wants us, and Alaska, to do all we can to help. We're up to the challenge on this one."

Todd knew how much our state and our family had to contribute to the campaign and, if we were successful, to the country. It went beyond common sense conservatism and traditional values to the fact that we are everyday Americans. We know what it's like to have to make payroll and take care of employees. We know what it's like to be on a tight budget and wonder how we're going to pay for our own health care, let alone college tuition. We know what it's like to work union jobs, to be blue-collar, white-collar, to have our kids in public schools. We felt our very normalcy, our status as ordinary Americans, could be a much-needed fresh breeze blowing into Washington, D.C.

—————

As the sun crept higher, I became increasingly aware that I was dressed for the North, wearing one of the three practical black Ann Taylor suits I always use to travel. Still, the desert air felt good as John began discussing his independence and how much he, too, was irritated with time wasted on games within the political world. We had that in common, and agreed that not being beholden to anyone gave us strength and the freedom to do what was right. No political establishment had propelled me to where I was—in fact, I had reached the governor's office in *direct opposition* to the political establishment.

I looked up to see Cindy walking down from the house to join us. She is one of the most striking women I've ever seen, and that day she reminded me of one of those perfect, elegant moms on a 1950s TV show: a sleeveless dress, a little sweater, not a hair out of place. So petite and pretty, with those intense blue eyes. I remember her clothes because I was there in my let's-discuss-the-issues suit while she breezed across the lawn like a walking summer day.

Cindy is sometimes painted as an ice queen, but that couldn't be farther from the truth. Yes, she can be guarded. But who can blame her? It's no wonder that people like Cindy, who are unfairly clobbered in the press with lies about them and their family, appear to say, "Forget it, I'm here to help, but I'm not going to offer myself up anymore." I've been there. After a while, some of the giddy gets knocked right out of you.

In Cindy's case, the press had been pretty merciless over the years. Because of her upmarket elegance, she'd almost been ostracized from working-class people, but I loved her life story, which began with her dad starting out poor. He'd pulled himself up by his bootstraps, and made a great life for his family. Cindy grew up wealthy but with a heart for those in need. In the 1980s she founded the American Voluntary Medical Team and has since led dozens of medical missions providing emergency surgery and supplies to impoverished children in third-world and war-torn countries. She even brought one of those children home to become part of her family.

More power to her! I thought.

When Cindy met us on the lawn at the ranch, she had just returned from the country of Georgia, which had been under military siege by the Russian army. She gave us an update on what she'd seen there, then she and John went for a quick stroll while I walked up to the deck of the main cabin to speak with Kris. Looking out across the lawn a few minutes later, I saw that Schmidt and Salter had joined John by the creek. The three men had their heads together and were deep in conversation. A few minutes after that, John walked up the lawn, climbed the steps, and offered me the job.

3

The tunnel thundered with ten thousand voices, and the air inside felt electric. I stood behind John and Cindy as he waited for the cue to step onstage at the Ervin J. Nutter Center in Dayton, Ohio. It was August 29, John's birthday, and we were pretty sure we'd pulled it off, managing, under the unblinking eyes of thousands of news cameras, to whisk me and then my family secretly from Wasilla, Alaska, to this moment.

I was so humbled and honored, so thankful, and so ready to get on the trail with the campaign. Now the crowd's roar poured backstage like a powerful locomotive. An electric guitar whined under the steady drum of thousands of stomping feet. I glanced at Todd, beside me, in a handsome blue suit, his ice blue eyes twinkling in the dark. I whispered to him, "You look sharp! Are you ready for this?" Four of our five kids crowded in just behind us: Bristol, seventeen; Willow, fourteen; Piper, seven; and four-month-old Trig, who cuddled sleepily as he was passed gently from sister to sister. I glanced down at Piper, who'd grown up with small crowds and campaign glitz, but in the grassroots fashion of Alaskan politics—nothing like this. She grinned up at me. There's always something in her eyes that says she's ready to get it done, but she's determined to have fun doing it. My big girls took deep breaths, smiled, and felt the energy of an anxious country waiting to see what was next for John McCain.

We passed a whisper between us: "Say a prayer!"

Glancing out through the end of the tunnel, I could see the crowd, and flashes of red, white, and blue. John's blue-and-gold posters, emblazoned with his campaign message, "Country First," rippled in the stands.

I was proud of the senator. *He is so bold, so out of the box,* I thought.

He didn't go with a conventional, safer pick. John believed in change, the power of independent and committed individuals, the power of women. He thought it was time to shake things up.

Cheers, whistles, foot stomping punched through the music echoing through the hall as the crowd waited to see John. I thought back to the greenroom, where, only a few minutes before, we'd greeted the McCains. He'd clapped his hands and rubbed them together. "This is gonna be fun!" he said, eyes sparkling. "Let's have fun! You're gonna do great."

The kids were awestruck. They'd seen John on television before and knew a bit about his heroic story.

"Are you excited?" John asked Willow.

"Yeah, stoked!" Willow said.

John was stoked too, and as he bounded up onto the stage, the noise in the tunnel became a deafening roar.

"I'm very happy, very happy today to spend my birthday with you and to make an historic announcement in Dayton, a city built on hard, honest work of good people."

Cheers and applause rolled through the arena in giant waves.

"Like the entire industrial Midwest, Dayton has contributed much to the prosperity and progress of America," John continued. "And now in these tough, changing times, after all you've done for our country, you want your government to understand what you're going through, to stand on your side and fight for you. And that's what I intend to do. That's why I'm running for president, to fight for you, to make government stand on your side, not in your way!"

It was moving to hear this man who had given so much for his country offer himself up to serve it again. As the crowd quieted, John explained his search for a vice presidential candidate.

"I found someone with an outstanding reputation for standing up to special interests and entrenched bureaucracies. Someone who has fought against corruption and the failed policies of the past. Someone who stopped government from wasting taxpayers' money on things they don't want or need, and put it back to work for the people . . . someone who grew up in a decent, hardworking middle-class family, whose father was an elementary school teacher and mother worked first as a lunch lady, and later as a school secretary."

As I listened, I thought, *Only in America! Me, an ordinary woman from a town at the top of the world, standing next to this American hero who truly deserved to be the next president!* This was a man who had not only survived more than five years of torture as a prisoner of war, but had *led* his fellow prisoners and even refused early release. I thought of Track and wished he could be here to see John, whom he admired.

"The person I'm about to introduce to you was a union member and is married to a union member, and understands the problems, the hopes, and the values of working people; knows what it's like to worry about mortgage payments and health care, the cost of gasoline and groceries . . ."

It was true. Todd and I had been single-income and dual-income, with and without basic health care coverage, and it wasn't unusual to still clip coupons in our home because a month's worth of diapers and formula cost about as much as a truck payment.

". . . An outstanding high school point guard; a concerned citizen who became a member of the PTA, then a city council member, and then a mayor, and now a governor who beat the long odds to win a tough election on a message of reform and public integrity . . ."

It struck me as ironic that the Obama campaign had captured the theme of change. I'd always run on a platform of change, and I quickly wondered how I could start interjecting that "We were change when change wasn't cool" theme.

"She stands up for what's right, and she doesn't let anyone tell her to sit down," John continued. "She's fought oil companies and party bosses and do-nothing bureaucrats, and anyone who put their interests before the interests of the people she swore an oath to serve. . . . My friends and fellow Americans, I am very pleased and very privileged to introduce to you the next vice president of the United States—Governor Sarah Palin of the great state of Alaska!"

That was amazing, not nerve-wracking, and even sort of funny to me, because it meant John had a little explaining to do right off the bat. *Who in the heck is she?*

I gave my speech, and it was an absolute blast. The kids had fun, and Piper waved to the world. And as my family left the stage, I whispered to my husband, "Happy anniversary, Todd! Twenty years ago today—who'd have thought?"

4

From Ohio, we headed to Minnesota, the site of the 2008 Republican National Convention. Our first day there was a whirlwind. Campaign staff whisked me from the airport to the downtown Hilton and up to an enormous hotel suite with two bedrooms, one for the girls and one for Todd, Trig, and me. Track would be there soon, so he and his cousins would stay down the hall.

In the center of the room, when you first walked in, stood a huge dining/conference table. On the left side of the main living area stood four racks packed end to end with clothes. Looking more closely, I could see that one rack was hung with young ladies' clothes, probably for Bristol and Willow. Another contained men's clothes. Then there was one rack devoted entirely to women's tops and jackets, and another to women's pants and skirts. At first glance, it appeared that the campaign already had all our sizes, as well as a good sense of my style, which involves a lot of straight skirts and solid-colored blazers.

Good, I thought, remembering that all I'd brought on my secret, whirlwind trip from Alaska was an overnight bag. *Somebody's going to hand me something to wear, I'll put it on, and that's that. Simple. One less thing to worry about.*

Eventually people started shuttling into the suite for introductions. Policy people. Communications people. Logistics people. Assistant people. Assistant-to-the-assistant people. They were like human flash cards, there and gone. I smiled and shook hands with each one, hoping I could remember them all.

During the first couple of days, I would meet the major players on the VP staff. There was Tucker Eskew, a clean-cut Southern gentleman who spoke with a South Carolina drawl. Tucker, whose McCain campaign title was "counselor," was part of the political team that torpedoed John McCain's 2000 primary campaign in South Carolina. I heard that McCain's people had hired him in the hope that he could do the same thing with Obama. Obama wasn't saying much in his speeches, but his oratorical skills were absolutely captivating.

I remember the first time Todd and I heard the Illinois senator speak on TV, during the run-up to the Democrat primary. Afterward, we looked at each other and said, "Wow. That was good." But even then I feared his smooth style would obscure what he was actually saying.

Other members of the campaign team included Tracey Schmitt and Chris Edwards. Tracey was a very smart woman who had served as press secretary at the RNC and had a gift for media messaging and for relating with reporters. Chris, a White House veteran, was so kind, polished and impeccably dressed.

I was also introduced to a married couple that was working for John, Mark and Nicolle Wallace. I was told the couple met during the 2000 Florida recount, when Mark was one of George W. Bush's attorneys and Nicolle was communications director for the Bush campaign. Mark, who went on to work as a deputy with Bush's U.N. Ambassador John Bolton, seemed to me half sunshine, half thundercloud. Always talking with his hands, he joked a lot to keep things light, but I would also learn he had a hair-trigger temper and often reacted to problems with a brief explosion ("This is f****d up! Fix it! Now!").

Blond and pretty, Nicolle was outwardly very affectionate, with a charm that some women in politics lack. She also had a television quality about her, always "on" and speaking in sound bites.

Also on the team were a pair of very brainy guys named Randy Scheunemann and Steve Biegun, the men who would be helping with foreign policy briefings.

Randy began with a smile. "I've been around John McCain for a long time and he's known for making a lot of bold choices. This might be the boldest one yet."

I laughed, glad he felt comfortable enough to joke with me. "I agree," I said.

Randy explained he'd done John's foreign policy briefings when John ran for president in 2000. He had also worked as a national security advisor for Republican lawmakers and consulted with Pentagon officials on Iraq and other major conflicts. I liked Randy from the start.

He then introduced his colleague, Steve Biegun. Steve had served as staff director for the Senate Foreign Relations Committee and spent three years as the number three man on the Bush National Security Council; he had been there on September 11, 2001. Steve was an expert on Soviet and post-Soviet Russia and had lived in Moscow for a number of years. I liked him right off the bat, too, especially when I saw an eight-by-ten glossy of his wife and kids taped to the inside cover of his briefing binder.

His boys were baseball players, he said when I asked about them.

"I hope you're not missing their games for this," I said.

He was.

Steve and Randy were good men, helpful and unpretentious. They reminded me that Obama didn't have foreign policy experience. As a governor, I had gained such experience as it related to Alaska's international commerce and energy issues, as well as our strategic national security position. Steve and Randy reminded me that after a decade and a half in public office, including serving as a city manager and governor, I had more administrative and executive experience than either Obama or Biden. We assumed it was the campaign press people's job to get that message out to the voters.

Most of the folks in this group would be affectionately known as "the B Team" because, with the exception of the Wallaces, they were all assigned to the VP half of the ticket. Most of the B Team turned out to be, unquestionably, first string.

Very early in the campaign, Schmidt walked into our suite, escorting a tanned, kind of tired-looking guy in a suit.

"Governor Palin, I'd like to introduce Andrew Smith," Schmidt said. "He'll be your campaign chief of staff."

I stood up and offered my hand. "Hi, Andrew, it's great to meet you."

"Tell the governor what you've done, Andrew," Schmidt said.

"What I've done?" Smith said in a thick East Coast accent.

Schmidt eyed Smith and made a kind of "Go on, tell her" motion with his hands.

"Yeah," Schmidt said. "You've worked on the New York Stock Exchange."

Smith turned to me. "I've worked on the New York Stock Exchange."

"Oooh . . . okay," I said, smiling. "Well, it's great to have you aboard. Have you managed campaigns before?"

Andrew swiveled his head between Schmidt and me. Finally Schmidt answered for him: "No. He's a financial guy."

It seemed odd that we were being put in the hands of a man who had never run a campaign before, but Andrew seemed like a nice guy, and it wasn't my call. I figured they were pros and knew what they were doing. It ended up being a learning experience for all of us.

5

In the suite, a beautiful, helpful lady named Coral had set up a sewing machine to tailor the clothes the campaign supplied. Nicolle had had a hand in hiring a team of New York stylists, one of whom had apparently worked for some big-name newscasters, including Katie Couric.

When we had a few minutes and the stylists helped me take a closer look at the clothes, the price tags almost knocked my eyes out.

I remember seeing one rather plain-looking blazer and thinking, *That cost more than a semester at the University of Alaska.* I also noticed that instead of decent $7 pairs of nylons, one fancy package's price tag read $70. I hated to break it to them, but I doubted I'd even wear them—it was still warm out, after all.

The campaign had also purchased real pearls for the girls to wear on the night of my speech. After the big night, I made my daughters put them back into the store boxes and hand everything back to campaign staffers. We didn't need fancy jewelry. (Not long after Todd and I married, we bought a $35 wedding band from a street vendor in Hawaii, and it still works!)

At one point, Willow asked a campaign staffer, "Who's paying for all this?"

"Don't know," the staffer said. "But it's taken care of."

After my parents arrived for the convention, campaign aides took Dad down to Neiman Marcus to browse $200 ties and $350 shoes. Ever the practical and frugal one, he, too, asked who was paying for it all and was told the same thing: "It's taken care of. It's part of the convention."

No one had a good answer, either, to a more general question: why was the Palin family being made over for the two days of the convention anyway? With smiles on our faces, we asked, Do we really look that bad?

We felt like we were starring in an episode of *What Not to Wear.*

I was told that Nicolle had worked with the stylists at CBS. She also assured me that all candidates traveled with hair and makeup artists, and eventually introduced me to Amy and Angela, the talented hair and makeup girls. I told them I was comfortable doing my own makeup, but I did look forward to someone else trying to do something with my hair, which I had worn in the same boring style forever. (I later heard that people thought I wore my hair in an "up-do" so I could look "chic." Nah, it just saves me a few minutes every morning to plop it on top of my head.)

I didn't see how I was going to get used to sitting still while someone primped me. I had five kids; I was used to *doing* the primping. Like any mom, that usually just meant making sure the kids were warmly dressed and relatively wrinkle-free, then we were good to go. Throughout the campaign, though, Amy and Angela worked their magic, repeatedly rescuing my hair and mess of a face after too many days of fast food, snatched sleep, and stale, indoor air.

As the stylists buzzed around me like helpful bees, I began briefings and speechwriting sessions. I'm sure they got a bit annoyed with me. They wanted to turn me slowly in front of mirrors to make sure the clothes fit perfectly . . . but I had convention events to attend, as well as opportunities for once-in-a-lifetime meetings with various people and groups. Also, I wanted to study

John's foreign policy positions with Randy and Steve. So, while being tailored to within a millimeter, I talked over my shoulder with them and other advisers. It was all very different from my inaugural ball in Alaska, when I had run out in the final two hours, literally, to buy a pair of shoes for the grand event. I felt all the fuss over clothes was a colossal waste of time, and I was usually ready to bolt during fittings, thinking, *Okay. Yep. That's fine, gotta go.*

I wondered who had strategized this part of the campaign. I knew it wasn't John. Never before had I been involved in a campaign that placed such an emphasis on packaging. When I ran for office in Alaska, I'd written my own script, usually traveled by myself, and, obviously, had worn my own clothes. I presented myself as I was and told people what I believed in. Now I was in the hands of "campaign professionals," and it was my first encounter with the unique way of thinking that characterizes this elite and highly specialized guild. In Alaska, we don't really have these kinds of people—they are a feature of national politics. Naturally enough, as the experts, they are used to being in charge. But no matter how "expert" any of them was, nothing had apparently prepared them for the unprecedented onslaught of rumors, lies, and innuendo that "packaging" would have on my candidacy.

———

I also wasn't used to the beautiful hotels we enjoyed on the campaign trail. In Wasilla, we have the Best Western Inn on Lake Lucille. We've used it for years, for everything from town hall meetings to the Wasilla Warriors high school prom. It has a gorgeous view of the lake backed by thick, forested parklands and jagged peaks, and it's only a few doors down from my home. But it's not what you would call fancy. As governor, when I traveled on state business, I made frugality a point, asking for only reasonably priced rooms. So it wasn't often that we had the whole high-end, robe-and-slippers hotel treatment. The convention accommodations were different from the place we had stayed to hide out the night before I was announced as the VP candidate, which featured pink carpet and at least one huge cockroach, the first one Alaska-born Piper had ever seen.

I especially wasn't used to over-the-top perks, such as the flat-screen TV *inside* the bathroom mirror, an innovation that drew cries of "Way cool!" from my girls. *Cool* was not what I thought, though, on the morning of September 1. I was standing in the bathroom, brushing my teeth, enjoying the novelty of watching the news at the same time, when a crawl scrolled across the bottom of the screen: "Breaking: Vice presidential candidate Gov. Sarah Palin's teenage daughter, Bristol, is pregnant."

I nearly gagged on my toothbrush. *Oh, God,* I thought. *Here we go.*

The news, of course, wasn't a surprise to our family and friends. And certainly it wasn't a surprise to the campaign, nor were we going to try to hide it, even assuming we could have. But we would have liked to announce the news in our own way.

I knew now we would be playing defense on an issue that I would rather have been out front on. It surprised me that the campaign, which had the information in the first place, had had no plans to raise it in a constructive way. After all, it is an issue that affects far too many American teenagers.

I also recalled Barack Obama chastising a reporter in a nationally televised interview, insisting that his family was "off-limits." And the press obeyed him. They left his kids alone, as has generally been the tradition. I couldn't recall much scrutiny of any of the candidates' children . . . Biden's, McCain's . . . and I was glad for them. But nothing about the campaign would be like others.

I walked out into the larger suite just as Maria, a shy young staffer assigned to the VP media team, entered the room.

Headquarters, Maria told me, had elected to issue a statement in response to news reports about Bristol. In my name. She didn't know who had written it.

Maria handed me a printout. "Statement of Gov. Sarah Palin on the pregnancy of her daughter, Bristol: 'We have been blessed with five wonderful children who we love with all our heart and they mean everything to us. Our beautiful daughter, Bristol, came to us with news that, as parents, we knew would make her grow up faster than we had ever planned. We're proud of Bristol's decision to have her baby and even prouder to become grandparents.' "

I was pretty shocked. " 'Bristol and the young man she will marry are going to . . .' " I stopped reading.

I looked up at Maria. "No," I said. "That's certainly not the message we want to send."

We were *not* giddy-happy that our unwed teenage daughter was pregnant, as the press release suggested. Todd and I were proud of Bristol's selfless decision to have her baby and her determination to deal with difficult circumstances by taking responsibility for her actions. But in no way did I want to send the message that teenage pregnancy was something to endorse, much less glamorize.

I got a pen and marked up the printout, drafting a more serious statement that balanced concern with a message of love for my strong, but, truthfully, embarrassed daughter. I knew we had only one shot to get the right message out there concerning this life-changing event. Then I handed it back to Maria, who relayed it to "headquarters."

My cell phone rang. It was Bristol.

"Mom! The whole world knows about this. It's bad enough that Wasilla knows, but now the *whole world* knows."

"I know, honey. It's going to be okay. I'm really sorry."

Bristol sounded heartbroken. "Why is this even *news? I'm* not running for anything! What do I have to do with this?"

"You're right, you're right. This shouldn't be top news, and I'm sorry it is. We're going to get through this together, okay?"

Silence on the other end, punctuated by deep breaths.

"Bristol?"

"Okay . . ."

"I love you, honey. You're brave and you're strong, and it's going to be okay."

"Thanks, Mom. I love you, too. But I hate this morning, and I feel like I'm going to throw up."

I hung up the phone and turned to the television in the living room, just in time to see a new scroll across the bottom of the screen: "Gov. Sarah Palin on teen daughter's pregnancy: 'We're proud of Bristol's decision to have her baby and even prouder to become grandparents.'"

What?

Maria was just coming back into the room. "I don't get it," I said. "This is the statement I specifically said I did *not* want released."

Maria stared at the screen and her mouth fell open. "I . . . don't . . . I gave headquarters your edits . . . they knew . . ."

The incident sent a clear message: Whoever "headquarters" was, they were firmly in charge. And if they weren't going to let me speak my heart and mind even about an intimate issue affecting my own family, what *would* they let me speak to?

Perhaps it was just an honest mistake, and I was willing to give them the benefit of the doubt. But after a few similar incidents, I questioned Schmidt about what headquarters would and would not allow me to say. Schmidt was a busy guy; he didn't have a lot of time to elaborate, no doubt. He replied coolly, "Just stick with the script."

Most campaigns prepare press briefing guides on their candidates—fat three-ring binders indexed into multiple categories, including a detailed bio, a history of accomplishments, policy positions, and copies of significant speeches and statements. The McCain campaign had evidently been very, very busy, and had not had time to compile any press material that explained who I was or what my record represented. I was told later that the McCain communications team learned the name of John's vice presidential pick at the same time everybody else in the country did. And to make matters a bit more challenging, my family, friends, and political associates were under strict instructions not to talk to the media. So when the avalanche of press inquiries tumbled in, the national media folks had *zero* information. What they did report, patchy factoids cobbled together from the Internet and a few left-wing Alaskan bloggers, was usually wrong.

Immediately after the August 29 announcement, planeloads of national reporters and opposition researchers descended on Alaska. There was genuine reporting, but also extensive dirt-digging, which included oppo researchers hopping from store to store in Wasilla asking clerks, "Does Sarah Palin buy liquor here?" These black-suited, laptop-toting flatlanders weren't hard to spot. They'd never been to Alaska before and needed a field guide to the local political scene. With their editors back in New York and Washington screaming for copy to feed hourly news cycles, they took whatever they could get and weren't too careful about vetting their sources, who included a defeated former opponent, a maniacal blogger, the falafel lady, and the Wasilla town crank. These "credible sources" didn't help the media's credibility in the eyes of Alaskans who knew them.

Remember John Stein, my mayoral rival in Wasilla? He got busy again, this time giving interviews about me right after my nomination on August 29, calling me a book banner in a *Time* magazine article:

> Stein says that as mayor, Palin continued to inject religious beliefs into her policy at times. "She asked the library how she could go about banning books," he says, because some voters thought they had inappropriate language in them. "The librarian was aghast."

That set off a firestorm. Suddenly I was the book-burning evangelical extremist sweeping down from the North on her broomstick. Reporters didn't bother to find out the facts and print the truth.

The book-banning story flared quickly and didn't completely fizzle out even after lists of books I'd supposedly wanted to ban circulated on the Internet. The list included books that hadn't even been published at the time. It was one lie after another— from rape kits to Bridges to Nowhere. All easy enough to disprove if the press had done its job. The campaign was immediately overwhelmed, though, and the Alaska GOP (still run by Randy Ruedrich) had apparently decided to sit this one out.

The Bristol story was a different matter. After news broke of her pregnancy, the media train jumped the truth track in record time. The tone some reporters (and many bloggers) seemed to want to set was one of "hypocrisy." I was amazed at how many liberal pundits seemed floored by a pregnant teenager, as if overnight they'd all snuck out and had traditional-values transplants. The talking heads began to parrot one line: "If Sarah Palin can't control her own daughter, how can she serve as vice president?"

Some reporters insisted I favored abstinence-only sex education in public schools. "And see?" they said. "It didn't even work for her own daughter."

The media got that wrong too. The only time I had commented on sex education was in an answer to a gubernatorial candidate question asking whether I supported abstinence education versus "explicit" sex education in public schools—what some call the "slip a condom on a banana" show-and-tell curriculum. Given the choice, I answered that I would support abstinence education over "explicit" sex ed. I never said I didn't support contraception; I did. I also explained about being a longtime subscriber to the philosophy of Feminists for Life, a group of pro-life feminists who do not oppose contraception.

At about the same time as the pregnancy story broke, another bullcrap story entered the wider media bloodstream: "Who Is Trig's Real Mom?" Formerly reputable outlets like the *Atlantic* ran with the loony conspiracy theory that I was not Trig's mother— perhaps it was Bristol or Willow, they suggested. Even *Anchorage Daily News* reporters, who knew better, couldn't get enough of the story. That, too, would have been almost funny had it not been damaging to McCain and a hassle for my doctor, who was continually harassed by reporters to repeat her response that, yes, indeed, I had given birth to Trig. Even to this day, the "Trig-truthers" won't let go of their bizarre, through-the-looking-glass fantasy.

Another one of these stories that surfaced early on was that I had been invited to visit Wasilla Assembly of God church to speak to graduates of a missionary program. I asked the congregation to "pray for our military men and women who are striving to do what is right. Also, for this country, that our national leaders are sending [U.S. soldiers] out on a task that is from God." The *Huffington Post* ludicrously described this as: "Palin painted the current war in Iraq as a messianic affair in which the United States could act out the will of the Lord." In reality, I was invoking Abraham Lincoln's admonition that we should pray that we are on God's side—not that He is on ours.

These baseless and frankly insulting stories dominated the news for cycle after cycle after cycle. Tabloids and mainstream publications ran their ugly headlines until people couldn't tell truth from fiction. Back home in Wasilla, Bristol could barely stand to look at the television as commentators started suggesting that her pregnancy might change the outcome of the U.S. presidential election.

My sister Molly was furious. "It's outrageous!" she told me. "It's so unfair to put that on a seventeen-year-old girl. Why aren't they talking about presidential issues? What's going on in our country?"

I told Molly that for the next couple of months, maybe our family would do well to return to the Chuck Heath strategy of our childhood: keep the boob tube off.

6

Writing my convention speech was really a team effort, and the captain of the team was an ace speechwriter named Matthew Scully. Scully had worked for Bush 43, Dick Cheney, and John McCain. He is, to use author Rod Dreher's term, a "crunchy con." A political conservative, he is a bunny-hugging vegan and gentle, green soul who I think would throw himself in the path of a semitruck to save a squirrel.

He reminded me of the classic absentminded professor. Intellectually brilliant, he walked around looking up at the sky a lot, as if there were ideas up there he was pulling down, jotting them on the loose slips of paper that always peeked out of his pockets.

Somehow all this blends into Scully's special gift for writing. Throughout the campaign, the speeches he handed me were like poetry, so smooth, such amazing flow. But the convention speech he wrote was in a league of its own. We worked on it together, and he was very generous about letting me add my own words.

I practiced the speech with a teleprompter in a downstairs room at the hotel, which I found kind of peculiar because I didn't think anyone would practice for hours with a teleprompter. My experience was that either you knew your speech and delivered it with notes, or you used a teleprompter because you didn't know your speech. When I was governor, we used a teleprompter only a handful of times in front of a crowd. At the convention, my experience giving a speech the old-fashioned way, speaking from the heart, turned out to be a good thing.

During rehearsals, there was one part of the speech I thought I might not make it through gracefully. Every time I got to the section about one of McCain's fellow POWs, a man named Tom Moe, I'd choke up. I just couldn't get through the mental imagery of a broken John McCain encouraging his fellow soldiers in a torturous POW camp. So, during the live speech, I planned to just pinch myself and grit my teeth when I came to that part.

Just before I left the hotel room to hit the convention stage, on the evening of September 3, I noticed that Trig needed changing. I also noticed that we had run out of diapers. After a frantic, hotel-wide search, someone found a stack, and the last thing I did before heading down to give the biggest speech of my life was to change the baby.

It's the kind of thing that keeps you grounded.

———

The excitement at the convention center was overwhelming. The noise was deafening—ten times what it had been in Ohio. I knew we'd have a great time that night.

When it quieted enough so that I could speak, I began.

"I am honored to be considered for the nomination for vice president of the United States. I accept the call to help our nominee for president to serve and defend America. I accept the challenge of a tough fight in this election against confident opponents at a crucial hour for our country. And I accept the privilege of serving with a man who has come through much harder missions . . . and met far graver challenges and knows how tough fights are won—the next president of the United States, John S. McCain!"

I reminded Americans that it hadn't been so long ago that the polls and pundits had written John off. He had been all but out of the primary race. But, I said, "They overlooked the caliber of the man himself—the determination, resolve, and sheer guts of Senator John McCain . . . Our nominee for president is a true profile in courage, and people like that are hard to come by."

I reminded America of John's military heroism, something he'd been reticent to talk about. Then I mentioned how proud I was of *all* our military men and women—the Armed Forces were a unifying and equalizing entity in America, and we had a son and a nephew following in the tradition of millions of military families.

"I'm just one of many moms who'll say an extra prayer each night for our sons and daughters going into harm's way."

When a wild round of applause for the U.S. military died down, I introduced Todd and the rest of our family, making special mention of Trig and all children with special needs who inspire a special love.

"To the families of special-needs children all across this country, I have a message: For years, you sought to make America a more welcoming place for your sons and daughters. I pledge to you that if we are elected, you will have a friend and advocate in the White House."

I wasn't too far into the speech when I realized technology had failed me. The upcoming lines of the speech were no longer appearing on the teleprompter. I knew the speech well enough that I didn't need it, which was a good thing, since the machine didn't sync up for the remainder of my time onstage.

"Long ago," I continued, "a young farmer and haberdasher from Missouri followed an unlikely path to the vice presidency. A writer observed: 'We grow good people in our small towns, with honesty, sincerity, and dignity.'

"I know just the kind of people that writer had in mind when he praised Harry Truman. I grew up with those people. They are the ones who do some of the hardest work in America, who grow our food, run our factories, and fight our wars. They love their country, in good times and bad, and they're always proud of America."

Applause boomed, and a chant broke out: "U.S.A.! U.S.A.! U.S.A.!"

I could feel the energy, electricity snapping in the air.

"Before I became governor of the great state of Alaska, I was mayor of my hometown. And since our opponents in this presidential election seem to look down on that experience, let me explain to them what the job involves. . . . I guess a small-town mayor is sort of like a 'community organizer,' except that you have actual responsibilities."

Applause erupted again, a shout-out to independent-minded Americans who didn't look to government for all the answers. I was so proud at that moment because I knew that even though the other ticket had looked down on my small-town mayor creds, the convention delegates clearly knew that national leaders are nurtured in the cradle of local service. There are only a few hundred people in Congress making "big" decisions, but tens of thousands of hardworking mayors and council members and commissioners and volunteers who keep this nation functioning every day.

They, not Congress, keep the roads paved and the sewers running and the schools open and the police force trained and firefighters equipped. Small-town involvement isn't something to be scorned; it's something to be upheld as the foundation of what makes this country great. Even so, an individual's commitment to his or her own business and family—*that* is significantly more important than any community leadership role.

A little later in the speech, I spotted a group of hockey jersey–clad delegates, waving their banners and cheering. I pointed to them, ad-libbing since the teleprompter wasn't working right anyway.

"I love those hockey moms!" I said.

They screamed and jumped as only hockey moms can. "You know, they say, what is the difference between a hockey mom and a pit bull? . . . lipstick!" I wasn't nervous. By God's grace I was having a ball, and that broken teleprompter was pretty liberating. Still, after the laughter died down, I got back on script. I discussed my record: fighting the oil company monopoly, working for energy independence, and my work on the Alaska natural gas pipeline.

Chants broke out in the crowd: "Drill, baby, drill! Drill, baby, drill!"

A bit later, I launched into a part of the speech that, since Barack Obama's election, has proved Matthew Scully prescient:

". . . when the cloud of rhetoric has passed . . . when the roar of the crowd fades away . . . when the stadium lights go out and those Styrofoam Greek columns are hauled back to some studio lot—what exactly is our opponent's plan? What does he actually seek to accomplish, after he's done turning back the waters and healing the planet?

"The answer is to make government bigger . . . take more of your money . . . give you more orders from Washington . . . and to reduce the strength of America in a dangerous world.

America needs more energy . . . our opponent is against producing it.

"And let me be specific, the Democratic nominee for president supports plans to raise income taxes . . . raise payroll taxes . . . raise investment income taxes . . . raise the death tax . . . raise business taxes . . . and increase the tax burden on the American people by hundreds of billions of dollars."

I was nearly finished. But now I was getting to the Tom Moe part. I steeled myself and began by talking about the journey of John McCain, "an upright and honorable man, the kind of fellow whose name you will find on war memorials in small towns across this great country, only he was among those who came home. To the most powerful office on Earth, he would bring the compassion that comes from having once been powerless, the wisdom that comes even to the captives by the grace of God . . ."

The crowd erupted again with cheers and applause for our candidate.

". . . the special confidence of those who have seen evil and have seen how evil is overcome."

My throat tightened. Thankfully, I was able to pause as more applause thundered through the hall, honoring America's veterans. It gave me time to brace myself and plunge in, though my throat closed even tighter.

"A fellow—fellow prisoner of war, a man named Tom Moe of Lancaster, Ohio . . ."

Now the applause was deafening and extended, and there was a commotion right in front of me in the first row. A group of people were pointing to a handsome older man, alternately clapping and patting him on the back. The distinguished gentleman had tears in his eyes that I could barely see through my own. His friends were ecstatic and I could make out what they were saying: "He's here! This is Tom Moe!"

This brave man had suffered vicious torture at the hands of the North Vietnamese. Like John, he had been locked in tiny cells for five years with rats, bugs, excrement, brokenness, and constant pain. I knew it would be only by the grace of God that I would make it through the next part of our message because words in a speech don't do our veterans justice.

"Tom Moe recalls looking through a pinhole in his cell door as Lieutenant Commander John McCain was led down the hallway by the guards day after day," I continued. "And the story is told, when McCain shuffled back from the torturous interrogation, he would turn toward Moe's door and he'd flash a grin and thumbs-up, as if to say, 'We're going to pull through this.' My fellow Americans, that is the kind of man America needs to see us through the next four years!"

Seeing Tom Moe standing there made our message about national greatness so real. This wasn't campaign hype. Here was an authentic American hero standing right in front of me. I'd had no idea he was going to be there. It was an honor to be in his presence. I'm not sure how the next lines flowed because I was so overwhelmed with American pride that the rest of the speech was a blur.

I've never seen a replay of that night, but I remember that as soon as I wrapped up the speech, I looked around for Todd and the kids to join me onstage. They had argued over who would get to carry Trig. It was a good thing Piper lost the argument and had her hands free so she could pump her fist in the air and wave hello, again, to the world.

Immediately after the speech, John surprised everyone by joining us onstage and embracing my family. I was so proud of them. The kids looked great—even in a bunch of borrowed clothes.

The next night, John McCain accepted the nomination. My family and I walked with John's mom, the precious and resilient

Mrs. Roberta McCain, to join him onstage. As I headed down the stairs toward the stage area my high-heel shoe fell off! *Great,* I thought, figuring the media caught my first stumble! But if they did, they didn't broadcast it around the world, bless their hearts.

7

During the convention, yet another story started bubbling in the press. It was about the state troopers and Walt Monegan. The story would eventually achieve proper-noun status: Troopergate, or as those who knew the facts called it: Tasergate. I was heartened to see that by September 4, the last day of the convention, *Investor's Business Daily* had already seen the handwriting on the wall. An un-bylined op-ed on the editorial page said this:

> Palin's political enemies have a stink bomb set to go off late in October, just before the election. That's when voters will see fruits of a legislative investigation into the charge that the governor fired Alaska's Public Safety Commissioner Walter Monegan because he wouldn't get rid of Mike Wooten, a state trooper and Palin's ex-brother-in-law.
>
> We can see where this is headed. Palin will be found to have done nothing illegal in firing Monegan, since public safety commissioners serve at the governor's pleasure. But the media will frame this case in vague but sinister terms: Think "abuse of power." It will also bury the back story that explains why Palin was so concerned.

The op-ed then laid out the key facts: the trooper's marriages and divorces (by this time, there were four); his threat that my father "would eat a f***ing lead bullet" if he hired a lawyer for Molly; his tasering my nephew; and other unethical and illegal behavior, including hunting wild game illegally—a big deal in Alaska, where people ethically harvest game to eat. *IBD* also noted the finding of Alaska State Trooper Director Colonel Julia Grimes that the trooper's actions demonstrated "a serious and concentrated pattern of unacceptable and at times, illegal activity occurring over a lengthy period, which establishes a course of conduct totally at odds with the ethics of our profession." She also warned him, *IBD* noted, that he would be fired if he didn't shape up.

> Now ask yourself this: If you were Sarah Palin and had such a revealing look at Wooten, would you have wanted him on the force? Palin was acting as any concerned citizen should after a close encounter with an unfit cop. If there's abuse of power in this story, it lies on the side of bureaucrats and unions protecting officers whose behavior makes them a danger to the public.

In 444 words, the *IBD* editorial board had explained the essence and the eventual outcome of a case on which the State of Alaska would spend half a million taxpayer dollars and the mainstream media would spill untold gallons of ink. It would have saved everyone a lot of time if they'd just read *IBD* and moved on. But unfortunately, no election cycle is complete without the throbbing drumbeat of scandal to distract voters from the issues—even if politicos have to gin one up.

———

As we hit the road, three of the campaign staffers I'd met during convention week would become friends. Jason Recher, a special assistant to President Bush, took leave from the White House and joined us a couple of days in. A dyed-in-the-wool New Englander from an Irish Catholic family, Jason, twenty-nine, had two choices while growing up in New Hampshire: sports or politics. He chose politics, but I didn't hold that against him. He had shined as a volunteer during the 2000 primary and become a permanent member of the Bush team at age nineteen. Jason was a calming presence on the trail and was very kind to our kids.

Jeannie Etchart, one of the trip coordinators, was a beautiful, soft-spoken young lady from Minnesota. We wore the same size clothes, and as the weeks went on she would keep loaning me her black Theory pants that she'd bought four years earlier. I kept telling her to find a duplicate pair on the Internet and I would order them for her because I was wearing hers out. My daughters instantly loved Jeannie's sense of style and enjoyed hanging out with her and another of the assistants, Bexie Nobles.

A quiet country gal from Texas, Bexie was tireless and great at anticipating what we'd need next on the trail. I don't think she *ever* slept. It was pretty comical the first time I met her. I walked into the Hilton suite, and there was this young woman I'd never seen before kneeling on the floor packing my suitcase. She looked up and smiled.

"Hi, my name is Bexie," she said in her Texas twang as she tucked in a stack of my T-shirts. "I'll be assisting you, and I'll be doin' this from now on."

"Hi!" I said. "It's Betsy?"

"No . . . but you can *call* me Betsy."

She was that accommodating.

Jason, Jeannie, and Bexie were there at one of our first campaign stops after the convention, a stop I'll never forget. It was at a rally in Cedar Rapids, Iowa. The town was a slice of Americana, with its quaint town square with mom-and-pop stores; red, white, and blue bunting; moms and dads; kids in strollers; seniors; and people of every color. I was astonished at the number of people who had come out. These people were there when they could have been somewhere else; they were there because they wanted to be involved.

Maybe it seems kind of sentimentally patriotic, but the scene stirred in me a great appreciation for the American system of democracy that stretches all the way back to 1776: regular people from all walks of life turning out peacefully to hear which candidates have the best ideas, then going on election day to the courthouse or a local school or a firehouse to cast a ballot. Simply beautiful.

Afterward, in the rope line, I was moving through the crowd, shaking hands and signing posters and hats and shirts, when I suddenly came to a stop. Standing on the other side of the rope were a woman and two teenagers whom I could not miss. The kids had Down syndrome. A boy and a girl.

"Hi, what's your name?" I said to the girl, smiling.

The girl stammered for a minute and finally managed to say, "Sarah."

"Sarah!" I said. "That's my name, too! It's so great to meet you, and we have the same name. Isn't that amazing?"

Then I turned to the boy, and my heart just melted. Trig's face flashed into my mind, and I thought, *This could be my son fifteen years from now.*

By then, Trig was going on five months old and we were still learning the ropes of having a child with Down syndrome. We were so enjoying this little guy with his just-happy-to-be-here demeanor and his silly smiles, and watching him get stronger, chubbier, and more fun every day, just like any other baby. Still, we were curious about what was ahead. We were managing well with him as a baby, but what about a toddler? As a teenager?

I reached across the rope and laid my hand against the boy's face. "Let me look at you," I said. "I want to get a good look at how beautiful my Trig is going to grow up to be."

That was a significant turning point for me, personally. At that moment, I realized in awe that these precious ones *are* all brothers and sisters. Before Trig was born, I didn't know what to expect and we had a natural uncertainty about perceived "imperfection." There on the rope line in Cedar Rapids, I realized that my Trig is part of a large and very special community. And look how this mom was making it work with these two precious teenagers! Look how she cared so much to bring them out to a crowded, hectic, but fun rally and give them what might be a once-in-a-lifetime experience, a presidential campaign event in their own hometown. And I just knew there was no need to fear anymore. At this rowdy rally in Iowa my world became a more peaceful place. Todd was right: everything was going to be all right.

As it turned out, the number of special needs kids and adults who began showing up at events along the trail was spectacular. It was one of the absolute best parts of the campaign. I heard from experienced staffers that organizers would typically need maybe a sign language interpreter and a handicapped area large enough to accommodate a few dozen wheelchairs. But it seemed that at all our stops, the number of wheelchairs multiplied, as did the number of kids and adults with various challenges. At a rally in Fairfax, Virginia, I remember looking about and seeing scores of wheelchairs. In the middle of my speech it started pouring rain. Within five minutes, I looked like a wet dog and my makeup was running off my face. I wanted to keep going and finish because I didn't want to disappoint all those people who had been waiting for hours to hear our ticket's message. Even more, I was inspired to see that not one of the people in wheelchairs made a move to leave.

I thought, *This is inspiration!*

On rope lines across the country, I remember making eye contact with special needs families and caretakers. This connection was a kind of mutual acknowledgment that said, Yes! Their lives are precious! They're worthy! And now we're going to let America know that there's no need to be afraid or hesitant. Instead, let's work together to make this world a more welcoming place for everyone with special needs.

I remember another rally down in Pensacola, Florida. Up in the stands, I spotted a group of fifteen kids with Down syndrome wearing shirts that said, WE LOVE TRIG! and TRIG IN THE WHITE HOUSE! I thought, *Wow!* How great that these precious people have someone associated with a national campaign that they can identify with. I asked an aide to see if someone could go get that group and bring them down so we could have our picture taken together.

Down syndrome comes in a range of severities. Some people with Downs can live self-sufficient lives. Others may be totally dependent. They spend their lives *knowing* they are different from other people. So it blessed me in ways I can't even describe to be able to help bring them from the fringe into the bright spotlight that most often seems reserved only for the privileged.

It was after meeting all these amazing people that Todd and I proudly displayed the bumper sticker a very cool group from Arizona sent us, which read, MY KID HAS MORE CHROMOSOMES THAN YOUR KID!

8

John was a maverick, and he said he had picked me because in many ways I'm wired the same. So early in the campaign, I called Bob Lester and Mark Colavecchio, talk radio hosts on KWHL in Anchorage. We used to call each other often, along with another great host, Eddie Burke, on a rival station, KBYR—when I had some state news to announce or when they had a hot topic to bounce around on their shows.

I had always had a fine relationship with the state and local media. They could call me up and within five minutes be up in my office to talk about any topic. Many reporters had my personal cell phone number, and I had theirs. That's the way we operated. It helped us govern.

So, as the campaign bus barreled down a freeway somewhere in the middle of America, I punched up KWHL on speed dial.

"Hey, Bob, it's Sarah!"

"Governor!" Bob said. "Good to hear from you! Finally!"

"Hey, I wanted to touch base, and I've got a true American hero sitting right here with me, and you should feel honored to hear him say hello. I'm going to put him on the line so he can say hi to Alaska."

So I handed John the phone, and he was very funny and gracious and engaged in an upbeat, informative interview with KWHL and a whole lot of constituents.

Afterward, one of the campaign higher-ups told our staff, "Don't ever let her do that again."

Oops.

It was a treat for Alaskans to hear from their governor's friend, the top of the GOP ticket, but I suppose my handing John the phone with a radio host on the other end could be considered breaking their proper protocol. Since people did that to me all through my time in public office, it didn't seem particularly improper, especially for a man whose campaign bus was called the "Straight Talk Express." That's what John was known for—giving the press incredible access and allowing them to ask him any question at any time.

I suspect it wasn't that big a deal to John at all. But the lectures from on high began about my talking to the media, especially Alaska media. I told the campaign staff that part of my job as governor would be keeping in touch with my constituents via local media contacts.

"Alaska has three electoral votes," Schmidt told me. "You don't need to contact the Alaska media again."

I would learn that this was typical of Schmidt. This was business, and I respected that aspect of his personality. Not a lot of camaraderie or rah-rah optimism. And that describes most others in the professional political caste. I was focused on meeting constituents every minute of the day and conducting State of Alaska business, so I didn't pay much attention to what the paid operatives were doing and orchestrating. But I did notice that there was a jaded aura about some of them. Funny things that even Piper commented on—such as tumbling out of the bus in a pack, lighting cigarettes as they went so it looked like a walking smoke cloud with legs.

My Alaska spokeswoman, Meghan Stapleton, kept pushing for official campaign permission to grant interviews to the reporters I'd been talking to at least weekly for years. Recognized for her intelligence, hard work, and political acumen, Meg had a huge following from her days on the air in Anchorage, and I had never met anyone like her. She had worked in my governor's office, so she knew my top priority was continuing to communicate with my constituents even during the national campaign.

She noted that an Alaska station was willing to spend whatever it took on a trip to Minnesota so a local reporter could report on the VP candidacy. Meg kept trying to negotiate with the campaign staff. She pleaded with headquarters to let me answer just *three questions* for the guy: How do you feel? What is it like? What's your message to Alaskans? Not only was this guy a decent person whom we knew well, but these were simple, softball, *scripted* questions. It was tough for her, even as my Alaska spokesperson, to get in touch with the VP of the campaign. But when we finally connected, the answer came back from headquarters: No. Not allowed. Too dangerous. The national media might pick up the interview.

Well, exactly, we thought. Wasn't that okay? Meg and I agreed that the better strategy would be to *let* the national media pick up information about me from journalists who knew me and had been reporting on me for years. Maybe that would help counter the negative spin of so many other stories.

It was not to be. As the weeks wore on, Meg kept reaching out to the McCain people, but she couldn't get anywhere close. Ultimately, this hurt the campaign to a degree the "experts" could never grasp. By that time people from across the country were busily inventing reasons to label us "unethical." And slowly but surely, the Alaska press decided that I was ignoring them and maybe thinking I'd grown too big for my britches. Back in Wasilla, my friend Kristan Cole spoke often on my behalf, hosting many reporters in her home during my time on the trail. Her job would have been a lot easier if headquarters had embraced the idea of local reporters getting to cover their governor's efforts.

I remember one day walking into an event to speak with other governors from across the country. They were standing behind me, cheering—"This is good! We've got a fellow governor who's

out there fighting for the little guy on the national ticket." Afterward, I walked into a press availability and saw that Anchorage
reporter. He'd made it Outside to track us down!

I thought, *Alaska is finally here! Right on!*

I moved to go speak with him, but a campaign handler grabbed
my elbow and said, "No, no, no . . . this way." A few minutes later
on my way out of the building, I saw the same reporter and photographer back behind a rope line.

He yelled out "Alaska!" But as I tried to holler back, different
pairs of hands hustled me into the campaign's Suburban. It was
not a respectful thing to do. I had turned my back on our own
local press. Right then and there, I knew it wasn't going to be
good.

It wasn't. In a televised report about the campaign, that reporter wrapped it up this way: "And the Sarah Palin we once
knew, is gone."

I wasn't. But I couldn't blame him for thinking so.

———

By the third week in September, a "Free Sarah" campaign was
under way and the press at large was growing increasingly
critical of the McCain camp's decision to keep me, my family
and friends back home, and my governor's staff all bottled up.
Meanwhile, the question of which news outlet would land the
first interview was a big deal, as it always is with a major party
candidate.

From the beginning, Nicolle pushed for Katie Couric and
the *CBS Evening News.* The campaign's general strategy involved
coming out with a network anchor, someone they felt had
treated John well on the trail thus far. My suggestion was that
we be consistent with that strategy and start talking to outlets
like FOX and the *Wall Street Journal.* I really didn't have a say in

which press I was going to talk to, but for some reason Nicolle seemed compelled to get me on the Katie bandwagon.

"Katie really likes you," she said to me one day. "She's a working mom and admires you as a working mom. She has teenage daughters like you. She just relates to you," Nicolle said. "Believe me, I know her very well. I've worked with her." Nicolle had left her gig at CBS just a few months earlier to hook up with the McCain campaign. I had to trust her experience, as she had dealt with national politics more than I had. But something always struck me as peculiar about the way she recalled her days in the White House, when she was speaking on behalf of President George W. Bush. She didn't have much to say that was positive about her former boss or the job in general. Whenever I wanted to give a shout-out to the White House's homeland security efforts after 9/11, we were told we couldn't do it. I didn't know if that was Nicolle's call.

Nicolle went on to explain that Katie really needed a career boost. "She just has such low self-esteem," Nicolle said. She added that Katie was going through a tough time. "She just feels she can't trust anybody."

I was thinking, *And this has to do with John McCain's campaign how?*

"Katie wants people to like her," Nicolle said. "She wants *you* to like her."

Hearing all that, I almost started to feel sorry for her. Katie had tried to make a bold move from lively morning gal to serious anchor, but the new assignment wasn't going very well.

"You know what? We'll schedule a segment with her," Nicolle said. "If it doesn't go well, if there's no chemistry, we won't do any others."

Meanwhile, the media blackout continued. It got so bad that a couple of times I had a friend in Anchorage track down phone numbers for me, and then I snuck in calls to folks like Rush Limbaugh, Laura Ingraham, Sean Hannity, and someone I thought was Larry Kudlow but turned out to be Neil Cavuto's producer. I had a friend call Bill O'Reilly after I was inundated with supporters in Alaska asking why the campaign was "ignoring" his on-air requests for a McCain campaign interview. I had another friend scrambling to find Mark Levin's number. Aboard the campaign plane I was within twenty-five feet of reporters for hours on end. Headquarters' strategy was that I should not go to the back of the aircraft and talk to the press. At first this was subtle, but as the campaign wore on, Tracey or Tucker would call headquarters to request permission, and someone in D.C. would respond, "No! Absolutely not—block her if she tries to go back."

All of us admired Tracey, who was an endearing multitasker. She was always so busy thinking about her next strategic move that mundane details—such as luggage, laptops, her purse—fell in her wake.

One day on the trail, she and I were walking toward the campaign plane with the ever-present camera crews filming us as we went. We had been told that the protocol is that the candidate walks up the stairs alone, turns and waves, then boards the plane. Well, that day as Tracey walked across the tarmac with me, we were deeply engrossed in conversation, laughing as we went. We both just sort of forgot the protocol and she walked up the stairs with me. Then when I turned to wave, she did, too.

When Tracey got inside the plane, she was absolutely mortified. "Omigosh! I can't believe I just did that!"

I thought it was very human and hysterically funny, and I honestly didn't even notice it until headquarters told us we screwed up. That was just Tracey, this kind of fun, distracted brainiac. She did her best to try to manage the communications nightmare that became our half of the ticket, but her hands were tied by others higher up.

In my quest to connect with reporters, I did find that I had a tiny little press ambassador, and her name was Piper Palin. The reporters loved her, and whenever they would pass her seat on the plane, they'd ask how she was doing. At first she was a little shy, but as days passed and reporters' friendly faces grew more familiar, she started asking if she could go back and visit with them.

One day, Jason took an orange and wrote on it, "Hi, How are you? From Piper Palin." Then he rolled it down the aisle to where the press was sitting. One of the reporters picked it up, inked a reply on the orange, and rolled it back: "Come visit us! Please!"

Jason showed it to me, and I said, "Of course!"

So Piper and Willow both went back with Tracey and introduced themselves. After that, it became a bit of a routine that the kids would go back and chitchat with the press. From where I was sitting, it seemed like a win-win. The kids enjoyed getting to know new people, and the reporters got to be around at least two smiling, unguarded human beings who weren't stressed out and suspicious all the time. Sometime early in the campaign, Piper must have asked someone if they could print up special stickers with hearts on them. They did, and then whenever we'd get a new batch of reporters on the plane, she would go back and pass out stickers that said, "Vote for Piper's Mom."

─────

In New England and other parts of America, fall foliage burns in the colors of fire, but autumn in Alaska shimmers in white and gold. By mid-September, the birch leaves have turned from bright green to rich yellows and golds, and the mountaintops are powdered with "termination dust," the first snows that signal summer's end. The alpenglow is pinker on the mountains late in the evening, casting the prettiest light.

September 11, 2008, was one of those gorgeous fall days in Fairbanks, the home of Fort Wainwright. The Stryker Brigade's 3,500-soldier unit was set to deploy to Iraq, and I had committed to keynoting the deployment ceremony long before being tapped as the GOP's vice presidential candidate. In fact, I knew I would speak at the event even before I found out that my son would be one of the soldiers going to war with the brigade. Still, in the days after the convention, the campaign questioned my commitment to speak there.

"It could be perceived as 'political,'" Tucker said.

"Really?" I said. "I think it would actually *be* political to cancel on the Army and be off somewhere politicking instead of fulfilling my promise."

As the campaign unfolded, Tucker stuck to me like gum on a shoe. Nice guy. I'd see him in the hotel in the morning. Throughout the day, he'd usher me from building to SUV to building to SUV. I'd see him before each event, and afterward he'd be waiting for me on the campaign bus steps with an indulgent smile that said, "Come over here and let me tell you what you did wrong, bless your heart."

I assured Tucker and the rest of the campaign folks that I knew how to explain in my opening remarks that I was speaking as Alaska's governor and not as a vice presidential candidate. I also pointed out that as governor, I routinely attended deployment exercises and welcome-home ceremonies, as well as far too many memorials for fallen troops. The whole country, and especially Alaskans, knew that I firmly supported our military.

Besides all that, there was nothing in the world that could keep me from saying good-bye to my son. The campaign finally agreed to honor my committment and we all flew to Alaska.

On the day of the ceremony, I sat on the field in the shade of an awning with the military top brass, waiting for my turn to speak. It was chilly because once summer gives way to fall in Fairbanks, winter chases the mild temperatures out fast. I longed to sit out in the last remnants of warm sunshine with the military families who had gathered to honor their deploying spouses, sons, and daughters.

As usual, I had to swallow hard when the military band played, the honor guard presented the colors on the tarmac, and our troops marched by in formation. I scanned the thousands in uniform, hoping to spot Track, but I couldn't pick him out.

Once again, I marveled out loud, "They sure do look alike." And as before, an officer smiled and whispered, "That's the point!"

What a strangely incongruous but perfectly appropriate place for my son to be at this moment in his life—no special attention, completely blended in with the crowd, just one of many who had volunteered to serve his country. Sharp, disciplined, uniformed, Track was incognito—just as he wanted to be.

In conversations leading up to the ceremony, he had emphasized that he did not want to be singled out, especially at his deployment, something I had known before he said it.

"And whatever you do, Mom, don't say 'Hooah,' " he told me on the phone one day. He meant that I shouldn't embarrass him by trying to imitate the Army's trademark rally cry.

"I *have* to say it! It's a tradition!"

"But you never say it right."

Now, sitting under the awning, I leaned over to my escort again. "It's okay if I say 'Hooah' at the end, right?"

"Oh, yeah, you gotta say it!" Colonel Daly said. "They'll love it!"

"So how do *you* pronounce it?"

"*Hoo*-ah."

"*Hoo*-ah. Okay. Got it." Thinking about Track's warning, I still wasn't sure if I was going to say it, but now I had the confirmed pronunciation in my back pocket, just in case.

Todd and the kids, along with our extended family, had traveled to Fairbanks for the ceremony and planned to hook up with Track afterward for see-you-soon hugs and pictures. But I had to content myself with seeing them all from a distance. It was a weird feeling: A couple of weeks before, I could have—and would have—made a special point of gathering with my own. But now I felt like a bit of a captive, pulled away from my loved ones in favor of a "higher priority," as though in the final analysis there is any such thing.

As the ceremony unfolded, I mentally rehearsed my speech. The campaign was worried that the press would spin or misinterpret it, so I was asked to submit my talking points to headquarters in advance. Throughout the campaign, the Schmidt-Wallace tag team would continually invoke the all-powerful "headquarters," a mysterious, faraway entity whose exact identity and location were never fully explained. By the end of the campaign, my VP teammates and I would look at each other and say, "Who *is* headquarters?"

Thankfully, headquarters was content with the message I was determined to convey. I took the podium of burnished oak and looked out at the thousands of young Americans who had all volunteered to put their lives on the line in defense of our freedoms. I praised their bravery, commitment, and sacrifice. I couldn't say enough about them and our country. I asked for God's hand of protection over them.

And then, at the end, I just couldn't help myself. I shouted out the forbidden word: "*Hoo*-ah!"

I took one last look at the Stryker Brigade and grinned, knowing that somewhere amid the troops standing stock still in perfect formation, there was one soldier rolling his eyes.

9

On September 17, John and I held a joint town hall session in Michigan at the Grand Rapids Community College Ford Field-house. John was in his element, with such an easy way of connecting with a Main Street audience. He was witty, charming, and in complete command of the issues. I was excited to participate in this format for the first time during the national campaign. Town hall meetings are my comfort zone, too, and were one of the keys to my administration's success on energy issues in Alaska: just get out and talk to the people. I was eager for more of them, hoping to campaign in ways my experience had shown me was most effective, instead of the orchestrated events the campaign operatives wanted to put us through.

I wound up with a personal connection in Grand Rapids: the Holmes family—the gracious and patient hosts whom Track had stayed with while playing hockey in Michigan during the 2006 season. It was a chance to give them a hug and tell them how much Todd and I appreciated their kindness to our son. On a larger scale, I felt the Holmes family represented the kind of people our ticket could resonate with in a state filled with hard-working, patriotic Americans, hockey moms, union members, and veterans. Obama was leading by double digits there, but the Grand Rapids meeting gave me hope that we could bounce back and turn the state around. I got to tell Michigan, "Thank you for taking care of my son—now he's taking care of *you!*"

Todd and I were sitting in a Michigan hotel room where the campaign staffers were enjoying an emotional lift from the town hall meeting, when Schmidt, flanked by security personnel, walked in grim-faced and announced he had something important to discuss. I had just seen on TV a sickening report that my personal e-mails had been hacked into, and I figured that's what he wanted to talk about. A cold hand squeezed my heart, though, as I wondered if something else had happened with the kids back in Alaska. Bristol had been reporting strange vehicles creeping up and down our long gravel driveway. Secret Service agents had just stopped a local reporter-photographer team sneaking through the bushes toward our house. Reporters had taken to camping out near our family members' homes. Had one of them crossed the line between reporting and invading privacy?

That was partially right. "Your personal e-mails have been hacked," Schmidt confirmed. "The hacker is broadcasting your personal e-mails on the Internet right now. And photos, too." And it wasn't just Todd's and my e-mails—it was the kids', too. And personal contact information. This came on the heels of my Social Security number and other private information being broadcast.

It was another fine how-do-you-do: *Hi, Governor, welcome to the blood sport known as presidential politics.*

The TV was on in the background. We could see on a news channel the contents of my private correspondence scrolling across the screen. The network showed the "To" and "From" fields, thus making my family's and friends' private e-mail addresses visible to the world. Recognizing one of the names that flashed in front of me, I was horrified to realize that millions of people could read my personal messages, including the thoughts of a friend who had written of her heartbreak over her pending divorce.

My mind raced to other messages I knew were stored in one of my e-mail accounts: Bristol and I discussing her pregnancy. Todd and I discussing Trig's medical challenges. My farewell prayer and encouragement before Track's deployment. Me telling Willow that no, she absolutely could *not* get a ride home with a high school boy. All kinds of sensitive discussions, including political ones, the kind of unguarded talk you have only with the people who are closest to you and don't take what you say out of context. Obviously our discussions weren't meant for public display. But because I had no home-based headquarters my e-mails *were* my campaign headquarters.

As I watched message after message float across the screen, I thought, *What kind of creep would break into a person's files, steal them, read them, then give them to the press to broadcast all over the world in order to influence a presidential campaign? And what kind of responsible press outfit would broadcast stolen private correspondence?*

Standing beside Schmidt was Tony Ball, a patient soul wrapped in a tough, muscle-bound Secret Service agent body. Even as I was staring at the screen, he was already on the phone, working with the FBI. It didn't take long for the feds to identify the source: a college student who was the son of a Democrat Tennessee state legislator. The excuses made for this invasion of privacy were disgusting and nonsensical. "Sarah Palin is a public figure," the spin went. "She should expect this kind of thing, and if she's worried about it, what is she trying to hide?" We had to cancel all our e-mail accounts. My friends' and families' personal and business accounts had to be changed too, as they'd all been compromised. And once again, the campaign confiscated the kids' phones.

The incident was, to me, the most disruptive and discouraging of the campaign. It created paralysis in my administration because it cut off an easily accessible form of communication between me and my Alaska staff. Worse, I could no longer contact my kids, even Track, who would shortly leave for Iraq. Also, thanks to the hacker's disclosing all of our contact information, the kids began receiving vulgar e-mail threats and phone calls, which scared me for all of them. It was all sickening.

The incident put tremendous stress on the campaign. Schmidt and others acted as though they believed scattered reports that my hacked e-mail contained incriminating messages that would "destroy the McCain campaign." There were no such messages, of course, but the episode ratcheted up paranoia and distrust inside the campaign. The hacker later admitted he was looking for something damaging. It reminded many of us of a modern-day break-in of campaign headquarters.

―――

The nationwide momentum that was building didn't become clear to me until we stopped at The Villages, near Lady Lake, Florida, one of the largest retirement communities in the United States. The Villages is like a city unto itself, with restaurants, lakes, and shopping, and golf courses. The residents there are very politically aware and active, so the community has become a must-stop stomping ground for politicians in the Sunshine State—especially for the GOP. Florida seniors tend to vote Republican.

The place is also famous for golf carts. Instead of getting around in cars, most residents toodle around in carts, decorated and jacked up to fit the owner's personality. My family and I had never seen anything like this and thought it was the Florida version of Alaskans congregating with their boats or snowmachines.

The morning of our event, Jason and Doug McMarlin, the campaign's advance guy in Florida, drove to the venue to take a quick look at the setup.

"How many people do you think we'll get?" Jason asked.

"Probably ten or twelve thousand."

Jason was satisfied. That was a great number for a vice presidential candidate.

A few hours later, he joined us on the bus as the whole crew headed down to The Villages for the rally. About an hour and a half before the event, Jason called Doug again. "How many people do we have now?"

Jason shared the number with rest of us: fifteen thousand.

Twenty minutes later, he called Doug again. "Wow," I heard him say.

The crowd had doubled to thirty thousand.

"Wow," I said myself. Something big was happening.

When the bus reached the edge of the retirement community, all I could see were golf carts. It seemed like miles and miles of them lined up along the side of the road. As we drove on, I could see and feel momentum building, energy radiating from the growing crowd of patriotic Americans who had gathered because they wanted to be involved. As we got closer to the venue, the strings of golf carts became a sea of golf carts, double- and triple-parked, bumper to bumper on the sidewalks, security teams with flags waving long chains of carts into makeshift parking areas.

When I stepped off the bus at a Villages community center, humidity dropped over me like a hot, wet blanket. We trailed Jason into the community center, where he found Doug.

"How many people now?" Jason said.

Doug, an experienced campaign advance man, shook his head in wonder. "Fire marshal's saying fifty to sixty thousand people."

Jason's jaw dropped and his eyes grew wide, and I was a little surprised myself. Obama had drawn a couple of similar-sized crowds to this point, but the McCain campaign had previously been averaging only a few thousand people. This was a rock concert–sized crowd. Some football stadiums didn't hold that many people. What was going on?

The advance team had set up a walkway that led from the center's door out to the stage. Jason opened the door to take a peek, and a huge, overwhelming roar crashed in like an ocean wave. Jason quickly let the door swing shut.

"Wow, this is going to be a blast!" I said. "I can't wait to meet these folks!"

Then Piper chimed in. "I want to say something!" So Jason grabbed a handheld mic to take out onstage.

At go time, he opened the door, and another tidal wave of sound rushed in. I looked out at the sea of people, so large and stunning that I had nothing to compare it to. We walked out, and with all the hand shaking on the way, it took at least ten minutes to make our way to the stage. I had by that time been doing public speaking for going on two decades. But the only time I'd ever seen a crowd this large, even as a spectator, was at a Broncos-Seahawks game in Seattle twenty years before.

When we finally reached the stage, I just wanted a moment to take it all in, so I looked for a momentary savior, and there she was, standing four feet six.

"Piper, do you have something to say to the nice people of Florida?"

She grinned and waved and took the mic, and then she said, with a last-minute flush of shyness, "Thank you for letting us be here!"

That was exactly how I felt.

I gave my speech with my face sliding off in the Sunshine State's humidity and 90-degree heat. Then the kids and I worked the rope line, grinning the entire time. It was overwhelming.

It took us an hour and a half to make our way through all the people. In the campaign's opinion, that was way too long. In one way I understood, because there were a lot of events each day and a schedule to keep. On the other hand, tens of thousands of everyday Americans had waited for hours in steaming tropical heat to share their day with us.

Women shouted out, "My husband's in Iraq!" I knew how they felt.

"I have a special needs granddaughter!" I wanted to hug that grandma.

"I want to stay in business!" A guy in coveralls hollered.

"I skipped school to see you guys!" one kid called out. I playfully scolded him, then gave him a big thumbs-up.

Oil workers, schoolteachers, home builders, homemakers, doctors, truck drivers, waitresses, police officers . . . how could I just blow by? I couldn't, so I didn't. Instead I zigzagged back and forth, shaking hands and signing everything in sight. It drove the Secret Service a little crazy, but I wasn't worried about an assassination attempt on Sarah Palin from Wasilla. I felt the least we could do was spend some time really connecting with voters, promoting John McCain's values and commitment, showing our appreciation for all of them, not just whisking through and dashing off a couple of autographs like Hollywood celebrities on a red carpet. We owed them.

After the rope line, the agents and staffers hustled us onto the bus and it was just incredible to see: as we were driving out, people lined both sides of the street for miles, waving and shouting, holding up U.S. flags and lipstick tubes. Hundreds of golf carts followed the bus, honking their support. The kids were whooping and hollering on the bus because they'd never had so much fun.

I didn't consciously plan to, but we would treat the rope line crowds the same way throughout the campaign. It was not until after the campaign that I heard my spending so much time with the people who came out to see us had irritated the schedulers and made them think we were being "uncooperative." I had hoped they might share my viewpoint, that the voters deserved that connection with the candidates. Throughout the campaign, the people's response at these rallies was incredible. Our rallies continued to number in the tens of thousands. Once, during a bus trip from West Virginia through Ohio, we stopped at an Ohio Wal-Mart to buy diapers and formula for Trig. Nothing scheduled, just a necessary stop. It turned into a rally. Only when we got out of the bus did we learn that a caravan of 150 cars had been following us for six hours, all the way from West

Virginia! We on the B Team just looked at each other, humbled and astonished and ready for more!

10

In selecting the slogan "Country First," the McCain team had hoped to make national security the central theme of the campaign and differentiate itself from what always sounded like the other side's "Blame America First" impulse. This seemed especially important after Michelle Obama's statement during the Democrat primary in February 2008 that she felt proud of her country "for the first time in her adult lifetime." To me that was an incomprehensible statement. The campaign also hoped to position John, a legitimate war hero, as the best candidate to lead a nation currently fighting two wars.

But even with our American troops still dying abroad, by early September the nation's financial meltdown had pushed Iraq and Afghanistan below the fold. The housing market was already in the tank, with the number of foreclosures hitting record highs. Major financial giants had declared bankruptcy earlier in the year, sending shock waves through the markets. Then, on September 7, the feds seized control of the mortgage lenders Fannie Mae and Freddie Mac. A week later, the Wall Street heavyweight Lehman Brothers collapsed. In the same week, news broke that the insurance giant AIG was on the verge of bankruptcy.

John briefly suspended his campaign in order to attend an emergency economic summit in Washington. The VP half of the ticket didn't know the strategy on that one; most of us heard the announcement in the news. There was initially some doubt as to whether the first presidential debate would even go on as scheduled. So we scrambled to make plans either to take John's place at his scheduled events or to travel back to Alaska to catch up on my gubernatorial duties. But it soon became obvious that there were no quick fixes to the economic crash, and the campaign resumed the next day. It was an odd strategic call on someone's part, but we all learned lessons along the trail.

The debate went on as planned, and John did great. The post-game analysis in the media, though, was that the coolheaded Obama had won the night, displaying a firm grasp of the facts, while John, they tried to convince voters, had seemed irritable and condescending. Granted, 90 percent of the newspeople covering the debate were liberal.

Three days later, the House of Representatives rejected a Bush-backed economic bailout plan in a vote in which two-thirds of Republicans voted no. The impression this made on the electorate was not helpful to our cause. Millions of Americans were poised to go bankrupt or lose their savings, and the perception was that Republicans had failed to respond.

On September 24, the day John announced he was setting politics aside to deal with the financial crisis, we were four points ahead in the polls. By September 29, the day of the bailout vote, we had fallen behind. That bracket of time also included my seemingly endless serial chat with the lowest-rated news anchor in network television, CBS's Katie Couric.

As it turned out, ABC's Charles Gibson did the first major in-terview, connecting with us up North while I was back in Alaska to speak at the Army troop deployment ceremony. There we stopped along the Trans-Alaska Pipeline to discuss substantive issues that I dealt with as governor. He didn't seem as interested as I thought he would be.

At one point we jumped out of the van to film in front of the pipeline when a truck full of hunters swung in on their way to a moose camp up the highway. They asked for a picture, and I was delighted. Charlie straightened his collar, but the guys in their hunting gear and camo vests just handed their camera to Charlie and asked him to take snapshots of me standing with them by their truck.

Then we headed to Wasilla, where Charlie wanted to interview me inside my old high school gym. Same thing happened. Some teachers and students stopped us, handed Charlie the camera, and he patiently snapped the pictures of me in Warrior territory. They seemed not to recognize him—or maybe they just figured, hey, he's the media guy, let *him* take the picture. Charlie was a great sport and appeared to take it in stride, but he did seem a bit grumpy during the later segment filmed at my home in Wasilla, where he peered skeptically at me over his bifocals like a high school principal.

As for Katie Couric—where do I begin? If all you know of me comes from that interview, then you don't know me. Needless to say, I have had better interviews. Out of the many, many hours of tape, I had bad moments just like everyone else. I choked on a couple of responses, and in the harried pace of the campaign, I mistakenly let myself become annoyed and frustrated with many of her repetitive, biased questions. What I didn't know was that those few moments would come to define the interviews; they were repeated and mocked so often that everything else has seemingly been forgotten. And that is unfortunate.

The campaign scheduled Katie during that last week in September. The prep was minimal. The team of people who usually hustled information before these types of things wasn't very involved in this one. But I was told this was to be a pretty mellow interview, short and sweet, about balancing motherhood and my life as governor. I was also led to believe this interview would be the only one, but if things went well, we could consider adding more.

The first stop was a segment at a hotel near the United Nations, which then turned into a walk-and-talk in front of the UN itself. It didn't go well. I readily admit I did what no politician should ever do—let her annoyance show. I was anxious to get this interview over with and you could tell, which was my mistake.

Ironically, as all this was going through my head, when the walk-and-talk ended and the cameras clicked off, one of the CBS producers, a nice New Yorker with a big presence and a loud voice, walked up to me and started singing my praises. "You did *great*, Governor, just great! I mean, you just got better and better as you went!"

Then Nicolle walked over. "That was great! Now, for tomorrow what we're going to—"

"There's going to be a 'tomorrow'?" I asked.

"Yeah, there's another segment—you were really good today."

I thought, *Dear Lord, if that's what you call a good interview, then I don't know what a bad one is.*

As I walked away, I glanced back and saw Nicolle and Katie share a friendly hug. Then they posed for pictures.

I couldn't have known it then, but what transpired during the series of interviews and what CBS actually aired were two different breeds of cat. Camera crews shot hours of footage across the U.S.; Katie and her producers decided on which fraction America would see—and let's just say the emphasis was on my worst moments. Editing footage is nothing new, of course; I created video packages when I worked as a sports reporter. But responsible editing means you keep substance and context, and trim out fat. When I saw the final cut, it was clear that CBS had sought out the bad moments, and systematically sliced out material that would accurately convey my message. The sin of omission was glaring.

For example, when John and I sat down with Katie for a segment in Columbus, Ohio, she started with an energy-related question. "Governor Palin, it will take about ten years for domestic drilling to have an impact on consumers," the anchor said. "So isn't the notion of 'drill, baby, drill' a little misleading to people who think this will automatically lower their gas prices and quickly?"

I said, "And it's why we should have started ten years ago tapping into domestic supplies that America is so rich in. Alaska has billions of barrels of oil and hundreds of trillions of cubic feet of clean, green natural gas onshore and offshore. Should have started doing it ten years ago, but better late than never."

That's the part CBS left in. They edited *out* a discussion of the need to wean ourselves off hydrocarbons and a call for America to stop spending billions of dollars on foreign oil when we could be investing it at home. Did Katie think Americans wouldn't be interested to know that I was in favor of alternative energy sources and reducing our carbon footprint? Or that I might be a conservative who was both pro-development *and* pro-environment? Perhaps my answer didn't fit her agenda.

Katie then moved on to ANWR. "Experts say it will take almost twenty years . . . to achieve peak production," she said. "And it would still only cut foreign oil dependency by about two percent and only for a little while . . . so is it really worth . . . the risk?"

I replied that I didn't know which experts those were. But I explained that as the chair of the AOGCC and IOGCC, I knew from the geologists and petroleum engineers with whom I had worked that it could be done a lot quicker. I also pointed out that ANWR is a 2,000-acre plot that's in the midst of 21 million acres. Americans needed to know how unconscionable it is that anti-development radicals use ANWR as their fund-raising poster child. They use bogus Photoshopped pictures showing mountains and waterfalls and lush forests with Bambi prancing to and fro.

That's all fake and these fund-raisers know it. It is an absolutely barren, permanently frozen, remote sliver of land that requires a minimal drilling footprint, and its development parameters are equivalent to the size of L.A.'s airport. But neither Katie's question nor my answer wound up on the air.

I knew the media would distort my responses on social issues. But I thought surely they couldn't distort my economic and energy-related responses, because they would have to stick with the facts. I was mistaken.

Though Katie edited out substantive answers, she dutifully kept in the moments where I wore my annoyance on my sleeve. For instance, when she asked me how living in Alaska informed my foreign policy experience, I began by trying to frame the geographical context. Lower 48ers grow up seeing our state tucked with Hawaii in a little square off the coast of Mexico on the nightly news weather map. So I began by trying to squeeze a geographical primer into a ten-second sound bite, explaining that only a narrow maritime border separates Alaska from Russia, that we're very near the Pacific Rim countries, and that we're bordered by Canada.

But Katie interrupted and I did not complete my answer. I wish now I had stopped her and said, *"Here's the geographical context. Now may I answer your question?"*

There was so much I could and should have said, and I later kicked myself for not doing so. There was much Katie appeared not to know, or care to hear about. For instance, that Alaska's geographic position makes our relations with Pacific Rim countries of great strategic import, and that we're the air crossroads of the world. That Russian bombers often play cat-and-mouse with our Air Force near Alaska's airspace. That I dealt with Canadian officials on a weekly basis and have signed agreements concerning everything from security to salmon fishing, and that NAFTA has significantly affected our economy. That melting polar sea ice has created new trade routes but has also created security threats to North America. That Alaska takes on Japanese and Russian fishing trawlers that want to ravage the ocean floor. That Chinese and Russian energy companies had both sought access to (and possible control of) our natural gas resources. That these and other countries were staking their own resource claims in Arctic waters while the U.S. sat on its hands. And that, yes, you can indeed see Russia from Alaska.

And those were just the foreign policy issues (though issues certainly foreign to most governors). How much more I would have liked to say about Alaska's contribution to the U.S. economy, its potential to help the nation reduce its dependence on foreign energy sources, and the delicate balancing act required to manage and responsibly develop our abundant wildlife resources.

But Katie wasn't interested in discussing these issues. And when I did, she didn't air them. Instead, when I tried to describe frequent Russian incursions by figuratively referring to Vladimir Putin entering our airspace, CBS researched the Russian leader's actual flight plan over the United States and called my statement inaccurate. And when I referenced Alaska's narrow maritime border to describe our close proximity to other nations, CBS reported that the Coast Guard monitored the border and not the governor.

But Katie's purpose—shared by most media types—seemed to be to frame a "gotcha" moment. And it worked. Instead of my scoring points for John McCain, I knew that I had let the team down.

You'd have thought the ordeal would have been over then. Nope, there would be more. The next interview segment would take place backstage immediately after I finished speaking at an inspiring, raucous rally and working a packed rope line. We were over-the-top energized! We were pumped! I was also sweating like crazy and ready for a minute to breathe and drink an icy Diet Dr Pepper. But when I finished with the rope line and Bexie opened the curtain to let me backstage, there was Katie. Again. With microphone in hand.

I tried really hard to smile, but wondered again about a media strategy that involved ignoring objective journalists and continuing with a reporter who clearly had a partisan agenda. In a situation like this, I'd have thought expert political strategists would realize that you don't drown by falling in the water; you drown by staying there. But that's what we did.

Katie began her walk-and-talk. "When it comes to establishing your worldview," she asked with a cock of her head, "I was curious, what newspapers and magazines did you regularly read before you were tapped for this to stay informed and to understand the world?"

Trying to ignore the heavy dose of condescension, I replied matter-of-factly, "I've read most of them, again with a great appreciation for the press."

"What ones specifically, I'm curious . . ."

"All of them. Any of them that have been in front of me all these years."

It wasn't that I didn't want to—or as some have ludicrously suggested, *couldn't*—answer her question; it was that her condescension irritated me. It was as though she had suddenly stumbled on a primitive newcomer from an undiscovered tribe. But I should not have let my irritation show. Doing so was disrespectful to viewers who had tuned in to the interview to decide how to cast their votes.

She asked me a third time, and I told her that I got my news from a variety of sources.

Over the past several months, especially as AGIA news broke, I had been interviewed on energy and security issues by numerous national media outlets, including her hometown newspaper, the *New York Times*, for whom I had also penned an op-ed earlier in the year on another issue. *Had* she *read* those, I wondered?

This interview ended only to immediately give way to another segment, this time on the campaign bus. Nicolle had said we wouldn't spend more time with this crew if things weren't going well, and I knew that moment had long passed. How was this moving our campaign forward?

On the bus, the topic turned to social issues. Katie asked me if I thought it was possible to "pray away gay"—to convert homosexuals to heterosexuality through prayer. *Hmmm*, I thought. *Odd question.* I don't think she really wanted to hear my answer because she interrupted me five times as I tried to give it. *The badgering had begun. This is really annoying me,* I thought. Then she asked me about abortion and the morning-after pill twelve times. *Twelve* different times.

I answered as graciously and as patiently as I could. Each time, I reiterated my pro-life, pro-woman, pro-adoption position. But no matter how many ways I tried to say it, Katie responded by asking her question again in a slightly different way. I began to feel like I was in the movie *Groundhog Day.*

The line of questioning began, of course, with an extreme, horrific example: "If a fifteen-year-old is raped by her father, you believe it should be illegal for her to get an abortion. Why?"

I answered there were good people on both sides of the abortion debate, but that I was unapologetically pro-life, and that I would counsel someone to choose life. I also said that we should build a culture of life in which we help women in difficult situations, encourage adoption, and support foster and adoptive families.

Katie jumped in, "But, ideally, you think it should be illegal . . ."

"If you . . ."

". . . for a girl who was raped or the victim of incest to get an abortion?"

I answered again: I would personally counsel such a girl to choose life, despite these horrific circumstances, but I absolutely didn't think anyone should end up in jail for having an abortion. Katie included that but didn't include another important part of my answer: that we should support women in these difficult circumstances and give them the resources necessary to give their children life. And that the real extremism came from those who supported partial-birth abortion, those who didn't believe parents should have a say in whether their minor daughters underwent abortions, and those, like Barack Obama, who opposed laws that would protect babies born alive after botched abortions.

But that wasn't enough. Katie asked it again. And again. And again. I had been out of journalism for a long time, and it was pretty obvious the rules had changed. I felt sick about the depths to which some in the press had apparently sunk, not because it was unfair to me and John, but because it was unfair to the American electorate.

Afterward, a staffer noted that Katie had been much more forgiving during an interview with Joe Biden around the same time, not even asking a follow-up question when Biden let loose with a real clunker: "When the stock market crashed, Franklin D. Roosevelt got on the television and didn't just talk about, you know, the princes of greed. He said, 'Look, here's what happened.'"

Of course, FDR wasn't president in 1929 and television had barely been invented. There were no White House broadcasts in those days. But Katie never pointed out these glaring historical errors. Instead, the sound bite aired as a factual statement and was used to denounce Bush's handling of the economy.

Still, my biggest disappointment wasn't the badgering, or even the selective editing. It was that the interviews ended up wasting time. There were any number of productive things I could have been doing instead: meeting with constituents, greeting the thousands of good Americans who waited in sweltering lines and stuffy hangars to hear from us, or speaking with the many good reporters who just wanted to do their jobs.

Later a public remark of Katie's came to my attention that told me everything I needed to know—and the campaign should have known. The occasion was a National Press Club event where she spoke to fellow journalists about the patriotic atmosphere following the 9/11 attacks. "The whole culture of wearing flags on our lapel and saying 'we' when referring to the United States and, even the 'shock and awe' of the initial stages, it was just too jubilant and a little uncomfortable," she said.

Unbelievable.

11

I love Philadelphia, its energy, its history. It was also the city where a supporter gave me a very cool T-shirt that said, SARAHCUDA, which I wore to a rambunctious meet-and-greet the campaign organized in a Philly bar.

But a few people in the City of Brotherly Love weren't the most loving on that trip. During a motorcade ride, my children looked out the windows of the Suburban and saw people wearing T-shirts that said lovely things like SARAH PALIN IS A C—.

Willow was astonished. "Mom, did you see that?"

"Don't worry about it" was all I could muster.

In Philly, Mark Wallace caught up with the B Team because the VFW debate between Senator Joe Biden and me was right around the corner. Mark sequestered a small debate prep team in a hotel room with the curtains drawn, blotting out the sunlight. My experience had taught me that you can work well with a diverse team, even people you don't know, if you make the atmosphere upbeat and positive. Whoever was leading this team, though, turned it into a high-pressure penalty box.

I understood the stakes. I knew that the McCain ticket was on the ropes and that top campaign staffers were unnerved. I got that. But I had a different perspective than some of the principals on the team as to how we should deal with this reality.

We were all wired pretty much the same way—intense and focused—but when things weren't going well, the last thing I wanted to do was sit in a darkened room and hear strange people yelling at one another. Seemed pretty unproductive to me. Finally, after an inconsistent strategy of trying to guess what would be asked in the debate, I thought we all needed some fresh air.

As a lifelong runner, I craved breathing in the outdoors and pounding the pavement hard enough to make my thighs hurt and my lungs burn. Coming from the grand, sparkling mountains of the North, I was inspired and energized every time I stepped outside. I repeatedly requested that headquarters carve out some time so I could run—just half an hour would do. Campaign managers would promise to do so, and once in a while they did write it into the schedule—usually at the exact hour when we were barreling down the freeway in the bus.

That day, I didn't care that I was in downtown Philly with protestors lining gray streets, chanting their support for anyone but us under the perpetual shadow of skyscrapers. At this point, I'd take it.

I'm glad I wasn't reading my own press at that time. Weeks out, pretty much the entire Washington–New York media constellation was predicting that I'd make a complete fool of myself in the VP debate.

Meanwhile, the B team heard that Schmidt and others at head-quarters were outraged about the choice of Gwen Ifill as debate moderator. Ifill, a former *New York Times* correspondent, was in the process of writing what was assumed to be a pro-Obama book. I wasn't worried about it; I was debating Biden, not the moderator. In any case, if Gwen showed any bias, viewers would pick up on it in a heartbeat. It made no sense that the campaign spent so much time firing off talking points and quasi-coordinated strategies for surrogates to make a big deal over something we couldn't control.

During debate prep, I had been given stacks of five-by-eight index cards, bound in rubber bands, and we lugged them around everywhere. Someone had gone to a lot of trouble to type them up, which I appreciated, but it was funny because on one side of each card, there was a question and on the other side there were a whole bunch of what most people would consider nonanswers:

FRONT OF CARD: What is America's role in the world when it comes to global security?

BACK OF CARD: *"Senator McCain and I are optimists. We love our country, and John has proven that more than any other leader in America."*

Or . . .

"I see the United States as a force for good in the world. As has already been so beautifully said, we're a shining city on a hill."

Or . . .

"We don't apologize for who we are or what we stand for, even if we're not perfect. We learn from our mistakes, but we don't doubt our goodness."

Right. But *what is our role in the world and how does that relate to national security?*

Another card asked:

What will it take to win the war in Afghanistan?

BACK OF CARD: *"The world is better off for the fact that the Taliban no longer rules Afghanistan."*

I said to the prep people, "Okay, but what they're asking is, what will it take to win the war?"

"Right," somebody said. "But you don't have to answer the question."

"Why wouldn't I want to answer the question?" I said.

The bottom line was that these were political answers—and I couldn't force myself to play it safe and sound like a politician. On top of that, there were probably ten cards for a single topic with a different set of nonanswers on every one. So in the end I'm thinking, *Okay, which nonanswer do you want me to give?*

Or here's an idea—I could give a *real* answer: "Yes! America should lead the world in global security. We should be developing our own resources and leveraging our power for good, not apologizing for being the strongest nation in the world. . . ."

I kept a stack of the cards as a souvenir. I wish I had kept them all because I scribbled a lot of notes in the margins, probably some not fit for public consumption, such as "Just let me answer the question, dang it."

It was as though they were saying "We love you just the way you are—now change."

After a while, this caused me to question my answer-from-the-heart style, the way of dealing with the public and the press that had helped me to serve my constituents. I liked my simpler style because it meant I never had to spin, I never had to B.S., and, good or bad, I never had to struggle to remember what I had said the last time. Local reporters liked it, too, because I didn't tiptoe around the issues.

Here, though, it sounded as if the strategy was to listen to a question and then try to pull out a scripted nonanswer. Only to a couple of the guys, it was never the *right* nonanswer. At one point during prep in Philly, I gave one of the scripted nonanswers and Mark shouted out, "Wrong, Governor! Wrong, wrong, wrong!"

"What do you mean 'wrong'? What do you want me to say? Everybody has different input in this room. Here, read the card yourself. You guys *wrote* it."

What I should've said was, "Look, I get it. Our numbers aren't good, this debate is a big deal, but this stuffy, dark hotel room with a bunch of crabby guys isn't working. So get some fresh air and let's come back and tackle this with clear minds."

But I didn't say that, and there was disagreement on how to proceed with all the different input the staff was throwing around. I remember it well because I was wearing a Rangers hockey jersey that morning and as the process of sifting through hundreds of note cards grew more frustrating for the team leader, I couldn't help but think of my petulant son the year he had spent so much time in the penalty box. Game after game, it seemed Track couldn't figure out how to react productively to irritations on the ice. I used to knock on the Plexiglas behind the box and ask him, "What good does it do the team to have a scorer stuck in the box? Get back out and skate hard—and clean—do what you're put there to do!"

I didn't need a multiple-choice selection of nonanswers. All I needed to hear was what John's position was on any particular issue. Then I could either formulate a response that would support it wholeheartedly or carefully articulate my own slightly different perspective.

At some point, someone must have told Schmidt that debate prep wasn't going well. He and McCain's campaign manager, Rick Davis, came in and cleared the room. They sat down at a round conference table and motioned me over to join them. Suddenly, I felt like I was on thin ice.

Schmidt leveled his eyes at me. "We don't have the money Obama does and the numbers don't look good. We've got to change things up."

I agree. I was eager to hear a new strategy.

"So," he continued, "headquarters is flying in a nutritionist."

There it was again, the mysterious "headquarters." On the B Team, folks had taken to making quote marks with their fingers every time they said the word. I had visited the physical headquarters once in Washington, D.C., and met amazing volunteers working round the clock for the GOP ticket. But somehow I must never have met the tight inner circle of shot callers. We joked that perhaps they didn't even exist. Still, they were flying in a nutritionist.

Interesting.

"Oh, good . . . the team could probably use a nutritionist," I said. The chain-smoking, junk-food-packing, recirculated-air-breathing habits of some of the staffers were probably catching up to them. They'd been on the road a long time. The more I thought about it, the more I realized Schmidt really did have a great idea.

"No, it's for you," he said. "You gotta get off that Atkins Diet."

Huh?

I had to do a mental double take.

The Atkins bars—that must be it. They were everywhere, in every hotel room and on every snack table along the trail. They were great when I didn't have time to slow down and eat, but I didn't know why they were all over the place.

"I'm not on the Atkins Diet, Steve."

"Don't you know what a high-protein diet does?" he asked, ignoring what I had just said. He then launched into a discussion of nutrition physiology, holding forth on the importance of carbohydrates to cognitive connections and blah-blah-blah. As he lectured, I took in his rotund physique and noted that he used nicotine to keep his own cognitive connections humming along.

I interrupted his lecture. "Steve, you know what I really need? Half an hour to go for a run in these beautiful cities we're visiting. Also, seeing my kids does wonders for my soul."

He barreled on as if I hadn't spoken. "Headquarters is flying in a nutritionist, and for three days you're going to be on a diet balanced in carbohydrates and nitrates and—"

I'm a forty-four-year-old, healthy, athletic woman raising five kids and governing a large state, I thought as his words faded into a background buzz. *Sir, I really don't know you yet. But you've told me how to dress, what to say, who to talk to, a lot of people* not *to talk to, who my heroes are supposed to be, and we're* still *losing. Now you're going to tell me what to eat?*

I suppose if headquarters had flown in a nutritionist, I would've listened to what he or she had to say. But as with much of what headquarters said, it never happened.

———

There was a bright spot in Philly and his name was Joe Lieberman. Usually, the tense, dark hotel room was a revolving door for tired operatives and well-meaning experts. At one point, Senator Lieberman stopped by the room, and I think he could sense that the prep was overly scripted, with no room for productive give-and-take. A moment came when the only people in the room were me, Senator Lieberman, and Kris Perry.

Senator Lieberman sat down in front of me and regarded me kindly. "Be yourself," he said. "Don't let these people try to change you. Don't let them tell you what to say and how to think."

Kris and I both nodded and laughed; she was thinking the same thing I was—*Well, we're glad it's not just our imagination.*

"God is going to see you through this," Senator Lieberman said. "Just put your faith in Him and let Him take care of it."

Then he repeated our mutual friend John's words of wisdom: "Just have fun!"

It was so heartfelt, so genuine, so sincere. In a campaign swirling with professional handlers and operatives, Joe Lieberman, the Democrat-turned-Independent senator from Connecticut, reminded me exactly how to do this.

Meanwhile, Cindy McCain broached the good idea of moving debate prep to their ranch in Arizona. Todd went on ahead with the kids, and I planned to meet them there. I looked forward to seeing the comfortable home again where McCain family artwork adorned the walls. And especially getting to visit the creek; John once told a reporter he liked to pursue his favorite form of exercise there: wading. The whole aura of the ranch was so refreshing that I asked if we could move the debate podiums outdoors.

We made sure that ace debate prepper Randy Scheunemann, the foreign policy adviser who'd briefed me at the convention, took the leadership role in this new locale. Randy had also been on hand for meetings at the United Nations when I had been privileged to meet people like Henry Kissinger and the leaders of Pakistan, Afghanistan, and India, plus several congressmen and former President Clinton. It was interesting to meet President Clinton, with whom I spoke a couple of times. In him, I sensed what I believed was an unspoken mutual disappointment with the media's serial unfairness to some presidential candidates in the 2008 race. I don't think anyone can argue that Obama didn't get a free pass compared to the treatment of Bill's wife, Hillary Clinton.

In February 2008, Hillary publicly pointed out some of this media favoritism. Weeks later, I responded to her comments during a *Newsweek* Women and Leadership Event in Los Angeles: "I say this with all due respect to Hillary Clinton . . . but when I hear a statement like that coming from a woman candidate, with any kind of perceived whine about that excess criticism . . . I think, man, that doesn't do us any good."

I wasn't really accusing her of whining. Still, before criticizing her on this point, I should have walked a mile in her shoes. I can see now that she had every right to call the media on biased treatment that ended up affecting her candidacy. In fact, I should have applauded her because she was right—Democrats deserved to see a fairer picture of what they were getting into before they cast their primary votes.

Should Secretary Clinton and I ever sit down over a cup of coffee, I know that we will fundamentally disagree on many issues, but my hat is off to her hard work on the 2008 campaign trail. Compared to the guys she squared off against, a lot of her supporters think she proved what Margaret Thatcher proclaimed: "If you want something said, ask a man. If you want something done, ask a woman."

12

During debate practice under the Arizona sun, we worked our way through questions for a couple of hours and then took a brief break with the kids down by the creek. Randy had watched all of Biden's debates during the primary, read his autobiography, and studied him; he had the senator's voice down pat, including some of his semifolksy sayings ("As my mom used to say, 'God love ya, Joe, but you are *wrong!*'").

"Remember," Randy told me, "Biden is a truly experienced debater. He's been through thirty-five years of legislative debates, foreign policy debates, and Supreme Court nominees. He has spent literally decades on the art of political talking." He characterized Biden as someone who definitely liked to hear himself talk, but also made clear that he respected the senator on a number of foreign policy positions. (Not including, of course, Biden's harebrained idea to divide the nation of Iraq.)

I too respected Biden's decades of experience, but I also knew him as one of just a handful of members of the U.S. Senate who way back in the 1970s had actually voted *against* the Trans-Alaska Pipeline, an economic lifeline that would ultimately result in thousands of American jobs, 15 billion barrels of oil pumped into the economy to date, and a huge chunk of domestic energy production. The day before the debate, Ann Coulter was spot on, calling Biden's vote against domestic energy production "the equivalent of voting against the invention of the wheel."

"The only argument against the pipeline was that it would harm the caribou, an argument that was both trivial and wrong," Ann wrote. "The caribou population near the pipeline increased from 5,000 in the 1970s to 32,000 by 2002. It would have been bad enough to vote against the pipeline bill even if it had hurt the caribou. A sane person would still say: *Our enemies have us in a vise grip. Sorry, caribou, you've got to take one for the team.*"

Over the years, I had occasionally listened to Biden's discussions of energy and realized he had not changed. He still seemed opposed to sensible innovations, from clean coal to nuclear energy to responsible new directional drilling techniques in places like ANWR. On one issue after another, Obama's VP choice was loaded with government experience but still seemed to have no understanding of logical steps we could take to capitalize on American energy resources.

During prep, we spent a lot of time on foreign policy and national security issues involving Afghanistan, Iraq, Pakistan, and various aspects of the war on terrorism. We knew the press would portray these as Biden's strengths—and they *were* strengths, thanks to his thirty-five years of foreign policy experience.

During rehearsals, I accidentally called Randy "Senator O'Biden"—a slip-of-the-lip combination of Obama and Biden. The blunder struck too often, even tripping up campaign staffers. (Jay Leno later made the same slip on his new talk show, so we were in good company.) We laughed about it but knew that if I said it even once during the debate, it would be disastrous.

Then somebody said, "You ought to just call him Joe."

"Oh, I can't just call him Joe!" I said. Senator Biden was a senior statesman. He'd been sitting in a U.S. Senate seat since I was nine years old. I believed calling him by his first name without his permission would be disrespectful.

Randy seemed to read my thoughts and offered a solution. "In every debate, you cross the stage and shake hands with your opponent," he said. "When you shake hands, just ask him for permission to call him Joe. He's certainly going to say yes, because he's a gentleman."

So that's what we decided I would do. We had no idea my mic would already be hot when I walked onstage, crossed over to his turf, and said, "Can I call you Joe?"

The "expert" postdebate analysis was that my question was a cleverly devised strategy to disarm my opponent. Yeah, right.

At the ranch, things got more serious when we started the first of two formal practice debates: indoors, cameras rolling, under the lights, and each a fully timed ninety minutes long. The first session was intense. No breaks. No commentary or suggestions on refining answers. Just back and forth with Randy playing his attack-dog Biden role so convincingly that I wanted to reach over and clobber him for his baiting and twisting of my words and record. When the ninety minutes ended, there was a pause, then the room burst into spontaneous applause. That took me aback— I'd been so focused on the battle that I really wasn't paying attention to whether or not the McCain team thought I was doing well. But it felt fine to know they all thought so, especially after the gloom and friction of the Philadelphia trials.

Through all this, I had continued to request time to run. At the ranch, I decided I would just take the time, period. The Arizona weather and the hot, dusty trails heading into the McCains' property were too good to pass up. I couldn't wait to slip into my ASICS and work up a sweat. One afternoon when the guys stopped for a bountiful lunch Cindy had prepared, I laced up and headed out.

Of course, I wasn't alone. We were never alone. Secret Service agents ran with me, and a couple more followed us in a golf cart. I loved those guys to death and got a kick out of watching them adjust to this tornado assignment called the Palin clan. But I still wished I could go solo, just have some space to breathe. This time, they knew best.

I ran along a road lined with plants that were exotic to a Northerner, such as purple sage and cactus. A gray-green lizard darted across my path, and I couldn't wait to tell Piper about it—there are no lizards in the wilds of Alaska.

The sun warmed my back, the earth crunched under my feet, and I breathed in the late-summer quiet. We crested a hill and I started striding down the other side, feeling freer and less burdened than I had in days. Then I stumbled.

I lost traction and crashed, tumbling into the dirt, gravel slicing into my hands and knees. It took a second to register what I had just done. One of the Secret Service agents helped me up. It was quite embarrassing.

My hands and knees were a bloody mess, and one thigh was scarlet with road rash. Suddenly I was very thankful for the agents. They helped me into the golf cart, and I tried to manage a laugh—between winces.

"Okay, you guys, you have to *swear* to secrecy!" I said. *"Please* don't tell anybody I crashed. I feel like a fool!"

The guys were so sweet. They promised.

When we got back to the ranch, one of them helped me clean up, picking gravel out of my palms. Although I probably needed it, there was no way I was going to a doctor for stitches because I knew it would be instant national news. I could imagine what headquarters would say about that. So the guys fixed me up and we covered the damage with giant flesh-colored bandages.

Later, I saw Piper at the guesthouse. "Mommy! What happened to your hands?"

I knew she would go around bragging about my crash, so I told her, "Well, when we were out running, I had to save your Secret Service guys from a rattlesnake! I tackled it!"

No dice. "You crashed, didn't you?" she said and offered me a Hannah Montana Band-Aid.

During the rest of our time at the ranch, debate prep went well because Randy and Steve Biegun basically took over. When we finished, the kids' babysitter, Penny Stielstra, helped pack up the car seats and the bright pink Bumbo chair that Trig learned to sit up in during the Arizona stay; then the kids and Todd and I all headed in different directions that would ultimately converge in St. Louis. We'd come full circle with Penny. She was the meticulous and trustworthy babysitter I'd relied on nearly two decades earlier when I worked as a proofreader at the *Frontiersman* when Track and Bristol were tiny. We were thankful she was back in this chapter of our lives for our little ones.

We left the ranch and hummed down the road toward the airport and the jet that would whisk us to the face-off with Biden.

As I watched the arid landscape glide past, my hands and knees stung and I reflected on my fall. It was like anything else I'd encountered in life that didn't go as perfectly as planned. You stumble. Yep—it hurts. You're bloodied. So what? You get back up and get on with it.

The vibration of my cell phone pulled me back into the vehicle. And when I answered, my heart leaped. It was Track. Finally. We talked for a few minutes from wherever he was in Iraq—he wouldn't tell me, exactly—and I was so thankful for the Providential timing of his call: now of all times when I had just a few uninterrupted minutes, what would be the only quiet moments for many days to come. That he called at just that time from half a world away was, to me, a miracle.

I told him I was headed to a debate.

"Yeah, I heard something about that on the news," Track said. "Did you study?"

I laughed. Talk about a mother-son role reversal. "I did," I said.

"I'll be praying for you." Another role reversal, the same words I'd said to my son so many times over the years. It was a "Right back atcha, Mom," moment.

"You're gonna do great," he said. "I love you."

"I love you so much, son."

I hung up the phone and a peace settled over my heart: For me, no matter what happened in the debate, I could keep it in perspective. *My son called from Iraq. He is safe. Life is good.*

———

We touched down in St. Louis, piled into vans, and headed straight for the debate venue at Washington University. From the second we arrived, I felt carried along on a wave of technicians, directors, and producers. We went straight into what they call a "technical walk-through," and a series of people were introduced to me: stage manager, lighting manager, production manager. Mic guy, podium-height guy, get-the-shine-off-your-nose guy.

I was standing onstage when a campaign consultant whispered some last-minute advice on voice inflection. I hated to drop a bomb on her, but I'd been talking the same way for forty-four years and doubted our few moments alone would miraculously reform my style. Besides, I thought of all the money Tina Fey was making imitating me; I didn't want to screw up her *SNL* thing by changing up on her midstream. I'm all about job security for the American worker.

Then began a kind of odd, orchestrated photo op that I learned is customary before a big campaign event. Photographers come in and snap pictures as you pretend to be doing something important. In the middle of that, Bexie and Chris Edwards appeared onstage. Chris was holding two different suits, skirts with blazers, and he held them up in the lights. Cameras continued to flash.

"What do you think?" Chris asked.

"What do I think? I'm wearing the blue one, that's what I think. Remember—the one we ironed?"

Flashbulbs popped. Chris smiled and said through his teeth, "Just play along. They're recording this Historic Moment."

"Of me picking a suit?" I whispered.

"Exactly."

I tried to put a comparing-suit-colors look on my face. But finally, when Chris and I made eye contact, I broke into a big grin. I loved this guy, another B Teamer who deserved to be on varsity. We called Chris "the Candy Man" because his family owns Edward Marc, a gourmet chocolatier founded in Pittsburgh with headquarters in D.C. What a great way to top off an energizing day on the trail, with a milk chocolate truffle or peanut butter meltaway; Chris kept the bus stocked, and we loved him for it.

Later on, I was sitting in the greenroom surrounded by a buzzing crowd of people doing their best: Amy and Angela doing their miracle work, keeping the hair plopped up and the makeup troughed on; communications people answering press phone calls; and lots of people with last-minute tips on what to say and what not to say. Piper sat in the corner, quietly sipping on my Diet Dr Pepper. Andrew Smith, bless his heart, was doing his best to keep more people from crowding in.

I looked up to see Schmidt barrel through. Immediately, he began to bellyache about Gwen Ifill. "You know she's going to f*** with you?"

I'm thinking, *Why are you telling me this? Last minute . . . what's the point? And no more f-bombs around Piper, please?*

I wanted to focus on the points I planned to make about getting the economy on the right track with free-market principles, not government growth and bailouts. I wanted to focus on a message of military strength and support for our allies, especially Israel.

In the greenroom, various preppers kept quizzing me. Comm people flitted in and out. Schmidt was thumping around, mad about something. Meg had flown in from Alaska and was watching all the hubbub. Kris gave her a meaningful glance: time to herd the cats out of the room so there could be a minute of peace.

I wasn't nervous, but I could always use some divine inspiration, so I looked around for someone to pray with before I walked onstage. I spotted Piper in the corner, still sipping my pop.

"Come here and pray with Mama, Pipe," I said. No surprise for her; all my kids were used to my praying through life's roller-coaster ups and downs and competitions.

Piper walked over and we clasped hands. She looked up at me with her sweet, round face and freckle-dusted button nose. "Okay, Mama, what should we pray?"

I wanted to say that we should humbly seek the Lord's strength before I explained to 44 million viewers why they should vote for John McCain. I wanted to say that my heart's desire was that our Lord would guide my words in a way that would be truthful and honoring to Him.

But I said, as simply as I could, "Just pray we win the debate."

She drew a deep breath. "Mom!" she said. "That would be cheating!"

———

The debate commission had assigned a poised and serene woman to escort me to my toe mark, the spot just offstage where I would wait to be introduced before emerging from behind the curtain. As she led us down a hallway, she calmly reeled off times in hours, minutes, and seconds, speaking to debate producers through a mic and earpiece she was wearing. When we had nearly reached the stage, she turned to Jason and said, "I did the same job you're doing for Geraldine Ferraro in 1984."

Wow! I thought. What an amazing piece of American history— that there had been only two women in debates at this level of national politics and the same dedicated woman had worked behind the scenes to help shatter the proverbial glass ceiling both times, on both sides of the aisle. I admired Geraldine Ferraro's accomplishments. During the campaign, I sometimes spoke about her contribution to the advancement of women in public service. Shortly after one of those acknowledgments, Ferraro called me on the campaign bus and we had a nice conversation. What struck me most was that she said my shout-out to her was the first time, in all those years, that she had been so publicly acknowledged for her historic step for the United States and for women. I don't believe in voting according to gender or color of skin, but Ferraro's vision and efforts helped a lot of women reach higher than they'd reached before.

Jason and I hit my toe mark precisely on time. On the other side of the stage, Biden was supposed to hit his at the same moment. But when I looked across, his spot was empty. Seconds ticked by, an eternity in a tightly scripted television production schedule. Still no Joe.

Dang, I thought. *He's still running on Senate time.*

An aide poked his head into the empty space where the senator was supposed to be, swiveled his head, withdrew. Looking back, it could've been backstage chaos causing the delay, or it could've been a strategy, sort of like icing the kicker just before a field goal.

Finally Biden appeared, as usual looking impeccable in his dark suit, tall and confident, his distinguished silver hair flawlessly groomed. I had never met him before, but now I tried to catch his eye, to give him, I don't know, a friendly nod, a thumbs-up, something to acknowledge that, hey, ultimately we're all on the same team. Go, U.S.A.! But Senator Biden didn't make eye contact.

Instead he looked past me. His features then hardened into what can only be described as a "game face." I could respect that. I knew what it was like to get into a zone before a big game.

Then the senator started to stretch. Literally.

He put his hands on his hips and, staring grimly at some point behind me, began to bend at the waist, bouncing first to the right, then to the left. Then the neck rolls started, presumably to get rid of all that nasty tension from being the front-runner. After that, the senator from Delaware began stretching his quads, grabbing his dress shoe and pulling it up behind his designer-suited rear end. Right leg, then left.

I'm thinking, *O-kay. Didn't know this was going to get physical.*

I looked at Jason to mouth, *What the heck? Should I be doing that, too?*

But Jason was looking at his watch, counting down to go time. He didn't tell me then, but his plan was to push me out five seconds early so that I could cross more than half the stage and meet Biden, symbolically, on "his" turf.

Seconds later, Jason gave me a gentle nudge. "Go!" he said. "And remember, think 'hair plugs'!"

I hustled out onstage, where I shook hands with Senator Biden and asked, "Hey, can I call you Joe?"

The debate went well—from my perspective, anyway. It was a relaxed and comfortable atmosphere, and the time zipped by much too quickly. Gwen was fine as moderator. I wrapped it up by stating that I had always been proud to be an American, and closed with a quote from Ronald Reagan, who once said that freedom is always just one generation away from extinction: "We don't pass it to our children in the bloodstream; we have to fight for it and protect it and then hand it to them so that they shall do the same, or we're going to find ourselves spending our sunset years telling our children and our children's children about a time in America back in the day when men and women were free."

That's what I wanted Americans to remember.

After the debate, my family and Joe's family joined us onstage. He has the most beautiful wife and daughters and granddaughters. We all hit it off for those few minutes, and it was nice to unwind with a casual chat. Senator Biden and I reflected on the debate and laughed about a couple of the lighter moments. After a few minutes, I looked up to see that Dad had wandered down to Gwen's moderator chair. They seemed engrossed in an earnest discussion. Was he thanking her for her fair handling of the debate? I walked over in time to hear Dad, always a coach at heart, advising Gwen on how to ice and elevate her ankle. She had broken it the day before and shown up for the evening in a wheelchair. Now, *that's* my kind of tough.

For a few moments, we shared old war-wound stories about bum ankles and sprained fingers, and Dad spoke for me when he wished Gwen well.

13

We kicked the next morning off with a lot of prep for the day's events, including an on-camera interview atop the hotel with Fox News reporter Carl Cameron, with the St. Louis Gateway Arch framed in the shot behind me. Among his other questions, he asked what I thought of the campaign pulling out of Michigan.

"Yes, I read that this morning," I answered, then said I wished we *weren't* pulling out of Michigan—that every single person and every single vote mattered, and I sure didn't want anyone to give up anywhere. No harm giving a little shout-out to the Great Lakes State, I thought. No one had mentioned to the VP staff or me that the campaign was even considering pulling out of Michigan, much less that we already had. So when I was asked about it, I was caught a bit off guard, but I answered truthfully about having read about it in the newspaper. We moved on to the next question and wrapped up the interview. No big deal.

But we soon heard that back at headquarters, it *was* a big deal. The word came hurtling down that I had been "off script" with Cameron. Of course, it's pretty easy to issue candid, off-script messages when there is no script to begin with. It wasn't the end of the world, though, and I hoped headquarters would forgive me and move on.

They didn't. One or more McCain senior staffers would later anonymously tell reporters that I was "going rogue."

The VP team had been scheduled to do another event in Michigan, but it was canceled, disappointing a lot of us who had appreciated that September 17 town hall meeting with John. Still, we understood that funding was limited, so I suggested to the VP staff that the next time we had an official event near Michigan, we pass the hat for gas money and just do a quick trip across the border to snap one off-the-record photo at a café or gas station, maybe hold a quick grassroots rally. I thought we would send a positive message to the state that way, show the people that our campaign really did care about their votes.

It would be fast, it would be free, it would be . . . mavericky. What was the worst that could happen? We'd maybe get a few more votes? Headquarters said no. With the strange pushback we were getting by then, we were tempted just to sneak across the border. More than once, Nicolle had summarized the campaign organization well when, during chaotic moments, she turned to the B Team and said with a resigned smile, "Welcome to the pirate ship."

But we didn't want our throats cut, so we dropped the road trip idea and tried to find a copy of the script so we could stay on it.

———

When we first got on the campaign plane, it was just a plane. But by the time the staff got through with it, the interior was like a flying motivational poster. All through the rope lines, people would hand us stickers, signs, and pins they'd spent their own money to make.

PIPER FOR PRESIDENT!
HEELS ON, GLOVES OFF
TRIG IN THE WHITE HOUSE
I'M JOE SIX-PACK
COME BACK TO MICHIGAN!

Dad presented our JetBlue pilots with a pair of moose antlers, which they proudly displayed in the cockpit throughout the campaign, like the bull horns some Texans liked to wire to their Cadillac grills. Jason taped a U.S. map to the ceiling, and it was tradition that every time a visitor came aboard, he or she would reach up and sign it upside down with a Sharpie.

The Democrats had quite a bit of extra positive media coverage thanks to the various celebrities appearing at their events, and the steady stream of liberal stars beating a path to Obama's door had the B Team asking why we weren't doing the same with the common sense conservative celebrities who had offered to help our ticket. There were plenty who sent us word that they would do so. I don't subscribe to the idea that celebrity endorsements are necessarily weighty or significant to public policy, but neither do I think politicians can ignore the influence of popular culture in the age of the instant image and streaming sound bite.

Staff started working the phones, and within a few hours we had a number of events lined up with some courageous, independent-minded actors, musicians, and athletes. Kid Rock, for instance, is very pro-America and has common sense ideas. We heard he was going to come out and do a rally with us, but headquarters said he could participate only in a McCain rally, so that never materialized. Still, the kids were happy—they got to talk to him on the phone.

We very much appreciated Robert Duvall and his wife helping at our events, and Jon Voight blew us away with his articulate and passionate reasoning for the real change America needs. Actress Janine Turner was an eloquent supporter, particularly on the subject of women in politics and the strength and value of single moms who are committed to raising solid citizens. We also welcomed "Redneck Woman" Gretchen Wilson aboard the campaign plane. We knew all her songs, and I loved that she loved to talk about her daughter.

Along with other patriots, Hank Williams Jr., John Rich, Naomi Judd, and Lee Greenwood joined us on the trail. When Lee jumped onstage with us the first time, Kris Perry, who would wrestle a grizzly bear if it got too close to one of her kids or her BlackBerry, just about melted when she heard him sing his famous song "Proud to Be an American." We all choked up.

Mike Ditka, Brady Quinn, Aaron Tippin, the Bellamy Brothers, and many others also joined us on the trail at different points. And some fund-raisers would attract big names—supporters not as visible to the national media but wildly appreciated by us.

The Orange County Choppers guys were outrageously bold—which is why people love them. They roared up to a Media, Pennsylvania, rally on a hot, custom-made bike that they honed to honor POW and MIA vets. Senators Lieberman, Lindsey Graham, and Arlen Specter were onstage when John highlighted the rally with his promise that "Sarah and I are going to get on that chopper and ride it right to Washington and raise hell when we get there!"

After the event I looked at the bike, then at the campaign bus, then back at the bike . . . it was so tempting. What do you think headquarters would have said to that?!

Seven months later, Orange County Chopper founder and Vietnam Vet Paul Teutul Sr. and his sons—all tattooed up and looking good—visited Alaska to honor our state's fiftieth anniversary. I invited them to come back and we'd go ride together . . . on snowmachines.

Meanwhile, other people called. I talked to Bono. And John's friend Warren Beatty. These were interested folks with good intentions who wanted to share ideas and insights, and I was happy to hear from them.

One morning, I was showering when Bexie knocked on the door. "Rick Warren's on the phone again," she called out. "He's been trying to track you down and has called twice."

She handed me the phone in the shower, and I turned off the water so it wouldn't be so obvious where I was standing. The well-known author and pastor shared some encouraging words, then offered to pray right then for strength during the campaign. I said, absolutely! Pray away! I would never turn down prayer even with limited hours in a campaign day, standing in a few inches of water with a shower curtain for a wardrobe. You do what you've got to do.

Without a doubt, though, the real stars of the campaign were the people who contacted us along the trail to encourage McCain and those who packed the rallies—everyday, hardworking Americans. Bexie, Jeannie, and other staffers would collect notes from supporters on the rope lines, and it was an absolute joy—sometimes heartbreaking, always heartwarming—to read them. On the plane I'd read them one by one. Parents sending pictures of their precious children. Prayer warriors writing to say they were interceding for us. And, so tragically, a Blue Star mom writing to tell me she had become a Gold Star mom.

I read those notes and kept them with me. They inspired me, helping to strip away all the sound bites and the slick, orchestrated political theater, and reminded me whom we were fighting for. Sometimes, supporters would jot their e-mail address, and I could stop right then and tap them a note. There are some families that Todd and I still keep in touch with—like Charlie Walling, a very confident and handsome young man who had scored an extra chromosome too. We met him in Florida, and he asked me not to call him "darling" because that wasn't "tough." And Joshua Wold, another precious child we met in Minnesota. Todd has his picture on his cell phone—Josh snowmachines with his dad!

The Providential appointments we experienced on the trail were many, and they kept us going with good attitudes and the right perspective.

In late September, Todd and Cindy traveled to Los Angeles for a campaign event. Todd enjoyed meeting comedian and radio host Dennis Miller there, along with actors Gary Sinise, Kelsey Grammer, and John Ratzenberger. Another special guy Todd met was a young war veteran who was wearing his buddy's memorial bracelet. "My friend was killed in action four years ago and I haven't taken off this bracelet since," the combat veteran said. He slipped the C-shaped metal band off his wrist and handed it to Todd. "But now I want you to give it to your wife."

When Todd returned to Arizona and handed me the bracelet, it was an overwhelming moment. I put this precious memento on and wore it for the rest of the campaign. Not long after that, we hit Orange County, California, for another rally, and I heard a voice behind me in the crowd calling out, "That's my bracelet! That's my bracelet!"

I turned around to see a fit, dark-haired young man waving furiously a few rows up in the bleachers. After the rally, I hustled over to meet him—and thank him. We still have his buddy's memorial bracelet, a cherished reminder of things that really matter.

All of those elements—the stickers and signs, the proud parents, the enthused, curious, attentive folks showing up at events by the thousands—suggested an idea: in addition to meeting with movers and shakers in towns on the trail, and doing obligatory face time with big-money donors who were going to vote for John anyway, why couldn't we focus more attention on the everyday folks who attended our rallies?

This occurred to us after the umpteenth time we rolled into a town on the campaign bus to pick up a group of supporters who were already solidly in John's camp. We'd spend hours chatting with them and posing for pictures. ("Okay, now, I want one with you, Sarah—pretend like we're talking. Now I want one with Trig. Okay, now, you and Trig. Now, Todd, you get out of this one. Okay, Piper, you next. Here's my cell phone, could you call my mother?")

I enjoyed these friends of the campaign immensely, and I know how important donors are. I sincerely appreciated every one of them. But with such a short timeline and as we were trailing in the polls, I thought, instead of putting me on a bus with ten "friends of John" for hours, put me with ten friends of nobody in particular and I'll sit with them and convince them to vote for John.

———

Three days before the final presidential debate, a man named Joe Wurzelbacher was out in his front yard playing football with his son when Barack Obama walked past his driveway. The Democrat candidate for president had made a campaign stop in Holland, Ohio, to visit with residents and take questions. Joe had a question about his plan to buy a company that makes $250,000 to $280,000 a year.

He said to Obama, "Your new tax plan's going to tax me more, isn't it?"

The Illinois senator's short answer was yes, and he finished with this revealing comment: "I think when you spread the wealth around, it's good for everybody."

An ABC cameraman recorded the exchange, and on October 12, 2008, "Joe the Plumber" was born. Our campaign quickly realized that Joe Wurzelbacher, a plumber by trade, typified the everyday American laborer who had worked hard to make his own way, was trying to improve his economic lot, and ought not to be punished by oppressive tax policies. Joe the Plumber reminded me personally of those Country Kitchen guys I'd sat with on Friday mornings in Wasilla when I was mayor. I liked him.

In the presidential debate three days later, both candidates made references to Joe the Plumber as a symbol of the American worker. Immediately, at all our rallies, we began seeing a whole new crop of signs: I'M RAY THE PRINCIPAL; JOSE THE HAIRDRESSER; PEGGY THE NURSE; and BOB THE COP. Then *National Review* ran an article about the Joe the Plumber phenomenon in which writer Byron York noted that regular workaday Americans were disgusted at how quickly the media tore Joe apart when he told a reporter that Obama's idea of "spreading the wealth around" sounded a lot like socialism to him.

One workaday American who was mad as hell and not going to take it anymore was Tito Munoz, a Colombian-born U.S. citizen. Dressed in a yellow hard hat and orange reflective vest and carrying a sign that said CONSTRUCTION WORKER, Munoz—the owner of a small construction company—pulled no punches when he told reporters why he'd come to an event. "I support McCain, but I've come to face you guys because I'm disgusted with you guys," he said about the press, speaking English with a thick Hispanic accent. "Why the hell are you going after Joe the Plumber? Joe the Plumber has an idea. He has a future. He wants to be something else. Why is that wrong? Everything is possible in America. I made it. Joe the Plumber could make it even better than me . . . I was born in Colombia, but I was made in the U.S.A."

A left-wing reporter from the magazine *Mother Jones* told Tito he didn't see anything wrong with the press coverage. But Tito and a feisty African American woman in the crowd hit back.

"Tell me," the woman said to the reporter, "why is it you can go and find out about Joe the Plumber's tax lien and when he divorced his wife and you can't tell me when Barack Obama met with William Ayers? Why? Why could you not tell us that? Joe the Plumber is me!"

"*I* am Joe the Plumber!" Munoz chimed in. "You're attacking me."

"Wait a second," the reporter said. "Do you pay your taxes?"

"Yes, I pay my taxes," the woman said.

"Then you're better than Joe the Plumber."

That set off a general free-for-all. "I'm going to tell you something," Munoz yelled at the reporter. "I'm better than Obama! Why? Because I'm not associated with terrorists!"

Tito the Builder sounded like the kind of guy who wasn't going to be told to sit down and shut up, something I'd basically been told to do when I spoke on the trail about Obama's associations with questionable characters, including Obama's long association with Bill Ayers.

A student radical and member of the Weather Underground, Ayers had helped bomb New York City police headquarters in 1970, the Capitol Building in 1971, and the Pentagon in 1972. When Ayers's memoir, *Fugitive Days,* was published in 2001, he told the *New York Times,* "I don't regret setting bombs. I feel we didn't do enough."

In a horrible irony, that *Times* interview with Ayers hit newsstands on the morning of September 11, 2001. Disgustingly, Ayers posed in the article stomping on our American flag.

In relation to the breaking news about the friendship between the unrepentant domestic terrorist and the Democrat candidate for president of the United States, headquarters issued an approved sound bite about Obama "palling around with terrorists," and I was happy to be the one to deliver it. As more information was made public concerning Obama's associations and the fact that he had kicked off his political career in Ayers's living room, the sound bite was written into a rally speech. The left went nuts, accusing me of lowdown rhetoric unworthy of presidential politics. And although it was headquarters that had issued the sound bite, the folks there did little more than duck.

I did not apologize for calling it like I saw it and wondered out loud why I was prohibited from calling the other ticket out on more of its strange associations. I was told not to discuss Obama's pastor of twenty years, Jeremiah "God Damn America" Wright. I will forever question the campaign for prohibiting discussion of such associations. All the more since these telltale signs of Obama's views, carefully concealed with centrist campaign-speak, have now been brought into the light by his appointments and actions in office.

By the time Joe the Plumber started making news, we were about ten days out from election day, and Jason told us he had an idea. We were about to do a campaign swing through Virginia, so why not turn it into a Joe the Plumber tour? Along with local dignitaries onstage, we'd have regular folks. After some tug-of-war with headquarters, we got the idea approved and, in the midst of planning, got a call from Matthew Scully.

"Hey, guess who lives in Northern Virginia?" Scully said. "Tito the Builder!"

Right on!

None of us had ever met Tito, but someone tracked him down. He rolled up to our Leesburg rally in his big old construction truck, decked out in his job site gear, looking totally, ruggedly Alaskan, and gave perhaps the most rousing introduction of the entire campaign. It was so absolutely real—not orchestrated or stage-crafted. No pipe-and-drape or stylists or scripts or $150,000 borrowed wardrobe. Just a real American who was excited about what John McCain represented.

Our Joe the Plumber tour played out like that all across Virginia with thousands of regular Americans coming out with their signs—NGUYEN THE GROCER, THERESA THE TEACHER, TOM THE REAL ESTATE AGENT, GREG THE TELEPROMPTER GUY, WENDY THE WAITRESS.

Speaking of waitresses, in Ashland, Virginia, we made a scheduled visit to Homemades by Suzanne and were warmly greeted with cookies, coffee, and plates of chicken salad—a real hometown spread. I sat down to talk with Suzanne, the business owner, about how John's lower tax policies would help grow her company. We shared coffee with her employees, and they shared their concerns over health coverage. We had owned a business. I had worked as a waitress, struggled with obtaining health insurance, balanced family and work. I had been in their shoes and had no doubt that I might someday be there again.

14

For years people told me, "You look like that lady on *Saturday Night Live*." One Halloween I dressed up as Tina Fey—it didn't take much costuming to do it. So when Tina started playing me on *SNL,* I told the B team, "Hey, I was Tina Fey before she was me."

I had liked some seasons of *SNL* since I was a teenager, sneaking around to watch it so my parents wouldn't catch me. So when she began impersonating me, it was a bit surreal. But from the beginning, I liked the idea that John and I might appear on the show.

"Let's *do* this," I said. "Let's go on and neutralize some of this, and have some fun!"

Of course, the idea was met with massive back-and forth haggling. Had we done it back in September, I think we might have had a shot at evening the odds with the *SNL* crew. As it stood, though, Tina's impression of me became so omnipresent—and so unchallenged—that some people blurred *SNL* skit dialogue with what I had actually said.

The classic example was Tina dressed up as me, saying, "I can see Russia from my house." Which of course I've never said. After that episode, many Alaskans sent me photos of themselves standing on the Alaska shore with Russia visible over their shoulders. (Not only can you see it—you can *swim* to Russia from Alaska, as hard-core athlete Lynne Cox did in 1987.)

Finally, when it was much too late from a tactical standpoint to say no, headquarters agreed to let us do the show. I was glad about it, but as time passed, I worried that we still hadn't seen a script. Word filtered down from on high, "Don't worry about it. We've got it under control. John and Lorne Michaels are good friends. They're not gonna screw you." So we'd wait some more, and we'd bug headquarters some more and . . . nothing. And there was still nothing on October 18, the morning we flew into New York City to do the show.

"Okay, guys, the show's tonight," I said to the staff. "Where's the script? What if it's raunchy? Worse, what if it's not funny?"

This was make-or-break stuff. Yet still no script, and with just hours to go, I wanted to see what millions of viewers were going to see.

So, finally, we B Teamers started brainstorming. What about a skit where I pretended to be a journalist and asked Tina condescending questions: "What do you use for newspapers up in Alaska—tree bark?" "What happens if the moose were given guns? It wouldn't be so easy then, eh?" "Is 'you betcha' your state motto?" We sent our ideas up the line, and somebody smacked 'em down. Word came back that Lorne was leery of letting Tina and me share the same stage because Tina's liberal politics might cause her to ad-lib something snarky that would stick like a burr to the campaign. Obviously he knew his NBC star better than I did, but I honestly didn't think that was plausible.

Finally, someone got us a copy of the script. We were sitting in the Suburban and Tucker was reading it, laughing out loud. "This is the funniest thing I've ever read, Governor. You have *got* to read this! Seriously, you're going to laugh your butt off!"

I looked at the script. It wasn't all that funny. *SNL* writers had taken the campaign's "Drill, baby, drill" mantra and turned it into a risqué double entendre about Todd and me. I thought, *Nah. C'mon, New York talent, we can do better than that.*

We checked into a hotel before the show. It was Bristol's eighteenth birthday, so the staff treated her to Magnolia Bakery's famous cupcakes. I think I ate six. Then we headed for the studios.

The campaign's "Fey Fears" turned out to be overblown. Instead, when I met her, she was friendly and gracious. Fresh-faced, very petite, and wearing jeans, Tina was standing near the wings holding her adorable little girl, Alice, who was about three.

"Don't worry!" Tina said when I walked up. "They'll put makeup on me!"

Then I noticed Alice turning her head back and forth, first to Tina, then to me, then to Tina again.

I smiled. "We're confusing your daughter."

Tina laughed. Without managers and handlers swarming around—"Don't say this, don't say that"—it was just a nice mom moment.

"Believe it or not, I've got Republicans in my family," Tina said, smiling.

"Believe it or not," I said, "I've got Democrats in mine."

She told me that her husband's parents were GOP loyalists. I enjoyed meeting them later when they came backstage at a rally. Tina and I chatted for a couple more minutes, then someone came and whisked me off to a tiny windowless dressing room crammed with a couch, a styling chair, and a brightly lit vanity. Then it seemed for a nice little stretch that I finally had a moment to take a break. Since August 29, the campaign had been burning fuel at breakneck speed, and now, in this cramped room, that almost faded to the background. The spotty cell phone coverage in there probably helped a bit. In addition to my duties as governor, we'd been plugged into updates and news and headlines and polls and people and headquarters' instructions 24/7 for weeks, and now suddenly, it just . . . stopped. And it was nice, in that little window of time, to be doing just one thing.

Not that the room itself wasn't jumping. Hair and makeup people buzzed in to quiz Amy and Angela on how they did my hair. Wardrobe people popped in; they wanted to make sure Tina looked exactly like me, so somebody had to go out and find a flag pin that matched mine. In the hallway I ran into a kid from Wasilla who had moved to New York and was now a stylist for the show. Another Alaskan, one of John Reeves's daughters who had grown up in Fairbanks, was an extra on *SNL*.

At some point, Amy Poehler came in. She was very pregnant. She and Bristol compared belly sizes and chatted about all the biological details expectant moms swap. *Very nice of Amy,* I thought. Very down to earth. And funny, of course. Really, everyone in the cast was so friendly and kind to us. There was nothing to fear.

I loved Amy's energy. During the first dress rehearsal, they unveiled a clever skit, a "rap" on the "Weekend Update" set, featuring two Eskimos, a fake Todd, and a moose. When the scene opens, I'm sitting at the anchor desk with Seth Meyers and Amy. The setup was that I was supposed to do a rap, but I announce that I've changed my mind, so Seth has to ask Amy if she remembers the lyrics from rehearsal. Amy acts like, well, maybe, she *sort of* knows it.

Then, wearing all black, she stands up with her *big* belly, and belts out, "One! Two! Three!"

My name is Sarah Palin you all know me
Vice president nominee of the GOP
Gonna need your vote in the next election
Can I get a "What? What?" from the senior section
McCain got experience, McCain got style
But don't let him freak you out when he tries to smile
Cause that smile be creepy
But when I be VP
All the leaders in the world gonna finally meet me.

Then the Eskimos jump onstage, flanking Amy, and she keeps rapping:

How you feel, Eskimo!
(Ice cold!)
Tell me tell me what you feel, Eskimo!
(Super cold!)

Then the guy dressed up as Todd joined the rap. He had the dark hair, the goatee, the Arctic Cat gear—he had most every-thing right.

After the dress rehearsal, I walked up to him and said, "Let me check you out."

Then I reached up, grabbed a strand of hair, and curled it down on his forehead. "There," I said. "Go, Todd!"

To this day, I still hear Piper rapping around the house: "You say Obama, I say *Ay*ers! Obama . . . *Ay*ers! Obama . . . *Ay*ers!"

During all this, the writers, the producers, and the campaign continued to hammer out the script. Josh Brolin, Mark Wahlberg, and the singer Adele were also on the show that night, as was director Oliver Stone, who made a cameo appearance. Unbelievably, he is a supporter of Communist dictator Hugo Chavez, who in a 2006 speech to the United Nations referred to the president of the United States as "the devil himself." I did not shake Stone's hand.

Alec Baldwin also guested on the show that evening. The bigwigs haggled back and forth over my appearance with Alec, the writers sending down some lines where Alec was basically supposed to perform a comic dissection on me. Then I was supposed to passively take his arm and stroll offstage.

From a political messaging standpoint, the campaign could see that wasn't going to work. We put our heads together and sent the producers a counteroffer: Alec would still get his barbs in, then I would say, "Hey, Baldwin, weren't you supposed to leave the country after the last election?"

Uh . . . no, producers said.

We tried another idea. It happened that I had recently talked with Alec's brother, Stephen, at a GOP fund-raiser. So we sent back another counteroffer based on my actual conversation with Stephen. "Hey, Alec," the proposed line went, "I saw Stephen at a fund-raiser last week and asked him when he was going to knock some sense into you."

Uh . . . no.

What's that line about being able to dish it out?

We went around and around until finally the *SNL* folks agreed to a version of the Stephen line that ultimately appeared in my bit with Alec.

It was watered down, but I still thought it was a funny piece; I'm standing with Lorne, and Alec walks up and pretends to think I'm Tina-as-me.

"Hey, Lorne. Hey, Tina," Alec says. "Lorne, I need to talk to you. You can't let Tina go out there with that woman. She goes against everything we stand for. I mean, good Lord, Lorne, they call her . . . what's that name they call her? Cari . . . Cari . . . What do they call her again, Tina?"

"That'd be Caribou Barbie," I said.

"Caribou Barbie. Thank you, Tina. I mean, this is the most important election in our nation's history. And you want her—our Tina—to go out there and stand there with that horrible woman? What do you have to say for yourself?"

Lorne turned from Alec to me and back again. "Alec, this is Governor Palin."

"Hi there . . ." I said. "I must say that your brother Stephen is my favorite Baldwin brother."

Then I stepped onto the famous set and got to say the words that have become a permanent part of American culture: *"Live from New York, it's Saturday Night!"*

15

The first wardrobe story hit on October 22: "RNC Shells Out $150K for Palin Fashion." The headline was highly misleading, as was the article itself, which said that according to campaign financial disclosures, the McCain campaign had spent $150,000 "to clothe and accessorize vice presidential candidate Sarah Palin and her family."

I never asked the New York stylists to purchase clothes, many of the items were never worn, many others were intended for the use of other people, and in the end the wardrobe items were all returned. It certainly wasn't true that I or my family had been on any kind of "big-time shopping trips." A *Los Angeles Times* fashion critic referred to me as a "pampered princess" and suggested that I had personally spent the money in a "one-woman economic stimulus plan." Katie Couric even weighed in on the trumped-up "controversy," writing: "There aren't a lot of Joe Six-packs out there who can drop six figures on a new wardrobe, so Gov. Sarah Palin's $150,000 shopping spree seems excessive to some people."

This was especially ironic coming from Katie, whose own stylist, the B Team was told, was part of the team the campaign hired to do the convention shopping before I even arrived.

I didn't care so much about the petty potshots because I knew they weren't true, and people who knew me laughed out loud when they read the "diva" accusations. But my family was made to look like a herd of hillbillies who had come to the big city and started living high on the hog, and that hurt me for them. My family is frugal. We clip coupons. We shop at Costco. We buy diapers in bulk and generic peanut butter. We don't have full-time nannies or housekeepers or drivers. So the portrayal of my family as wasting other people's money on clothes was a false one. And many wondered at the same time why no other candidates or their spouses were being asked a thing about their hair, makeup, or clothes.

Elisabeth Hasselbeck had a theory. In late October, the bold and talented *View* cohost joined us for a bus tour in Florida. I had met her at the GOP convention and found out we had a mutual friend from Wasilla. Elisabeth joined us at a huge rally in Tampa that took place right after the ridiculous wardrobe story hit the news.

"Now, with everything going on in the world, this seems a bit odd," Hasselbeck said from the podium before a crowd of thousands. "But let me tell you, this is deliberately sexist."

The crowd went crazy. Then she joked that the thing that impressed her most about my wardrobe were my accessories—my American flag pin and the blue star military pin I wore in honor of Track. The pundits peddling the story that I was this big-spending clotheshorse "didn't list that accessory," Elisabeth said, "because they know it's priceless!"

I was thinking, *Amen, sister!*

It was also ironic that at the Tampa rally that day, I was wearing a Dolce & Gabbana jacket that I had personally purchased—used—at an Anchorage consignment store months before the campaign. And earlier that day I was wearing a pair of my own Paige jeans, designed by the talented Paige Adams Geller, a Wasilla native who has made it big as a fashion designer in L.A.

The fact was, I would have been happy to wear my own clothes for the whole campaign. But I had a humbling experience while we were back in Wasilla for the Charlie Gibson interview in September. While the crews turned my kitchen into a television studio, I took Nicolle into my bedroom and showed her what I thought I should pack for the trail. She flipped through my wardrobe with raised eyebrows.

"No . . . no . . . no," she said as she slid each garment aside on its hanger. But I did manage to sneak that pink Dolce & Gabbana jacket plus other pieces onto the trail with me.

After Elisabeth introduced me in Tampa, I decided to take the wardrobe story by the horns. But it would just be a quick mention, a candid quote to set the record straight.

"I'm glad now that Elisabeth brought it up because it gives me an opportunity without the filter of the media to tell you the whole clothes thing," I told the cheering crowd. "Those clothes, they are not my property. Just like the lighting and staging and like everything else the RNC purchases. I'm not taking them with me. I'm wearing my own clothes from my favorite consignment shop in Anchorage, Alaska." There, simple, it was over, and it was truthful.

Word quickly came back from headquarters that I'd done it again—I'd gone rogue. What I had actually done was speak up to defend my ethics and my family, but still, the hammer came down.

Now, my friends and family sure knew the truth about the clothes. And the campaign folks, especially those who had vetted and chosen me, also knew the truth. But as the story grew legs, they didn't lift a finger to correct the record. I couldn't understand why until I realized that by the end of the campaign, the wardrobe fairy tale had become convenient. By then, with Obama soaring and our own ticket in free fall, one or two of the campaign's big dogs were already packing their parachutes.

By late October, with our numbers bad and some gears inside the campaign definitely out of whack, Nicolle sent around an e-mail suggesting that staffers all get on a conference call to discuss how to improve things. One thing we B Teamers thought was really off kilter was that the campaign wasn't telling voters everything they needed to know about the other ticket's records, past associations, and future plans. Nor was it holding the press accountable for biased reporting.

You could feel it—voters were clamoring for us to take the gloves off, yet the B Team was reprimanded for trying to shed light on some of these important questions.

I later learned from Randy Scheunemann that complaints were voiced against me, my family, and most of the B Team by a few folks on McCain's senior staff. They were angry that anyone in my family or group of Alaska friends had tried to set the record straight in the media without consulting with the campaign first. And they were still furious with me for speaking candidly on the Michigan withdrawal and the clothes issue.

To this day, Randy—ever the gentleman—won't tell me everything that was said about the B Team. But a couple of examples tell the story. "They're screwing up," Schmidt told Randy one day in Schmidt's office. "And the governor's not doing serious homework." Schmidt told Randy he thought I might be suffering from postpartum depression.

"That doesn't make any sense to me," Randy told Steve.

"What do you mean?"

"I really don't understand. I've had significant interactions with the governor during the campaign—at the convention, in New York, all the days of debate prep under tough conditions, I'm with her a lot—you are not," Randy said. "The Sarah Palin I've seen is not the one you're describing, and I don't understand how you're claiming that she's behaving this way *except* when I'm around. It doesn't make any sense to me."

Randy and others told me after the campaign that it appeared a couple of the paid operatives were building up a stock of half-truths and innuendoes concerning not just me, but *each other* to ensure that in the case of defeat, blame could be laid at somebody else's feet. Randy wasn't the only one who thought so. At around the same time, the Internet site *Politico* ran a story that claimed that Schmidt and his operatives had already put into motion a plan to destroy my reputation in order to save their own. He attributed his story to an "unnamed source" inside the McCain campaign. Other media outlets started reporting the same thing.

Then, somewhere high inside the campaign, the gloves came off. Randy, I later learned, walked into a communications meeting in the campaign office and found about eight comm people sitting around a U-shaped table, all buzzing over something big. One of the guys pointed to a computer screen and said, "Read this."

It was a CNN story, byline Dana Bash:

PALIN'S OFF-SCRIPT COMMENTS IRK McCAIN AIDES

Several McCain advisers suggested that they have become increasingly frustrated with what one aide described as Palin "going rogue." A Palin associate, however, said the candidate is simply trying to "bust free" of what she believes was a damaging and mismanaged roll-out.

McCain sources say Palin has gone off-message several times, and they privately wonder whether the incidents were deliberate. They cited an instance in which she labeled robo-calls—recorded messages often used to attack a candidate's opponent—"irritating" even as the campaign defended their use. Also, they pointed to her telling reporters she disagreed with the campaign's decision to pull out of Michigan.

Bash went on to note that "tensions like those within the McCain-Palin campaign are not unusual; vice presidential candidates also have a history of butting heads with the top of the ticket."

Randy finished reading the story. "I don't believe this!" he yelled. "Those guys have gone too far this time!"

It may not be unusual for major-ticket advisers to struggle internally over who calls the shots, or to offer only tepid public support to one half of the ticket or the other, Randy later told me. But it is unheard of for campaign staffers to brazenly throw a candidate under the media bus with sleazy anonymous comments.

Randy stormed toward Schmidt's office and confronted his secretary. "Where is he? I want his cell number *right now.*"

The door to Schmidt's office opened, and suddenly he was standing there.

Randy glared at him. "We've got to talk."

They stepped inside. Randy slammed the door and told Schmidt what he really thought. "It is unbelievable that advisers—*senior advisers*—are calling the press and telling them the vice presidential candidate is a diva! This is unprecedented! It's unacceptable!"

Schmidt looked at Randy, poker-faced. "Who do you think it is? The leak?"

"Is it Mark or Nicolle?"

"No, it's not," Schmidt said.

"Who the hell else is it? You guys have all been criticizing the governor like crazy!"

"Well, what about the *Politico* story?" Schmidt was referring to the piece in which an anonymous staffer had warned that McCain insiders were going to start taking me apart.

"You think I was the source for that?"

"No," Schmidt said.

"Well, I wasn't. But that's minor. Now you've got these lies all over CNN."

"It wasn't Nicolle," Schmidt said.

Randy laid out a very simple case: "Picking a running mate was John's most important decision, and being loyal to John means being loyal to his pick. That makes what's going on absolutely atrocious!"

Schmidt started in again, telling Randy what an awful pick I was—the "postpartum" problems, the wardrobe "scandal," "legal exposure" for Todd on Troopergate, whatever he meant by that. Somehow the Palins were responsible for all of the campaign's problems.

"This is absolutely outrageous!" Randy said. He started to walk out of the office but Schmidt stopped him.

Then, Randy says, Schmidt issued a threat that was veiled enough for deniability but as clear as day if you were on the receiving end: if there were any more leaks critical of anybody in the handling of Sarah Palin, then a lot more negative stuff would be said *about* Sarah Palin.

I knew none of that then, and Schmidt would later contradict Randy's account. At the time, I was just focused on finishing strong. I want to believe the tension between Schmidt and the B Team was a result of less-than-ideal circumstances in the pressure cooker of a national campaign, and that it wasn't personal. But as I realized back in my Wasilla mayor days, life is too short to hold a grudge. If I ever see Schmidt again, maybe I'll bring him a pretty white Peace Lily.

———

At the start of the campaign, I had discussed with McCain senior staffers my giving three key policy speeches—one each on energy, women's issues, and people with special needs. But September sped by, then October. Finally, with just two weeks to go before the election, I was scheduled to present our policy on special needs issues. *Very good,* I thought, remembering what had actually been my first campaign promise: that if John and I were elected, the special needs community would have an advocate in the White House. I could write the speech myself, weave in a lot of my family's experiences with Trig and with my nephew Karcher.

I heard we were to give the speech in a hotel ballroom. "We'll find a small campaign audience to show up," headquarters said.

The B Team thought, come on, we can do better than that. What's the point of getting forty Republicans in a room to listen to me talk? We've had thousands from the special needs community show up at our rallies, and surely there was such a community in Pittsburgh who would honor us with their presence at this event. Why not invite them to participate?

Headquarters was actually receptive to that idea and got to work on making it happen.

Then we found out, for the first time, that headquarters had employed a special needs coordinator who had provided a speech. (The special needs coordinator also called the B Team to say that we should no longer use the term "special needs people" because special needs families find it offensive. I guess I was behind the times.)

I looked the speech over and thought it was fine, but I also thought, *Anyone could give this speech. Where's my own connection to it? Where's Trig? Why should anyone care more about the issue after hearing this?*

So I reworked it and continued rewriting right up until the time I gave it, with the good people of the Woodlands Foundation, the Down Syndrome Center at the Children's Hospital of Pittsburgh, AutismLink, the Children's Institute of Pittsburgh, and others in attendance.

"Too often, even in our own day, children with special needs have been set apart and excluded. Too often, state and federal laws add to their challenges, instead of removing barriers and opening new paths of opportunity," I began. "Too often, they are made to feel that there is no place for them in the life of our country, that they don't count or have nothing to contribute."

I continued by saying that I loved it when the families of children with special needs came out to rallies and events. "You bring your sons and daughters with you, because you are proud of them, as I am of my son," I said. "My little fella sleeps during most of these rallies, even when they get pretty rowdy. He would be amazed to know how many folks come out to see *him* instead of me." I loved that fact!

"You know that there are the world's standards of perfection, and then there are God's, and these are the final measure," I said.

"Every child is beautiful before God, and dear to Him for their own sake. And the truest measure of any society is how it treats those who are most vulnerable."

I went on to discuss specific policies a McCain-Palin administration would implement for special needs kids. For example, we would reprioritize some of the $18 billion a year Congress spends on its pork projects and instead fully fund the Individuals with Disabilities Education Act.

"We're going to get our federal priorities straight and fulfill our country's commitment to give every child opportunity and hope in life."

I talked about my efforts as a governor. I told them I knew John's and Cindy's hearts were with me on this issue. I wanted White House people and policies to show the respect and dignity these families deserved. We still get e-mails about that speech today, saying, "This is why we connected with you. We felt you understood us."

There wasn't much promotion of that message. I didn't want that for my own sake, Lord knows, but it needed to be shared. Republicans are often stereotyped as a pack of politicians without compassion. Here was a chance to show that caring hearts did beat at the center of the common sense conservative movement. And in effective ways that don't only call on government to deliver caring solutions, because government *can't* deliver caring solutions. We needed to explain that under GOP leadership, caring people would not be shut out by policies that discourage nonprofits, churches, and generous individuals, but instead would be empowered to continue their good work.

I gave two more policy speeches, one on energy and one on women's issues, with a similar lack of promotion. That was a surprising strategy. I wished we could have done more. We asked whether we could expand the message, but by then it seemed, at least according to reports like the *New York Times Magazine* piece by Robert Draper, that headquarters might already have given up. The article telegraphed a defeatist mentality among some of the campaign operatives. That surprised the rest of us, because we still had more than two weeks until election day—an eternity in politics.

16

As October 31 neared, the press pool on the plane kept asking Piper, "What are you going to be for Halloween?" Piper played it kind of coy and wouldn't let anyone in on her secret: she was going to dress up as a snow princess. Her plan was that she'd get to be a princess all day long at whatever campaign stops were scheduled. Still, we all felt bad that the kids were going to miss Halloween. At our house we milk every holiday and birthday for all it's worth. Todd always says that only the Heath family can stretch a single birthday over three days' time.

When you're a kid, October 31 is all about one thing: candy. So, instead of passing out her stickers on the rope line, Piper would pass out candy. The B Team called headquarters to secure permission for the kids to trick-or-treat, but they wanted it to be politically useful by picking a neighborhood of swing voters. I hoped it wouldn't turn into merely a photo op because the kids had been so patient through all this, managing school schedules during the week in Alaska, then meeting up with us when they could for once-in-a-lifetime life lessons all across the country. Jason said it would get pretty clustered up if it stayed in the hands of someone in headquarters, so he kicked it over to the Secret Service.

The staff threw a Halloween party for the kids at the hotel. Nothing fancy, but so thoughtful! Chris brought in Chinese food and the advance team bought six pumpkins and carving equipment so the girls could make jack-o'-lanterns. Then on Halloween night, we all dressed up—Piper as the snow princess, Trig as a cute little elephant, me as Tina Fey again.

We were in Harrisburg, Pennsylvania, and the whole costumed crew jumped on the bus and drove over to an all-American neighborhood the Secret Service picked out. Piper was so excited. Here she'd thought she was going to miss out on Halloween and all these people had pitched in to make the night special after all. It really was nice.

For the first couple of houses, things went along fine. I carried our little elephant and held Piper's hand. It was dark by then. We rang doorbells and the kids yelled, "Trick or treat!" Nice, normal people greeted us, told the incognito kids "how cute," and doled out candy, just like at home. But it didn't take long for the people in the neighborhood to wonder why there were photographers walking backward and flashes popping in front of a snow princess, an elephant, and a comedienne, who were also being followed by a phalanx of large, serious-looking men in suits with wires sticking out of their ears. Before we knew it, a crowd had clustered around, taking pictures and shouting out questions.

I felt guilty as heck. This was supposed to be Piper's night, but she was shuffled off to the side to get her out of the path of the surging crowd that moved forward when I did, stopped when I did, and would've probably moved backward if I had, too. In the end, we got to go to only a few houses, and when the Secret Service hustled us back onto the bus, Tony, the head of the detail, had to confiscate Piper's candy.

"May I have your candy?" he said to Piper. "I need to check it, honey, make sure it's safe." To Piper, those were fighting words. Man, I felt sorry for Tony, because he was so caring and kind, but he was also a professional, which meant he was forced to be the bad guy. He had to sit there and screen the candy piece by piece, discarding anything unwrapped, whittling down the tiny amount Piper had collected while she stared . . . and glared.

A couple of well-meaning reporters on the bus asked her, "So, how'd you do?"

Always candid and keeping it real, Piper said, "It was the worst Halloween ever!" She then returned to her duty, watching poor Tony, bald head down, spectacles on, and broad shoulders curved, sadly doing his job, holding each treat up to the light like a potentially poisonous scientific specimen.

Jason and Tracey had earlier telephoned the press pool, who were waiting for us on the campaign plane.

"Things didn't go too well here," Jason told one of the reporters. "Could you guys make sure there's some candy for the kids on the plane?

"Are you kidding?" the reporter said. "We've been planning this for weeks!"

When we got back to the plane, the press pool had mounds of candy and treat bags and fun stuff for the girls, so much that when they finished "trick-or-treating" down the aisle, their baskets were overflowing. Piper hit the roof with happiness! When we took off, she sat in the back giggling with her reporter buddies and eating as much candy as she wanted. I think she stayed up all night.

———

The next day, November 1, the bus was rolling through Florida when Bexie handed me a cell phone. We were heading from a rally in New Port Richey to another in Polk City, near Lakeland. Florida Governor Charlie Crist was aboard, sitting up front. Todd and I were in the back.

"It's Nicolas Sarkozy," Bexie said, holding out the phone.

Oh, that's right, I thought. *It's on the schedule.* When headquarters let the B Team know the president of France would be calling, I'd immediately regretted not having paid more attention in Mrs. Lawton's high school French class.

By that time I'd received calls from presidents of other countries and our own, and had met elder statesmen and other dignitaries, so it didn't surprise us too much that we'd be speaking with the French leader.

"This is Nicolas Sarkozy speaking," said a deeply accented voice. "How are you?"

"Oh, it's so good to hear from you," I said. "Thank you for calling us."

"Oh, it's a pleasure." Sarkozy pronounced it *ple-zhur.*

We exchanged some pleasantries and discussed our campaign's performance in the polls.

Then Sarkozy said, "Well, I know very well that the campaign can be exhausting. How do you feel right now, my dear?"

My dear? That, and a few other things, were a little off. I wondered what time it was in France—maybe he was sipping a bit before he placed the call?

"I feel so good, I feel like we're in a marathon and at the very end of the marathon you get your second wind and you plow through the finish."

"You see, I got elected in France because I'm real, and you seem to be someone who's real as well," Sarkozy said.

Weird thing for a president to say. What to say back? "Yes, Nicolas, we so appreciate this opportunity."

I laughed, keeping it light.

Then Sarkozy started talking about hunting, and suggested we get together and hunt from helicopters, which Alaska hunters don't do (despite circulated Photoshopped images of me drawing a bead on a wolf from the air). He finished his comment with a long French phrase.

He's got to be drunk, I thought.

"Yes, you know we have a lot in common because from my house I can see Belgium. That's kind of less interesting than you."

It was getting weirder. The man on the phone began singing some freaky song, saying his wife was jealous of our phone call. He made some reference to *Hustler* magazine, which I didn't quite catch—I didn't want to offend the president of France, but this was getting stupid. I kept thinking, surely, someone will pop up and say something like, "Okay, the five minutes are up," but the call just went on and on and on. By now, I was thinking *exit strategy*. And I kept trying to laugh, even though it was increasingly unfunny.

"I really love you! . . ." the Frenchman was saying. And finally: "You've been pranked . . . we're two comedians from Montreal."

I pulled the phone away from my head and announced to the staff. "We've been pranked."

Bexie turned white.

"Oh, we've been pranked," I said into the phone. "What radio station is this?"

"Hello?" the man said. "If one voice can change the world for Obama, one Viagra can change the world for McCain."

I handed Bexie her cell phone.

"I'm sorry, I have to let you go," Bexie said, near tears, already imagining the heat about to come down from headquarters. "Thank you."

That's when the *merde* hit the fan.

Right away, the phones started ringing. One of the first calls was Schmidt, and the force of his screaming blew my hair back. "How can anyone be so *stupid?!* Why would the president of France call a vice presidential candidate a few days out?!"

Good question, I thought. *Weren't you the ones who set this up?*

As Schmidt's rant blazed on, I pictured cell towers between D.C. and Florida bursting into flame. I held the phone slightly away from my head.

Then I got another call. "Governor, I am *so* sorry," a campaign adviser said. "I put the call on the schedule. I thought it was vetted, but I was fooled, and I am *so* sorry."

I felt bad for him because he was an absolutely stellar professional, so I knew these radio guys had to be really good to get around him. We later found out that these same deejays had pranked a lot of leaders and celebrities, including Bono, Mick Jagger, Donald Trump, and Bill Gates. So we were in good company.

His explanation was so heartfelt.

"Don't worry about it, you don't need to apologize," I said. "It really is no big deal. We just need to dust off and move on."

When we reached Lakeland, Tucker bounded aboard the bus. "This is terrible! Terrible! I need to know everything you said in that phone call!"

I said, "Tucker, I already told Bexie and Jason what I said. Now, why don't we focus on how to fix this problem?"

"Well, this is just terrible!" he said, his face flushed red.

With the higher-ups still foaming at headquarters, the B Team swung into action. Jason called a friend who worked for the Canadian prime minister and within five minutes had a transcript of the call. Then Tracey Schmitt wrote a terrific statement, which had already hit the press by the time the Lakeland rally began.

"Governor Palin was mildly amused to learn that she had joined the ranks of heads of state, including President Sarkozy, and other celebrities in being targeted by these pranksters," Tracey wrote. "C'est la vie."

———

As the campaign drew to a close, my family and I were still pumped. We were having the time of our lives, and we ramped up our efforts to make clear to voters the distinctions between a McCain administration and an Obama administration, working to win a few more votes. In the final day before the election, John and I crisscrossed the nation separately in order to hit as many states as was physically possible. John touched down in Florida, Tennessee, Pennsylvania, Indiana, New Mexico, Nevada, and Arizona. The VP team moved from the east to the west, also chasing the sun, and hit seven rallies in Ohio, Missouri, Iowa, Colorado, and Nevada. Our families provided incredible support that day, speaking all over the nation at campaign events in key states.

On November 3, we joined Chuck and Sally and Chuck Jr., and Jim and Faye for a final late-evening event in a high school gym in Elko, Nevada, then flew through the night to Alaska to cast our votes. Todd and all our parents were, in my opinion, some of the campaign's best advocates for John McCain's message. It was perfect that we got to wrap it all up, together, in a high school gym just like the one we'd all been joined together in when Todd and I met twenty-seven years earlier. We had begun the journey when we landed in Arizona for vetting on a pitch-black night. Now, in the early hours of November 4, we landed in Anchorage in darkness, too. A fleet of Suburbans whisked us fifty miles from the airport to Wasilla, and when Todd and I arrived at City Hall, we were overjoyed to see crowds of friends and supporters standing in the frigid arctic darkness cheering on one of their own. I was so humbled—and so excited to see everyone after the weeks away. It felt good to be home.

After a round of handshakes and hugs, I stepped into City Hall. It was a full-circle moment: the place where Todd and I cast our ballots for president and vice president of the United States was where I had attended the second grade and, later, all those city meetings. I was even wearing the same wardrobe I had often worn back then—jeans, a Carhartt jacket, and a relieved smile. I marveled at life's Providential paths. Others may call such events "coincidences"; I believe they are miracles.

Despite the previous all-nighter and the pundits' swan song for our ticket, I felt great. I felt *thankful.* After voting, we jogged across the street to the well-lit line of partisan demarcation to greet some dear friends . . . and a large gathering of international reporters.

Well, this is good! I thought. *Our tiny town making news around the world!*

Jason took a couple of phone calls and I saw him shaking his head. Someone from headquarters was calling to tell the B Team to "put her back in the truck!" The instruction was not to allow Todd or me to talk to the reporters who had traveled all the way to Wasilla.

Nah, not this time, I thought, and walked over to finally say hello. Afterward, we scooted back to the trucks and began the police-escort motorcade back to Anchorage. After a quick run through a couple of coffee stands, we stopped at my brother-in-law's gas station for snacks. It seemed fitting that after some hundred-plus interviews across a hundred-plus cities, plus 130 campaign events, some of them glitzy, our last off-the-record campaign stop was at an ordinary family business.

As we boarded the campaign plane bound for Phoenix, I was confident but prepared to accept America's decision. Kris and I talked about the possibility of miracles. We honestly believed it could happen. We would not be surprised if voters entered the booth and pulled the lever for the GOP despite what the polls said.

No matter what happened, though, I knew that personally I was much better off depending on God's plan, not my own. It's easy to forget that in the chaos of a national election. But when life invariably leads me back to that truth, my perspective changes and I find peace amidst all storms. Stepping back onto the plane, I silently acknowledged my human weaknesses, consciously handed my future over to God, and asked for His wisdom, strength, and grace.

17

In the week leading up to the election, Matthew Scully and I, along with a quiet, levelheaded speechwriter named Lindsay Hayes, worked on a speech I would give on election night. The national media had already given the McCain campaign last rites. But the B Team refused to give up.

By election day, Matthew, Lindsay, and I had two speeches in our back pockets—one victory and one concession. I wanted to make sure that in either case, the speech focused on two things: reminding Americans of what kind of man John McCain is and what he had promised to do for the country—and moving forward, uniting with a new administration, while still holding it accountable where we disagreed. We were committed to this, to stand strong for America. Either way, I wanted to focus on giving a shout-out to John and to tell our nation, "Thank you for the honor of a lifetime for my family and me. We are so proud to be Americans!" I also wanted to say a word—finally—in appreciation of the Bush-Cheney administration's efforts.

I was so happy to have my family and friends in Arizona with me. Todd's parents had flown in all the way from Dillingham. Mom and Dad and my siblings and their families. Todd's siblings and step-siblings. Martin Buser, the Iditarod musher, had flown down with his wife. Todd's Iron Dog partner, Scott Davis, and his wife made the trip. Meg Stapleton, Kris and her family, some of the kids' friends. And they were from all these different little towns across Alaska where you have to drive for hours or fly in a puddle jumper just to get to Anchorage so you can then leave the state. After that, it's a four-hour trip just to get to the Lower 48. Then *another* flight to get down to Arizona. I was glad that they'd all endured the journey to be together on this amazing day, especially since I'd hardly had time to give anyone the time of day since August 29. I promised to make it up to everyone, and someday I will.

During the crush of the campaign, family and friends unfortunately didn't always come first, a fact that nagged at me the whole time. Now I was looking forward to being able, finally, to take a deep breath and enjoy the last part of this ride together, no matter how it turned out. And we'd be enjoying it in this beautiful, warm desert city, instead of in subzero land, where even daylight was scarce this time of year.

The Biltmore Resort was more like a complex than a traditional hotel. That meant that the rooms for everyone were spread out among the different buildings, with candidates and staff and family flung all over the place. In our room, Todd and the kids and I were with Kris and Meg as the election returns rolled in from the East to the West and flashed across the screen.

We prayed for a miracle. But finally the moment came when it was clear to all of us in the room that we were not going to win. It was very, very disappointing. Yes, it had been a great contest and a historic election. And I still believed we had the stronger, smarter agenda for the country. It was unfortunate that our message didn't seem to take hold. As Vince Lombardi said, "Winning isn't everything, but wanting to win is." Yes, we had wanted to win. Very much, for America.

In any case, I knew Matthew and Lindsay had done the campaign proud. It was time to step aside, but at least I was going to have this last moment to acknowledge my debt to John and thank him for giving me and my family—and Alaska!—this incredible experience. I wanted to tell Americans to keep on fighting for what is right—*and not to let anyone tell them to sit down and shut up.*

As I got ready for the concession speeches, I noticed a lot of BlackBerry traffic—even more than usual. It was then that Jason said, "This is unbelievable. It sounds like you're not going to be giving the speech after all." Other staffers' mouths fell open.

Someone poked their head into the room and said, "Governor, they want you over at Senator McCain's suite."

I carried the speech to John's suite, wondering why headquarters would have had us spend all this time drafting a speech if I wasn't going to deliver it.

John's suite was packed with campaign staff when we walked in. A senior staffer came over to me. "You know you won't be giving a speech," he said.

"It's a powerful message," I told him. "Scully did a great job. It's a shout-out to John McCain and reminds the country that he's an American hero. This is all about unity and bringing the country together now."

Then Schmidt waded in. "You're not giving one because it's never been done in the history of presidential politics," he said. "The vice presidential candidate does not give a concession speech."

I knew he was wrong about that. But I wasn't going to argue with him. So I just said, "Steve, a lot of things have never been done before." John hadn't earned his reputation for independent thinking by doing things the way they'd always been done, and neither had I.

"Don't think of it as a concession speech," I said. "Think of it as a way of honoring the man we've been working for all these months."

"Absolutely not," Schmidt said. "I don't even know why you wrote a speech. Nobody told you to."

That set me back on my heels. I was surprised that he was surprised. I didn't find out until after the campaign where the idea of a concession speech had originated—it had come from the most natural source: Matthew Scully. About a week out from election day, he had realized that since I'd been a bit more visible than some vice presidential candidates, there was a good possibility I might be asked to speak on election night. John Edwards had spoken in 2004, and one of Scully's responsibilities as a speechwriter was to be proactive, to make sure that the candidate was never caught without something to say.

In Phoenix, on election day, he met separately with both Rick Davis and Mark Salter and told them he'd been working on the speeches.

"I have these ready, just in case," Scully told Davis.

"Okay, so she would speak before he does? . . ." Davis said.

"We could do it that way. She could introduce him."

"Okay, that could work," Davis said.

Nothing was decided.

Later, Scully told Mark Salter about the speeches. Salter, exhausted from flying all night, said something like, "Great, that sounds great."

Again, nothing was decided.

But of course, I didn't know any of that. Since headquarters had micromanaged everything I did and said for weeks, I had no idea that they hadn't been the origin of the speech. So when I got the news I wasn't speaking, it felt to me like some kind of punishment, a slap in the face.

In truth, it was all a tangle of miscommunication and misunderstandings between worn-out people trying to cope with a shattering defeat.

But in the heat of the moment, the conversation with Schmidt ended abruptly. I was ushered into a room where John was waiting; he sat in an upholstered chair, and other guys sat on the edge of the bed. Schmidt came in too, and slouched in a chair like a pile of laundry. I felt bad for him—all his energy and efforts—he said he was leaving in the morning for some island.

John had a conciliatory look on his face. "Hey, Sarah," he said. "We fought a good fight and I'm going to just get out there and thank America." John smiled.

"Well, you worked hard, and I want to get out there and thank *you*," I said.

"No, these guys have it covered," he said, nodding in Schmidt's direction. "They've got it handled."

I knew that was that. I thanked John again for everything and walked out of the room. I was still absorbing the no-speech decision when campaign handlers starting rounding us up. "Let's go! Time to go to the stage! John's ready to go!"

Wait a minute, I thought. Where's my family? We're hardly dressed. Aunts and uncles and cousins had gathered from Washington to Texas for the final night, and no one knew where they were supposed to be or even when the speech was. The B Team was scattered all over, too. Todd and I shook our heads—the "experts" still didn't get it. What mattered to us was showing respect for the everyday, hardworking folks who had put their lives on hold and dedicated everything they had, everything, to fight for what's right. It had been the most spectacular ride—a roller coaster, yes, but we'd do it all over again in a heartbeat— and we'd learned some lessons along the way. I felt this ending in Arizona deprived a lot of people of some joy that could still be salvaged from the night.

"Wait a minute," I told the handlers. "My family . . . let me get them organized."

"No! No time! We have to go *now!*"

This isn't the way it's supposed to end, I thought. I walked toward the stage with just Todd and some of the kids, with a rolled-up speech in my hands that I wasn't going to give. I glanced around the area for any more of the five generations of our American family to share in this. Not many were around.

It was a warm, starry Arizona night. The expansive stage had been set up with a spectacularly huge American flag behind us.

"Excuse me, Governor," one of the McCain handlers said. "Just want to let you know, last-minute changes, Todd and the kids won't be allowed on the stage."

"Oh," I said. Now they weren't just in the back of the bus, they were in the luggage compartment. Todd was again relegated to the belly of the plane. I chuckled at the imagery because he'd been there before, *exactly* twenty years earlier, and we'd loved our simple life then.

Piper wasn't thrilled when I had to shoo her and her cousins away. Todd came up onstage anyway. And we stood with the senator and his wife. John gave one of the most gracious concession speeches a political candidate has ever made.

He was his patriotic and inspiring self. He talked about how far America had come. He thanked Cindy and the rest of his family and urged his supporters to unite behind the new president, then finished strong: "Tonight—tonight, more than any night—I hold in my heart nothing but love for this country and for all its citizens . . . I wish Godspeed to the man who was my former opponent and will be my president. And I call on all Americans, as I have often in this campaign, to not despair of our present difficulties . . . Americans never quit. We never surrender. We never hide from history, we make history."

The crowd responded with sincere applause, and I embraced John with affection and gratitude.

Back at the hotel, Jason, Andy Davis, and other staffers went to a couple of postelection parties in different suites and hotel bars. I guess it was the traditional election night letdown and data dump of people who had been going for weeks at light speed finally getting a chance to unwind. In addition to seeking campaign staffers and booze, reporters attend these parties as a matter of ritual, looking for colorful quotes and inside stories. But at gatherings tonight, Jason told me later, things were different: reporters already had their inside stories.

"It's going to get really, really bad tomorrow," several reporters told Jason at different times, in different ways. "You know that, right?"

"No, I don't know that. What's the deal?" Jason said.

"A few McCain senior staffers have been going around the campaign plane feeding stories to reporters on background. They knew McCain was going to lose. The staffers were telling us all we could run with the stories right after the election."

"What kind of stories?" Jason said.

"Negative stories, mostly about the governor and her family."

The whole family had been set to fly back to Alaska the next day, but we pushed the flight back a few hours so that we could pack up and take advantage of a few hours of morning sunshine. As the kids reminded us, how often did they get a chance to sit by an outdoor pool in early November? Todd, the grandparents, the kids and cousins set up camp on lounge chairs. Trig napped on my chest while I called my Anchorage and Juneau offices. Kris and Meg were also there, cell phones humming. My chief of staff, Mike Nizich, and his wife joined us poolside. Jason and Jeannie joined us, too. When Trig finally stirred, I went over and sat on the edge of the pool with my baby boy, listening to his giggles as I dipped his tiny toes in the pool. It was peaceful.

Then I looked up and saw Mark and Nicolle walking toward Todd.

"We just came over to say good-bye," Nicolle said. "It's been *so* great working with you. We really love you guys!"

Todd said something nice back. Then Nicolle said, "I think you should know that for the next few days it's going to get really nasty. Negative stories in the press. You should just be ready, that's always how it goes. Hang on to your hats!"

That made no sense to Todd—why would anything "get nasty"? And how could anyone know what would be coming in the media?

But the Wallaces waved good-bye, and that was that.

Chapter Five

The Thumpin'

*The Democrats seem to be basically nicer people, but they have
demonstrated time and again that they have the management skills of
celery. They're the kind of people who'd stop to help you change a flat,
but would somehow manage to set your car on fire. I would be reluctant
to entrust them with a Cuisinart, let alone the economy.
The Republicans, on the other hand, would know how to fix your tire,
but they wouldn't bother to stop because they'd want to be on time for
Ugly Pants Night at the country club.*

—DAVE BARRY

B ack in the campaign season of 2004 some Alaskans had
suggested that I challenge incumbent Lisa Murkowski in
the U.S. Senate race. The seat was vulnerable because of
the nepotism issue, and the GOP would have trouble holding on
to it. As always, I polled my family. Everybody thought it was a
decent idea, until I asked Track.

"I don't want you to run for U.S. Senate, Mom," said Track.
"Who would be our hockey manager?"

It sounds trivial now, but . . . who *would* be the hockey manager? At that point in his life, having an involved mom was more
important to him—and to me—than having a mom with a powerful position in Washington, D.C. So it was a pretty easy decision not to run.

I remember telling that to the same local radio host who gave me a hard time when I tried to make it to Track's boot camp graduation four years later. He treated it as if that were the phoniest excuse he'd ever heard.

"You're lying," he said. "You're chicken to run."

"Why would I lie about that?" I said. "If anything, admitting the real reason just opens me up to more criticism. It sure isn't for political gain."

There was no need to validate myself with the radio host, but he left the impression with listeners that women couldn't do more than one thing at a time. He wanted to portray me as a too-simple mom who was not serious about serving the public. He didn't understand that there is no greater service than mothering. I always admired Karen Hughes, President Bush's former adviser, because she left the White House so she could be close to her teenage son and spend quality time with him. At a crossroads, she was candid and courageous enough to tell the public she wanted to teach him how to drive. She had the right priorities.

Now, five years later, I found myself at a crossroads.

On November 5, 2008, I flew home to a political landscape that had permanently changed. The VP race had been an incredible, extraordinary ride, and I was still the same governor who had enjoyed tremendous—and humbling—citizen support just sixty-eight days earlier. But that had all changed on August 29, 2008, when John McCain and I teamed up to challenge a charismatic political figure who inspired worshipful loyalty from his supporters.

The fallout was immediate: the governor's office was inundated with frivolous ethics complaints. Literally scores of Freedom of Information Act (FOIA) and Public Records Act requests rolled in, generating thousands of pages that required hours of work to process. Reporters abandoned actual reporting in favor of tabloidizing my family, my record, and me. As the number of lawsuits filed against us mounted, and depositions, declarations, attorney time, staff time, and legal bills piled up, I asked Track again what he thought when he called home one day in the summer of 2009. The call came at noon my time, but it was the middle of the night in Baquba. For the first time in the nine months he'd been over there, my soldier sounded kind of beat.

Track was a man by then, twenty years old and serving a yearlong deployment as an infantryman. Though he didn't like the political spotlight, he had been supportive of my vice presidential bid. Now, though, he could see the beating our family was taking from half a world away, and in that summer phone call, my oldest son would once again weigh in on my political future.

2

Naturally enough, I had assumed that after the election everything would go back to the way it was before. John McCain would go back to the Senate, and I would go back to the job I loved. But what a difference ten weeks can make. Before my plane even touched down in Anchorage, shocking character assassinations of those I love had begun. Anonymous McCain campaign staffers were feeding lies to FOX News' Carl Cameron, who reported them without hearing our side of the story. I could roll with cheap shots against me, but the new blows against my family, my administration, and our state were over the top.

Other inaccurate stories followed, including one in which it was reported that RNC lawyers were flying to Alaska to retrieve clothes "stolen" from the campaign. Ironically, the campaign had *ordered* the B Team to pack the fancy RNC wardrobe into the belly of our JetBlue plane and fly it back to Wasilla. There Jason,

Jeanie, and Bexie joined us in immediately inventorying it all, right down to the $70 nylons. Then he and Todd FedExed some thirty boxes of clothes and fourteen empty suitcases to the RNC.

The media's constant pelting reminded me of the times we kids used to go out in the canoe with Dad near the Knik mud-flats early mornings before school. Fall was duck-hunting season. There would be hunters all around us, and I would huddle up, trying to stay warm, as lead pellets rained down around us in the water. I'd peer through the dark early-morning fog and grumble, "Geez, Dad! There's bullets flying around my head!"

He'd say, "Nah, that's just buckshot. Duck."

It was almost funny, certainly ridiculous, the political buck-shot critics fired our way. Nationally, pundits and reporters would criticize me for focusing on Alaska and not attending the celeb-rity-packed events we were invited to Outside; locally, the oppo-sition would criticize me for focusing on national issues—as if I suddenly needed to become parochial and think of Alaska's issues as irrelevant to the nation. In Juneau, one Democrat lawmaker complained that I wasn't as "sparky" as before and that Piper and I no longer brought around bagels like we used to. The few times I hustled out of the state to attend, for instance, a fund-raiser for kids with special needs, my Juneau critics cried that they were being abandoned.

Perhaps in another time and place it would have been endearing to know that lawmakers, mostly Democrats, wanted me nearby. ("There's a pothole that needs repair on the Seward Highway! If she goes, who will fill it?") But it was obviously disingenuous and absurd. Somehow my predecessors had been able to take extensive trips in the continental U.S. and abroad without anyone worry-ing that the state was at imminent risk of complete collapse the moment they left.

But since August 29 we were living in a "new normal."

Pundits seemed to assume that I was thinking only of my future on the national stage. And no matter how many times and in how many ways I repeated the plain fact that Alaska came first, the opposition interpreted every position I took through the prism of my supposed "national ambitions."

Even my previously positive relationship with local media changed. For example, during a routine interview for a story about a Thanksgiving turkey pardoning, our old friends at KTUU set up an odd camera angle to capture turkeys being decapitated behind me as I stood there discussing Alaska's relatively strong financial standing during the current recession. The photographer couldn't post it to the Web fast enough. The video became an instant YouTube hit.

Now, I'd be the first person to tell you where your Thanksgiving meal comes from, but this was a deliberate move to make some noise. My deputy press secretary, Sharon Leighow, was appalled after it aired and called the photographer to ask him why he'd done that. We'd worked with this photog for years and had known him (and the station) to have integrity.

The KTUU news director told Kris and me later that he was profoundly sorry for the station's lack of professionalism and that he had not known his employee to have ever engaged in that kind of tactic before. Kris told him he needed to catch up with the times: his photog and one of his reporters had approached her that day about an idea they had for a reality TV show starring me. We declined.

"Oh," the news director said quietly. "No, I didn't know my guys were doing that."

That was an ultimately harmless incident (for everyone but the turkey), but there were others that left us truly appalled.

In February, an Associated Press reporter asked Sharon if our commissioners could attend a press conference with me because it was more convenient for the media to have all of us there at once. I thought it was a great idea. This reporter and her colleagues piled into the room, laden with notebooks and tape recorders.

It worked out very well. I encouraged the commissioners to chime in anytime, and I had three sheets of paper in front of me that gave the most recent data on energy prices and projections that I knew we'd address. Sharon was so pleased with the press conference and thought this AP reporter brilliant for her suggestion—until we read her story claiming that I had to "rely on [my] commissioners and notes to answer questions."

Sharon read it and shook her head. She knew we'd been set up.

Another time this same reporter stopped Kris and me in the Capitol hallway for a quick interview. She wanted to discuss a string of what she considered "failures," including the sudden acceleration of ethics charges and the (illegal) leaking of those claims to the public. Pen and pad in hand, she asked, "How do you handle so many setbacks? How do you get through such a lousy week?"

"A 'lousy' week? Really?" I said. "My son just called from Iraq. He is safe today. We just found out the holes in Trig's heart are closing up on their own, thank God, and he won't need open-heart surgery. My daughters are good, my husband is good. Alaska is healthy and strong. No, ma'am, it hasn't been a lousy week—it's been *great*."

Meanwhile, members of the national press continued to hang out in Alaska sniffing for tabloid stuff. In one early press conference we noticed that our local reporters were flanked by a couple of reporters from the Lower 48 who'd been hanging around Juneau in search of material for their own Sarah Palin book. We never shut our doors to anyone, so people of all kinds attended these press availabilities. We didn't check credentials.

But glancing along the side wall, I recognized these particular folks as the same ones who had cornered Piper on her walk home from Harborview Elementary School and talked to her for who knows how long about who knows what. That day Piper had come to my office and said, "Mom, remember those reporters who came on the campaign plane with us? You know, the ones Nicolle said didn't like us very much? They just interviewed me on the sidewalk."

That was Piper's last independent walk from school.

Reporters from across the nation camped out at the end of our driveway in Wasilla and on the ice in front of our home. They incessantly called and stopped by my parents' and siblings' and in-laws' homes and businesses. Hostile political operatives barraged Meg and her husband's home, medical practice, and neighbors, and bugged my attorney, my doctor, and anyone else who might have anything to do with us. Every once in a while a friend or family member would think they could trust a reporter, and so they'd talk to them. And almost 100 percent of the time Todd and I would get a call later from a panicked loved one saying, "Geez! We can't win! That reporter took what I said all out of context." Or even worse, "I never said that!" We assured them we knew, it was okay, it was just the unproductive game some chose to play.

Challenges with the traditional media were one thing, but in addition there were the "new media"—the left-wing bloggers. The lines between the two were often blurred, with stories starting in the blogosphere and leapfrogging to old-media channels. And some of the strangest, the conspiracy-nut "Trig Truthers" were still at it, harassing my attorney and my doctor.

I loved my dad's straight talk on the subject when he had to respond to one Truther: "I know Trig is hers, dumbass. I was there when he popped out!"

When the bloggers weren't busy pushing fairy tales, they would post threatening stories about any number of looming scandals that would drive me out of office. Such threats were meant to wear at our credibility, so people would believe that I was always on the brink of political destruction. During a trip to central Texas for a gasline meeting in June 2009, Meg broke the news about one such Internet rumor, though I had a hard time hearing her through her peals of laughter. A group of left-wing bloggers had been yakking about porn pictures and videos of me that they threatened would soon be released to the public.

"And these sexy videos were supposedly shot between *which* pregnancies?" I asked.

Every action we took—or didn't take—was fodder for the national media. It was a pathetic and chilling thing to watch because I knew we weren't the first this had happened to, and won't be the last—until Americans say *enough*.

I don't like to hear people complain; I am the first to say, "Buck up or stay in the truck." You have a choice about how to react to circumstances. But I will state this complaint for the record: what used to be called "mainstream" national media are, in many respects, worthless as a source of factual information anymore. The sin of omission glares in their reporting. Perhaps national press outlets just don't have the resources anymore to devote to balanced coverage. Perhaps they've all just given up on themselves, so we've given up on them, too, except to treat their shoddy reporting like a car crash—sometimes you just have to look. The time has come to acknowledge that it is counterfeit objectivity the liberal media try to sell consumers. A period in the great American experiment has passed. We are moving into a new, more intelligent realm to gather information differently in order to hold our government accountable. Thank God there are still a few credible broadcasters on cable news, plus informative talk radio, common sense blogs, and some fine, fact-based print publications. Beware of the left's attempts to silence these—as they have already with the bogus "Fairness Doctrine," which attempts to blunt the force of conservative talk radio—and join me in being all over it when censoring efforts crop up.

To be fair, there were other channels of misinformation, too. In ordinary times, there would not be national interest in issues like my Alaska State Supreme Court appointments. But I had just appointed a well-qualified woman to serve on the highest court in the state, and now I got a call at midnight from the pastor of a large ministry in the Lower 48. I had never met this man, but he told me that he'd been at a conference when he received a message that threw the conferees for a loop. The problem? I had appointed a judge who this pastor didn't think was pro-life enough.

The kids were asleep so I tried to keep the conversation quiet. "How could you have done that? Our church has been praying for you," the pastor said, sounding exasperated. "I can't tell you how disappointed we are."

I felt bad for him as he spoke because I knew where he was going with the conversation. I hung in there, hearing him out until he came up for air. I finally tiptoed out of the bedroom so I wouldn't awaken Trig, who was snuggled in his crib next to our bed.

"Sir, with all due respect, let me tell you what the circumstances are." I then explained what I used as criteria for my judicial appointments, and that I chose judges who were strict constitutional constructionists, since those who were not often undermined public trust by making law from the hip.

"Alaska follows the Missouri Plan," I explained. That system of judicial appointments was designed to remove political biases from the process, but instead adds to it by limiting governors to a small group of appointees to choose from. So here I was, in the early-morning hours, explaining a process in which politics and personalities often outweigh experience and merit because someone thought spreading misinformation about my judicial philosophy was a smart thing to do.

By then, the pastor seemed to understand the circumstances. The woman I nominated didn't pass the litmus test he wanted to apply, but the other guy wouldn't have passed it either. The pastor had been falsely led to believe—by a local pro-family group—that I had chosen the woman candidate simply because she was a woman.

"I'm going to assume this group will choose to react differently now that they know the circumstances," I told the pastor. "They can put their energies into changing the law that dictates how the Judicial Council selection process works."

Thankfully, a few months later the group said it was working on exactly that.

3

On June 7, 2009, Rudy Giuliani and his wife took Todd, our fourteen-year-old daughter, Willow, and me to a Yankees game. Willow's friends back home texted her teasing messages because they saw her on TV—she was there in Yankee Stadium with Giuliani! Baseball, hot dogs, sunshine, and family time—it was one of the most incredible afternoons we got to spend together that summer.

Later that week, in Texas, I met with representatives of Exxon-Mobil and TransCanada-Alaska to discuss their proposal to partner in building the natural gas pipeline under AGIA. This partnership between the largest corporation in the world and the best pipeline construction company in the world would be a historic agreement. I was confident Alaska would be protected, and excited for the agreement to be announced the next day. No doubt, it would also be the biggest news to hit Alaska and certain sectors of the world's energy markets in years, and a strong step toward achieving energy independence for America. My family had joined me in Texas after the meeting, and they were eager to play for a day at our friends' house in the quaint all-Western town of Giddings. I promised to join them after a couple of interviews to get the word out about the gasline agreement. We would set up interviews with NBC's Matt Lauer and CNN's Wolf Blitzer that morning. Matt had been decent to date, and we liked his producer, Matt Glick.

Wolf? Well, I like his mom.

We negotiated the one mandatory term of the interviews: the first question had to be about the gasline, not the tabloid stuff that people were making up. By then we were fielding questions from reporters across the country who wanted a comment about a "joke" David Letterman had told on his CBS late-night show about Willow's visit to New York. He had made a crude reference to her having been "knocked up in the seventh inning by Yankee infielder Alex Rodriguez."

We had already learned that the national media's game was to bait us with caustic, untrue reports just so we would comment and they could make a story out of it. But this time I was caught off guard when radio host John Ziegler asked me about the Letterman clip, because I hadn't seen it. I gave a quick answer, and from there the left turned it into a firestorm of accusations that we couldn't take a joke and that I had exploited my daughter because she had attended a ball game with me.

No, I guess I can't take a joke that suggests it's funny to humiliate a young girl and pretend that statutory rape by a thirty-four-year-old man is something to laugh about.

More telling, though, was the reaction by some women's groups and feminists, who, as usual, stayed silent too long. If they couldn't articulate some concern, if not outrage, that this kind of "humor" was still acceptable—to the detriment of young women, who are already too often made to feel like sex objects by sexist older men—then these women's rights activists were hypocrites.

Not long after this, gossipmongers began spreading lies that Todd and I were divorcing. The kids saw the pictures on the front page of glossy tabloids, and we were forced to waste time fielding network news questions because they were running with the "story" whether it was true or not. They used as evidence a picture of my ringless left hand. I often didn't wear my $35 wedding ring because I often didn't wear any jewelry at all. Todd didn't even have a ring, and neither one of us worried about that, nor did we think media personalities should worry about it either.

That day in sunny Texas when the divorce rumors were rampant in the tabloids, I watched Todd, tanned and shirtless, take the baby from my arms and walk him back to the ranch house so Trig could nap while I made calls. Seeing Todd's blue eyes smiling, I chuckled.

Dang, I thought. *Divorce Todd? Have you* seen *Todd?*

⸻

Stuff like this makes you wonder why anyone would keep coming back for more in public service—especially when you get an up-close and personal look at the popular political blood sport called the "politics of personal destruction."

Prior to the VP campaign, my administration had received a normal number of legitimate FOIA requests from the public and media pertaining to official communications. This is good; this holds government accountable. But over the next ten months, the FOIA requests swelled into a tidal wave, and my administration was hit with *hundreds* of demands for all communications: months' worth of e-mails between me, Todd, and my staff, and every other combination of e-mail addressees you can imagine. Only the opposition really comprehends the work involved with FOIA requests—from the retrieval of all correspondence and e-mails, to copying them for lawyers and staff to review in order to remove confidential or privileged information, to assembling and packing them, and on and on. Just *one* of these requests for a certain batch of e-mails generated 24,000 individual sheets of paper. So instead of doing our jobs, my staff, including attorneys, spent thousands of hours and wasted more than $2 million of public monies to sort through it all one sheet at a time.

The FOIAs were fishing expeditions—just attempts to see what could be seen, then pick it over to see if something, anything, might generate another story. Meanwhile, opponents filed many baseless ethics complaints and lawsuits against me. Combined with the FOIAs, the sheer volume of paperwork and legally required responses brought the business of governing the State of Alaska to a grinding halt. Eventually, it overwhelmed us—and was obviously meant to.

Amazingly enough, a significant share of the complaints and information requests came from just two people. One was a reporter with the Associated Press. The other was Andrée McLeod, the falafel lady. She was a disgruntled former state employee who made an art of filing frivolous ethics complaints and leaking them to the media in violation of state law. Andrée inspired a group of cobelligerents who also learned how to disrupt our agenda, and these gadflies actually became "legitimate" news sources for the state and national media.

We tried to keep a sense of humor about the fact that the media took Andrée seriously, especially after Mike Nizich, my chief of staff, received a fresh complaint from her, this time alleging that women in state service wore their clothes too tight. Breasts were apparently spilling from blouses all over the 49th State and Andrée demanded I *do* something about it!

After the string of nutty complaints she'd already hit us with, this one just cracked us up. I told Nizich and Kris: "Yep, that's my job. I'm the state Cleavage Czar. I'll get right on it."

We shot a few e-mails back and forth on the topic, even typed in a couple of smiley faces, copying Sharon, who I knew would appreciate the absurdity. She passed it along to a columnist at the local paper who thought Andrée's newest gripe about inadequate state breast management was hysterical. It also put some things in perspective for her.

We always suspected that someone was funding and directing Andrée's efforts. During the spring of 2009, she was actually still begging my administration for a job and led others to believe she hadn't worked for a couple of years. Yet somehow she had enough time and money to turn harassment of the governor's office into a full-time vocation. Over time, the wording of her ethics complaints became more and more sophisticated, and we later found out why: prominent liberal attorney Don Mitchell was advising her. As early as September 2008, weeks before the presidential election, Mitchell had already detailed the ethics attack strategy in an article in the *Huffington Post*. Later he sat with Andrée as her counsel at one of her hearings.

Andrée wasn't the only complaint filer, just one of the most prolific. As per the conventional left-wing playbook, disgruntled political operatives twisted the ethics reform process that I had championed into a weapon to use against me. They were relentless—and shameless. I was charged with violating ethics laws for wearing a jacket with the logo of Todd's Iron Dog sponsor. I was charged with accepting "bribes" of chocolates and a kids' hockey stick when I gave a speech at a charity event in Indiana. I was charged with holding a fish in a photo for a state fishing pamphlet. I was served with a complaint filed under the name of a fake British soap opera character. I was charged with conducting an interview with a national media figure in my state office. I was charged with answering reporters' questions *in the lobby* of my state office the day I returned to work and found a herd of reporters congregated near the doorway to my office. As I tried to make my way through, I stopped to answer questions—and got slapped with an ethics accusation.

These relentless time-sinks shook my staff's confidence and forced us to question our every decision. Instead of concerning ourselves with legislation and problem solving, my staff had to worry, *Will we get in trouble if I answer that reporter's question? Will she get hit with another complaint if we speak out on an issue?* I had to wonder, *Will I be punished for wearing these clogs, or this label on my jeans today?*

Sometimes the complaints were so ridiculous it's hard to believe we even had to litigate them. Take the complaint about my warm winter jacket. I was accused of "abusing my power" as governor because the coat featured the green-and-black logo of Arctic Cat—one of the Iron Dog race sponsors and the snowmachine brand that Todd rode. I'd been wearing the logo and team colors for years. FOX News' Greta Van Susteren interviewed me outdoors that day at the Iron Dog race and captured video of me wearing the notorious coat. After I was hit with the complaint, I argued about it with my attorney, Tom Van Flein. "What the heck? Let's just plead guilty if that's the accusation. Of course I wore my warm coat, on that cold day, and it happened to be the team's colors. I wore it proudly in front of God and FOX and everybody, so what? Let me pay the piddly ethics fine instead of this costing me thousands of dollars to fight."

Tom would have none of that because he knew there was nothing illegal or unethical about wearing a jacket with a logo on it.

Keep in mind that anyone anywhere in the world could file an Alaska ethics complaint free of charge. It cost them nothing to do it. And even though leaking was against the state ethics laws, they still leaked the complaints to draw headlines. In short, they could flood the system at will and without consequence to themselves, but we had to formally process each and every complaint—and I had to pay personally for my own defense.

We never imagined our critics would be so unscrupulous as to make a mockery of a serious issue like the ethics act. My state had been rocked by *real* ethical violations. We had lawmakers taking bribes and going to prison, the former administration's chief of staff pleading guilty to a felony, and oil service executives ready to go to the clink. But now partisan operatives were using the reformed ethics to level charges against me that were as trivial as they were absurd—charges that were eagerly reported by the press as though they were actual news.

What a bass-ackwards way of doing the people's business.

4

We've all got megaphones, they just come in different sizes and styles. The one I was handed during the campaign gave me a platform to speak from regarding the path our nation is taking. I didn't ask for this megaphone and, obviously, after the campaign ended, the opposition would rather I didn't use it. But how can I be silent in the face of the serious issues facing my state and our country? What a selfish thing it would be to just zip my lips and coast comfortably along with a nice job, a secure paycheck, and government perks, when I share the concerns of so many Americans.

For example, I considered the Obama administration's panicky effort to stimulate the economy by spending enormous amounts of borrowed money shortsighted and ill conceived. It defied the lessons of history and common sense. His nearly $1 trillion stimulus package was patently unfair both to future generations who will inherit our wasteful debt and to the everyday Americans who work very hard to pay the taxes that the administration seeks to spend at breakneck speed.

While I was driving through Anchorage commuter traffic one evening, a radio news update reported that the White House was considering a second stimulus plan, even though the first had not been measured for success, and deficit and unemployment rates were going through the roof. I turned that depressing news off.

"Bristol, answer me this," I said as we drove from her barista job at an espresso café over to her aunt Molly's house, where my grandson, Tripp, was waiting for his mama. Bristol woke up at 4 a.m. most mornings to get to work, then took college classes late in the afternoon. We got to commute home together that day. She was working hard and, like any new mom, not getting much sleep.

"You want to buy a coffee shop someday, right?" I asked. "Say you investigate markets, scout locales, take business classes, you work on the side to invest in that coffee shop, and all along you know you'll be rewarded for your hard work to meet a demand for a quality product and good service. And you know you'll have to be brave enough to fail, right? This business would be *your* responsibility. You can't look to anyone to bail you out if you make poor decisions. You have to spend within your means and save for the future."

"I know, Mom. It's going to happen someday," she answered. "Lauden and I are going to do it. What should we call it?"

"Doesn't matter. Call it Bristol's Beans."

"Sounds dumb. But what's your point?"

"The point is, it's a great goal for you and your cousin to own your own business—but this administration hasn't figured out how to encourage small businesses, and that's the backbone of the economy."

She lay back in the truck seat and closed her eyes.

The more I heard about the new Democrat administration's economic philosophies, the more I feared for the future of free enterprise. Now, I put a finer point on my advice to Bristol on opening a business: "In fact, don't do this until this administration understands government's role in private business. Or wait until they're out of office."

I told Bristol she had a lot to consider in creating her business plan. Can you imagine setting up a business while the Democrat-led Congress is dictating how you should invest your money, the color of your roof, your source of energy generation, and what kind of health insurance you must offer, and even the kind of cars you can have in your company fleet?

My point was that government should get *out* of private enterprise as much as possible, not take it over. My administration had done so with the dairy industry in Alaska with the result that a once limited, failing enterprise is now out from under government's thumb.

All this went through my mind as I was driving through town with Bristol. Suddenly she opened her eyes and looked over to teach me a lesson. "What do you mean, 'don't do it'? If everyone gives up their dreams to own a business just because someone in the White House is clueless about free enterprise, our country's going to tank," she said. "You're always 'rah-rah America,' so why say, 'Give up now'?"

Bristol was wide awake now. "You're always preaching that government 'can't make you happy, healthy, wealthy, or wise.'

Business owners are smarter than politicians give them credit for, and President Obama is wrong to think more government control is the answer. Pay attention to the tea parties, Mom. You're not alone in this. That's what they're saying."

Bristol's barista wage: $7.25 an hour.

Her advice to the president (and her mom): priceless.

My daughter closed her eyes again as we drove toward Molly's, and I thought of the long road ahead for Bristol and Tripp. She'd be fine because she was independent and strong and loved to work, and I loved her and her cousin Lauden's enthusiastic plans to own coffee shops as a side business while they were busy going to school and growing up. But Bristol and Tripp wouldn't be fine if pandering politicians buffaloed Americans into believing some utopian promise that big government could "fix" everything through more of the same meddling that had caused the economic failure in the first place.

I didn't have a problem with sound, necessary projects to stimulate the economy that could be funded by our tax dollars. In Alaska, we'd use infrastructure funds to tackle deferred road maintenance and build access for more resource development. My problem was with the bureaucratic mandates attached to the programmatic part of the package. These were short-term, debt-ridden funds that would grow state government and hand more states' rights to the federal government. Many economists could see where this was headed. They described these rushed-through, barely read proposals as nothing less than an assault on the free market.

On the campaign trail many had been hesitant to talk about legitimate fears that Obama's past comments and associations with anti-capitalist radicals would influence his economic policy. The press gave the impression it was the wrong thing to do. I was "going rogue" when I answered reporters' questions about candidate Obama's associations and pals. I wish we had talked more about them, and about Obama's close relationship with ACORN, the voter-fraud specialists. But we did not elaborate on any of that during the campaign.

Americans with common sense and a passing acquaintance with history do not agree that you can build a strong and sound economy by spending money we don't have and redistributing wealth. Common sense conservatives recognize that not only is there no justice in taking from one person to give to another, it doesn't work. Abe Lincoln reminded Americans that you can't lift up the poor by pushing down the very people who create jobs for them. The rich will simply move their wealth elsewhere, and the poor will wind up even poorer.

———

Bristol slept and as I drove I got to think about her future and the country's future. America was built on free-market capitalism, and it is still the best system in the world. No one explained this better than Margaret Thatcher, who noted that there's no alternative to capitalism because it's the system that ensures the most prosperity for the most people. Thatcher acknowledged that capitalism is not controllable or even predictable—but neither is human nature: "Since its inception, capitalism has known slumps and recessions, bubble and froth; no one has yet dis-invented the business cycle, and probably no one will . . . [What are] called the 'gales of creative destruction' still roar mightily from time to time. To lament these things is ultimately to lament the bracing blast of freedom itself."

My cabinet agreed that in challenging the stimulus package, we'd have to deal in reality. Legislators did hold the purse strings, after all, as they reminded us every day. Conservative governors all over the country were getting hammered for questioning use of the stimulus funds. Some legislatures, through threats of litigation, made it impossible to refuse the money. Litigation would be the next step for those either truly wanting to grow government or just wanting to obstruct a conservative agenda. I told our commissioners we'd have to appeal directly to friendly lawmakers and help educate the others.

I highlighted a couple of obvious examples, such as the package of funds earmarked for the National Endowment for the Arts inside the general "Education Funds" package. I pointed out that there were higher priorities for our kids housed in leaky-roofed classrooms with underpaid teachers than funding more NEA projects. The other example was universal energy building codes that we'd have to adopt if we accepted a $25 million earmark for energy conservation.

"I feel like I'm beating my head against the wall trying to get legislators to understand there are fat strings attached to this," my Deputy Chief of Staff Randy Ruaro said.

Randy was a smart, mild-mannered young attorney who lived in Juneau. He had adopted an adorable child, a Native boy named Dylan, who played hide-and-seek with Piper in the Capitol hallways when we worked weekends. Randy was frustrated with the legislators' claims that the federal cash was as good as free money. He printed sections of the stimulus package, as well as current federal energy department guidance, highlighted specific pages, and handed them out to lawmakers and reporters. The documents clearly stated that acceptance of the funds required the adoption and enforcement of energy building codes.

Universal building codes—in *Alaska!* A practical, libertarian haven full of independent Americans who did not desire "help" from government busybodies. A state full of hardy pioneers who did not like taking orders from the feds telling us to change our laws. A state so geographically diverse that one-size-fits-all codes simply wouldn't work.

I vetoed those building code funds. After a Fairbanks speech on the subject, I knew I'd be criticized for sounding like the mom that I am, but so be it. I had to remind Alaskans one last time of our opportunities: "We don't have to feel that we must beg an allowance from Washington—except to beg the allowance to be self-determined. See, in order to be self-sufficient, Alaska must be allowed to develop, to drill and build and climb to fulfill our statehood's promise! At statehood we knew that we were responsible for ourselves and our families and our future, and fifty years later we cannot start believing that government is the answer. It can't make you happy or healthy or wealthy or wise. What can? It is the wisdom of the people and our families and our small businesses and industrious individuals. And it is God's grace helping those who help themselves. And then this allows that very generous voluntary 'hand up' that we are known to enthusiastically provide those who need it."

The crowd that attended the speech in the warm Fairbanks sun that day humbled me by giving those words a standing ovation. The unaccustomed warmth must have worn out a few of the legislators in the audience, though, because they remained seated. And just weeks later, after Sean Parnell took over as governor, the Democrat-controlled legislature overrode my veto.

An hour later, now driving across the Palmer flats with Bristol, I turned the radio back on just in time to hear talk of another anti-tax tea party. Just what I needed to hear to spark hope again! I had to believe enough Americans were listening, watching, learning what was going on in *their* White House, with *their* Congress, and that they weren't going to just sit quietly and buckle up while those in Washington took the country for a ride.

We were almost home when Bristol stirred and yawned. She

must have been reading my mind the whole ride. "'Bristol's Beans' is dorky, Mom," she finally mumbled. Okay, she was right about that, but I was at least right about our economy.

<h1 style="text-align:center">5</h1>

In early 2009, as our legal defense bills piled up, Todd and I retreated to my quiet bedroom office and sat down for a sobering look at our finances. By then, we were faced with attorneys' bills that would grow to more than $500,000—a lot more than my total salary for all the time I'd served as governor. Then Meg broke the news that a large chunk of those bills—nearly $50,000—was courtesy of the campaign. It was our portion of the bill *for having been vetted!* I had no idea, nor was I ever told, that we would have to pay personally to go through the VP selection process. (If I had, I would have kept my answers shorter!) Meg and Tom made polite inquiries with the RNC and the remnants of "headquarters" to see whether the McCain campaign could help with these expenses. The word came back from on high: if we had won the election, they would have paid; but we lost, so the responsibility was mine. Looking on the bright side, though, if anyone questions whether I was properly vetted, at least now I can tell them, "Yes, and I have the bill to prove it!"

As the number of complaints mounted, I remembered the observations of the left-wing-radical-turned-conservative-activist David Horowitz in his treatise *The Art of Political War.* I'd been following Horowitz's work ever since I met him a decade earlier at an Alaska GOP convention at which we both spoke. His book explained the stark difference between the left's expert use of the weapons of political warfare and the right's high-minded but ineffective approach. One of the left's favorite weapons is frivolous ethics complaints. That's what they used to bring down the architect of the 1994 "Republican Revolution," Newt Gingrich.

Prior to the election of 1994, the Democrats had held a majority in the House of Representatives for four decades. Working with a team of grassroots activists, Newt selected and trained candidates, shaped a political message, and became what Horowitz called "something rare in Republican politics—a genuine movement leader."

To the left, that meant one thing: he had to be eliminated. There are many fine Democrat public servants, but sadly many in the party have moved increasingly to the left, and often the beating heart of their political warfare has been the personal destruction of their enemies. Generally speaking, after decades of failed social policies and weak national security positions, the party doesn't have a strong base of success from which to win political arguments. So it targets people instead of ideas.

Back in the 1990s, Democrats had Newt in their sights. And strangely enough, the more influential he became, the more "unethical" he became—at least if you counted the number of complaints filed against him. Horowitz wrote, "Eventually, Democrats lodged seventy-four separate charges against Gingrich, sixty-five of which were summarily 'laughed out of committee.'"

Over time the cloud of ethical questions hanging over Newt reached critical mass. Instead of defending their own, Republicans on certain committees forced Newt to concede to one charge.

In my case, one by one, every ethics charge filed against me and my staff was tossed out. But there was one that was settled with a finding of no wrongdoing.

It concerned First Family travel. Since we live in a huge state with few roads linking rural communities, flying to another city usually isn't just a day trip. Before, when I'd travel on the road system for a state function, any of the kids who were not tied up with school or a sport could just jump into the truck and off we'd go. When we had to fly somewhere for a First Family event, the state would pay for it; otherwise, I would pay for the kids out of my own pocket. Sometimes we could hop on the state's prison transport plane, the King Air, and zip somewhere to attend one of the many First Family events we were constantly being invited to. It wasn't as though they were bumping anyone—the seats were empty, and it was usually only Piper displacing forty pounds of air on this old state aircraft. I loved traveling with the kids because they needed me and I needed them. They got to share in some of the joys of public service and to see what hard work it is. Often constituents were happier to see, say, Todd at an outdoor Alaskana event or Trig at a senior citizens' event, than they were to see me.

However, a complaint was filed about my kids' travel. It targeted trips that appeared to have questionable benefits to the state—trips such as Piper's travel to wave the starting flag at one year's Iron Dog race (though apparently her travel to two other Iron Dog races was fine—go figure).

All of my kids' travel requests had been authorized by the Department of Administration and approved by the ethics supervisors who had worked for previous administrations on both sides of the aisle. We had disclosed and announced all of our travel. Nothing was hidden. And here's the kicker: I had spent less on travel and personal expenses than my last two predecessors, despite having a much larger family.

The Personnel Board investigator for this complaint was a Democrat, and though he had been fair to my administration in the past, the word was that he was feeling some pressure not to let us off. Still, he admitted that the travel guidelines were vague and circular, and that I had correctly followed the law and the historical precedent established by past governors in their family travel. However, because the travel guidelines were so vague, he asked me if I would hold myself to a future law that could one day be written to establish clearer travel guidelines. I'm always in favor of holding myself to a high standard. I agreed. He reviewed my kids' trips and presented me with a list of the ones he found "questionable" according to the new (and as yet unbinding) guidelines he established for judging their benefit to the state. He then offered me two options to settle the case: I could reimburse the state for the eight or nine trips, or I could present my case to the Personnel Board and wait for the board to provide clearer guidelines or tell my administration what to do.

I saw the second option as an utter waste of state time and public resources. The proceedings would be a major distraction and would only prolong a complaint process that was obviously out of control. Besides, it wasn't fair to have yet another complaint distract us from doing our job—and distract Alaskans from the progress being made for the state.

I signed a settlement that stated clearly that I had not violated any law, travel regulation, or protocol. I agreed to reimburse the state for the trips in question, even though they were First Family functions that the kids were invited to—my staff had all of the e-mails and invitations proving this. One of the trips I reimbursed never actually took place. It was the one listed as "Bristol: Travel to Attend Valley Performing Arts *Beauty and the Beast*, Opening Night." I was pretty sure she hadn't attended the play, and later I confirmed with her that she hadn't. But I reimbursed the state for it anyway because my Department of Law told me to just sign the settlement and get it over with, even though I knew how the media would spin it.

And spin it they did. The result is that instead of reporting that an independent board of review found me not guilty of any wrongdoing and that all the ethics charges filed against me have been dismissed, the media made statements like: "Gov. Palin has been dogged by ethics complaints, most of which have been dismissed."

Most of which. Now an asterisk will forever accompany the issue because of this one settlement. Although, the fact is, all have been dismissed. Indeed, the resolution of the travel issue expressly concluded that no rule was violated and that the law needs to be rewritten because even lawyers could not explain what it said.

In the end, Newt Gingrich lost his battle on one complaint and was assessed a $300,000 fine. Three years later, the IRS exonerated him. But it was too late: the image of Newt as ethically challenged had become part of the media record. Democrats had neutered their nemesis and pushed him to the back burner—at least for a while.

Now they were trying to consign us to the same fate. Thus, although it was illegal to do so, Andrée and her acolytes leaked to the media every time they filed another charge. The leaked complaint would get front-page coverage. Our vindication would be buried next to the obituaries, if mentioned at all.

The saddest part of the whole travel issue is that these complaints broke up my base of support by separating me from my family. The critics had already succeeded in keeping Todd away. He kept his distance from the office now because they had accused him unfairly of being the "Shadow Governor." Now travel questions forced us to minimize our trips. Piper, Trig, and I stayed in Juneau while Todd, Bristol, and Willow lived in Wasilla.

The ethics complaint insanity came to a head when the obstructionists started targeting my staff. *My team.* If they answered a press question about, say, a national event I was invited to, they would be charged with doing "partisan work on state time." Andrée charged Kris with accompanying me on the campaign trail as the liaison with my state office, although she had full clearance to do so, and I was obviously not going to abandon my full-time responsibilities as an elected official while on the trail, though many candidates do. Kris had to pay to defend herself out of her own pocket. Randy Ruaro was charged and also had to pay personally to defend himself for merely doing his job. Others were in the same boat. Why would any rational citizen want to put himself through this? You wonder why good people stay out of politics? This is why.

The method of attack we were combating seems to have come right out of Saul Alinsky's activist manual *Rules for Radicals*— the revolutionary handbook that taught leftists how to effectively harass and obstruct their opponents. Alinsky's tactics had seemingly been updated by a new generation of left-wing activists.

In March, a group from the Republican Governors Association traveled north to warn us that I was being "Emanuelized" or "Thumped." As evidence, they pointed to a book called *The Thumpin': How Rahm Emanuel and the Democrats Learned to Be Ruthless and Ended the Republican Revolution*. It's the story of how the Illinois congressman, now President Obama's chief of staff, had crafted and executed the ruthless 2006 campaign strategy that won back Congress for the Democrats. The RGA told us that Alaska was being given the "Chicago treatment."

Their arguments fit the bill. Those who have seen this before traced the ethics attacks back to the period when I was being vetted for the vice presidential slot and also linked them to the partisan investigation known in the media as "Troopergate." Walt Monegan knew that I was well within my rights to remove him, and in normal times it would have been a nonissue. But a few days later, the troopers' union and a group of Democrats with close ties to a senior adviser to the Obama campaign, Pete Rouse, then Senator Obama's chief of staff, were demanding an investigation.

Rouse had lived in Alaska many years before, returning only on a couple of occasions over the last decade. Yet, somehow, though he actually resides on the East Coast, and has for years, he still votes in Alaska through a voter registration address on Main Street in Juneau—an address once shared by Alaska State Senator Kim Elton on voter rolls. Elton, who played a key role in advancing the Monegan issue as a ginned-up "scandal," has since moved to Washington and joined the Obama interior department as director of Alaska Affairs.

As I mentioned earlier, after the Democrats got involved, Walt dramatically changed his story about the reassignment. Meanwhile, the legislature's investigative panel decided to pay an independent investigator to find something to charge me with while I was being vetted as a VP candidate. I would later learn that similar groups were doing this across the country for the other GOP hopefuls, too. After I was named to the ticket but before the Troopergate investigation had even been completed, Democrat Senator Hollis "Gunny" French actually announced nationally that an "October Surprise" was coming. He told the *New York Times* that an outcome of the investigation could be my impeachment.

Early on, CNN reported that the Obama campaign had contacted the troopers' union to talk about the Troopergate investigation. One prominent Democrat lawmaker even bragged to a fellow senator that he was the conduit between the higher echelon of the Obama campaign and the investigating committee.

The "independent" investigator ultimately issued a strained and nonsensical decision in October that actually declared that I had been well within my legal rights to reassign Commissioner Monegan. It wasn't until the day before the election that the Personnel Board dismissed the ethics charges surrounding Troopergate. That circus was finally over.

Was I "Thumped," as some suggested? Others can decide. One does have to wonder, though, what Kim Elton did to earn his new job in Washington.

6

"It's still best for the state that you're there," Todd encouraged me. "The people who are ticked off just cannot stand that with all the darts and arrows they throw, your team is still making progress. Do you kind of get a kick out of that aspect of all this?" He grinned.

"Well, hmm . . . what a perspective," I said, not grinning. "Hey, just keep reminding me of Grandpa Sheeran's favorite Latin tag: *Illegitimi non carborundum!*" which, loosely translated, means, "Don't let the bastards get you down."

It was easy to take Grandpa's advice when it concerned my own hide. But the attacks on my family? Those cut deep. I would ask only this of others: imagine if your family were the subject of relentless attention from a hostile press. Surely there is at least one person or incident the press could seize on to embarrass your loved ones; perhaps there is a messy divorce, or even an adored child whom you are proud of but who maybe made a mistake and is now taking responsibility and doing so with quiet grace and hard work. If your extended family doesn't fit that description, count your blessings. I've never met anyone like you.

The questions for me became: How do I respond to attacks on my children? Do I respond? Do I ignore them? And if I ignore them, will that encourage more or allow the cheapening of our national discourse to go unchallenged? I still don't know the

Sally herds up part of the family for a blueberry-picking day at Hatcher Pass in the Mat-Su Valley. We make jam and freeze a lot of our wild organic produce for the winter, plus bake plenty of pies and muffins with the fresh berries. Wild game, local vegetables, and berries grown under the midnight sun are our family's food staples. *Courtesy Chuck Heath*

In between salmon runs at our commercial fishing site in Dillingham, I try to squeeze in a few miles of running from my in-laws' house and usually try to make it a kid-friendly event. Here Todd watches a very young Track, with a traditional summer buzz cut, and Willow as we get ready for a jog. *Courtesy Chuck Heath*

Fireweed grows wild and gorgeous throughout many parts of Alaska. Willow stands in a field of it, probably ready to nibble on a blossom because they're sweet and can be made into honey. Legend has it that when the flower reaches the top of the stalk, then summer is over and a quick autumn lets us gear up for winter. *Courtesy Chuck Heath*

ABOVE: I'm taking in the day's news while Payton; my brother-in-law, Kurt Bruce; and Karcher surround me, modeling fur hats at my parents' kitchen table. The hats are the best for keeping heads warm in the cold northern climate. *Courtesy Chuck Heath*

February 2002. Todd holds Piper in the city garage in Nome, the halfway point of the 2,000-mile Iron Dog snowmachine race. Todd and his partner won that year. Some remnants of duct tape protected Todd's exposed skin during the 100-miles-per-hour rides in frigid conditions. Racers apply new tape at checkpoints along the way to avoid inevitable frostbite. *Courtesy Sarah Palin*

Easter brunch at my old house on Wasilla Lake. Bristol, me (I'd just had Piper), Sally, Willow, Molly, and Payton join hands as Mom leads us in saying grace. It's always been our faith's tradition to join together in thanking God for His blessings, and asking for His strength and guidance. *Courtesy Chuck Heath*

Opening the door to Alaska wildlife in the Heaths' home. Dad refused to let Molly invite the moose any further into the house. Dad has a massive fishing lure collection, and just a few of the many thousands of "snags" he's found in local rivers adorn the wall next to the door where the moose peeks in. *Courtesy Chuck Heath*

LEFT: Piper, wearing a colorful Eskimo parka made by Great-Great-Grandmother Lena Andree, tries to stay upright with a hockey stick on the ice in front of our Lake Lucille home. I pretend to be able to play the game while Todd, behind me, finesses the puck. *Courtesy 2009 © Judy Patrick/ AlaskaStock.com*

BELOW: October 2006. Three of five generations of beautiful Yupik women, all dressed in traditional bright Native clothes. Gathered around Lena, the matriarch, are Willow, Blanche, Piper, and Bristol. Todd and I are blessed knowing that our kids have Lena and other esteemed elders to look up to. *Courtesy Chuck Heath*

ABOVE LEFT: Judy shot this of Todd and Piper (in backpack) marching with me in a local parade as I campaigned for lieutenant governor in 2002. *Courtesy 2009 © Judy Patrick/AlaskaStock.com* ABOVE RIGHT: Autumn 2006. Gold miners stand in front of a bar in Chicken, Alaska, to help in the campaign. Constituents like these at the Chicken Creek Saloon made the campaign perpetually exciting and unconventional! *Courtesy Judy Patrick*

LEFT: November 6, 2006. Piper gives a thumbs-up with her cousins McKinley and Heath crammed in the booth as I vote for governor. We won the six-way race with more than 48 percent of the vote. *Courtesy Chuck Heath*

December 2006. My first day in the governor's office in Juneau. The Wasilla Warriors presented me with their team ball. It was joined by John Stockton and Jerry Tarkanian basketballs, a John Wooden inspiration pyramid, a Fred Crowell Golden Ruler, a Jack Lambert jersey, a Scottie Gomez puck, Great Alaska Shootout schedules, and as much high school and college sports memorabilia as I could fit on my desk. *Courtesy Sarah Palin*

December 4, 2006, inauguration ceremony in Fairbanks. Todd, Piper, and Bristol are shown here, having just witnessed Superior Court Judge Niesje Steinkruger swear me into office as governor of Alaska. Piper was as patient as most five-year-olds could be but could barely muster one last hand on the heart at the end of the ceremony. *Courtesy AP Images*

Todd and I dance the first dance at Juneau's Governor's Inaugural Ball. I'd run out to Shoefly just two hours before to grab a pair of heels so we could kick them up at the event. *Courtesy © 2009 Christopher S. Miller/ AlaskaStock.com*

Early lessons in life.
Here in Juneau, reading to Trig
about his Native culture.
Courtesy State of Alaska

Track visited Juneau after his
Michigan hockey tour and before
his U.S. Army enlistment. Here we
were getting ready for an official
First Family photo, but we weren't
ever able to have a portrait taken of
the entire family at the Governor's
Mansion because Track was gone by
the time Trig was born.
Courtesy State of Alaska

The kids have always been
such good sports! For three years
running, Piper's birthday was
celebrated in the Capitol. One year
I brought a cake into a meeting and
pretended that was her birthday
party—even though the visitors
didn't speak English.
Courtesy State of Alaska

A behind-the-scenes look at the AGIA ceremonial bill signing in Fox, underneath the Trans Alaska Pipeline. Piper and McKinley stood near me (Piper was still grooming my wardrobe) while my gasline team and other dignitaries surrounded us. This historic piece of legislation would progress the largest private-sector energy project—ever.
Courtesy Todd Palin

Dad and Mom, married forty-eight years, stand in front of a house of prostitution (long abandoned, of course) in the ghost town near Bonanza, Alaska. This house served the gold miners during one of many Alaska gold rushes.
Courtesy Chuck Heath

LEFT: January 18, 2008, Fort Benning, Georgia. We made it to Track's U.S. Army boot camp graduation ceremony in time for Todd to put the blue cord on our son's right shoulder. The young soldier, along with thousands of others in a Stryker Brigade, later deployed to Iraq for a year. This was one of our proudest days. *Courtesy Sarah Palin*

At the 2008 GOP convention in Minneapolis, both the McCain and Palin families were on stage after John's inspiring acceptance speech! We teased the Secret Service about their "volunteering" for the campaign assignment, perhaps not realizing all the kids (and their energy) were part of the gig. Note my dad's head in the bottom right of this picture. Always grinning ear to ear! *Courtesy Sally Heath*

Dad and Mom with Henry Kissinger at the 2008 GOP convention in the Twin Cities. It was an honor for me to meet with Mr. Kissinger a few times, and even after the campaign to return back East for another visit with him. *Courtesy Chuck Heath*

Pictured here at the GOP convention, Todd's parents, Jim and Faye Palin, lived the maxim 'I'll sleep when I die' as they traveled all over the country working tirelessly for the campaign—putting their passion for golf on hold. *Courtesy Chuck Heath*

Television crews interview Dad, some of the eighty-one reporters who descended on the Heath house immediately after the VP announcement. We were glad for the economic boost provided to Alaska during that time, even if some reporters' purpose in being there wasn't altruistic. *Courtesy Chuck Heath*

Todd, Piper, and I prepare to depart Anchorage airport en route to Reno, Nevada, in September. *Courtesy 2009 © Shealah Craighead*

Shed moose antlers that I signed were given to our pilots, who proudly displayed them across the nation on the instrument dash panel of the McCain-Palin jet. Todd's a private pilot, so he was pretty intrigued with our pilots' missions. A lot of other people were pretty intrigued with the ungulate dashboard decoration. *Courtesy Chuck Heath*

Piper gets a call from President Bush on board the campaign plane. A lot of callers asked to speak with her. My mom, Matt Scully, Fred Malek, and Governor Rick Perry are behind us. *Courtesy 2009 © Shealah Craighead*

Moments like these brought the campaign into perspective. On this day, we paid tribute to all those who lost their lives during the terrorist attacks of September 11th. This photo was taken near Ground Zero with New York City firefighters. *Courtesy 2009 © Shealah Craighead*

Our bus was actually quite homey and comfortable. Heading down the road to the next campaign stop, this was a typical scene—balancing family, work, and campaign. *Courtesy 2009 © Shealah Craighead*

This picture says it all. A dark hotel room in Philadelphia and a frustrated Mark Wallace trying to tell me which of his nonanswers I should give during debate prep. The atmosphere immediately turned around when we headed to Arizona for more prep in the great outdoors at McCain's ranch. *Courtesy 2009 © Shealah Craighead*

Behind the scenes, so many good laughs with friends like Senators Graham, Lieberman, and candidate McCain. *Courtesy 2009 © Shealah Craighead*

Heading down the hotel hallway on the way to debate Joe Biden, it's all laughs with Todd. Behind Todd is his assistant, Ben Veghte, with whom he had so much fun hanging out, especially at a NASCAR race and at Broncos-Chargers and Penn State football games! *Courtesy 2009 © Shealah Craighead*

It was a thrill to meet so many courageous Americans on the trail, including well-known patriot Hank Williams Jr. We brought our own from Alaska—four-time Iditarod champ Martin Buser and four-time Iron Dog champ Todd. *Courtesy 2009 © Shealah Craighead*

During our time with the Clinton Global Initiative on the campaign trail, Cindy and I stopped to talk with our usual gang of merry followers. *Courtesy 2009 © Shealah Craighead*

Piper takes the mic from me as Willow, holding Trig, laughs at her "speech" to tens of thousands of Floridians at The Villages. It was one of the most fun stops on the campaign trail, and Piper wanted to take the opportunity to say, "Thanks for letting us be here!" *Courtesy 2009 © Shealah Craighead*

A "Country First" rally to let American voters know where John and I stood on the issues. I loved talking at these events about energy independence, our need for strong national defense, and ending the self-dealing in Washington. I could palpably feel Americans' hunger for change at the rallies. *Courtesy 2009 © Shealah Craighead*

I got to return home for the 1-25th's deployment ceremony, then hit an Alaska rally where we were joined by, from left to right, front row: Mayor Curt Menard Sr. and his wife, Senator Linda Menard. And behind them: Rachel, Grace, Sandy, and Governor Sean Parnell. This picture was taken six months before Curt passed away. *Courtesy Chuck Heath*

On the last day of campaigning, we hit seven rallies across the United States. Here on the steps of the Missouri State Capitol, I met one of our most energized crowds. *Courtesy 2009 © Shealah Craighead*

We returned to cast our votes in Wasilla on November 4, 2008. I was met by friends who braved the freezing-cold morning hour, including Capi Coon (on my right), Roberta Niver, and Lavancha Lankford (from the Beehive). It was great to have so much of the Mat-Su Valley's support! *Courtesy Roberta Niver*

Before voting for president and vice president, I finally got to stop at my house to pick up my own coat before heading to Wasilla City Hall. This vote was cast in the same place that I attended second grade, then all those City Council meetings, and then later served six years in the mayor's office upstairs, in the former schoolhouse. *Courtesy AP Images*

John gives his concession speech in Arizona on the night of November 4. My family and I were able to fly through the night to vote in Alaska, then return in time for John's wrap-up at the Biltmore Resort. His speech inspired the country to unify for a stronger nation and a bright future. *Courtesy 2009 © Shealah Craighead*

The day after! Working via BlackBerry on November 5, I chill with Trig next to the big kids splashing in the pool before we head back home. My ever-present BlackBerrys kept me in constant touch with my governor's staff and constituents while on the trail. *Courtesy Chuck Heath*

At the cold finish line of the 2009 Iron Dog, Piper by my side, wearing my warm winter gear with an Arctic Cat logo, which turned into the infamous coat that was the subject of the ethics charge leveled for "advertising" in public. It was one of many bogus charges filed after I was named the VP candidate. *Courtesy 2009 © Al Grillo/ AlaskaStock.com*

It's a celebration—Palin-style! July 27, 2009, the day after my farewell address in Fairbanks. Tripp (the bald one) and Trig (the hippie) wrestle with Todd while I hug these precious boys in our Wasilla home. *Courtesy Bristol Palin*

answer, but I responded as any mother would—with that mama grizzly thing again.

Bristol was criticized from all sides as a hypocrite because she took up the cause of helping prevent teen pregnancy. Critics couldn't understand how she could love her precious son, Tripp, with all her heart, and still wish that he had been born ten years later. She wanted teens to know that though they had choices to make about contraception, the only surefire way of preventing pregnancy is not to have sex. This pragmatic position was attacked by both the right and the left—the left because abstinence seems to be a dirty word and the right because even mentioning the word "contraception" "sends a mixed message." Bristol wasn't trying to draft a national sex-ed policy. She just wanted to help her peers. She simply told teens what she has told her sisters: "Don't make the same mistake I did. Wait."

She graduated from high school on time with great grades, while raising her son and working two part-time jobs to pay for his diapers and formula, and then immediately started college classes. You don't read about any of this positive progress in the tabloids and scandal rags, though.

Bristol wasn't the only target. Using partisan bloggers as their primary sources, some reporters questioned Track's enlistment, suggesting that he had joined the Army because he was "hiding from the law."

Also, unbelievably, hurtful attacks were directed at Trig. On the Internet, a fake Planned Parenthood ad showed a photo of me holding Trig. In one corner there was a coat hanger and in the other a slogan: "Better luck next time." What kind of a person creates something like that? Maybe the same kind who would Photoshop distorted images over Trig's pretty face in order to make him look monstrous. The person who did this proudly displayed it on her Web site; she was also the official Alaskan blogger for the Democratic National Committee during the 2008 election.

It was reported nationally that a New York federal judge named Naomi Reice Buchwald blasted me for bringing Trig onstage during the campaign: "That kid was used as a prop. And that to me as a parent blew my mind," she said. Apparently she missed it when the Obamas appeared on stage with their lovely daughters. Or the Bidens. Or the McCains. Or most every other public servant/parent in living memory. Imagine if I hadn't been a proud mom—those same individuals would have said I was ashamed of Trig.

I'm a mom. He's my baby. Who is this woman to say I cannot hold my baby in public? No one told me that running for office means a woman candidate has to switch off her maternal instincts and hide her children from view. If that's required, then count me out.

Let's debate ideas. Let's argue about legislation and policy. Let's talk about political philosophy. But leave my children alone.

By the summer of 2009, Kris was ready to leave state service because of the nonstop harassment. She finally had enough when, while caring for her dying father-in-law as the family stood at his bedside, she received another harassing FOIA request. The official demand for action was presented to Kris just an hour after her father-in-law passed away.

She knew she couldn't serve the state effectively anymore because her days were spent fending off wasteful charges, putting out partisan fires, and managing the avalanche of paperwork purposefully generated by the hit squad since our return from the campaign trail. No one blamed her when she decided she'd had enough.

I knew exactly how she felt. It got to the point where I thought, *To do this job, you either have to be rich or corrupt.*

Rich enough not to care that even though you've been found innocent of all the charges your political enemies have filed against you, your legal bills now exceed several years' income. Or corrupt to the point of being able to sleep well despite knowing you are collecting a paycheck but have ceased being effective in your job.

My approval ratings plummeted from nearly 90 percent to 56 percent during the one-sided public discourse over "the governor's ethics problems." Slowly and steadily, my record, my administration's efforts, and my family's reputation were shot to hell.

The hit squad had successfully created a mirage, a kind of "where there's smoke, there's fire" illusion. Friends told me they saw blog comments from ordinary, well-meaning citizens around America saying things like, "Well, how could Sarah have a $500,000 legal bill if she didn't do anything wrong?" and "If she has a legal defense fund, doesn't that mean she must have done something?"

The truth is that the obstructionists figured out a way to inflict a heavy personal financial toll on their opponents at no cost to themselves. In Alaska, the governor and the executive staff have to hire attorneys at their own expense to defend themselves against ethics charges, no matter how frivolous, malicious, or ill conceived an ethics complaint may be. The state attorney general cannot provide representation under the law because these types of complaints are considered "personal" even though they arise from government service. The liberal mentality is that if a charge doesn't stick, personal bankruptcy has to eventually. While some in Alaska have recommended changing this, legislators have yet to do so. There isn't really a sense of urgency for them because the legislative branch is protected; if you utter a word about a legislative ethics complaint, it's automatically dismissed. My biggest concern is that the prospect of personal financial ruin through the abuse of our ethics process is going to discourage good people from working in state government.

In response to the ethics attacks against me, my friend Kristan Cole led supporters in setting up a legal defense fund to help defray my attorney costs. But my opponents began twisting even that. Despite the fact that Kristan made sure the fund was vetted by expert East Coast attorneys who were in the business of setting up such funds for politicians on both sides of the aisle, I was charged with yet another violation for having the fund at all, and for paying bills out of it—even though the fund is not mine and I have not drawn a dime from it.

Financial hardship is painful but bearable. Loss of reputation I can take. But I could not and cannot tolerate watching Alaska suffer. One by one, each ethics complaint against me was tossed out. But a new one quickly sprouted to take its place. I knew it wouldn't stop and the ongoing cost to our system plagued me. My loyal staff who had accomplished so much with me in our years in office were beseiged.

No one could paralyze my administration before, and I wouldn't have been told to sit down and shut up, but these frivolous and expensive complaints were effectively doing what no one else could. I knew I could just hunker down and finish out a final, lame-duck year in office—but I'm not wired for that.

At some point, you have to say "Enough." You have to pick your battle. Pick your hilltop. And hold the position of your own choosing. My state was being shaken by one partisan earthquake after another. Every time we found steady ground, another avalanche of FOIAs, ethics complaints, and lawsuits crashed down. My team had been targeted for destruction because of who the team leader was. I began to think it was time to pass the ball. And, after many months of consideration and prayer, a phone call from the other side of the world helped me clarify it all at last.

7

"This isn't good, Mom," Track told me from a desert outpost 6,000 miles away. "I just saw another dumbass 'expert' on TV telling the world who he thinks we are."

A year earlier if Track had said that to me I would have argued with him and said, "Come on, it's not that bad."

But for the first time, he sounded tired, and I could tell he wasn't in the mood to be lectured. This time, I heard him out.

"I know you, Mom. You want to protect us. You want to say, 'Screw this, I won't put my family through this.'" Track did know me. "But are you going to let those idiots run you off? You can't tap out!"

He talked about watching his sister be humiliated on national television as her former boyfriend went on his fact-free kiss-and-tell media tour. Track knew the kid was making things up.

When he started giving example after example of all he had watched and read, I interrupted. "Those are political potshots, son," I reminded him, thinking of my recent trip to the medical facility in Landstuhl. "The shots that really hurt are felt by people losing their livelihoods, losing a loved one in battle—"

He interrupted me. "That's my point, Mom!" Then he hushed his voice because there were always fellow soldiers around. "Don't let the jerks get you down!" His view was that you don't quit. You don't violate your contract. There is pain, you push through it, you stick it out.

Then he brought it home: "No dishonorable discharge. You only leave if it's honorable—that means you move up to something more worthy."

Then it was my turn. I asked him if he thought protecting Trig and his sisters was "more worthy." I asked if fighting through the bull so that I could reveal truth and fight for what is right for our state and our country was "more worthy." I asked if breaking free of the bureaucratic shackles that were now paralyzing our state was "worthy."

I finally said out loud what I knew I had to do.

"I'm not a quitter, Track," I finished. "I'm going to fight. And that's the point."

By the end of the conversation Track understood more. He knew this was one of the most important decisions I would ever make, and he also knew that I knew what I was talking about.

"I hear you, Mom," he finally said. "I'm praying for you."

"Fast about it for a day," I said.

"Eat nothing for a whole day? Holy crap!"

"Okay, forget fasting food," I conceded. "Fast from cussing for a day, then."

"Hell, no. Impossible over here. Next?"

He agreed to give up chew for a day. That was a big darn deal.

I remembered again the advice of my dear friend Curtis: "In politics, you're either eating well or sleeping well." Was I sleeping well knowing that I was incapable of serving my state effectively— that I had become an obstacle to progress because I was the target of out-of-control obstructionists? No. I wasn't sleeping well at all. A politician is supposed to be a public servant, but in our current understanding, a politician would have just gone with the flow, collected the paycheck, padded the résumé, and finished the term as a lame duck. But that's not what a public servant would do. How would a lame-duck session benefit Alaskans? How would millions more in FOIAs and ethics complaints and lawsuits benefit Alaskans? I prayed hard because I knew that if I resigned, it might very well end any future political career.

But then I thought, *This is what's wrong with our political system. Too many politicians only consider their next career move. They don't put the people they are serving first.*

In the end, I decided, politically speaking, if I die, I die. I had to do the right thing. It might be the end of my career, but it wouldn't be the end of my work to make a difference. No one can make me "sit down and shut up." I don't need a title to effect positive change.

On July 3, 2009, I announced our decision in a speech from my backyard, with my cabinet members lined up alongside the Parnell family on one side and my family on the other. It was a gorgeous summer day and the waters of Lake Lucille shimmered behind me. I was thankful to have my family with me, because they had been there four years before, on Alaska Day, to begin this journey. Most of them had, anyway. Trig cuddled in Piper's arms, cooing and squirming, until finally being handed off to his aunt Heather, then to his aunt Molly as his fourteen-month-old "talking" grew louder during the press event. Tripp slept in Uncle Chuck's arms.

As cameras rolled, I announced my conclusion that it was best for Alaska if I stepped aside. "We will be in the capable hands of our lieutenant governor, Sean Parnell. And it is my promise to you that I will always be standing by, ready to assist. We have a good, positive agenda for Alaska. In the words of General MacArthur, 'We are not retreating. We are advancing in another direction.' "

Or, as my dad later put it, "Sarah's not retreating; she's reloading!"

I wanted to leave no doubt that I wasn't running from political shots. In my inaugural address, I had asked Alaskans to hold me accountable. But I wanted to be held accountable for doing my job. I wanted to be challenged to serve the state better, not have to prove that I'm Trig Palin's mom.

We had invited only local press, and one station sent its satellite truck out from Anchorage. I figured it must be quite a slow news day to warrant that. The station blasted my speech across the country. Though we knew my announcement would make news, we did not expect the wall-to-wall national coverage that exploded over the next week.

As Kris, Mike Nizich, and family members stood in my kitchen, my brother turned up the television just to get a read on what kind of bizarre theories the press was cranking out this time. Before long we told him to just turn off the news. And we just had to say it: "What a bunch of buffoons."

I knew resigning was the right thing to do, the same way I had known it was right to run for mayor, right to take on the party at the AOGCC, right to run for governor, and right to say yes to John McCain. I knew we had just done the right thing for Alaska. We were now going to get to fight for what is right for our state and our country. I was at peace and confident in my decision. I felt a renewed sense of excitement and freedom—so, of course, we ate cake.

———

The reaction to my announcement was instructive. The same people who had wanted nothing more than to throw me out of office were suddenly outraged that I was obliging. Right away the scandal rumors broke. Left-wing bloggers began feeding stories to their friends in major media that the FBI was investigating me. NBC's Norah O'Donnell was the first to e-mail us asking for details about the embezzlement scandal that she'd heard would lead to my FBI indictment the following week. The *New York*

Times and the *Washington Post* stalked my parents at a July Fourth parade to ask how they felt about the pending indictment. Meg and Sharon were inundated with press inquiries demanding confirmation. Kristan Cole, Heather, and the rest of the family were snowed under again by media calls. Soon reporters from every major media outlet were abandoning their Fourth of July barbecues, hopping on planes, and heading to the Last Frontier to report all the juicy details.

It was a major letdown for them, though. Even as their planes were cruising above "flyover country," the FBI's Alaska spokesman went on the record to declare that I was not under investigation and had never been under investigation.

Poor press. At that moment, the *B* in "FBI" stood for "Buzz-kill."

The reporters landed in Anchorage anyway, looked around, and said, "Well, now what? Where is she?"

It was an early July weekend, and I was where I always am at that time of year—at our set-net site in Bristol Bay slaying salmon during the quick two-day peak of the run. We had no cell phone coverage, and there was only one landline in my mother-in-law's home where the fishing crew crashed. I had a satellite phone for state communications during my annual two days away from the office, but the reporters had traveled all the way from the East Coast and they weren't leaving without a personal interview.

So we decided to invite them to join us: "Welcome to Dillingham!"

Secretly, I must admit that I really wanted to see the likes of Andrea Mitchell on my home turf witnessing how happy and at peace my family was. The last time I had seen Andrea was many months prior at our friends Fred and Marlene Malek's Virginia home with a number of distinguished "inside the Beltway" guests, such as Dick Cheney, Alan Greenspan, Dianne Feinstein, Madeleine Albright, Walter Isaacson, Jeb Bush, and my friend John McCain. Now I wanted to see Andrea and her colleagues sporting fish-slimed waders, banging around in a skiff, stuck in the mud, and trying to pull themselves back over the bow. At the very least they'd see there's no diva in me. Bring on the mosquitoes and horseflies, the wind and the driving rain!

We issued an open invitation for the press (except for CBS). If they wanted to come, they could, but we could spare only a half hour between tides to anchor up and speak with them. We also told them to bring their own rain gear and prepare to be introduced to a few fish scales. The major media outlets took us up on the offer and within a few short hours landed in Dillingham, along with their crews, and accepted rides with our family and friends or hired local guys to drive them onto the gravel beach nearest our site.

I always love introducing reporters to remote areas of Alaska: it gives them a better sense of our state's vastness, diverse people, and subsistence lifestyles as well as an appreciation for Native culture. The reporters were told they would have ten minutes each on the beach before the tide changed. Then Todd and I would skiff them down to our site. We'd grab Piper on the way so she could teach a couple of them how to drive the boat—and she did.

But the question they all asked was the one I had already answered: "Why?"

They just couldn't believe that a politician would willingly give up power and title for good reasons. Instead, there had to be some huge scandal chasing me out of office. But there was no scandal. There was no FBI investigation, no greedy grasp for money, no divorce. And it sure wasn't because I disliked my job—I loved my job. The decision wasn't about me. It was about Alaska. It was as simple as I'd said it was.

They didn't act as if they believed me, of course. They asked if my decision had to do with seeking higher office. No. If that alone had been my ambition, I would have finished out my term, as all the talking heads had said I should. I knew full well that resigning might be a political death sentence. One of the only commentators who called it right was Mary Matalin, who noted that my strategy would disarm my opponents and free me up to travel and raise money and awareness for worthy causes.

The reporters headed home, many still shaking their heads. Their whirlwind visit had provided a little economic stimulus for Dillingham, but it was not a great day for the hard-core, messy fishing I had wanted to show them. Instead of typical Bristol Bay weather, it was sunny, hot, and flat calm, so—dang it—none of them got slimed.

Chapter Six

The Way Forward

Sarah's not retreating; she's reloading!

—CHUCK HEATH SR.

My last trip to Fairbanks as governor was pretty magical. We spent a busy three weeks finalizing the smooth transition of power. Then we filled the motor home with kids and coffee and headed up to Fairbanks, where the Palin-Parnell administration had been inaugurated in the Nanooks' hockey arena. The late-July weather was perfect, and thousands of Alaskans and tourists were there to enjoy the ceremony.

A number of the Alaska reporters who made the trek to the Golden Heart City told Meg they wanted to say good-bye and expressed concern that they would be out of a job once we left. Apparently we were good for business. And, really, that's got to be the nicest compliment you can give to a pro-free-market fiscal conservative.

In my farewell speech, I reminded Alaskans of how we'd moved the state "North to the Future," as our state motto says. I said good-bye to the governor's office but hello to new opportunities for the people. I got to thank the state I dearly love.

Our drive back to Wasilla was full of cranked-up Southern rock music, and we stopped along the highway to roast hot dogs and make s'mores over a campfire. I took a few minutes to tell my family how much I appreciated them riding that roller coaster with me, and we looked forward to driving down the road to whatever was ahead.

Since leaving office I've frequently been asked, "What does Sarah Palin stand for? What's your vision for the future?"

I welcome the opportunity to share it. Keep in mind, I tell my parents the greatest gift they ever gave me, besides building a foundation of love for family and for healthy competition, was an upbringing in Alaska. The pioneering spirit of the Last Frontier has shaped me.

I am an independent person who had the good fortune to come of age in the era of Ronald Reagan and Margaret Thatcher. I am a registered Republican because the planks in that party's platform are stronger than any others upon which to build Alaska and America. I disagree with some of the characters in the party machine, but the GOP stands for principles that will strengthen and secure the country, if they are applied. I'm not obsessively partisan, though, and I don't blame people who dislike political labels even more than I do. My husband, for example, isn't registered with any party, for sound reasons, having been an eyewitness to the idiosyncrasies of party machines. I also don't like the narrow stereotypes of either the "conservative" or the "liberal" label, but until we change the lingo, call me a Commonsense Conservative.

What does it mean to be a Commonsense Conservative?

At its most basic level, conservatism is a respect for history and tradition, including traditional moral principles. I do not believe I am more moral, certainly no better, than anyone else, and conservatives who act "holier than thou" turn my stomach. So do some elite liberals. But I do believe in a few timeless and unchanging truths, and chief among those is that man is fallen. This world is not perfect, and politicians will never make it so. This, above all, is what informs my pragmatic approach to politics.

I am a conservative because I deal with the world as it is— complicated and beautiful, tragic and hopeful. I am a conservative because I believe in the rights and the responsibilities and the inherent dignity of the individual.

In his book *A Conflict of Visions,* Thomas Sowell explains the underlying assumptions or "visions" that shape our opinions and the way we approach social and political issues. He identifies two separate visions: the unconstrained and the constrained.

People who adhere to the unconstrained vision (the label applied to them is "liberal" or "left-wing") believe that human nature is changeable (therefore perfectible) and that society's problems can all be solved if only the poor, ignorant, disorganized public is told what to do and rational plans are enacted. And who better to make those plans than an elite bureaucracy pulling the strings and organizing society according to their master blueprint? No one can doubt that our current leaders in Washington subscribe to this unconstrained vision.

Conservatives believe in the "constrained" political vision because we know that human nature is flawed and that there are limitations to what can be done in Washington to "fix" society's problems.

Commonsense Conservatives deal with human nature as it is— with its unavoidable weaknesses and its potential for goodness. We see the world as it is—imperfect but filled with beauty. We hope for the best. We believe people can change for the better, but we do not ignore history's lessons and waste time chasing utopian pipe dreams.

We don't trust utopian promises from politicians. The role of government is not to *perfect* us but to *protect* us—to protect our inalienable rights. The role of government in a civil society is to protect the individual and to establish a social contract so that we can live together in peace.

We are currently in the midst of an economic crisis, and the recovery is slow in coming. But I do have fundamental faith in the American entrepreneurial spirit. We go through booms and busts, and America comes out stronger. Just as wildfires in Alaska burn away deadfall to make way for new growth, so too does the business cycle undergo a process of "creative destruction." We let some dying businesses fail as new businesses emerge. The horse and buggy gradually disappeared after Henry Ford introduced an affordable automobile. In my lifetime, we've gone from companies in the business of making LPs to eight-tracks to cassette tapes to compact discs to MP3s. My kids finally got me to retire the portable CD player I lugged around while jogging. I now carry an iPod, and I can't wait to see what comes next.

The marketplace changes. Often it's not easy for politicians to explain to their constituents this process of "creative destruction" with its booms and its busts, because more and more politicians prefer pandering instead. They complicate simple and sober truths, and make vague promises to get elected. It's easy to promise free medical care and a chicken in every pot. It's more difficult to explain how we're going to pay for it all and to explain why social programs that were supposed to help the poor have ended up hurting them, becoming unsustainable financial liabilities for all of us. Ronald Reagan was the last president to really explain this to us.

Somewhere along the way, these clear principles got lost. People look at the Republican Party today—the supposedly conservative party—and say, "What happened to the Reagan legacy?"

And we deserve that criticism.

The national GOP gambled away the progress of the Reagan years. Perhaps they meant well, but it looked to me as if they thought they could achieve a permanent majority by compromising their principles. In the end, they lost both.

That bled on down to the state level. I saw it happen in Alaska. It's why our GOP-controlled legislature, where the R's outnumber the D's, turned into a Democrat-controlled legislature. A few Republicans gave key committee assignments to the most liberal Democrats in Juneau, just so they could secure favors and big titles. It's why, even with billions of dollars in state savings accounts, we couldn't permanently repeal a fuel tax or a tire tax that hit the people in their pocketbooks. It's why I had to veto huge budgets. And why, when I vetoed a government expansion program, it was ultimately overridden. It's why an outnumbered Democrat, Hollis French, who was handed the Senate Judiciary Committee gavel by just a few Republicans, was empowered to kill a parents' rights bill that would have protected our daughters from invasive surgeries without parental notification.

When titles and personal power grabs are more important than fighting for the people, voters become discouraged and apathetic. Politics-as-usual continues, and the Reagan legacy cannot be revived.

You can't claim to be a fiscal conservative and then institute massive new spending programs without even attempting to reduce government in other areas. President Reagan used to speak of reducing the federal government. Now some Republicans barely bat an eyelash when helping create whole new federal bureaucracies. Today if you ask, "Why exactly do we need that federal program? Can't we do without it?" people will look at you as if you're from outer space—or perhaps from Alaska.

Many people had stopped questioning this federal government growth—until we elected an administration that is growing government at a rate unprecedented in our history. This "change" has awakened the curiosity and concern of all Americans. Now people are asking: "Why do we continue to add to our skyrocketing debt? How will our children pay these bills? We are already in a very deep hole; when will we stop digging?"

We have allowed the left, with its unconstrained vision, to convince us that America's current woes were caused by too little government involvement and regulation, and that the only way to fix our problems is for bureaucracy to regulate more, to stifle more freedoms, and to force itself even deeper into the private sector.

This is nonsense. We got into this economic mess because of misplaced government interference in the first place. The mortgage crisis that triggered the collapse of our financial markets was rooted in a well-meaning but wrongheaded desire to increase home ownership among people who could not yet afford to own a home.

Politicians on the right *and* left wanted to take credit for an increase in middle-class home ownership. But the rules of the marketplace are just as constraining as human nature. Government cannot force financial institutions to give loans to people who can't afford to pay them back and then expect that somehow things will all magically work out. Sooner or later, reality catches up with us.

———

Within six months of taking office, President Obama put the United States on track to double its already staggering national deficit. The new debt, which will burden future generations, is immoral. And all of it in the name of fixing an economy broken by too much debt in the first place.

Servicing the $11.5 trillion debt is a huge annual expenditure in the federal budget. Those who hold our debt, including foreign countries like China and Saudi Arabia, must be paid first. Last year we spent more than $400 billion to service our debt. At this rate, by 2019, that number is expected to be $1 trillion. Our overspending today could destroy our children's future.

Is that what the president meant by "change"?

Where is all of this money going to come from? It can come from only three places. Government borrows it, government prints it, or government taxes the people for it. So far the administration has done the first two. We've borrowed massive sums from foreign countries, and we've also simply printed money. Economists call this practice "monetizing the debt," and it's not something we hear much about. Higher taxes won't be far behind.

Our parents were right when they told us that money doesn't grow on trees. There are consequences to these massive spending plans. And we will be feeling them soon.

Is that what the president meant by "change"?

Washington is not done with its spending spree yet. Congress is talking about additional stimulus packages and bailouts. But we tried growing government to save the economy back in the 1930s, and it didn't work then either. Massive government spending programs and protectionist economic policies actually helped turn a recession into the Great Depression. New Deal–like spending plans aren't the only blast from the past we see today. With the government takeover of parts of the banking industry and the auto industry, we see the return of corporatism—government collusion and co-option of big business.

No one person is smart enough to control and predict markets. The free market is just that: free to rise or fall, shrink or expand, based on conditions that are often outside of human control. Government interference in market cycles is just as dangerous as government-directed programs that encourage permanent dependency. In both cases the rewards for responsible behavior and the penalties for irresponsible behavior are removed by the state. This is the lesson I tried to convey to Bristol when we discussed her plans for the future. It may look to her now that the rewards for her responsible behavior and sacrifices as a hardworking single parent will be a long time coming. But in time they will.

Our massive interventions in the economy today haven't "fixed" anything; instead, we're rewarding a few large firms for being irresponsible. We've told them they're "too big to fail"; we've told them that the bigger they are and the more trouble they get themselves into, the more likely the government will be to bail them out. Sorry, little guys. Bruce's Muldoon Chevron isn't big enough to save. Uncle Kurt, you're on your own.

The lesson in all of this is that we can't abandon free-market principles in order to save the free market. It doesn't work that way. The cure only makes the disease worse.

One such cure: Washington's misguided "Cap and Trade" plan. But let's call it what it is: a "Cap and Tax" program. The environmentalists' plan to reduce pollution is to tax businesses according to how much pollution they produce. Industries that emit more pollutants would have to pay more in taxes. Businesses that reduce emissions and thereby avoid all or part of the cap and tax hits could trade or sell their government credits to other companies.

There are big problems with this. We have the highest unemployment rate in twenty-five years, and it's still rising. American jobs in every industry will be threatened by the rising cost of doing business under cap and trade. The cost of farming, for example, will certainly increase, driving down farm incomes while driving up grocery prices. The costs of manufacturing, warehousing, and transportation will also rise. We'll all feel the effects of this misguided plan to buy and sell pollution.

The president has already admitted that the policy he seeks will cause our electricity bills to "skyrocket." Sadly, those hit hardest will be those who are already struggling to make ends meet. So much for the campaign promise not to raise taxes on anyone making less than $250,000 a year. This is a tax on everyone.

Is that what the president meant by "change"?

As more and more Americans understand that cap and trade is an environmentalist Ponzi scheme in which only the government benefits, they will refuse to tolerate it. They will make their voices heard at the ballot box, and any lawmaker who supports destructive legislation like this will soon be turned out of office. That's what we mean by "change"!

———

Our nation is facing great challenges, but I'm optimistic—and I know there is a way forward.

Ronald Reagan faced an even worse recession. He showed us how to get out of one. If you want real job growth, cut capital gains taxes and slay the death tax once and for all. And if we really want to help the poor and middle class get through this recession, how about cutting their payroll taxes? Giving people control over more of the money they've earned: now that's real stimulus. Get federal spending under control, and then step aside and watch this economy roar back to life.

The way forward is full of promise. But it takes more courage for a politician to step back and let the free market correct itself than it does to push through quick fixes. Reagan showed courage when he stayed the course through the long recession of the early

1980s. Critics even in his own party told him to abandon his tax cuts. He was confident they would work. And they did.

Reagan once recalled with amusement that economists in the 1970s never saw the tech boom coming when they made their gloomy forecasts. The personal computer revolutionized our economy, yet the "experts" didn't see it coming. Energy independence is a bit like that. I don't think people quite see how important it is and how much it can offer us. Energy touches every aspect of our lives. It lubricates the gears of our economy. Our prosperity has been driven by steady, abundant, affordable energy supplies. In Alaska, we understand the inherent link between energy and prosperity, energy and opportunity, and energy and security. I believe Alaska will lead the nation in developing both renewable and nonrenewable resources. I've always advocated an "all of the above" approach to energy production, and I support the harnessing of alternative sources of energy such as wind, solar, and geothermal. Using renewable sources means developing nuclear energy, too.

We will achieve economic growth and energy independence if we also responsibly tap conventional resources. God created them right underfoot, beneath American soil and under our waters. We must abandon the false dichotomy that says you can't be pro-environment and pro-development. We can responsibly develop our resources in a way that protects the environment. I speak as an Alaskan. We love our state. We live here. We raise our children here. Why would we want to foul it up? Alaskans are pro-development because we know from experience it can be done without harming the environment.

No one can deny that we need crude oil. It's not just for cars. We use petroleum for everything from jet fuel to petrochemicals, plastics, fertilizers, pesticides, and pharmaceuticals. We need petroleum, and if we don't drill for it here, we must import it from developing countries that have little to no environmental protections, that often ravage the earth to extract oil, and that exploit workers with little or no regard for human rights. In denying domestic energy development, environmental groups are effectively just supporting irresponsible development overseas.

Taken together, Alaska's energy reserves coupled with future discoveries on our continent could yield domestic energy supplies to cover America's needs for decades. Building the energy infrastructure necessary to bring these supplies to market is true economic stimulus. It means jobs. It means revenue. The bulk of America's trade deficit is fueled not just with plastic toys we buy from China, but also by the oil we import. Imagine how much stronger our economy would be if all of those billions of dollars we spend overseas were circulating here in the United States. Instead, our foreign energy purchases now help subsidize regimes that don't necessarily like us and can always use energy as a weapon against us.

In the end, it's not just about the environment or the economy. It's about our security and building a more peaceful world. Washington should work to clear the way for domestic energy projects that will ensure that our energy needs will never be at the mercy of madmen in possession of vast oil reserves.

The way forward lies in energy independence. It will make us a more peaceful and more prosperous nation.

And let's talk about peace. Today our sons and daughters are fighting in distant countries to protect our freedoms and to nurture freedom for others. I understand that many Americans are war-weary, but we do have a responsibility to complete our missions in these countries so that we can keep our homeland safe. America must remain the strongest nation in the world in order to remain free. And our goal in the War on Terror must be the same as Reagan's: "We won. They lost."

But military might isn't the only tool we have to guarantee peace and freedom. We are both the world's sword and its shield— we lend not just our strength but the support of a free people to others who are fighting for their freedom. They need to know that America is not indifferent to their struggles but will lend her considerable diplomatic power to their cause. Nations like Israel need to be confident of our support.

Some people ask whether we are still a republic, or whether we are becoming an empire, doomed to fade away like all the other empires once thought to be invincible.

We are still a republic. We are certainly not doomed to fade away. And we have no desire to be an empire. We don't want to colonize other countries or force our ideals on them. But we have been given a unique responsibility: to show the world the meaning and the rewards of freedom. America, as Reagan said, is "the abiding alternative to tyranny." We must remain the Shining City on a Hill to all who seek freedom and prosperity.

President Obama has reminded us that our security depends in part on reaching out to other nations. I certainly agree, and I respect his leadership on this. But it is not in our best interests or the interests of the peace-loving nations of the world for America to project weakness to terrorists and tyrants.

That's why I believe that the best way to avoid a fight is to be ready to fight. That sentiment is expressed in the simple yet profound motto on the seal of the USS *Ronald Reagan:* "Peace through Strength."

The world will not be more peaceful if we retreat behind our borders; it will in fact be more dangerous and violent. We don't go looking for fights, but we're ready to face them if necessary. If we ever lose faith in our ideals, the world will be a darker place for those who love peace.

That's what I stand for and what I see as the way forward.

The nation is at a crossroads. Will we take the path forward to a strong and prosperous future, or will we repeat failed policies of the past? Today millions of Americans are standing up and voicing their concerns about where our country is heading. Yet some belittle those who attend tea parties, or show up at town hall meetings, or dare to run for office without an establishment-approved résumé.

Like every other ordinary American, I'm tired of the divisions and the special interests that pit us against one another. It doesn't matter whether you grew up in Skagway or San Francisco, you're an American. Whether you're Bill Gates or Bill the Cable Guy, you're an American. Whatever your gender, race, or religion, if you love this country and will defend our Constitution, then you're an American.

As I said during the campaign, all that most of us have ever asked for is a good job in our own hometown and that government be on our side and not in our way. But too many of us have felt ignored and have become disillusioned. Many Americans don't even vote because they've come to expect government to be indifferent—or corrupt. I want to challenge those Americans to stand up with me.

The enlightened elites want to tell you to sit down and shut up. But the way forward is to stand and fight. Throw tea parties. March on Capitol Hill. Write letters to the editor. Run for local office—you never know where it may lead. And make your voice heard on every single election day, on every single issue. That is your birthright.

Stand now. Stand together. Stand for what is right.

Epilogue

AUGUST 2009

Twenty years from now you will be more disappointed by the things
you didn't do than by the ones you did do. So throw off the bowlines.
Sail away from the safe harbor. Catch the trade winds in your sails.
Explore. Dream. Discover.

—MARK TWAIN

It is one year ago this week that I got the call from John McCain at the Alaska State Fair. So this week, it's cotton candy and roller-coaster rides again.

As I write this, I put Piper on speakerphone and listen to the sounds of comforting chaos behind her at home in Wasilla. It's very quiet in the little apartment I'm in for a couple of weeks as I work on this book, and the curtains are open to invite in the California sunshine. Piper explains that she's trying to comb her hair but it's sticking up on one side.

"Yeah, and it was picture day on Wednesday and Bristol wouldn't fix my hair and I had to go to school soaking wet and I couldn't even find a comb!" Piper says.

"Well, right now just put water on it," I tell her from a few thousand miles away. "Or wear a hat."

"Oh yeah, a hat. I'm wearing a hat!" I figure she grabbed one of

Todd's baseball caps and is comfortable wearing it oversized and lopsided because she's not too worried about impressing anyone.

She interrupts me to holler for her sisters to lend her some money. "I'm broke! I had to pay for Mom's mocha again when we were down in California, and now I don't have any quarters!"

Our kids had been with Meg and me at the beginning of the trip. Then Todd and Meg's husband, Eric, flew home with the flock in time for the first day of school. Now Piper's mad because I'm not there to help. She knows if she doesn't get going soon she'll have to stand in long lines to ride the rides at the fair.

I listen to her take-charge commands and then tell her she needs to go help get the babies ready. "Pack Trig's stroller," I say. "He likes his Elmo thing, and bring a diaper bag—the big one, and make sure there's two of everything in there for Tripp, too, okay?"

I hear her offer to get the boys bundled up before they head out. I can picture what she'd choose for them to wear. She'd look for their matching fleece jackets, and I can count on her topping off the task with a lick of the palm and a slick of Trig's hair. I'll be home soon and can't wait to be smack in the middle of the comforting chaos of family life.

Before Piper hustles away from the phone, Todd gets on to tell me Trig slept through the night, so it was a good night.

"And it's close, Sarah! He's going to take his first step any day." I bite my lip. "You better hurry home. He's going to walk!"

Piper jumps back on to announce that she's found some change in a mason jar in the laundry room and she needs it desperately.

"I love you, Piper. Give everyone a kiss. See you in a couple of days."

"Bye, Mom, love you too. Gotta go."

Earlier I took a break and accepted the sun's irresistible invitation to get outside and run. I ran slowly, but my mind raced. After a couple of miles, I had to slow down to a walk. It was the first time I'd had to do that in years. Thinking about the past year with some emotion, I felt my throat tighten, and I thought I was going to hyperventilate, which hasn't happened since my high school cross-country days. I was thankful to be incognito on a bike path in a city where no one recognized me with salty sweat dripping under my sunglasses.

I thought of Track's call that morning. He'd be home soon. His brigade unit's replacement had arrived, and they were making the transition from a war zone to the States. His return would be a few weeks later than he'd thought, which wasn't great news for me, but he said that was fine—he knew his old truck with a new lift kit would still be there waiting for him. Oh, and the family was waiting, too. (A lot of these guys have to act like it's all about the truck.)

A long year for him. For every soldier. For all of us.

As I walked, my mind drifted from Track to Trig and every-thing in between. That included the politics of the past year. Oh, the politics.

I had to stop walking for a second. I rarely stop. I sat down on the grass and prayed, "God, thank You. Thank You for Your faithfulness . . . always seeing us through . . . I don't know if this chapter is ending or just beginning, but You do, so I hand it all over to You again. Thanks for letting me do that." Then I thanked our Lord for every single thing we'd been through that year. I believed there was purpose in it all.

Meg and I were staying in a quiet little apartment in California as I worked on my book for an early deadline and she ran my "office in exile," fielding phone calls from the media and stomping out crazy rumors (every week I was reportedly moving to a new state).

Someone asked her the other day, "Where exactly is the governor's office located now?" Meg looked up at me, both of us sitting at the kitchen table, typing away on our laptops, cable news blaring in the background, BlackBerrys buzzing nonstop from incoming e-mails, and she said, "I guess you could say it's virtual."

It was a bit surreal to go from a big state office and all the trappings of power to just a kitchen table. But being out of power can be very liberating.

Take an example: from this tiny apartment, I watched debates unfold in Washington, and I used my Facebook page to call things like I saw them.

These posts had an impact, and it made me think, *Isn't Facebook a terrific illustration of the power of American ingenuity?*

Facebook was created in a Harvard dorm room in 2004. No one gave its young creator a government grant—he just did it on his own, like generations of other American entrepreneurs. And here we have the president and his party telling us that the American system is broken and it's the government's job to fix it. What better refutation of the argument could there be than an innovation like Facebook, which sprang up out of nowhere and virtually overnight became a powerful tool for communication, commerce, and political action.

As I write this, Commonsense Conservatives are out of power in D.C. But that does not discourage me. I think of Reagan in 1976, when his conservative politics and his political future were declared all but dead. How did he turn things around in four years? By speaking to ordinary Americans about the ideas that bind us together.

These ideas resonate just as strongly today. Encourage the free market. Lower taxes. Get government out of the way. Put the people's money back into their hands so that they can reinvest.

Empower them to be generous. Respect honest work. Strengthen families. But because these are common sense ideas, they will be ignored by politicians until their employers—the American people—make them listen.

The green grass smelled so good, I couldn't believe all of California wasn't outside for a walk on an afternoon like this. I looked up the road and tried to see around the trees that lay ahead. The turnaround point wasn't far off, so I retied a shoelace and mentally shifted gears.

"Dang, I must be getting old," I mumbled. My knees creaked underneath me as I stood up. It had been a while since I felt that stiffening and hurt you first feel when you stop in the middle of a run before picking up again.

I started running again, and it wasn't long before I started feeling pretty good, because I started thinking about some pretty good things. We'd been through amazing days, and really, there wasn't one thing in my life to complain about. I felt such freedom, such hope, such thankfulness for our country, a place where nothing is hopeless.

Granted, I'm very concerned about our future. I question the road that Washington has us on with fundamental changes in economic policy that affect the free market and questionable shifts in national security priorities. And knowing that not many everyday Americans want to get involved in either major political party because we're just plain busy, I'm concerned that "ordinary" voices could be ignored. With so much going on in our lives, why would the Joe the Plumbers and the Tito the Builders want to waste time on what usually seems like a destructive exercise? Ordinary Americans feel that until both parties do some housecleaning, and until government gets back on the side of the people, their time is better spent on their families and their jobs and businesses.

But we must reawaken our belief in the principles that underlie our Constitution and the power we have when individuals stand together. And this does not mean an indifference to others. Far from it. We know that the most vulnerable among us deserve our protection; we value life and those who nurture it; and we want to make America a more welcoming place for those whom some may not consider "perfect." History has shown us that when we empower ourselves to stand up together, we become an even more blessed and prosperous nation. And we become a more generous nation, too—a nation that has proved for more than two centuries its willingness to share its blessings with others.

I believe in my soul that we will be a stronger and freer America when we walk that walk.

As I ran, these thoughts accompanied my steps. The nearer I got to the turnaround point ahead, the more energy I picked up. That is where America is today—nearing the turning point. Change, real change, is just around the corner. We are picking up momentum as more and more citizens rise up and say to government, "Trust us! Trust the people of this great country! Our government is supposed to work for us; we're not supposed to work for government!"

Our country is definitely at a crossroads. Too many Americans no longer believe that their children will have a better future.

When members of our greatest generation—the World War II generation—lose their homes and their life savings because their retirement funds were wiped out in the financial collapse, people get angry. There is a growing sentiment that says just "throw the bums out" of Washington—and by that, people mean Republicans *and* Democrats. Everyday Americans suffering from pay cuts and job losses want to know why our elected leaders aren't tightening their own belts.

I can't help but think of Michigan—the state where I "went rogue" trying to reach out to during the campaign. Some of the people in Michigan are hurting the most right now in our economic downturn.

Michigan is a good example of why we must stand up and not give up! We must fight for reform and fight to reclaim these places suffering under the weight of decades of failed big-government policies—the very policies that now threaten to overtake us all. We can't abandon Michigan and places like it. We're Americans. We don't give up on each other.

I turned the corner toward my goal, and it felt so good I didn't want to stop. I felt light and strong and joyful, with that kind of invigorating exhaustion that comes from hard work at the end of the day.

I've been asked a lot lately, "Where are you going next?" Good question! I'll be heading home to Alaska, of course. Back to that kitchen table. We'll discuss the day's news and the next stop. I always tell my kids that God doesn't drive parked cars, so we'll talk about getting on the next road and gearing up for hard work to travel down it to reach new goals. I'm thinking when I get back I'll bake the kids a cake. And I'll pull out a road map—I want to show Piper the way to Michigan.

As I was writing this book, a friend forwarded to me a widely circulated e-mail that describes one ordinary citizen's view of my governorship. It is so Alaska—I had to share. I hope you get a good laugh as well!

A View from Alaska

by Dewey Whetsell

The last forty-five of my sixty-six years I've spent in a commercial fishing town in Alaska. I understand Alaska politics but never understood national politics well until this last year. Here's the breaking point: Neither side of the Palin controversy gets it. It's not about persona, style, rhetoric, it's about doing things. Even Palin supporters never mention the things that I'm about to mention here.

1. Democrats forget when Palin was the Darling of the Democrats, because as soon as Palin took the governor's office away from a fellow Republican and tough SOB,

---

* After twenty-eight years as chief of Fire/Rescue in Cordova, Alaska, Dewey Whetsell moved to Eagle River, where he remains involved in disaster management. He is the author of *Fire and Ice* and *Lazarus on a Spur Line,* and is a familiar figure in the local music scene. Find him on the Web at www.dewey whetsell.com.

Frank Murkowski, she tore into the Republicans' "Corrupt Bastards Club" (CBC) and sent it packing. Many of its members are now residing in state housing and wearing orange jumpsuits. The Democrats reacted by skipping around the yard, throwing confetti, and singing "La la la la" (well, you know how they are). Name another governor in this country who has ever done anything similar. But while you're thinking, I'll continue.

2. Now, with the CBC gone, there were fewer Alaska politicians to protect the giant oil companies here. So Palin constructed and enacted a new system of splitting the oil profits called "ACES." ExxonMobil (the biggest corporation in the world) protested, and Sarah told it, "Don't let the door hit you in the stern on your way out." It stayed, and Alaska residents went from being merely wealthy to being filthy rich. Of course, the other huge international oil companies fell meekly into line. Again, give me the name of any other governor in the country who has done anything similar.

3. The other thing she did when she walked into the governor's office is that she got the list of state requests for federal funding for projects known as "pork." She went through the list, took 85 percent of them out, and placed them in the "when-hell-freezes-over" stack. She let locals know that if we need something built, we'll pay for it ourselves. Maybe she figured she could use the money she got from selling the previous governor's jet because it was extravagant. Maybe she could use the money she saved by dismissing the governor's cook (remarking that she could cook for her own family), giving back the state vehicle issued to her

(maintaining that she already had a car), and dismissing her state-provided security force (never mentioning—I imagine—that she was packing heat herself). I'm still waiting to hear the names of those other governors.

4. Even with her much-ridiculed "gosh and golly" mannerisms, she managed to put together a totally new approach to getting a natural gas pipeline built that will be the biggest private construction project in the history of North America. No one else could do it even if they tried. If that doesn't impress you, you're trying too hard to be unimpressed while watching her do things like this while baking up a batch of brownies with her other hand.

5. For thirty years, Exxon held a lease to do exploratory drilling at a place called Point Thomson. It made excuses the entire time for why it couldn't start drilling. In truth it was holding it as an investment. No governor for thirty years could make it get started. This summer, she told Exxon she was revoking its lease and kicking it out. It protested and threatened court action. She shrugged and reminded them that she knew the way to the courthouse. Alaska won again.

6. President Obama wants the nation to be on 25 percent renewable resources for electricity by 2025. Sarah went to the legislature and submitted her plan for Alaska to be at 50 percent renewable by 2025. We are already at 25 percent. I can give you more specifics about things done, as opposed to style and persona. Everybody wants to be cool, sound cool, look cool. But that's just a cover-up.

I'm still waiting to hear from liberals the names of other governors who can match what mine has done in two and a half years. I won't be holding my breath.

By the way, she was content to return to Alaska after the national election and go to work, but the haters wouldn't let her. Now, these adolescent screechers are obviously not scuba divers. And no one ever told them what happens when you continually jab and pester a barracuda. Without warning, it will spin around and tear your face off. Shoulda known better.

DEWEY WHETSELL
Alaska

Acknowledgments

I'm very glad this writing exercise is over. I love to write, but not about myself. I'm thankful now to have kept journals about Alaska and my friends and family ever since I was a little girl. That practice allowed an orderly compilation over the past weeks and let me summarily wrap up at least some of my life so far, but next time, the focus will not be on me.

The people I'll acknowledge here are more interesting and inspiring. I would much rather have written about *you*:

Mom and Dad, Chuck, Heather, Kurt, Molly, Payton, Lauden, Karcher, Happy, Kier, McKinley, Heath, and Teko—thank you for centering me and joining me every step of the way. Come along for the rest of the ride! And Lena, Jim and Faye, Bob and Blanche, Kristi, JD, D.D., and all of your families—Kasey, Kandice, Alex, Miranda, Denali, Tori, Brooks, Skyler, Camryn, and Isha—plus aunts and uncles and cousins on all sides, from the extended

Sheeran clan to those with the rich Alaska Native bloodline that flows across the Last Frontier, it's a privilege to be part of this full, diverse, blended family.

To those who supported the efforts for this manuscript: attorney Robert Barnett and the many folks at HarperCollins—Brian Murray, Michael Morrison, Jonathan Burnham, and my editor Adam Bellow: I appreciate the opportunity to write a book! (Next time may it be about everyone else?) Thank you for your advice, hard work, and dedication. Thanks as well to Lynn Vincent for her indispensable help in getting the words on paper. The skills of Lynn and Meghan Stapleton, and the assistance of Ivy Frye, Anita Palmer, and Kim Daniels helped in so many ways to communicate the message in a truly collaborative process.

I want to focus on those who helped build the road that I've been traveling, starting with all my teachers and coaches. Besides parents, no one influences a child more than a teacher. Thank you for letting me love to learn. And now all of my *kids'* teachers and coaches—thanks for your patience with our unconventional schedules, and despite some political opinions held by their mom, thank you for mentoring and loving the Palin kids anyway.

Thank you John Hernandez and John Carpenter for giving me a shot at sports reporting. You chiseled away an ice ceiling twenty-two years ago and let me in the locker room.

Roberta Niver! And Karen, Tiffany, DeAnn, Dawn, Christy, Barb, Juanita, Danielle, and other friends—I couldn't do a thing without your generous help with the kids, and I can't thank you enough for the babysitting, carpooling, overnights, diaper changing, storybook reading, arts and crafts and entertainment for the crew. Plus, the Elite 6, and Judy and Adele and the Menards, Ketchums, Dorwin and Joanne Smith, Kristan Cole, Kris Perry, Tom Van Flein and Meg (along with your patient families). I love you, my friends, and thank you for your support.

To Todd's Slope buddies—thanks for swapping work schedules and passing along the calls and messages all these years in the Gathering Centers. Your hard work for industry in America is unsurpassed. Todd misses you already.

I want to acknowledge the local and state employees (especially cabinet members and aides) whom I've been honored to work with for almost two decades. I've seen many true servants' hearts and Commonsense Conservative minds in the arena, from the City and Borough, to the Legislature, to statesmen in the Washington delegation. Thanks Kate, Sharon, Tara, Britta, Abbey, Janice, Kari, Carol, and everyone else serving for the right reasons. Huge kudos to the governor's campaign volunteers, too: Scott Heyworth and the Bensons, Seibels, Mary, Tara, Paulette, and everyone else who loves Alaska so much—I can't wait 'til we assemble again!

I note with sincere admiration the many good people who built the road we travel: the mom-and-pop businesses all across the country, like Big Dipper Construction and Finishing Touch, Atlee Dodge and The Carpetmen, and so many other industrious ventures. You are the backbone of our economy, so may your efforts to build and create and invent and produce be rewarded.

To the people of faith who sacrificially give their time, even their lives, to the mission of faith. May your prayers for this world be answered! And to the prayer warriors from Wasilla to Washington to Winnipeg, it is your intercession that allows me to stand today. Your letters of support, the Words you share, the prayers I sense . . . I fail in articulating how much I appreciate you, but I trust you'll have a double portion of blessings returned to you. Thank you Valley Pastors Prayer Network, Karl, and other supporters across the country.

I appreciate everyone who values good customer service, so a special shout-out to airline flight attendants (you know why). The same goes for law enforcement officials who take pride in serving the public with integrity. And to all the good ones we met on the VP campaign trail, especially the Secret Service, motorcade, and local public safety women and men all across the USA—my kids idolized you!

Speaking of the campaign, I thank Senator John McCain for his valor. He represented real change, pride in Country, and he lived out his belief in the power and ability of women. It was also an honor to meet John's many friends on the trail, including state party volunteers. I urge you to stand strong and get ready for formidable competition in upcoming races at all levels.

There's not room to list everyone here in acknowledgment of those who've touched my life, so please accept my apology, and I'll finish with a few words of admiration for some special people:

Special Needs community and your families—you are my most favorite people, ever. You are lucky because God touched each one of you in unique ways. Don't let anyone make you feel small. You are beautiful and worthy of all that is good, and I loved meeting all of you.

And to everyone else we met on the campaign trail—all you "ordinary" Americans who seek freedom and value our Constitution—you are the reason John McCain and I put it all out there, and still do. It was the honor of a lifetime to try to win for you. Thank you, America, for your involvement and enthusiasm, and for wearing your patriotism proudly on your sleeve. To everyone who helped with the events, from photographer Shealah Craighead to the hotel staffs, drivers, fund-raisers, musicians, technicians, and everyone else who put Country First, my family and I will cherish the memories we have of you forever. The messages of support we've received since coming off that trail have been overwhelmingly encouraging. Thanks for your patience as we endeavor to respond appropriately to you because we appreciate every single communication!

Thanks, too, to those who deserve credit for inspiring the fight to continue: Valley Republican Women's Club (thanks for helping with the mail!) and other state women's groups; and Fred Malek, Conservatives 4 Palin, Team Sarah, Vets 4 Sarah, 2012 Draft Sarah Committee, Sarah Palin Radio, SarahPAC . . . you are proving that we can make a difference in the world—and we don't need a title to do it.

To some media professionals whom I admire because you don't let anyone tell you to sit down and shut up, please keep making the idiots' heads spin. Thanks for not taking our Freedom of the Press for granted, you bold and patriotic, fair and balanced media folks. Keep calling it like you see it: Amanda, Andrew, Ann, Bill(s), Bob, Cal, Dennis, Dick, Eddie, Fred, Glenn, Greta, Hugh, Joey, John, Jonah, Larry, Laura, Lou, Mark, Mary, Michael, Michelle, R.A.M., Rich, Rush, S.E., Sean, Tammy, Walter . . . and there are more. I join you in standing up for what is right. Remember that as your voice is heard and your spine is stiffened, the spines of others are stiffened, too.

And finally, thanks to Todd, Track, Bristol, Willow, Piper, Trig, and Tripp. You are my reason for living. I breathe you. If everything else were to all go away, as long as I have you, then life is good. I look at you and see miracles in all your lives and know there is a God.

And I *do* know there is a God. My life is in His hands. I encourage readers to do what I did many years ago, invite Him in to take over . . . then see what He will do and how He will get you through. Test Him on this. You'll see there's no such thing as a coincidence. I'm thankful for His majestic creation called Alaska, which has given me my home, and for His touch on America, which has given us all so many opportunities. By His grace, an American life is an extraordinary life.